PREACHING THROUGH THE BIBLE

i

The Bible Study Textbook Series

NEW TESTAMENT

The Bible Study New Testament Ed. By Rhoderick Ice	The Gospel of Matthew In Four Volumes By Harold Fowler (Vol. IV not yet available)	The Gospel of Mark By B. W. Johnson and Don DeWelt
The Gospel of Luke By T. R. Applebury	The Gospel of John By Paul T. Butler	Acts Made Actual By Don DeWelt
Romans Realized By Don DeWelt	Studies in Corinthians By T. R. Applebury	Guidance From Galatians By Don Earl Boatman
The Glorious Church (Ephesians) By Wilbur Fields	Philippians · Colossians Philemon By Wilbur Fields	Thinking Through Thessalonians By Wilbur Fields
Paul's Letters To Timothy & Titus By Don DeWelt	Helps From Hebrews By Don Earl Boatman	James & Jude By Don Fream
Letters From Peter By Bruce Oberst	Hereby We Know (I-II-III John) By Clinton Gill	The Seer, The Saviour, and The Saved (Revelation) By James Strauss

OLD TESTAMENT

O.T. History By William Smith and Wilbur Fields	Genesis In Four Volumes By C. C. Crawford	Exploring Exodus By Wilbur Fields	Leviticus By Don DeWelt
Numbers By Brant Lee Doty	Deuteronomy By Bruce Oberst	Joshua · Judges Ruth By W. W. Winter	I & II Samuel By W. W. Winter
I & II Kings By James E. Smith	I & II Chronicles By Robert E. Black	Ezra, Nehemiah & Esther By Ruben Ratzlaff & Paul T. Butler	The Shattering of Silence (Job) By James Strauss
Psalms In Two Volumes By J. B. Rotherham		Proverbs By Donald Hunt	Ecclesiastes and Song of Solomon — By R. J. Kidwell and Don DeWelt
Isaiah In Three Volumes By Paul T. Butler		Jeremiah and Lamentations By James E. Smith	Ezekiel By James E. Smith
Daniel By Paul T. Butler		Hosea · Joel · Amos Obadiah · Jonah By Paul T. Butler	Micah · Nahum · Habakkuk Zephaniah · Haggai · Zechariah Malachi — By Clinton Gill

SPECIAL STUDIES

The Church In The Bible By Don DeWelt	The Eternal Spirit By C. C. Crawford	World & Literature of the Old Testament Ed. By John Willis	Survey Course In Christian Doctrine Two Bks. of Four Vols. By C. C. Crawford
New Testament History — Acts By Gareth Reese		Learning From Jesus By Seth Wilson	You Can Understand The Bible By Grayson H. Ensign

PREACHING THROUGH THE BIBLE

By

Edwin V. Hayden

College Press Publishing Company, Joplin, Missouri

Library of Congress Catalog Card Number: 81-82987
International Standard Book Number: 0-899000-145-9

To Hester,

whose courageous partnership

has made life pleasant

and ministry possible,

the following pages are

lovingly dedicated.

EVH

Table of Contents

vii

TABLE OF CONTENTS

TABLE OF CONTENTS

FOREWORD

YOU TAKE IT FROM HERE

The basic *Bible Book-of-the-Month preaching plan,* urging a marriage of Bible reading and Bible preaching, is presented with confidence. It fits the apostolic plea to "preach the Word." A *pattern* for month-by-month development is valuable. It works toward accomplishing the plan. A *procedure* for building sermons on an orderly development of the thoughts actually presented in the text Scripture is the best way we know to preach the Word. Thus far we are on solid ground.

The 208 sermon outlines in this book are samples, not models. They are reasonably strong, we think, in research and logical development. For the most part they are "meaty."

Users will need to add some flavoring to the fare. Many illustrations that were used in preaching the sermons have been deleted from the outlines because they were "dated," or of only local interest, or would be obscure to the reader. Poems used with the sermons have been omitted from the outlines for lack of space or because of copyrights.

At least one characteristic flaw is evident among the sermons. That is a lack of proportionate balance among their major parts. The reader will find some outlines built like bulldogs or bisons, heavy in the forequarters and dwindling away toward the end. Many lack a planned, climactic conclusion. That is partly because the Scriptural message, developed throughout, arrives at its own conclusion in the final point and requires no separate conclusion. But in some cases a greater development of the conclusion is to be recommended.

A study of the topical index. (529 to 533) will reveal a fair coverage of Biblical themes. The coverage in the sermons is better than it would appear from the index, as Biblical teaching on such matters as the Holy Spirit, and Christian baptism, and love, and Christ's coming again in judgment is woven into sermons on other themes. And the coverage in a forty-year ministry is better than will be found in two years' supply of publishable

xvii

outlines. It is a humbling and revealing experience, nonetheless, to keep and occasionally examine a topical index of one's own preaching. Such a record makes its own demands for correction.

Given another forty years—or even ten—we could produce a volume of sample sermons far superior to this. But to await that perfection would probably be to cancel the whole enterprise. So take the volume, dear reader, the way it is and make your own improvements. Meanwhile, may God use it to help you preach the Word.

—Cincinnati, Ohio, August 6, 1981.

Introduction
BIBLE BOOK-OF-THE-MONTH PREACHING

The outlines that follow have grown out of a lifetime ministry geared to expository preaching. The sermons themselves were prepared and preached for rural congregations in Indiana and Kansas, urban churches in Ohio, county seat churches in Pennsylvania and Illinois, and special meetings in a dozen states. They cover a forty year ministry beginning in 1934.

As a preaching minister and a ministering preacher I felt the need for God's people to read the Bible more for themselves, and also to hear more Bible teaching from the pulpit. Someone suggested a plan to secure both benefits at once: select a Bible book for the congregation's reading, and preach from that book while the people are reading it. I tried the procedure and liked it; first using books randomly chosen. Then I turned to an orderly procedure through the Bible, but without spending years on the Old Testament before coming to the message of Christ and the church in the New.

It seemed good to spend at least half the time in the New Testament, as well as to point out the New Testament implications in Old Testament readings. Thus we spent a month in the Old Testament and a month in the New, alternately. It seemed wise also to give major emphasis to the Gospel itself—the story of Jesus as told by Matthew, Mark, Luke, and John—but without repetition in successive months. So we scheduled one of the Gospels each sixth month, or each third period of New Testament study.

The Central Church of Christ in Mount Vernon, Illinois, provided the first hearing for the full program. Without announcing the whole plan we asked the members to sign a Bible-reading roster, agreeing to participate in the suggested readings of a Bible book (or group of small books) each month, amounting to one or two chapters a day. We agreed to preach the Sunday evening sermons from the assigned books, but usually chose to preach both morning and evening from the Bible Book-of-the-month.

Seventy-five members signed at our first appeal, but many others participated as the program developed. At the beginning of each month we distributed copies of introductory material, including background, introduction, major message, and outline of the assigned book, with announcement of sermon subjects and texts for the month. At the end of each month we asked for at least a show of hands to indicate who had completed the reading; and with the young folk we used quickie quizzes providing an opportunity to show their familiarity with the material.

As the plan developed I found in it a number of expected benefits and unexpected bonuses. As a preacher I couldn't very easily fall into a monotonous rut or ride a single-theme hobby when moving through the grand themes of Bible books, one after another. Neither could I play a one-string tone in preaching style or emotional level when presenting the pungent practicality of Proverbs or James on the one hand and the sighs of the Psalms or the songs of Luke on the other. My living with one inspired writer for an entire month enabled him to influence my manner as well as my message, to the benefit of my hearers.

The reading-preaching program made it possible for me to deal with difficult subjects, such as divorce, in their obvious Biblical context, protected from any charge of aiming viciously at one person. At the same time I was amazed to discover how readily special-day and special-occasion sermons presented themselves in the monthly program. Not only Thanksgiving and Christmas, but Mother's Day and Labor Day themes arose wherever we might be studying.

A wide variety of themes presented themselves for treatment in series: biographical series from the books of history, doctrinal series from the epistles, devotional series from the books of poetry, ethical-practical series from the prophets and the letters, a series on conversions from the book of Acts, and symbolic series from the books of law, to name a few examples.

The advantages to the hearers were fully as great, and sometimes surprising. Most commonly noted was the fact that Bible reading meant more to them by reason of the sermons developed from it, and the sermons were more meaningful by reason of the reading in preparation. The cult of preacher-personality was minimized; the hearers didn't have to like the preacher to enjoy the preaching. They just had to like the Bible. Folk who moved away before it was over, still received a balanced Biblical fare as the reading/preaching program dealt in rotation with the Gospels, history, epistles, and prophets.

The plan lent a wholesome discipline, I felt, to the relationship between preacher and people. In both it tended to develop a respect for and knowledge of God's Word. We became increasingly a "people of the Book," without the need for boasting or advertising the fact. Sermons, under the circumstances, were expected to grow naturally from their Scriptural context. Any tendency to use Biblical words and phrases to spark an explosion of dogmatic *parsonal* opinion was discouraged. The hearers had seen the Biblical tree from which the text twig was taken!

That does not mean that preaching became a Bible-study session of commentary with application, or that the whole of every month's reading assignment was dealt with from the pulpit. Far from it. Sermons each month were built on the eight or ten grand passages and themes that demanded attention that month in the life of the congregation and the over-all pattern of preaching as it developed. If some aspects of Biblical teaching were neglected in the process, the neglect was made up the next year and was still less than under any other preaching plan I know.

A brief introduction is provided for each Bible Book-of-the-Month. You may want to mimeograph this material for every person in the congregation to aid them as they read the book. A list of sermon topics and texts for each Sunday of the month could also be provided with the introduction.

Review questions have been provided with each Bible Book-of-the-Month. They may be used as a quiz over the Bible book on the last Sunday night of the month as a review of the month's Bible reading. They may be used in other ways to encourage the congregation to read the book of the month.

Following is an outline of a forty-nine months' program, based on thirty-seven segments of Scripture. Shown are the number of chapters included in each segment. You can make your own variation and application of the pattern.

xxi

PREACHING THROUGH THE BIBLE

FIRST YEAR

Month	Book(s)	Number of Chapters
January	Genesis	50
February	Matthew	28
March	Exodus	40
April	Acts	28
May	Leviticus	27
June	Romans	16
July	Numbers	36
August	Mark	16
September	Deuteronomy	34
October	I & II Corinthians	29
November	Joshua	24
December	Galatians through Colossians	20

SECOND YEAR

Month	Book(s)	Number of Chapters
January	Judges-Ruth	25
February	Luke	24
March	I Samuel	31
April	I Thessalonians through Philemon	22
May	II Samuel	24
June	Hebrews-James	18
July	I Kings	22
August	John's Gospel	21
September	II Kings	25
October	I Peter through Jude	16
November	Ezra through Esther	33
December	Revelation	22

THIRD YEAR

Month	Book(s)	Number of Chapters
January	Job	42
February	Matthew	28
March	Psalms 1-72	72
April	Acts	28
May	Psalms 73-150	78
June	Romans	16
July	Proverbs	31
August	Mark	16
September	Ecclesiastes through Song of Solomon	20
October	I & II Corinthians	29
November	I Chronicles	29
December	Galatians through Colossians	20

FOURTH YEAR

Month	Book(s)	Number of Chapters
January	II Chronicles	26
February	Luke	24
March	Isaiah	66
April	I Thessalonians through Philemon	22
May	Jeremiah-Lamentations	57
June	Hebrews-James	18
July	Ezekiel	48
August	John's Gospel	21
September	Daniel through Hosea	26
October	I Peter through Jude	16
November	Joel through Nahum	27
December	Revelation	22
	Habakkuk through Malachi	26

PREACHING THROUGH GENESIS

You are invited to join us in reading this book during the month, and to hear the discussion of it in sermon, morning and evening.

Hear how modern discoveries support the historic truth of the Bible record.

If your reading of Genesis arouses questions you would like to hear discussed, write your questions out and hand them to your preacher. They will be considered in the evening services.

The "Book of Beginnings" tells of:

Creation—the beginning of all things.
> The beginning of the human race.
>> The beginning of sin.
>>> The beginning of God's plan for man's redemption.
>>>> The beginning of God's promise finally fulfilled in Christ.
>>>> The beginning of the Hebrew nation.

The writer is *Moses,* who lived three centuries after the last event recorded in Genesis. He may have used ancient records, but was aided by the Spirit of God (Heb. 1:1).

The time covered—something like two thousand years, from Adam to Joseph.

A BRIEF OUTLINE OF GENESIS

Chapters	Characters	Events	Places
1- 5	Adam, etc.	Creation and Fall	Mesopotamia
6-10	Noah, etc.	The Flood	Mesopotamia
11-20	Abraham, etc.	The Beginning of the Nation and the Promise	Mesopotamia and Canaan
21-36	Isaac, Jacob, etc.	Founding of the Nation	Canaan
37-50	Joseph, etc.	Preservation of the Nation	Canaan and Egypt

Sermon Outlines Provided:

"The First Birth of Freedom" (Gen. 3:1-20)
"Cain and Abel - Hatred and Warfare" (Gen. 4:1-15)
"Mother Love in Trying Times" (Gen. 16; 21:1-21)
"Jacob and Esau - God's Sense of Values" (Gen. 28:10-22)
"Everybody's Business" (Gen. 41:25-43)

1

Other Suggested Sermon Topics:

"In the Beginning" (Gen. 1:1-13)
"Noah - Obedience and Salvation" (Gen. 6)
"Babel - Man's Way to Heaven" (Gen. 11:1-9)
"The Greatness of Abraham" (Gen. 13:1-13)
"Joseph - Used of God" (Gen. 45:1-11)

QUESTIONS OVER GENESIS

1. How many days did God use in creating the world? (1:3-31)
2. Who gave the animals their names? (2:19)
3. Adam called his wife Eve. What does the name Eve mean? (3:20)
4. Who said when asked about his brother, "Am I my brother's keeper?" (4:9)
5. How old did Methusaleh live to be? (5:27)
6. Who were the sons of Noah? (6:10)
7. Who closed the door of the ark? (7:16)
8. What was the sign of God's covenant with men after the flood? (9:13)
9. What does the word *babel* mean? (11:9)
10. Who was promised that he would be the father of a great nation? (12:2)
11. Who escaped from Sodom when it was destroyed? (19:16, 26)
12. Who is the only woman whose age at death is given in the Bible? (23:1)
13. The Arab nations are descendants of whom? (25:18)
14. Who were the children of Isaac and Rebekah? (25:25, 26)
15. Who helped Jacob steal the blessing from Esau? (27:6-17)
16. Who was Jacob's second wife? (29:28)
17. Who is famous for wrestling with an angel? (32:24)
18. Because of jealousy who was sold to the Egyptians by his brothers? (34:4, 19)
19. Name the two sons of Joseph. (41:51, 52)
20. What last request did Joseph make concerning his body? (49:29, 30)

FIRST BIRTH OF FREEDOM
(Genesis 3:1-20)

INTRODUCTION –

Abraham Lincoln, at Gettysburg, November 19, 1863, urged that "This nation, under God, shall have a new birth of freedom . . . ."

Whence comes freedom? (from preamble to Declaration of Independence)

When in the course of human events it becomes necessary for one people to dissolve the political bands which have connected them with another, and to assume among the powers of the earth the separate and equal station to which the laws of nature and of nature's God entitle them . . .

We hold these truths to be self-evident – that all men are created equal; that they are endowed by their Creator with certain inalienable rights; . . .

. . . We therefore . . . appealing to the Supreme Judge of the world for the rectitude of our intentions, do in the name and by the authority of the good people of these colonies, solemnly publish and declare that these united colonies are, and of right ought to be, free and independent states. . . .

I. "LET US MAKE MAN IN OUR IMAGE, AFTER OUR LIKENESS . . . AND GOD CREATED MAN IN HIS OWN IMAGE" (Gen. 1:26, 27).

   A. God indicated the freedom of His own choice – "Let us . . . ."

   B. The man, made in His image, is likewise free.

II. MAN IS COMMANDED, BUT NOT FORCED, TO ABSTAIN FROM THE FRUIT OF THE TREE.

   (All elements of freedom are here:)

   A. Man with the power of choice – no other creature has it.

   B. There is more than one way to choose.

      1. There must be an alternative or there is no freedom.

3

2. The presence of evil in the world is necessary to preserve the humanity of man.

C. God's command, guiding in the right way. Without it, the human family is like a ship without a rudder.

III. MAN CHOOSES TO DISOBEY.

A. Well-ordered nature, without choice, moves in the pattern set by God. Man blunders through history like a drunkard, because he must be free.

B. Wherever there is choice, some will choose the wrong course.

C. Read Edwin Markham's poem—"Man Test."

IV. MAN IS PUNISHED, BUT NOT DESTROYED, FOR HIS DISOBEDIENCE.

A. Here is evidence of God's value placed upon human personality. On this all human liberty rests.

B. The serpent and the ground are cursed for man's sin; man is not cursed.—The things of nature have suffered much for man's sin (Romans 8:19-22).

C. The punishment is discipline, not destruction.

1. Toil, to teach the value of life and God's goodness.

2. Pain—"Tribulation worketh patience, and patience approvedness" (Rom. 5:3, 4).

3. Death—But only after a time of testing and preparation.

D. Freedom remains.

V. GOD SETS IN MOTION THE PLAN TO SAVE MAN FROM HIS SINS.

A. The promise of the redeemer

B. The clothing of skin, preview of the covering for sins.

C. The plan of salvation itself must be accepted freely, or not at all.

4

CAIN AND ABEL - HATRED AND WARFARE
(Genesis 4:1-15)

INTRODUCTION —

A German school teacher says, "Hatred in the intellectual world is what the atomic bomb is to the physical."

Here is traced the beginning of hatred and warfare, and here are the words of God Himself on the subject—the story is too often told without them.

I. HATRED GREW OUT OF DIFFERENCES—CAIN A TILLER OF THE SOIL, ABEL A SHEPHERD.
   A. "I like everybody I know; it is just the ones I don't know that I don't like."
   B. Compare feuds between cattle men and sheep men in the old West.
   C. "We are different."—Reply, "We are brothers."

II. HATRED GREW OUT OF *CAIN'S OWN MORAL FAILURE.*
   A. "Jehovah said, Why art thou wroth, and why is thy countenance fallen? If thou doest well, shall it not be lifted up."

   Illus. —"I have noticed that the man who is doing his level best to live a Christian life knows how hard it is, and is usually generous of his fellow man. It is the one who has something in his own life to hide who wants to drag everybody else down to his level."
   B. Bitterness, frustration, quarrelsomeness, have the same source. — When one fails himself, he can trust no other.

III. HATRED IS EXPRESSED IN JEALOUSY AND RESENTMENT AGAINST THE BETTER OR MORE FORTUNATE. —Can one hate a baby, or a small kitten?
   A. Fear and lack of security make one dangerous—as a skittish animal.
   B. Jealousy of another in some way superior. (How popular is the star pupil?)

5

1. Materially—driver of a jalopy smashes the big car.
2. Morally—the resentment kindled against Jesus. "If they have hated me they will hate you also."
3. The Swiss said, "We see no reason to persecute the Jews; we do not feel inferior to them."

IV. THE TIME TO CONQUER THE THING WAS BEFORE IT TOOK SHAPE IN ACTION.

A. "If thou doest not well, sin coucheth at the door, and unto thee shall be its desire, but do thou rule over it." (See Matt. 15:11, 18-20.)
B. "Whosoever hateth his brother is a murderer.

V. THE ACT FOUND A TIME (DELIBERATELY) FOR FRUITION.

The Septuagint says ("Cain told Abel his brother") "Let us go out into the open field."

A. Sin grows up: Adam disobedient—his son a murderer.
B. "When inclined to work up a triple plated hatred for somebody, just pause, count ten, and think. If hate still lingers, sit down and write a letter to that half-forgotten man or woman who gave you a lift when you needed it most."—*Strickland Gillilan.*

VI. DISCOVERY AND PUNISHMENT ARE SURE. . . .
"The day when every secret thing shall be made known."

VII. GOD FORBIDS REVENGE.

A. "Beloved, avenge not yourselves, but rather give place unto wrath . . ."
B. The spiral revenge, like the spiral of inflation . . . "If ye bite and devour one another, take care that ye be not consumed, one of another" (Gal. 5:15).

CONCLUSION:

God's reply in Christ Jesus.
"God so loved the world"—"Blessed are ye"
Diff.—He broke down the middle wall.
"Do good unto all men—overcome evil with good.
Failure—If any man be in Christ, he is new.

6

MOTHER LOVE IN TRYING TIMES
(Genesis 16; 21:1-21)

INTRODUCTION —

One difficulty about Mother's Day is an excess of idealization. Mother is pictured as a Madonna or as a silver-haired ideal; either of which applies to relatively few mothers.

Let us recognize Mother for what she is, and honor her before God. One of the most memorable mother stories in the Bible is not one of an ideal character.

I. CHAPTER ONE —

    A. Abraham, childless at 85, has been promised a nation. Sarah, according to the custom of her nation, urges him to take her Egyptian servant, Hagar, as a secondary wife, with the exception that Sarah will bring up Hagar's child as her own.

    B. When Hagar finds that she is to become a mother, she bcomes proud and despises her mistress. Sarah becomes jealous and deals harshly with Hagar.

    C. God's laws are not set aside without tragic consequences.

        1. Abraham did that which was custom in his country, but his act controverted God's plan, and he and all his suffered for it.

        2. Broken homes and re-marriages are not according to God's plan, no matter what the laws of the state may say.

        3. Marriages of believers and unbelievers (mixed marriages) are not His plan.

        4. Hasty, thoughtless marriages are not according to His plan.

II. CHAPTER TWO —

    A. Hagar, unable to bear Sarai's mistreatment longer, flees into the desert, and is found at a fountain of water near Kadesh, on the way back to Egypt.

    B. The angel finds her, chides her, commands her to return; and promises a nation through Ishmael.

C. Here is born greatness.
   1. Hagar, the Egyptian servant, becomes a real heroine through mother love.
   2. She obeyed God's command and, for her son's sake, bore her trouble.
      a. Can we have the promises if we reject the commands?
      b. The mother who won't lose a little sleep to take her children to church may lose much sleep to get them out of trouble.
   3. (An obstetrician tells of seeing many frivolous girls respond remarkably to God's miracle of motherhood.)

III. CHAPTER THREE —
   A. Hagar returns, and sees her son brought up as Abram's heir; then Sarah bears a son Isaac, and there are two heirs; then at the feast of weaning, Ishmael makes fun of the baby Isaac, and Sarah demands his ejection.
   B. Abraham demurs, but God tells him that it shall be so, and, reluctantly hasty, he sends Hagar and Ishmael off with meager provisions to find friends among the wandering tribes of the desert.
   C. Water gone and thirst pressing down, Hagar resigns herself and the boy to death, making him as comfortable as possible; then an angel chides her again, and she is led to see a well of water.
   D. God relieves dark tragedy.
      1. Not only that we should do our best, but we must let Him do His best with us.
      2. The restoring fountain was always there — God pointed it out.

IV. CHAPTER FOUR —
   A. Ishmael lives, a rugged, independent life; genders a nation.
   B. How much more can God do with well-taught sons of godly mothers — sons of God in Christ.

CONCLUSION — "What aileth thee, Hagar?"

8

JACOB AND ESAU—GOD'S SENSE OF VALUES
(Genesis 28:10-22)

INTRODUCTION —

Why should God choose Jacob, rather than Esau, to establish His chosen nation?

"Please, God, make bad people good and good people nice!"

These twins are an astrologer's nightmare:

Born with one holding the other's heel; no way to explain their horoscopes.

The one the carefree, frank, and generous outdoorsman delighting his father.

The other the suspicious, crafty, quiet dweller in tents.

In popularity contest, then or now, Jacob would not have had a chance. But God—

The incident at Bethel may shed light on the subject.

I. JACOB LEFT BEERSHEBA.

That's the first chapter; he was escaping Esau's wrath.

A. The purchase of birthright (double portion of inheritance) for a bowl of chili.

1. Esau demonstrated absorption with present satisfaction—*now* generation. (red lentiles)

2. Jacob showed concern for roots in past and development in future. — His procedure was shady, but his sense of values was right.

B. The securing of the blessing from aged Isaac (the first place in the family).

1. Jacob's deception promoted by Rebekah. They both pay for it. Last time together.

2. Esau's bitter tears and Isaac's disappointment.

II. JACOB WAS ON HIS WAY TO HARAN.

Second chapter; he was going to establish a family.

A. God's directive was clear in later times: dont' marry idolaters. So find a bride among the family and keep the way of godliness clear.

9

B. The family to become the nation, through which to send God's son. The family to teach of God, to worship God, to serve God. Father the priest.

C. By contrast, Esau took Hittite girls, "which were a grief of mind unto Isaac and to Rebekah" (Gen. 26:34, 35).

D. This tolerant integration is very popular now.
   1. Love is all; religion, race, culture mean nothing. But what of the children?
   2. And what of the love of God?

E. In this case it was respect, or disregard, for God.

III. AT BETHEL
Third chapter; the place and the experience.

A. The place, a desolate area in the highlands of central Palestine. (Bears found among the scrub trees.)

B. Evidence that Jacob had turned his thoughts to God. He brought his family here to build an altar twenty years later, speaking of that former time: "God . . . answered me in the day of my distress" (Gen. 35:3).

C. The dream of access to Heaven could have answered to thoughts of the day.

D. God renews to Jacob in this dream the promise He had made to Grandpa Abraham.

E. "The Lord is in this place!" (Did he then recognize that God is everywhere? At least he was on the way.)

IV. FROM BETHEL
Fourth chapter; Jacob's response.

A. Set up and anointed the pillar; customary act.

B. Made a vow, expressing the worship reflected in the name and the place.
   1. "The Lord will be my God" (with him everywhere.) This was the key factor.
   2. "I will give a tenth." This was not mere yielding an agent's fee. It was recognition of Him who supplied.

CONCLUSION — Hebrews 12:16, 17 "Esau could bring about no change. . . ." *You* still can!

10

EVERYBODY'S BUSINESS (An election time sermon)
(Genesis 41:25-43)

INTRODUCTION –

    A. Politics is literally everybody's business, and as such demands intelligent participation.

    B. The story of Joseph as one who handled the affairs of Egypt during its trying time, to the salvation of many lives.

    C. Politics and vote-getting are not really the same.

    – See the kind of man Pharaoh sought to handle the affairs of Egypt.

I. JOSEPH SAID THERE WAS NEED OF A MAN "DISCREET AND WISE."

    A. He must be chosen for ability, not for popularity.

    B. He must rely on service to be rendered, not only on service already rendered in another capacity. (One may be a good soldier and a poor congressman.)

    C. One remarkably honest western Senator tells those who apply for appointments, "I can recommend you for character only as far as I know you, and you will have to prove your ability."

II. PHARAOH SAID, "A MAN IN WHOM THE SPIRIT OF GOD IS."

    (Illus. – The Virginia voters drafted Alexander Campbell to their legislature for the purpose of drawing up the state constitution.)

    A. A worshiping man – humble, knowing there is a Ruler above. (Compare the regal humility of George Washington.)

    B. A clean and upright man
    Prov. 31:4, 5 – "It is not for kings, O Lemuel, it is not for kings to drink wine; nor for princes strong drink; lest they drink and forget the law, and pervert the judgment of any of the afflicted." Eccles. 10:17 – "Blessed art thou, O land, when thy king is the son of nobles,

11

and thy princes eat in due season, for strength and not for drunkenness."

C. A courageous and uncorruptible man.
The office-seeker who is willing to take a stand on an unpopular moral issue automatically recommends himself for courage and integrity.

D. An unselfish man
Note that Joseph served for Pharoah and Egypt, not for himself. Wipe out greed in politics, and vice is half gone.

III. THE RING, THE ROBE, THE CHARIOT, THE HOMAGE SPEAK OF LOYALTY AND DIGNITY.

A. A curse to American politics is the unfair pressure and petty fault-finding exerted against office holders — they become targets.
1. It martyred at least two Presidents.
2. See Romans 13:1-7. Christian citizens ought to respect and be loyal to the laws and public men of the land. Either may be judged and perhaps changed by proper methods.

B. A curse to local politics is the undignified and unfitting series of displays, either forced upon, or chosen by, its protective officers, firemen and police (Raffles, benefits, drawings, dances, etc.).

IV. CONCLUSION

A. The power of Joseph lay in his trust in God, and God's help to him.

B. Christian citizens need to ask God's help for public servants — first being themselves Christian.
(A man taking high public office said to his friends, "Pray for me — I need it.")

PREACHING THROUGH EXODUS

You are invited to read and enjoy this part of God's Word with the rest of the congregation during this month.

Exodus — second of the five books of the Law, tells of:

1. Israel's four hundred years in Egypt (Exod. 1).
2. The preparation of Moses to lead them out of bondage (Exod. 2-4).
3. God's contest with Pharaoh (Exod. 5-11).
4. The Passover and the departure from Egypt (Exod. 12).
5. Israel's journey to Mt. Sinai (Exod. 13-18).
6. Their sojourn at Sinai and the giving of the Law (Exod. 19-24).
7. God's directions for the Tabernacle and the Priesthood (Exod. 25-31).
8. Israel's sin and Moses' intercession (Exod. 32-34).
9. The construction of the Tabernacle (Exod. 35-40).

Exodus — The name of the book means "the going out," signifying the going out of the children of Israel from the land of Egypt.

The writer is Moses, who is also the central figure in the account.

The first chapter tells of the doings of nearly four hundred years; chapters two to four cover a period of eighty years; and the rest of the book tells of the important events of a few months' time.

Of special interest: The Passover is a foreshadowing of the sacrifice of Christ (I Corinthians 5:7). The Commandments are the basis of all moral law (chapter 20). The Tabernacle, so carefully constructed according to pattern, foreshadows the Church, for which the pattern is found in the New Testament.

Sermon Outlines Provided:

"The Education of God's Man" (Exod. 2)
"Aaron, the Priest" (Exod. 4:10-17, 27-31)
"Christ, Our Passover" (Exod. 12; I Cor. 5:7)
"Ten Commands to Israel" (Exod. 20:1-20)
"The Wisdom to Work" (Exod. 35:30—36:4)

13

Other Suggested Sermon Topics:

"Author of Liberty" (Exod. 5:19—6:8)
"God's Conquest of the Idols of Egypt" (Exod. 9:33—10:6)
"The Going Out and the Going In" (Exod. 14:19-25)
"Out of Egypt Have I Called My Son" (Matt. 2:15)
"Christian Teaching in the Tabernacle" (Exod. 25:40)

QUESTIONS OVER EXODUS

1. What was the ruler of Egypt called? (1:9, 10)
2. Who named Moses? (2:10)
3. Who were Moses' parents? (6:20)
4. Who was Moses' wife? (2:21)
5. What was Jethro's other name? (3:1)
6. How did the Lord appear to Moses in Midian? (3:2)
7. Who said, "I am that I am."? (3:14)
8. Who was older, Aaron or Moses? (7:7)
9. What was the name of the part of Egypt where the Israelites lived? (8:22)
10. What was the first plague? (7:17-25)
11. What was the tenth and last plague? (11:4—12:30)
12. Name the feast that commemorates the angel of the Lord sparing the Israelites' first-born. (12:27)
13. How many Israelite men of war left Egypt? (12:37)
14. What is the meaning of Marah? (15:23)
15. What was the name of the bread God provided for the Israelites? (16:14, 15)
16. Who held up Moses' hands during the battle with the Amalekites? (17:12)
17. Where did Moses receive the Ten Commandments? (19:20)
18. On what were the Ten Commandments written? (24:12; 31:18)
19. How long was Moses on the mountain? (24:18)
20. How many lights were in the candlestick? (25:37)
21. What was the large brass basin where the priests washed before entering the tabernacle called? (30:17-21)

THE EDUCATION OF GOD'S MAN
(Exodus 2)

INTRODUCTION —

What did that man do when he trod the part of the path we tread? How did God prepare the man who was to lead?

I. RELIGIOUS EDUCATION IN THE HOME
   A. Identity with the people of God.
   B. Persistent reverence for Him as opposed to all other gods.
   C. Habit of prayer
   D. "First in thy grandmother Lois and thy mother Eunice . . ." (II Tim. 1:5). (Special need in the present day.)

II. FORMAL EDUCATION IN THE COURT OF PHARAOH
   A. It was an adequate education.
      Egypt strong in mathematics, astronomy, and many branches of science.
   C. Opportunities today . . . "Ask and ye shall receive, seek and ye shall find" (Matt. 7:7).
      What are you looking for in school?
      1. Earning power?
      2. Usefulness in community?
      3. Personal development?
   D. One man's idea about education:
      1. Know how to use language.
      2. Have important knowledge concerning world, and know how to learn.
      3. Appreciate the beautiful.
      4. To be at home with self and the world — fit in anywhere.
      5. To rise above provincialism and to see all of life whole.
   E. There was much in it that he could not use — paganism of Egypt.

15

IV. EXPERIENCE IN MIDIAN
   A. The formal education "plowed in," so as not to be obtrusive.
      The student needs experience, as new shoes need "breaking in."
      — adequate evaluation of what is usable.
   B. Application of knowledge to the things in which one lives.
      Much of training seemed to lie dormant, but the preparation of the prince came out later.
   C. Continuous gathering of information
      — he knew the geography of the Sinai peninsula.
      He knew how to observe and to apply.

CONCLUSION — "A prophet shall God raise up like unto me. . . ." (Deut. 18:15).

AARON, THE PRIEST (A Biographical Sermon)
(Exodus 4:10-17, 27-31)

INTRODUCTION —

What made Aaron the great figure in Bible history? Little is known of his life and character. He was three years older than Moses; an able speaker, companion and helper for the time of the wilderness wanderings; died some time before their end.

I. WE KNOW OF THREE OCCASIONS WHEN AARON SINNED.
   A. The incident of the golden calf—he erred in accepting the voice of the people above the voice of God (Exod. 32).
      1. It is required of the priest, chosen of God, that he be faithful to Him in all things.
      2. When "like priest, like people" becomes "like people, like priest," both are in grave danger.
   B. The incident of Miriam's murmuring, in which Aaron joined (Num. 12).
      1. One circumstance in which ambition and jealousy seem to have appeared.
      2. God did not still reject Aaron. See the incident of Korah's rebellion, and the budding of Aaron's rod (Num. 16).
      3. Even the members of the family are not to dissuade one from right course. "He that loveth father or mother more than me is not worthy of me" (Matt. 10:37).
   C. The incident of the striking of the rock at Meribah, denied both Moses and Aaron entrance to the promised land (Num. 20).
      1. Here the leader in the fault seems to have been Moses himself.
      2. The most trusted leaders may be wrong, and the man of God must follow the revealed will of God rather than follow any man.
   D. These incidents do not describe the character of Aaron; they contrast with it.

17

1. They are notable. (One says he would be greatly disturbed if the newspaper headlines should tell of honesty as a thing unusual.)
2. They are warnings. One foolish step can undo the fidelity of a lifetime. The foolish step is what is remembered.

II. THE TRUE MEASURE OF AARON WAS HIS FAITHFULNESS.
   A. The addresses to Pharaoh and to the people, in which Aaron resisted the temptation to be original, and lent himself to be the mouthpiece of another. (Cf. John Baptist—"The voice of one crying in the wilderness" Mark 1:3.)
   B. The loss of his personality in his priesthood.
      1. He is to us a faceless figure. We trace his priestly garb from mitre to breastplate, to robe, to sandals— but see no face.
      2. "He that loseth his life for my sake and the gospel's shall find it" (Mark 8:35).
   C. The years of precise faithfulness in performing duty in offering sacrifices.
      1. His sons showed disrespect to sacred things, and died (Lev. 10).
      2. Aaron was forbidden to mourn for them—he must choose God instead of family.
      3. Mid familiarity with things of the Tabernacle, he kept sense of sacredness.
      4. Christians face danger of becoming disrespectful through familiarity with baptism, Bible, prayer, Lord's Table.

CONCLUSION — Aaron the forerunner of the Great High Priest — Christians are priests.

18

CHRIST, OUR PASSOVER
(A Sermon in Type and Anti-type)
(Exodus 12; I Corinthians 5:7)

INTRODUCTION —

The theme of Christ is repeated in the Bible as the theme of a musical composition is repeated over and over. See the directions given for the Passover; the occasion and the story.

I. A LAMB FOR A HOUSEHOLD (vv. 1-3).
   A. Observe the personal and universal nature of Christ's atonement.
   B. The Jewish religion was taught to family units, and the New Testament speaks of the conversion of more than one "household."

II. A MALE WITHOUT BLEMISH, A YEAR OLD (v. 5).
   A. The best becomes the sacrifice.
   B. It was especially so with Jesus. The inspection was most severe, but no fault could be found in Him.

III. KEEP IT UNTIL THE FOURTEENTH DAY, HAVING TAKEN IT FROM THE FLOCK THE TENTH DAY.
   A. It was consecrated some time before it was given.
   B. It was taken into the house, and became loved as a pet. (David said later, "Neither will I offer burnt offerings unto the Lord my God of that which doth cost me nothing" II Sam. 24:24.)
   C. So Jesus "came and dwelt among us." We know the cost, because we know something of the gift before the giving.

IV. THE BLOOD ON THE DOOR POSTS (v. 7).
   A. The prescription by which the Children of Israel were spared.
   B. The suggestion of the Cross by the position of the strokes.
   C. The suggestion that the doors control the life. "The Lord shall preserve thy going out and thy coming in

from this time forth, and even forever more." (Compare the Jewish Mezuzah, on the doorpost.)

V. THE LAMB ROASTED WHOLE.
"Not a bone of him shall be broken."
   A. This, with Psalm 34:20, is applied by John to Christ (John 19:36).
   B. Even the manner of preparation is suggestive of the Cross.

VI. YE SHALL EAT OF IT.
   A. "He that eateth my body and drinketh my blood hath life" (John 6:50-63).
   B. Thus we feed upon Christ, taking His person and being into our lives.

VII. "WHEN I SEE THE BLOOD."
   A. Suggests the blood atonement — "without the shedding of blood is no remission" (Heb. 9:22).
   B. We come into fellowship with Christ's death in Christian baptism (Rom. 6:3, 4).

VIII. EAT IT WITH LOINS GIRDED AND STAFF IN HAND (v. 11).
   A. The Israelites needed to be ready to go, pilgrims to the promised land.
   B. So our Passover makes of us pilgrims, aware that we have no permanent dwelling on earth, and prepared to go to the home prepared for us.

IX. THE LAW OF UNLEAVENED BREAD (vv. 15-20).
   A. Exclusion of leaven is symbolic of purity.
   B. Mentioned by Paul in I Corinthians.
   C. See the inconsistency of having moral impurity in the body in which the perfect Lamb dwells.

CONCLUSION —

"Keep the feast!"

TEN COMMANDS TO ISRAEL
(Exodus 20:1-20)

INTRODUCTION — The reading of a will; everyone listens.

The Commandments were the center of the covenant:
Deut. 4:13: "And he declared unto you his covenant, which he commanded you to perform, even ten commandments; and he wrote them upon two tables of stone."

I. IMPORTANCE OF THE TEN WORDS
    A. Preparation (Exod. 19:7-25)
        Three days preparations; washings, clothing in best; encamped about — but not touching Mt. Sinai.
        Thunders and lightnings; mountain trembles; smoke of furnace; trumpet voice, louder and louder.
    B. Introduction: "I am the Lord thy God, who brought thee out of the land of Egypt.
    C. Giving of the commandments
        1. Spoken by the voice of God in the hearing of all Israel.
        2. Written on tables of stone and given to Moses.
        3. Rewritten "by the finger of God" on second tables.
    D. Kept in the ark of the covenant, beneath the Mercy Seat.
    E. Josephus: "Which it is not lawful for us to set down directly, but their import we will declare."

II. THE COMMANDMENTS
    — Two tables: One the duty to God; first four, maybe five, commands. Second, duty to man; last five, maybe six.
    A. No other gods "in my presence" (not simply in preference to Him).
        1. Not another nation which worshiped one God.
        2. Ye shall be a peculiar people.
    B. Not make unto thee any graven images or any likeness of anything, etc., etc.
        1. Come from Egypt, where imitations were worshiped.
        2. Into Canaan, where images were worshiped.
        3. There can be no likeness of God.

21

4. Commanded that altars be of earth or unhewn stone.
5. Jealous God—for the sake of the worshiper.
   The worship of any other brings suffering.
C. Not take the name of the Lord in vain.
   1. When God's name binds any, he must be really bound.
   2. Must not wear the name of the Lord lightly.
D. Sabbath—like circumcision a sign of covenant with Israel. (Already established. Read Exod. 31:13-17.)
   1. Basis—creation, God's rest.
      Servants also to rest. "You in Egypt" (Deut. 5:15).
   2. Observance—rest, refraining from specific duties.
      "A holy convocation"—later worship and reading.
E. Honor thy father and thy mother. (Heathens exposed and destroyed the aged.)
   1. Strength of the home in Israel.
   2. Obedience, respect, support, learning of both parents.
   3. That thy days may be long—limited promise.
F. Not kill—do no murder.
   1. Does not prohibit making food of living creatures.
   2. Does not prohibit capital punishment (another, *muth*, for "put to death"). Death penalty prescribed.
G. Not commit adultery
   1. God's standards are for our good.
   2. Heathen religions were simply not moral.
H. Not steal
   1. Private property is recognized and protected.
I. Not bear false witness
   1. Justice due to every one—a judicial term.
   2. Spirit of the command inveighs against all falsehood.
J. Not covet
   1. Josephus, "We must not admit of the desire of anything that is another's."
   2. Here the command is definitely in the spiritual realm.
   3. It points up the failure of the old covenant, powerless to save from the sin it uncovers.

CONCLUSION - Read Romans 7:7-11, 18, 19, 22-25.

THE WISDOM TO WORK (A Labor Day Sermon)
(Exodus 35:30 − 36:4)

INTRODUCTION −

The importance of labor − the doing of the world's work.

I. WORK IS OF GOD − "By the sweat of thy face shalt thou eat bread" (Gen. 3:19).
   A. For thy sake. Work is a blessing.
      1. "Greatness is drudgery well done."
      2. Greatest man is often the one who has been the greatest drudge, and keeps at it.
   B. Labor by necessity
      1. Keeps one out of mischief.
      2. Toughens the fiber of the man and the nation.
      3. Drives cares away.
   C. Labor by self-discipline.
      1. Builds moral stamina and sense of purpose. (See Thoreau on Walden.)
      2. Great secret of happiness
         (Illus. − Returned G.I., mechanic, says of things at home, "Everything is wonderful; the cars are in awful shape!")

II. THE SKILL OF CRAFTSMANSHIP COMES FROM GOD. (See text.)
   A. Wisdom, God-given, includes much besides Solomon's skill to rule well.
      1. Mental attainment is not necessarily better than craftsmanship.
      2. The heathen despise manual labor − the godly respect it.
   B. Handwork has its own dignity.
      1. Paul was not ashamed to be rough-handed (Acts 20:34, 35).
      2. Peter said, "We have toiled all night" (Luke 5:5).

23

III. THE SKILL TO LABOR IS A STEWARDSHIP SUBJECT TO THE WILL OF GOD.
   A. That it be used to the glory of God and the good of mankind. Be careful, then, to what purpose you work.
   B. That it be used honestly.
      1. Many who would not steal other things will cheat on labor.
      2. Henry Ford II said, "We will all be better off when we can pay five dollars an hour for five dollars worth of accomplishment than when we try to pay a dollar and a half for seventy-five cents' worth of work."
   C. A dollar should represent a hundred cents' worth of contribution to society.
      1. The contribution may be in constructive thought, invention, or labor.
      2. The evil of gambling is that it tries to get without giving. (Seth Wilson says it is "stealing by consent.")
      3. The same evil is seen in give-away shows, prizes, etc. (When one gets something for nothing, someone else must always get nothing for something. Valuable things don't come into being by magic.)

IV. ONE MAY WORSHIP WITH HIS HANDS.
   A. It is not as though God had need (Acts 17:25), but rather that men need to express their love of Him.
   B. Hand work made the tabernacle.
   C. Hand work is necessary in the church.

CONCLUSION —

Wisdom to work brings one into closer fellowship with Christ— "My Father worketh hitherto and I work" (John 5:17). "I have finished the work thou gavest me to do" (John 17:4).

PREACHING THROUGH LEVITICUS

Whether or not you are a member of this church, you are invited to share with us in the reading of Leviticus during this month. Most of the sermons during the month will be based upon it, giving special attention to the way in which the Jewish Law prepared for the coming of Christ. If your reading raises questions you would like to ask, write them out and hand them to the preacher. They will be considered in the evening services.

The name "Leviticus" comes from the name of the Tribe of Levi. The Levites were the priests and keepers of the Tabernacle in Israel. The book deals with the matters in which they were directly concerned.

It is the third of the five books of the Law, given through Moses. Very little history is related in it. It tells in detail of the laws given at Mt. Sinai.

A QUICK GLANCE AT THE BOOK:

1. The Law of Sacrifice: (Lev. 1-7). These foreshadow the perfect Sacrifice in Christ.
2. The consecration of the Priesthood: (Lev. 8-10). These prepare the way for Christ, the perfect High Priest, and for the priestly character of His whole church, in which all are priests.
3. The Laws of Clean and Unclean things: (Lev. 11-16). The early laws of health have also a spiritual significance.
4. The Law of Holiness: (Lev. 17-26). The abominations which caused heathen nations to be destroyed are forbidden to Israel, with awful warnings. Consideration for the weak is commanded.
5. Vows and Tithes: (Lev. 27). The Children of Israel had real responsibilities before God. How much greater do Christians!

FOR US RIGHT NOW: We can find in this book challenge and help for every church member.

1. To value more highly than ever the perfect sacrifice of Christ.
2. To accept the responsibilities of Christian priesthood in taking Christ to the world.
3. To take more seriously the obligation to consistent Christian living.
4. To accept our position as a stewards of God's possessions.

25

Sermon Outlines Provided:

"The Sacrifice Seasoned With Salt" (Lev. 2)
"Commencement" (Lev. 9:1-7, 22-24)
"Marriage Is Sacred" (Lev. 18:24-30)
"Cursing the Deaf" (Lev. 19:9-18)

Other Suggested Sermon Topics:

"A Holy Priesthood" (Lev. 10:1-11)
"These Ye May Eat" (Lev. 11:1-10)
"Ye Shall Be Holy" (Lev. 11:44)
"Cut Off From His People" (Lev. 17:8-14)
"God and the Fortune Tellers" (Lev. 19:30-37)
"The Choice of Two Ways" (Lev. 26:3-13)

QUESTIONS OVER LEVITICUS

1. When a male sheep or goat was chosen for a sacrifice it was to be without what? (1:10)
2. The person offering a lamb or goat for a peace offering was to put his hand on what part of the animal? (3:2, 8, 13)
3. Certain parts of some sacrifices was to be food for whom? (7:31-36)
4. Name the two sons of Aaron who disobeyed God. (10:1, 2)
5. Name two others sons of Aaron. (10:6)
6. Every male Israelite baby was to be circumcised on what day? (12:3)
7. Who functioned as health officers in dealing with diseases such as leprosy? (14:36-48)
8. God describes the promised land as a land flowing with what? (20:24)
9. Where were the Israelites to live during the Feast of Tabernacles? (23:42)
10. In the fiftieth year property was returned to rightful owners. What was this year called? (25:8-17)
11. Israelites were commanded to give one-tenth of the increase of their produce and other income to the Lord. What was it called? (27:30-33)

THE SACRIFICE SEASONED WITH SALT
(Leviticus 2)

INTRODUCTION —

The Prescriptions for Sacrifices in Leviticus — "Make a difference between that which is sacred and that which is not."

Sacrifices included specially: Meat — the life; Meal — bread and equivalent; Drink offerings; First fruits. The people recognized God as the giver of every essential thing.

The modern world speaks in terms of money — (Darrow answered, "How can I thank you?" with "There has been only one answer to that since the Phoenicians invented money.")

"Money is life, minted into coin."

"It is the coldest, deadest thing in the world until you change it back into life again. It is trivial if we use it in little ways — wicked if we use it in wicked ways — holy if we use it in holy ways."

I. THESE MEAL OFFERINGS WERE VOLUNTARY, BEYOND THE SIN OFFERINGS OF FLESH.
"If any man *will* bring a meal offering . . ."

    A. Irenaeus — "Those who have received liberty set aside all their possessions for the Lord's purposes, bestowing joyfully and freely not the less valuable portions of their property."

    B. After the war of Hadrian it was decreed that none should dissipate more than one-fifth of his wealth in generosity. Christians' generosity had to be restrained!

II. THE MEAL OFFERINGS WERE TO BE GIVEN OBEDIENTLY TO PRESCRIPTION.

    A. Though voluntary, they were still in the will of God.

    B. Rebuke to an age that thinks any good intention is acceptable with God.

    C. Salt — permanence, healing, and seasoning (v. 13 "salt of covenant").

III. THE OFFERINGS HAD AN EMOTIONAL SIGNIF-
ICANCE HAVING NAUGHT TO DO WITH VALUE.
— They were an expression of love. "Not grudgingly or
of *necessity*, but cheerfully" (II Cor. 9:7). (Man will spend
three times as much on the satisfaction of his vain and
social delights as he will for food.)

A. The giver who does no more than pay the bills is not
giving at all.

B. Cf. gifts to the family carefully wrapped, and in the
nature of luxuries — "Something she wouldn't buy for herself." (The doll that was not wrapped was not accepted!)

IV. THE OFFERINGS WERE USED IN THE SUPPORT
OF THE TABERNACLE AND PRIESTHOOD.

A. They that preach the gospel shall live of the gospel.

B. But get rid of the idea of "giving to pay the preacher."

CONCLUSION — Money talks about its possessors — what does
it say of us?

COMMENCEMENT
(Leviticus 9:1-7, 22-24)

INTRODUCTION —

A great day in Israel when Aaron entered on the duties of his priesthood; a great day for the school graduate as he enters the wider fields of education and work.

It is a commencement; a beginning and not an ending; an opening rather than a closing.

I. AARON AND HIS SONS ENTER UPON THE PRIESTHOOD—A LIFE OF SERVICE TO GOD.
   A. The priesthood of Aaron and descendants was in effect until the Cross. God needs men and women for His work under the new covenant.
   B. For full-time Christian leadership.
      1. It is a really constructive activity
         (A bomber pilot in World War II, turned during War to the ministry, for, said he, "The Gospel is the only thing that can keep it from happening again."
      2. There is a shortage, even of pulpit fillers—much more of real preachers.
      3. The life is a joyous one, as seen by the records of spiritual giants.
      4. Not all are giants, but all the faithful are great.
      —The little known preacher, in whom faith, humility, character unite.
   C. Christian workers in all fields.
      1. A mill worker finds a daily Bible study meeting centering around him.
      2. The Bible school teacher who is evangelist, teacher-mother, and generous friend to the teen-age girls in her class.
      3. There is a thrill of grand responsibility in the task. It is not for the timid.

II. AARON AND HIS SONS HAD ALREADY BEEN SET APART AND PREPARED.
   A. The general preparation was life-long, the special preparation a matter of many weeks.

29

B. There is danger of too hasty assumption of work and responsibility.
   1. One says, "Every dollar earned before age 18 costs a hundred later on."
   2. The foolish workmen plunges into the lawn with a dull mower; the wise one pauses to sharpen his blade, and uses a file to keep it sharp.

C. Preparation is needed, for—
   competition is increasingly keen;
   specialization increasingly needed;
   skill in living, as well as making a living.

D. Any education that leaves out religion is like a fly-wheel out of balance—the faster it turns the more surely it will wreck the machinery. (In 1933 there were graduates of 32 different universities in Sing Sing prison.)

III. AARON AND HIS SONS HAD TO BRING THEIR OWN OFFERINGS.

A. Humble recognition of own sins was part of their preparation.

B. Humility does not mean fear or timidity. It means a sound sense of values and a realization of difficulties.

C. "Boasting better befits a man taking off his armor than one putting it on."

IV. AARON AND HIS SONS ENTERED IMMEDIATELY INTO THE DUTIES OF THEIR OFFICE.

A. The consecration without the application would have been useless.

B. Many a race is won or lost at the starting mark. "Well begun is half done."

C. The first six weeks at college set the pace and make the rest easy or hard.

D. Some who are well trained accomplish little, for they never start.

CONCLUSION —

Your start for Christ—Read Edwin Markham's "Task That is Given to You."

MARRIAGE IS SACRED
(Leviticus 18:24-30)

INTRODUCTION —

A traveler to a decadent ancient land returned saying, "Thank God for moral problems in America! Some nations have no moral problems because they have no moral standards."

In Leviticus, God gives His moral standards to a people coming out of such a land.

I. THE NATIONS THAT GOD DESTROYED WERE CONDEMNED BECAUSE OF MORAL FAILURES.

   A. It is a characteristic of paganism, even in advanced civilizations.

   B. Egypt had religious orgies to the gods Isis, Apis, and Mnevis. Their worship was drunken and licentious.

   C. The Canaanites worshiped Molech, whose worship was equally immoral.

      1. They sacrificed their first-born to him, "passing through fire to Molech."

      2. Archeologists find evidences of unspeakable abominations in idols of Canaanite cities.

   D. At a later time Socrates could teach the world philosophy, but anyone having God's Word could have taught Socrates concerning morals.

   E. A dying nation is regularly characterized by a "rising divorce rate" and "lowering moral standards."

II. "YE SHALL NOT DO ANY OF THESE ABOMINATIONS."

   A. The moral law is *God-given*, making marriage as sacred as any other revealed thing (I Thess. 4:8).

   B. Just what is that law? (see the rest of the chapter).

      1. "Thou shalt not commit adultery." The intimate personal contacts of a man and a woman are reserved to the divinely instituted marriage.

      2. The Old Testament law here and elsewhere:

         a. Pre-marital intimacies are forbidden — Those guilty are obligated to marry and never to divorce.

b. Marriage with close relatives forbidden under various penalties. (In Egypt it was common.)
c. Unfaithfulness of married or betrothed folk forbidden. Punishment was death.
d. Unnatural acts of lust, perversions of the marriage instinct, punishable by death.
3. As given in the New Testament — "Husband of one wife" (I Tim. 3)
a. (Mark 10:11, 12) "Whosoever shall put away his wife, and marry another, committeth adultery against her. And if a woman shall put away her husband, and be married to another, she committeth adultery."
b. (Matt. 5:28) "Whosoever looketh on a woman to lust after her hath committed adultery with her already in his heart."
c. Punishment — "The wages of sin is death" (Rom. 6:23). "Adulterers . . . shall not inherit the kingdom" (I Cor. 6:9, 10).
d. Escape — Repentance and forgiveness in Christ (I Cor. 6:11). "Go thy way, and sin no more."

III. IF YOU COMMIT THESE ABOMINATIONS, YOU ALSO SHALL BE SPEWED OUT OF THE LAND.
A. The people of Israel generally heeded this warning better than most.
B. Our own nation is in danger. God's moral law is not repealed or amended.
1. Ungodly teachers scoff and some teach the opposite.
2. Popular media encourage sin.
C. Positive approach to the problem.
1. Respect for marriage, purity, and personalities, before courtship begins.
2. Those who are carefully taught in God's Word have what they need.

CONCLUSION —

Christ is our only Savior from sin, and Leader in the way of life.

CURSING THE DEAF

(Leviticus 19:9-18)

INTRODUCTION —

(Italian immigrant at the zoo hears crowd boo the bear that attacked the coon, then cheer as the keeper drove him off. Weeping, he said, "That'sa what I lika about America; she'sa all for the little guy, even if he'sa justa animal!") The spirit of fair play and consideration is a heritage from God's word.

I. THE THREAD OF UPRIGHT JUSTICE RUNS THROUGH THE LAW
  A. "Ye shall not steal; neither shall ye deal falsely, nor lie one to another. And ye shall not swear by my name falsely."
  B. "Thou shalt not oppress thy neighbor nor rob him."
  C. "Ye shall do no unrighteousness in judgment; thou shalt not respect the person of the poor, nor honor the person of the mighty; but in righteousness shalt thou judge thy neighbor."
    1. Occasionally some Robin Hood will rob the rich to give to the poor. Even that is not justice.
    2. Often laws are applied leniently to the rich and powerful.
  D. Talebearing forbidden—"Shalt not stand against the blood of thy neighbor."
    1. Reference to the false witness bringing judgment.
    2. When the story comes, ask if it has been witnessed and will be signed.
    3. The stealing of another's good name is theft!
    4. Good people may do more injustice with tongues than any other way.

II. ADDED IS A THREAD OF CONSIDERATION FOR THOSE UNABLE TO TAKE CARE OF SELVES.
  A. The farmer forbidden to take the corners and the gleanings from his field. In the vineyard, forbidden to take the gleanings and the fallen fruit.

33

1. These belonged to the poor and the sojourner.
2. This right used by Ruth, and Jesus' disciples, without shame or rebuke.
3. In it no incentive to laziness; no loss of independence.
4. Apply — in times of need, let there be work to do, not doles to give.
B. "Wages of the hired servant shall not abide with thee till morning." — Immediate need must be met!
C. "Shalt not curse the deaf nor put a stumblingblock before the blind." —
   1. Nor taunt the stutterer, the half-wit, the awkward.
   2. Nor let the quick-tongued and clever take advantage of the slow.
   3. How much different is it to talk about one in his absence?
   4. How shall we excuse tempting the weak, as the liquor business does?
D. The next chapter in Leviticus commands special consideration for the stranger. It might have been natural to afflict strangers, because Israel was afflicted when they were strangers in Egypt, but . . .

III. VENGEANCE, GRUDGES, AND HATRED ARE FORBIDDEN.
A. Thou shalt not hate thy brother in thy heart.
   "Keep thy heart with all diligence, for out of it are the issues of life" (Prov. 4:23).
B. Rebuke thy neighbor, and not bear sin because of him. Here is a hard test of love — do we care if the neighbor goes to hell?
C. Shalt not take vengeance, nor bear a grudge. Smoldering resentment poisons the one who bears it.

CONCLUSION — "Thou shalt love thy neighbor as thyself" (19:18).
"If God so loved us, we ought to love one another" (I John 4:11).

PREACHING THROUGH NUMBERS

While the Old Testament books do not have the same worth to the Christian as the New Testament has, there is in them much of value for "reproof, for correction, for instruction in righteousness." Christ, the fulfiller of the purposes of God, stands out in bold relief against the background of these books.

The name of "Numbers" comes from the statistical records of the Children of Israel, as those records appear in chapters one and twenty-six. The Hebrew title of the Book is "In the Wilderness."

This is one of the five books of Moses. Chapter 33 summarizes the wilderness wanderings of Israel in his diary-like account.

The book records the history of approximately forty years, beginning when Israel was still at Mt. Sinai, and continuing until the nation was ready to enter the land of Canaan. It falls naturally into three divisions:

I. The camp at Sinai and preparations for departure (Num. 1-10).
II. Outstanding incidents in the wilderness (Num. 10-22).
III. Experiences in the plains of Moab, east of the Jordan (Num. 22-26).

Inserted in the historical account are numerous laws given for the government of the nation.

Of special interest are the following accounts:

Celebration of the Passover in the wilderness 9
Moses' facing of jealousy and rebellion
   among his people 12, 16
The sending of spies into Canaan, their report
   and results 13, 14
Moses' disobedience and its results. 20:1-13
The story of Balaam, prophet in Midian. 22-24
The establishment of cities of refuge in Israel. 35

We invite you to share with us in the reading of this part of God's Word, and in the hearing of the messages based on it. There will be something here that you will be glad to receive.

35

Sermon Outlines Provided:

"The Right Use of God's Name" (Num. 6:22-27)
"Come With Us and We Will Do Thee Good" (Num. 10:29-32)
"We Are Well Able" (Num. 13, 14)
"Our City of Refuge" (Num. 35:9-15, 22-28)

Other Suggested Sermon Topics:

"Atonement for the People" (Num. 16:41-50)
"Cost of Disobedience" (Num. 20:1-13)
"What God Speaks" (Num. 22-24)
"Pricks in the Eyes" (Num. 33:50-56)

QUESTIONS OVER NUMBERS

1. The census numbered all Israelite males above what age? (1:2, 3)
2. Which tribe camped in the midst of all other tribes? (2:17)
3. The priest prepared a water of bitterness to test a woman accused of what sin? (5:12-31)
4. At what age were the Levites to retire from their service? (8:25)
5. The cloud over the tabernacle was like what during the night? (9:15)
6. What kind of meat did God provide for his people? (11:31)
7. Name the spy who said they should go, possess and overcome the land of Canaan? (13:30)
8. When the Israelites grumbled against Moses and Aaron they wanted to go where? (14:3, 4)
9. What happened to the man who picked up sticks on the Sabbath? (15:36)
10. Who led a rebellion of 250 men against Moses and Aaron? (16:1-5)
11. On what mountain did Aaron die? (20:25-28)
12. Who was appointed the successor to Moses? (27:18-21)
13. One guilty of manslaughter could go to certain cities for safety. What were these cities called? (35:6)

THE RIGHT USE OF GOD'S NAME
(Numbers 6:22-27)

INTRODUCTION –

The vicious evil of cursing is not only that it takes the name of the Lord blasphemously, but that it misrepresents God. It is His desire that His name be used for blessing and not for cursing.

This was central and very early in the commands given to the priests in the days of Moses.

I. HIS NAME IS TO BE USED IN BLESSING, NOT CURSING.

    A. The purpose of God is to bless and save mankind. "God who has saved us, and called us with an holy calling, not according to our works, but according to his own purpose and grace, which was given us in Christ Jesus before the world began . . ." (II Tim. 1:9).

    B. The Old Testament priesthood was designed to bless the people. ". . . To burn incense before the Lord, to minister unto him, and to bless in his name forever" (I Chron. 23:13).

    C. Christ came with the same purpose. "God sent not his Son into the world to condemn the world, but that the world through him might be saved" (John 3:17).

    D. The followers of Christ - "Bless them that curse you, and pray for them which despitefully use you" (Luke 6:28).

II. THE BLESSING IS TO EACH MEMBER OF THE COMMUNITY INDIVIDUALLY – "BLESS THEE"

    A. The priest blessing the whole people speaks the mercy of God to each one as an individual.

    B. The convenant made with the nation is applied to each one alone.

III. THE BLESSING IS EXEMPLIFIED.

    A. "Bless thee and keep thee."

1. "The Lord is thy keeper; the Lord is thy shade upon thy right hand" (Psalm 121:5).
   "A thousand shall fall at thy side, and ten thousand at thy right hand, but it shall not come nigh thee" (Psalm 91:7).
2. The greater keeping power is in Christ.
   "I pray not that thou shouldest take them out of the world, but thou shouldest keep them from the evil" (John 17:15).
   "To Him who is able to keep you from falling, and to present you faultless before the presence of his glory with exceeding joy, to the only wise God our Savior . . ." (Jude 24).
3. Therefore we should trust.
   "Casting all your care on him, for he careth for you" (I Pet. 5:7).

B. "Cause His face to shine upon thee and be gracious unto thee." Revelation says that the Lord Himself is the light of heaven. "Grace and truth came by Jesus Christ" (John 1:17).

C. "Lift up his countenance upon thee and give thee peace."
   1. The uplifted countenance the sign of recognition and welcome.
   2. Compare Paul's greeting: "Grace, mercy, and peace."

CONCLUSION —

Compare Luke 24:50 (Christ blessed them, and departed) with Acts 1:11 (He shall so come again, in like manner.) Will our High Priest bless us at His return? Yes, if we are part of His congregation.

38

COME WITH US AND WE WILL DO THEE GOOD

(Numbers 10:29-32)

INTRODUCTION — THE STORY —

Moses and Hobab probably standing on a hill overlooking the camp as it breaks up.

Flash-backs:

Moses' 40 years in Midian, probable nights together at the camp fire.

Moses goes into Egypt and returns with the thousands of erstwhile slaves.

Jethro's help in the wilderness; his assistance in matter of organization.

The camp at Sinai, for the space of a year, approximately. Events engraved in the memory of the world, and the books of eternity—The law, Tabernacle, Priesthood, organization of the camp.

Now, the orderly removal of those who came as a disordered mob.

Judah first; then the Levites with the things of the Tabernacle; then the other tribes, and Dan last.

Moses is unwilling to part with his friend, but desires him to go the journey, too.

I. MOSES, SETTING OUT, INVITES.

A. So the Christian oft best evangelist at conversion. The way is fresh and challenging.

B. His own life is new-committed; there is a deep sincerity in his invitation.

II. MOSES INVITES HIS IN-LAWS.

They were known imtimately for forty years, companion of former journeys. So with us.

A. Our keenest interest ought to be in those closest to us.

B. They test:

1. The genuiness of our faith—is it important?

2. The consistency of our life—our power is greatest or least with them.

39

III. MOSES INVITES TO "GOOD."
   A. God has promised many things to Israel; share the promises.
   B. The Church offers good to its people
      1. A fellowship, without regrets, wearing well, and always richer.
      2. The satisfaction of spiritual hunger.
      3. The fulfillment of man's highest purposes.
      4. Eternal life.
   C. This invitation appeals—
      1. To the sense of need—humility—but some feel that they can get on right well without any help.
      2. To self-interest (on the other hand)—but some noble souls are far more interested in helping others than themselves.
   D. It didn't work with Hobab—maybe he thought he was needed worse at home.

IV. MOSES INVITES TO OPPORTUNITY—"You shall be to us instead of eyes." "You will do us good. We need you."
   A. God guided with the cloud, but there was need:
      1. To find forage for the flocks.
      2. To gain protection from enemies.
   B. No one else was qualified as Hobab was to give just what was needed.
   C. The cause of Christ needs you.
      1. Eyes to seek out the need in your own place, hands to work His work, a tongue to speak kindly and give courage.
      2. The cause of Christ may get on without you, but your contribution, if missing, cannot be made up, either for the church or for you.
         Illus.—Story of the man who was "well represented" by his family at church, was told at heaven's gate that he wasn't needed there, either.

CONCLUSION — Hobab heeds the invitation, and his posterity have an inheritance in the promised land.

40

WE ARE WELL ABLE
(Numbers 13, 14)

INTRODUCTION – THE STORY

The camp at Kadesh Barnea
Location, the Negev
The place that would support the camp, while establishing good attack point.

I. THE DIRECTIONS FOR THE SPYING EXPEDITION WERE GOD'S DIRECTIONS.
   A. Instructions to the spies to learn
      1. Land — good or bad, water, and terrain.
      2. Fruit — bring it!
      3. People — number, kind, how protected.
   B. The Christian, observing what needs to be conquered for the Lord.
      1. In self — greed, worry, selfishness, pride, evil habits.
      2. In the church — indifference, lack of faith, lack of fellowship.
      3. In the religious world — ignorance of, and indifference to the Word.
      4. Community and the world — unchurched, ungodly, unholy, unrighteous.

II. THE MAJORITY REPORT LOOKED ONLY AT THE DIFFICULTIES, AND WAS AFRAID.
   A. It meant lack of faith in the promises and the power of God.
   B. It meant lack of faith in themselves (as grasshoppers).
   C. Cf. Peter walking on the sea.

III. THE MINORITY REPORT SAW GOD'S POWER AND TRUSTED.
   A. They had full appreciation of the land and of the difficulty.
   B. The basis of their confidence lay in God (Num. 14:8, 9).

41

IV. THE FAITHLESS LOST THEIR OPPORTUNITY.
   A. Forbidden to enter the promised land—a new generation must rise.
   B. Remorseful, they then attempt an invasion contrary to the Word of God, and without the leadership of Moses, or presence of the ark. Amalek exercises a "defense in depth" and puts them to rout.
   C. Like this is the defeat of the "Christian" who attempts to build the good life without a sound foundation in faith.
   D. Similar is the apparent success, but real defeat, of the church which builds on the sand foundations of men's wisdom contrary to the Word of God.

CONCLUSION — The Reward of the Faithful.

See later writing about Caleb—the man in everything obedient to God—enough reward to make up for the brief refusal of his people (Josh. 14:6-15).

"Are ye able," said the Master, "to be crucified with Me?"
"Yea," the sturdy dreamers answered. "To the death we'll follow Thee."

"Are ye able?" still the Master whispers down eternity,
And heroic spirits answer now as then in Galilee,

"Lord, we are able; our spirits are thine;
   remold them, make us like Thee, divine.
Thy guiding radiance above us shall be a beacon to God,
   to faith, and loyalty."

OUR CITY OF REFUGE
(Numbers 35:9-15, 22-28)

INTRODUCTION —

The wisdom of God is seen in His provisions for people.
Provisions are realistic — He knew that offenses would come.
Provisions are hopeful — He provided a way of escape for the penitent.
Provisions are centered in the Savior who was to come.

I. THE PUNISHMENT FOR MURDER
   A. Death could come at the hand of the avenger of blood.
   B. The murderer who planned to kill because of hate was not protected.
   C. Blood feuds (such as in our Eastern highlands) were avoided.

II. THE WAY OF ESCAPE FOR THE UNINTENTIONAL KILLER.
   A. A place of asylum until guilt or innocence could be established.
      1. The cities of refuge were levitical cities; there would be men there who knew the law and could apply it.
      2. Trial of the escaped manslayer was provided, and the guilty were turned over to the avenger of blood.
   B. Cities of refuge so located that they were within reach of all.
      1. A day's journey would reach one from any place in Palestine (30 miles).
      2. Locations east of the Jordan were named by Moses:
         a. Bezer in the wilderness for Reuben.
         b. Ramoth-Gilead for the children of Gad.
         c. Golan in Bashan for the Manassites.
      3. Locations west of Jordan were established later by Joshua.
         a. Kedesh of Naphtali, north of sea of Galilee.
         b. Shechem of Ephraim (between mounts Gerizim and Ebal).
         c. Hebron in Judah, south Bethlehem.

C. The fugitive had to enter the city and stay there.
   1. Going forth before the death of the current high priest subjected him to death at the hands of the avenger of blood.
   2. After the death of the high priest, the fugitive went free.

III. THE THEME OF REDEMPTION IN CHRIST IS SOUNDED HERE.
(Read Hebrews 6:17-20)
   A. There is a contrast.
      1. Cities of refuge protected only the innocent or unintentional killer.
      2. Christ provides salvation for the penitent, even though guilty.
   B. There are comparisons.
      1. Judgment is not removed. God's realism is constant. There will be a reckoning and destruction of the wicked.
      2. There is a way of escape in Christ, to whom we flee in refuge.
         a. He is within reach of all, the same escape available to all. (As equal number of cities on each side of Jordan, so there is equal salvation to Jew and Gentile, or bond and free.)
         b. Each must avail himself of the means of escape. "Save yourselves from this untoward generation!" (Acts 2:39).
         c. Each must remain in the place of safety.
      3. The death of the high priest is the event which sets one free. (Here the figure is changed; Christ is priest as well as city; but the theme of salvation is the same.)

CONCLUSION —
"Other refuge have I none;
Hangs my helpless soul on thee.
Leave, ah, leave me not alone
Still support and comfort me.

All my rest on thee is stayed;
All my help from Thee I bring;
Cover my defenseless head
With the shadow of Thy wing."
— *Jesus, Lover of My Soul*

PREACHING THROUGH DEUTERONOMY

This book, with the Psalms, was quoted by Christ more often than any other. It is made up principally of three addresses delivered by Moses to the children of Israel as they encamped in the plains east of the Jordan River, just before he died and shortly before they went into the promised land. Its name is taken from a Greek word meaning "second law," since it repeats and enforces many of the laws found in Exodus, Leviticus, and Numbers.

ANALYSIS OF THE BOOK

First Discourse — 1:1—4:43
A review of the liberation and wanderings of the Children of Israel.

Second Discourse — 4:44—28:68
The commandments repeated...........................5
Provisions for godly teaching in the home 6, 7
Reminders of God's goodness, and command to put down all idols 8-13
Repetition of certain ritual laws.....................14-19
Miscellaneous moral laws..........................20-26
Prediction of things to come to the Jewish nation 27, 28

Third Discourse — 29, 30
Renewal of the Covenant, with promises and warnings.

Concluding portions — 31-34
Moses delivers the book of the Law to the Levites 31
Song of Moses 32
Moses' blessing on the Children of Israel 33
Death of Moses...................................34

GREAT PASSAGES

For pure eloquence these addresses of Moses have never been surpassed.

Deuteronomy 6:3-9 is used to the present time as the creed of the Jews, recited daily in the homes of the pious.

Chapters 8 and 9 tell how and why God dealt with the nation of Israel as His chosen people.

45

Chapter 18 (15-19) gives one of the clearest predictions of Christ to be found in the Old Testament.

Chapter 28 predicts with amazing accuracy and in amazing detail the fate of the rebellious Jews even to the present time.

Sermon Outlines Provided:

"Ask of the Days That Are Past" (Deut. 4:32-40)
"Taking God Home" (Deut. 6:1-9)
"Put Away the Evil" (Deut. 13:1-5; 21:18-21)
"The Law for the Family" (Deut. 22:13-21)

Other Suggested Sermon Topics:

"Lest We Forget" (Deut. 8:11-20)
"The Later Prophet" (Deut. 18:15-19)
"Amen" (Deut. 27:15-26)
"The Word Is Nigh Thee" (Deut. 30:11-14)

QUESTIONS OVER DEUTERONOMY

1. The book of Deuteronomy consists mainly of speeches of what man to the Israelites before they entered the promised land? (1:1)
2. Who was to lead the Israelites after Moses' death? (3:28)
3. What reason is given in Deuteronomy 5:15 for obeying the Sabbath commandment?
4. Why were the Israelites forbidden to intermarry with the tribes in Canaan? (7:4)
5. What did Moses do with the golden calf? (9:21)
6. Why does God say to show love to strangers? (10:19)
7. Clean animals that could be eaten must meet what two requirements? (14:6)
8. What kind of bread is not to be eaten during the Passover feast? (16:3)
9. What command is given about men wearing women's clothing and vice versa? (22:5)
10. Where did Moses die? (34:1, 5)
11. At what age did Moses die? (34:7)

ASK OF THE DAYS THAT ARE PAST

(Deuteronomy 4:32-40)

INTRODUCTION —

Moses an historian

Here is an interesting comment on his place as the recorder of history "since God created."

He would not speak slightingly of the "dead past."

"The past alone is complete and universal, and only through it can the fulness and richness of life be savored; the grains must be well ground before we can eat the wheat bread."

— *Aubrey F. G. Bell*

Moses knew a greater truth; the history he recalled was written by the finger of God.

I. HE CALLS ATTENTION TO THE FACTS (IN ALL TIME AND IN ALL PLACES).

    A. There may have been those who would call his method cold, irreligious, unfeeling.

    B. They are God's facts.

    C. The New Testament church appeals to facts.

        1. The apostles preached facts . . . Pentecost . . . Antioch . . . Mars Hill.

        2. They recorded basic facts in their writings. See contrast of modern preaching with this.

        "I would not have you to be ignorant, brethren, concerning them which are asleep, that ye sorrow not, even as others which have no hope. For if we believe that Jesus died and rose again, even so them also which sleep in Jesus will God bring with him. . . ." (I Thess. 4:13; cf. I Cor. 15).

        3. Personal salvation is established in the facts of Christ.

        4. Pattern for the church is laid down in facts.

        "added about 3000 souls" (Acts 2:41).

        "The number came to be about five thousand men" (Acts 4:4).

        "Then had the churches rest . . . and . . . were multiplied" (Acts 9:31).

47

II. HE SETS FORTH THE PURPOSE OF HISTORY.
   A. "That thou mightest know that the Lord, He is God; there is none else beside him" (Deut. 4:39; cf. Luke 1:1-4; John 20:31).
   B. "Be ready always to give an answer to every one that asketh thee a reason for the hope that is in you, with meekness and fear" (I Pet. 3:15).

III. THE PURPOSE OF KNOWING IS *DOING*
   Ask of yesterday that you may *know* today how you should *order your life* tomorrow.
   A. Paul uses history in the same way . . . I Cor. 10:6.
      "I would not that you should be ignorant, how that all our fathers were under the cloud. . . . Now these things were our examples, to the intent that we should not lust after evil things as they also lusted. . . ." (I Cor. 10:6).
   B. The conclusion of the whole matter is found in doing...
      "Behold I set before you this day a blessing and a curse, a blessing if ye obey the commandments of the Lord your God, which I command you this day; and a curse if you will not obey the commandments of the Lord your God, but turn aside out of the way which I command you this day, to go after other gods, which ye have not known" (Deut. 11:26-28).

CONCLUSION —

"Go ye into all the world and preach the gospel [tell the facts of the good news] to every creature. He that believeth and is baptized shall be saved; but he that believeth not shall be condemned" (Mark 16:15, 16).

TAKING GOD HOME (A Family Week Sermon)
(Deuteronomy 6:1-9)

INTRODUCTION —

This passage the creed of the Jews, recited by the orthodox. Used, with Exod. 13:9, 16 and Deut. 11:18, in phylacteries ("preservation") and mezuzah.

These uses came into being with the Talmud of the Pharisees, but the truth which is as old as time is the foundation stone of the Jewish home.

I. THE ON-GOING OF THE FAITH BECOMES THE ON-GOING OF THE NATION.
  A. "Fathers, provoke not your children to wrath, but bring them up in the nurture and admonition of the Lord" (Eph. 6:4; cp. II Tim. 1:5).
  B. Says Geo. A. Buttrick:
     "The New Testament church was in a house before it was in a church. It must, perchance, be revitalized in houses, before it can be revitalized in churches — or rather, home and church must revitalize each other.
  C. It is hard to say which is more necessary to the other — faith, or the home. They lean heavily on each other.
  D. To have a faith which will mean much in the home, it must be learned at home.
     But religion cannot be inherited; it must be taught to each individual.

II. "TEACH THEM . . .TO THY CHILDREN."
  a. One must first learn before he can teach.
  b. Much is caught by example in the home, but not all.
  c. Family worship —
     Possibilities — a few verses read and explained.
       Prayer — get off crutches of rote prayer.
       Songs and discussion of them.
       Talk about Christian leaders.
  d. Reading — Bible, story book *Christian Standard.*
  e. Talk of them — If family eats without discussion of the Law, it is as a heathen feast.

    f. Bind them for a sign. Mottoes of the mind.
      Guide the hand, the eye, the life.

III. "WHEN THY SON ASKETH THEE . . ." (6:20-25).
    A. Here is a lad who has been into religion over his depth; modern educator shudders: "Primary children cannot understand the adult ministry of Jesus."
    B. Expose to the things that will bring up questions about Christianity.
      The Bible—preaching—the ordinances.
      Then be sure you know the answers.

IV. BRING NO ABOMINATION INTO THY HOUSE
    A. Heathen image, perhaps of precious metal.
    B. Now—Drink, indecent pictures, decorations, literature. Shall it be, "Mother taught me to dance" or "Mother taught me to pray"?
    C. What shall we bring into the house?
      Christian friends—Christian workers.
      See Acts and Epistles for hospitality.

V. GIVE NOT YOUR DAUGHTER TO THEIR SON IN MARRIAGE.
      The tragedies of those "married out of the church" . . .
    A. Marriage is acquaintance and friendship come to fruition. —Where are friends made?
    B. God made marriage, and protected the home by law, that children might have a chance.
    C. Home is for the children—your home is for your children—their home for theirs.
      "Will he make a good father for my children?"

CONCLUSION — God our Father invites us home.

PUT AWAY THE EVIL
(Deuteronomy 13:1-5; 21:18-21)

INTRODUCTION –

Military authorities during World War II said that France was defeated early in that war because she saved too much of her equipment from World War I. Germany, having suffered destruction of all arms in the First World War, started fresh with modern implements, and conquered.

Many a Christian, holding to the traits and habits of the "old man," is spiritually defeated, whereas ruthless destruction of the old in making the fresh start would bring victory.

I. PUT AWAY THE EVIL
- A. The command is repeated nine times in Deuteronomy.
   1. Eight times it refers to the stoning of the lawbreaker: false prophet (13:5); idolater (17:7); rebellious son (21:21); harlot, adulterer, attacker of woman (22:21, 22, 24); kidnapper (24:7).
   2. The false witness to be requited in kind (19:19).
- B. The judgment of God is equally severe against the same things, with the difference that in Christ there is a way of repentance.
   1. The sinner can let Christ destroy the sin before it destroys him.
   2. Read I Cor. 6:9-11 for same condemnation of—
   Moral impurity in all its forms
   Idolatry, or false worship
   Covetousness and stealing
   Intemperance
   False witness or reviling.

II. STERN MEASURES ARE IN ORDER FOR THE SAVING OF THE NATION.
- A. Israel was in a life-and-death struggle between truth and heathenism.
   —A tender plant, it had to have the ground cleared relentlessly.

51

B. Ours also is a personal life-and-death struggle. The idea of coasting into heaven is not in God's book. "What shall it profit a man if he gain the whole world and lose his own soul?" (Matt. 16:26).
"If thy right hand offend thee, cut if off" (Matt. 5:30).
"He that loveth father or mother more than me is not worthy" (Matt. 10:37).
". . . the loss of all things, that I may know Him . . ." (Phil. 3:7-11).

C. Stern measures are in order as a community.
(Farmer unhesitatingly shoots and kills prize bull when it attacks his daughter.)
The liquor traffic claims more lives than war.
A nation gives to the limit and seeks to destroy cancer because it kills many, but liquor destroys ten times as many, soul and body.
Shall we continue to feed and pet this monster?

III. THERE IS DEATH IN REFUSAL TO PUT AWAY THE EVIL.

A. Achan kept a wedge of gold, 200 shekels of silver, and a garment, thus bringing defeat to Israel at Ai, and death to his own household.

B. One man refuses to leave his beer, another his gambling, to accept Christ.

C. A whole nation becomes complacent and tolerant of sin — "If no one ever did any worse than I do . . ." But sin is sin. "Every one else does it . . ." But everyone else won't stand with you when you are judged.

CONCLUSION —

The blessings of Christ are worth any sacrifice. (John Chase says Korean Christians make no sacrifices — all they give up is their material possessions, family, and friends — and look at what they gain!)

52

THE LAW FOR THE FAMILY

(Deuteronomy 22:13-21)

INTRODUCTION —

There are a multitude of funny stories about marriage and in-laws — tell none.

Laughter and jesting are a double-edged sword without handle; can cut wielder.

The text is about marriage — and it is no laughing matter. Neither is the creation, the Law, the Gospel, the Church. Jesus covered the whole matter admirably in Matthew 19:3-6.

I. GOD MADE THEM MALE AND FEMALE — THIS MAY BE SAID OF THE WHOLE CREATION.

 A. Purpose is, in most cases the continuance of the species. "Be ye fruitful, and multiply . . . and replenish the earth" (Gen. 1:28).

 B. "For this cause shall a man leave his father and mother, and cleave to his wife."

  1. A home is for the sake of the children, and because children need protection, guidance, spiritual training. The home is permanent.

  2. A "help meet" — spiritual union.

  Two personalities merge into one, which is greater and finer, richer than either or both together — each bringing out the best in the other — neither complete without the other — "so then, neither is the wife without the husband, nor the husband without the wife."

 C. That which is given for a blessing is often used for a curse — the best things, misused, become the worst. "For this cause shall a man leave — and cleave unto his wife" becomes:

  1. Men make merchandise of this God-given passion — make slaves and playthings of women, and make beasts of themselves.

  2. Young people make a toy of the love of man for maid, and so exercise it that both real love and self-respect become impossible.

53

3. The entertainment world makes merchandise of this sacred gift.
4. Men, inflamed by enticements of entertainment and social world, leave wife and family to keep company another.

II. GOD HAS HIS NAMES FOR THESE THINGS— NOT BEAUTIFUL, BUT NOT SO UGLY AS THE SIN.
   A. Lasciviousness—lewd and lustful, immoral thought and action in general.
      Fornication—the unlawful union of man and woman.
      Adultery—such unlawful union, violating a marriage already established.
   B. They are all in the catalog of sinners that "shall not inherit the kingdom" (I Cor. 6:9) and "shall have their part in the lake which burneth with fire and brimstone" (Rev. 21:8).

III. GOD HAS HIS LAW CONCERNING THESE THINGS:
   A. Old Testament
      1. The harlot was to be stoned.
      2. Adulterers to be stoned, both man and woman.
         Betrothal binding as marriage.
      3. The man who forces a woman against her consent shall die—if she consents, both.
      4. Those who come together before marriage are required to marry.
   B. Present relation to Old Testament law
      1. Many think that a thing is right if society does not condemn it. *Society* is condemned.
      2. The control of sex is an emotional matter, to be accomplished by a greater emotion—Christian love.
      3. Real answer is in I Thessalonians 4:1-8 "It is of God."

CONCLUSION — There is only one who can say, "Go thy way, and sin no more" (John 8:11).

54

PREACHING THROUGH JOSHUA

Join with the rest of the church in reading this book in this month. Be in the worship services to hear the sermons based upon it.

HISTORY

The book of Joshua is the first of the "Books of History" in the Old Testament, but it follows closely and logically the "Books of Law" preceding it. It tells how the children of Israel entered and conquered the land of Canaan after their release from bondage in Egypt and their wanderings in the wilderness. Joshua, its hero, wrote a "book of the law of God" (see 24:26), but there is nothing in it to tell who wrote the book of Joshua. The book covers a period of about thirty years just prior to 1400 B.C.

Chapters 1-12 tell of the conquest of Canaan.

Chapters 13-21 tell of the division of the land among the Israelites.

Chapters 22-24 tell of closing scenes in the life of Joshua.

ARCHAEOLOGY

Archaeology, the study of remains from ancient human occupation, helps us much to understand the book of Joshua. Many have wondered why God commanded Joshua to destroy the Canaanites. Archaeology suggests an answer. Many of the idols and other objects that have been found are very obscene. One writer says, "Archaeologists who dig in the ruins of the Canaanite cities wonder why God did not destroy them sooner than He did!"

Excavations at Jericho and at Hazor have shown that these places were violently destroyed and burned at the end of the late Canaanite period (the Middle Bronze). For a long time no discoveries from Joshua's time were found in the area of Ai. Recent discoveries of Canaanite objects in the Ai area give evidence of the truthfulness of the Bible.

IMPORTANCE TO THE CHRISTIAN

The Book of Joshua:

Shows the hand of God in the history of men.

Warns of the punishment in store for men and nations which reject the right ways of God.

Demonstrates the need for a clear-cut, courageous choice to be made by each person individually.

Shows how God acted in preparing for the coming of His Son through the Israelites.

Points out our own need of a Savior, that forgiveness, and not punishment, may be our portion.

Sermon Outlines Provided:

"Go Forward!" (Josh. 1:1-9)
"After the Battle" (Josh. 8:30-35)
"A Dangerous Altar" (Josh. 22:10-34)
"Witness Against Ourselves" (Josh. 24:14-28)

Other Suggested Sermon Topics:

"The Conquest of the Crossing" (Josh. 3:14—4:14)
"One Sins; All Suffer" (Josh. 7:1-26)
"What Remains to be Possessed" (Josh. 13:1)
"A Man Alive at Eighty-five" (Josh. 14:6-15)

QUESTIONS OVER JOSHUA

1. Before the children of Israel crossed into Canaan Joshua sent two spies into what city? (2:1)
2. What memorial was placed at Gilgal? (4:20-24)
3. Whose sin caused Israel to suffer defeat at Ai? (7:1)
4. For whom did the sun stand still? (10:12, 13)
5. Name the two sons of Joseph who share in the land of Canaan. (16:1, 4)
6. What did the sons of Reuben and Manasseh call the altar they built? (22:34)
7. How old was Joshua when he died? (24:29)

GO FORWARD! (A New Year Sermon)
(Joshua 1:1-9)

INTRODUCTION —

Entry to the Promised Land was fulfillment of long preparation.

    A. Moses' death left responsibility with Joshua.
        1. He must continue what Moses had begun.
        2. Thus the theme of the text: "Be strong and of good courage." It was Moses' attitude.
    B. God declared a promise.
        1. He would support Joshua as He had Moses.
        2. He would fulfill the promise of a homeland.
        3. He would require active faith and obedience.

I. "ARISE, GO OVER JORDAN" (v. 2).

    A. God required a definite commitment.
        1. Israel must cross the Jordan in the sight of all.
        2. Similarly, definite commitments are required in business; through purchases, rents, contracts, etc.
        3. A strong faith will make commitments in morals and religion.
        Resolutions made are not so soon broken as those not made at all.
    B. God required a definite action.
        1. The riverbed became dry only after the priests' feet became wet.
        2. Breaking and making of habits requires doing, according to determination.
            a. Formally it applies to Bible reading, prayer, church attendance.
            b. Informally it applies to words and deeds in personal relationship.

II. "OBSERVE TO ALL THAT MOSES COMMANDED" (v. 7).

    A. God required continuing course of obedience.
        1. The law must be spoken and taught.

2. The law must be kept continually in mind, by thoughtful meditation.

3. The law must direct the doings of the people.

B. A breakdown in obedience would nullify the promise: "Then you shall succeed."

1. Israel was defeated at Ai because of disobedience.

2. So we must beware the tendency to set aside the revealed will of God in favor of a general enthusiasm for "doing good."

3. Observe the condemnation of some who have even "done many wonderful works in the name" of Christ (Matthew 7:22).

III. "I WILL NOT FAIL THEE NOR FORSAKE THEE" (v. 5).

"The Lord thy God is with thee whithersoever thou goest" (v. 9).

A. The promise was interwoven with the command; neither is complete without the other.

B. "I will give the land." God set the boundaries.

C. "None shall stand before you" (v. 6). The conquering power was God's.

D. "The Lord thy God is with thee" (v. 9).

1. His presence with us cannot be maintained apart from our presence with Him.

2. Some doubt the presence of God because they expect the wrong things in evidence that He is there.

CONCLUSION —

God's commission to Joshua was echoed in Christ's commission to His apostles (Matthew 28:18-20).

A. Commitment and action are required in teaching and baptism.

B. Obedience is required in "observing all . . . I have commanded."

C. Presence is promised: "Lo, I am with you always."

AFTER THE BATTLE (Veterans Day Sermon)
(Joshua 8:30-35)

INTRODUCTION — Historical

A. The first great part of the campaign for the conquest of Canaan ended in a religious service.

B. Are we troubled at the ethics involved in the conquest?

  1. There was moral necessity for drastic action. Survival of worship of the true God was at stake, not for the sake of God, nor for the sake of Israel, but for the sake of all. Indescribable abominations of Canaanites crept in when Israel "went easy."

  2. Joshua's practice gentle according to practice of his day. No willful torture; pillage kept at a minimum.

C. Jericho, taken by a miracle. Ai, attempted, but Israel defeated because of the sin of Achan. Ai taken by strategy, one group drawing army out; other putting town to torch. Then came obedience to the command of Moses to establish covenant.

D. The occasion —

Half the tribes on the slope of Mt. Gerizim, half on Mt. Ebal (60 rods apart). Altar of whole stones erected on Mt. Ebal; altar plastered and the Law imprinted in the plaster. Valley of Moreh echoed to the sound of the blessing and the curse. (Travelers still note how sound travels in still clear air there.) Read from Deuteronomy 27:16-26.

Application to our own situation after crises.

I. OBEDIENCE TO THE DIVINE COMMAND GIVEN THROUGH MOSES.

A. Command given at a time of trial kept in an hour of success.

B. We have not special commands given at any one hour, but His commands remain.

  1. A service man writes, "I'll be in church."—Not yet.

59

2. What of the promises we made then—?
"When war is over and I am less busy—"
Work for the church—attend evening service.
Read Bible—have family prayer.

II. THE SHARED CONFESSION (SIN OFFERINGS) AND WORSHIP.

A. The victor is tempted to think that his goodness has won the battle.
B. We have humbling reminders in the form of strikes and crime.

III. LEARNING THE WILL OF GOD.

A. Israel served notice that ongoing national program was concerned with the will and law of God. That will must be learned before it can be done.
B. Shall we say, "Run along, God, until we need you again to help us win another war?"
C. Until we learn from Him the art of getting on with people in spiritual relationships, every other art is self-destructive. "If ye bite and devour one another, take heed that ye be not consumed one of the other" (Gal. 5:13).

IV. COMMITMENT TO THE WILL OF GOD.

A. The people were there and said, "Amen."
B. No great program can succeed if it is adopted *for* a nation only by a few men in conference—the people must be solidly behind it.
C. The *people* of the church must be committed to the program of the church.
Do we desire a flourishing church?
A program that will serve the needs of all?
Do we wish to escape the horrors of a crime wave?
Do we wish to see a real spiritual revival?
Let all the people say Amen, not only with words, but with deeds of devotion.

In Christ there is that which will meet our needs, but until we commit ourselves to Him we receive no blessing.

60

A DANGEROUS ALTAR
(Joshua 22:10-34)

INTRODUCTION —
Things are not always what they seem.

    A. Jesus admonished, "Judge not according to the appearance, but judge righteous judgment" (John 7:24).

        1. Righteous judgment demands investigation.

        2. Righteous judgment demands an honest report.

    B. What shall we say, then, of these:

        1. "What do you suppose he was doing in *that* place?"

        2. "But he reached into his pocket as though he was drawing a gun!"

    C. The answer is in an altar that almost started a war. The story has a happy ending because it includes patient inquiry before action.

I. THE EASTERN TRIBES BUILD AN ALTAR AT THE FORDS OF JORDAN (vv. 10, 11).

    A. The background.

        1. Reuben, Gad, and half of Manasseh had chosen the land of Gilead, east of Jordan, for their dwelling.

        2. They had continued with the other tribes to conquer the land of Canaan.

        3. Now they were dismissed to take up their homes.

    B. The altar they built.

        1. It was at the riverside, a natural boundary.

        2. It followed the pattern of the altar in the tabernacle.

        3. The offering of sacrifices was forbidden in any other place than tabernacle.

    C. The incident reported.

        1. It looked like forbidden worship, or idolatry.

        2. Israel remembered how the whole nation had suffered for the idolatry or rebellion of a few at Ai, or at Baal-Peor (Num. 25:1-9).

II. THE WESTERN TRIBES PREPARE FOR WAR (v. 12).

    A. They took the matter with utmost seriousness.

1. As an affront to God, it must be punished.
2. Moses had commanded the destruction of any city that practiced idolatry (Deut. 13:12-18).

B. They gathered at Shiloh, the place where they had received Joshua's commission.

III. PHINEHAS LEADS AN INQUIRY (vv. 13-20).

A. The inquirers were capable men; leaders of the tribes.
B. They emphasized the seriousness of the situation.
   1. Idolatry had brought God's wrath, and would bring it again.
   2. Application: Leaders who wink at evil share its responsibility.
C. They offered a way of reconciliation.
   1. If they could not remain free of idolatry in Gilead, the other tribes would make room for them in Canaan.
   2. Foreshadows New Testament: "Ye that are spiritual, restore . . . (Gal. 6:1).

IV. THE EASTERN TRIBES RESPOND (vv. 21-29).

A. They acknowledged that idolatry was a deadly sin.
B. They explained the purpose and nature of the altar they had built.
   1. It was not to another god, nor for offering sacrifices.
   2. It was for testimony and a link with the other tribes. All must know that God was worshiped on both sides of the Jordan.

V. THE RESPONSE BROUGHT REJOICING.

A. First Phinehas, then all Israel, welcomed the explanation as made known.
B. The nation was unified and saved from war.
C. The incident strengthened Israel against idolatry.
D. So understanding and reconciliation can strengthen any community.

CONCLUSION —

We rejoice with Phinehas the priest, but more with Christ our High Priest, who brings, not an explanation of innocence, but cleansing from guilt.

62

WITNESS AGAINST OURSELVES
(Joshua 24:14-28)

INTRODUCTION —

Nothing is so terrible as self-condemnation. (Illustration — A politician discredited in the eyes of his people by re-broadcasts of his old speeches.)

American courts, in policy of protecting innocent, will not force one to testify against himself.

I. CHOOSE YE THIS DAY!

    A. The situation of Israel, surrounded by idolatrous people; if they allowed themselves to be indecisive, it would end in drifting wrong. Let your choice be of your own making, and stand by that choice!

    B. Many make final choice without knowing it — they think they are not choosing. — A refusal to choose the right is to choose the wrong.

    C. To drift brings the evil of a wrong choice without the courage of it.

II. "WE WILL SERVE JEHOVAH" — Naturally.

    A. Any other reply would be unthinkable under the circumstances.

    B. Nearly every one approves the good, and "would like" to be on the right side.

        1. He approves an upright family, community, and national life.

        2. If he does wrong, he rationalizes it to make it look right, or harmless.

    C. Many, faced with the challenge to make a decision, have come into the church, and then have done nothing more about it. "Many profess Christianity with far more irreverence than others keep aloof from it."

III. "YE CANNOT SERVE JEHOVAH" — Not that easy; not the line of least resistance.

    A. Read Luke 14:25-33.

B. See marriage service—"It is not by any to be entered into lightly or unadvisedly, but reverently, discreetly, soberly, and in the fear of God."

C. "He will not forgive your transgression nor your sin." (If you declare yourself for Him, you leave yourself without excuse if you then turn away from Him.) See Hebrews 10:26-29.

IV. "NAY, BUT WE WILL SERVE JEHOVAH."

A. Ready now to accept the greater obligation with open eyes.

B. We ourselves have declared in favor of:
   1. The Christian life: "How shall we, that are dead to sin, live any longer therein?" (Rom. 6:2).
   2. The Lordship of Christ: There is no easy way to escape His commands.
   3. A personal faith: "Be ready always to give an answer to every man that asketh you a reason of the hope that is in you with meekness and fear" (I Pet. 3:15).
   4. Non-sectarian Christianity.
      a. Root out the sectarian spirit within and among us.
      b. Learn the doctrines of Christ, not the doctrines of the church.

V. "YE ARE WITNESSES AGAINST YOURSELVES."— You will be judged by your own statements.

A. "Thou art inexcusable, O man . . . " (Rom. 2:1).

B. See Romans 2:21-23 for application of self-judgment.

C. (A fitting sort of judgment would take place if a moving picture should show the things we did and said.)

CONCLUSION —

We are led to say with the apostles, "Who then can be saved?" "With men it is impossible, but with God all things are possible." (Matt. 19:25,26).

PREACHING THROUGH JUDGES AND RUTH

Judges and Ruth deal with the same period in the history of Israel—approximately 1400 to 1100 B.C. Judges tells of public events at various times; Ruth tells of the doings of one family at Bethlehem at a time about midway of this period.

After Joshua died the nation had no strong government, but formed a loose confederacy. They were surrounded by enemies. Among themselves they were united and protected principally by their faith in God. Many times they slipped into indifference and idolatry, and then God allowed their enemies to afflict them, sometimes in one part of Palestine, sometimes in another. When Israel repented, God raised up leaders, called "judges," to overthrow the oppressors and to lead in paths of peace. The Book of Judges records seven periods of oppression under seven nations, and it tells of fourteen judges.

Archaeologists have found evidence of many places and events recorded in Judges, thus again establishing the truth of the Bible record.

OUTLINE OF JUDGES

Chapters 1,2 Final conquests, Israel's forgetfulness and punishment.

Chapters 3-16 Stories of the Judges
    3 Othniel, Ehud, and Shamgar
    4,5 Deborah and Barak
    6-8 Gideon
    9 Abimelech
    10-12 Tola, Jair, and Jephthah
    13-16 Samson

Chapters 17-21 Stories of the tribes.
    17,18 Migration of the Danites.
    19-21 Feud between Benjamin and the other tribes.

IMPORTANCE OF THE BOOKS

The hand of God is clearly seen in the history of the people. God's Word does not whitewash the sins of His people; it tells the truth. The ugly doings of the days when "every man did that which was right in his own eyes" (17:6) prove that "there is a way which seemeth right unto a man, but the end thereof are the ways of death" (Prov. 14:12).

The book of Ruth shows that God did not scorn the righteous foreigner in building the nation through which to send His Son. Ruth was an ancestress of Jesus. The fields where she gleaned at Bethlehem heard angel voices twelve centuries later.

Sermon Outlines Provided:

"The Hand of a Woman" (Judges 4:1-10)
"The Men Who Kept On" (Judges 8:1-6)
"Orpah, Who Almost—" (Ruth 1:6-18)
"Ruth, the Friend" (Ruth 1:5-18; 2:1-13)
"Naomi, the Faithful" (Ruth 1:19-22; 4:13-17)

Other Suggested Sermon Topics:

"The Man Who Faced Judgment" (Judges 1:7)
"The Politician's Parable" (Judges 8:7-21)

QUESTIONS OVER JUDGES AND RUTH

1. Caleb gave his daughter for a wife to what man for capturing a certain city? (Judges 1:12,13)
2. Who was the second judge, who killed the King of Moab? (3:14-22)
3. Who put out a fleece to test the Lord? (6:36,37)
4. After the death of Gideon the Israelites worshiped what gods? (8:33)
5. Who vowed that if victorious in battle he would sacrifice whatever first came from his house to meet him? (11:30,31)
6. What was unusual about the 700 men accurate with slings? (20:16)
7. Name the wives of Naomi's sons. (Ruth 1:4)
8. Which daughter-in-law left Moab and returned to Israel with Naomi? (1:16-19)
9. In whose field did Ruth glean? (2:1)
10. Who was the great-grandson of Ruth and Boaz who became king of Israel? (4:22)

THE HAND OF A WOMAN
(Judges 4:1-10; Cf. I Tim. 2:8-15)

INTRODUCTION —

(Thesis): There is such a thing as too close attention to one's own business.

I. ISRAEL NEEDS A LEADER.
- A. After Joshua, no central leader: "Each did that which was right in his own eyes."
  —Chief immediate need of the nation was for protection.
- B. Leaders of limited ability were found and used where they were.
  1. Othniel
  2. Ehud   Now no leader appeared.
  3. Shamgar
- C. Present affliction was at hands of Canaanite king Jabin, whose commander, Sisera, had 900 chariots at his disposal.
- D. Application: Not all whom Christ involved, came to serve under Him.
  1. "Whosoever will come after me . . ."
  2. The harvest is still plenteous, and the laborers still few.
     a. There is need for preachers, teachers, youth leaders, etc.
     b. Many still "prefer not to be in the prominent places."

II. A LEADER TAKES OVER, AND SUCCEEDS.
- A. Deborah, of Ephraim (some distance removed from the danger spot), prophetess, sees the need, and attemps to stir resistance.
- B. Calls Barak to gather the forces of Naphtali and Zebulon.
- C. He agrees, on condition that she will go with him; she succeeds, but says the glory for the victory will go to a woman.
- D. Israel camps at Tabor; Sisera comes; Israel attacks,

67

withdraws, engulfs the Canaanites. (Josephus tells of rain and hail coming from behind the Israelites into the faces of the Canaanites.)

E. Sisera finally falls to the hand of another woman, Jael.

F. Application—One hears occasionally of a church held together and the doors kept open through difficult times by unlikely leadership, even that of a woman—and no credit to the men who made it so.

III. GLORY IS GIVEN TO THE LEADER, AND CONDEMNATION TO THE ONES TOO BUSY WITH THEIR OWN AFFAIRS TO TAKE THE RISK OF HELPING GOD'S CAUSE.

A. Honor to Deborah.

B. Song of praise includes Jael (See Judges 5:24, for stronger statement honor than that given to Mary, the mother of Jesus!)

C. The people of Meroz are cursed because they remained conveniently neutral.

D. See the courageous commitment of Paul. "He that is not with me is against me" (Matt. 12:30).

CONCLUSION —

Invitation to courageous commitment, which does not wait for someone else to shame one into doing his duty.

68

THE MEN WHO KEPT ON
(Judges 8:1-12)

INTRODUCTION —

The less well known sequel to the well known story of Gideon and the three hundred who routed the hordes of Midian. Here they were finishing what they started in the plain of Jezreel with their pitchers, torches, and trumpets.

    A. Preparation and onslaught had given them a sleepless night. Pursuit of the fleeing enemy had occupied the day, and some twenty miles to the Jordan.

    B. Men from the tribe of Ephraim had cut off the main force of Midianites at the Jordan, but some 15,000 of the original 120,000 had gotten past.

    C. Gideon's three hundred arrived at the Jordan, "faint, yet pursuing them" (v. 4).

    —The battle not over until victory is complete.

    D. Gideon's company gained the victory against three evident obstacles.

I. TEMPTATION TO ACCEPT A PARTIAL VICTORY.

    A. Marauders from far-off Midian had been plundering the Israelites in Gideon's homeland near the Sea of Galilee. Now only one-eighth of the Midianite army remained, running pell-mell for home with their kings, Zebah and Zalmunnah.

    B. Surely no major threat remained; but God's plan required total destruction of the enemy.

    C. So now a partial victory over Satan and sin is not sufficient: ". . . Till we all come in the unity of the faith . . . unto a perfect man, unto the measure of the stature of the fulness of Christ" (Eph. 4:13).

    D. Partial cleansing from sin leaves the sinner still guilty, and a partial commitment to Christ leaves the rebel still rebellious.

II. TEMPTATION OF WEARINESS AND HUNGER.

    A. The strenuous exertions of the night and the day, without time or opportunity for refreshment, left them understandably "faint."

B. The physical stamina and endurance of the three hundred must be noted.

C. Compare with the distance runner, "when feet are lead, the body aches, the stomach burns, the breath comes in gasps, and you have to comfort yourself with knowing that the man ahead and the one behind feel the same way."

D. "Let us not be weary in well doing: for in due season we shall reap, if we faint not" (Gal. 6:9).

E. Paul's example fits his advice: Even after he had written, "I have finished my course," he added, "When thou comest, bring . . . the books" (II Tim. 4:7, 13). There was still learning and work to be done!

III. TEMPTATION TO DISCOURAGEMENT FROM "FRIENDS."

A. Ephraimites pouted because they were not in on the beginning of victory (vv. 1-3).
   1. They had to be mollified with extravagant praise for what they did.
   2. Selfishness and childishness among the saints can be discouraging.

B. Men of Succoth and Penuel (another ten miles beyond Jordan) refused to help because they weren't sure Gideon was going to succeed.
   1. These were in the tribe of Gad, whose ties with other tribes were questioned.
   2. In the church, some are reluctant to become involved unless immediate rewards are assured.

C. Gideon finished the job at hand before "taking care" of these discouragers!

D. Compare Paul's loneliness; "Demas hath forsaken me . . ." (II Tim. 4:10).

CONCLUSION —

God's men press on to victory, confident in the assurance written in Isaiah 40:29-31. "He giveth power to the faint . . ."

70

ORPAH, WHO ALMOST —
(Ruth 1:6-18)

INTRODUCTION —

The story of Christ's coming reaches in every direction. Ruth is a part of it. But consider Chilion's wife, who also seems to have been faithful, dealt kindly with Naomi, and started to leave her homeland with her. The story is about Ruth. The blessing is hers, not Orpah's. Why?

I. ORPAH HAD GOOD INTENTIONS AND MADE A GOOD START.
   A. In Moab:
      1. Faithful wife, grieving with others at loss of husband.
      2. Affectionate to Naomi, dealing kindly with her.
      3. Hearing of Jehovah, and blessed by Naomi in His name.
   B. On the journey.
      1. At least followed the custom of seeing a traveler to the border.
      2. Seems to have intended to go to Bethlehem with Naomi.
      3. Affectionate and reluctant in parting.
   C. She did all that was reasonable and natural — perhaps more.
   D. In this she is the picture of most people associated with churches.
      1. They are attracted to the good and righteous.
      2. They follow it a certain way, perhaps all that is reasonable.
      3. These are the two soils, shallow with rock, and choked with thistles.
      4. These are the multitudes who followed Jesus.
      5. These are the Christians who are enthusiastic about one phase: Mother's Bible; baptism; blood atonement; creeds; fellowship; social reform; peace of mind.

71

6. These are they who attend church when it is convenient; read the Bible occasionally; pray when in need; and give what is reasonable.

II. ORPAH WAS TESTED.
   A. Naomi's suggestion that she return.
      1. Was it a deliberate test, as Jesus' challenge to the Syrophoenician woman?
      2. The suggestion reminded of home, family, friends in Moab, and the lonely life of a stranger in Bethlehem, without normal rewards.
   B. There come testing times.
      1. The multitudes following Jesus were offended at His "hard sayings."
      2. The apostles were offended at the sight of the cross.
      3. The rich young ruler couldn't take the challenge.
      4. Presently—
         a. There is difficulty, or ingratitude, in the church.
         b. There are financial reverses at home.
         c. "It isn't easy"—
            To forsake the religion of one's family.
            To go to church when no one else your age goes.
            To go to the small church in the community.

III. THERE WAS A LIMIT TO ORPAH'S LOVE, AND SHE RETURNED (It was reasonable).
   A. She to her family, her nation, her god Chemosh, and oblivion.
   B. Jesus said to the apostles—"Wilt thou also go away?" (John 6:67).
   C. "Demas hath forsaken me, having loved this present world" (II Tim. 4:10).
   D. How often do you hear, "There's a limit . . ."?

CONCLUSION—

Christ comes to earth and we get acquainted (not by famine in heaven). He returns, and we say, "I will follow thee whithersoever thou goest." Will we, to His home with the Father?

72

RUTH, THE FRIEND
(Ruth 1:15-18; 2:1-13)

INTRODUCTION — The name Ruth means "friend."

    A. A quick glance at the story tells why:

        Got along well with her mother-in-law, before and after death of husband.

        Gained smiles and favor in the fields where she gleaned.

        Gained a good name in the village of Bethlehem, though she was a stranger.

        Gained the favor, later to become wife, of the wealthy hero of the story.

    B. Surely she knew how to "Win Friends and Influence People." To have friends one must show himself friendly" (Prov. 18:24). A closer study reveals the *deeper meaning*.

I. FRIENDSHIP IS MORE THAN FRIENDLINESS.

    A. There is a surface friendliness, often mistaken for friendship. —"Never sees a stranger" (Does he make friends, or acquaintances?) (Illus. "I buy all my Christmas presents in October." "But how do you know in October who your friends are going to be in December?")

    B. That is not the stuff of Scripture and poetry:

        "There is a friend that sticketh closer than a brother."

        "A friend is like ivy; the greater the ruin, the closer he clings."

        "A friend is one who comes in when all the world has gone out."

    C. True friendship is of heroic, lasting stuff:

        "Because of your firm faith, I kept the track

        Whose sharp set stones my strength had almost spent—

        I could not meet your eyes if I turned back,

        So on I went."

II. OBSERVE THE BLESSINGS OF FRIENDSHIP.
  A. It made home with Naomi a pleasant place in spite of Naomi's dreary pessimism. — Homes need more than love and duty; they need the brightness of congeniality.
  B. It gained an entree among strangers, in Bethlehem.
  C. It made work with others a pleasure, and avoided jealousies.
  D. It avoided any employer-employee troubles . . . So every relationship is blessed by it.

III. THE CHARACTERISTICS OF FRIENDSHIP.
  A. A solid basis in mutual self-giving: Two principles of the friendly approach:
    1. Every one I meet has something I need.
    2. I have no right to claim that something without first offering something better in exchange.
    Ruth needed the deep faith that was Naomi's; she offered love and helpfulness.
  B. Spirit of courage and good cheer; not critical or fault-finding. "It is one of the charitable provisions of Providence that perfection is not essential to friendship." — Alexander Smith.
  C. Unselfishness, not quick to take offense or feel slighted.
  D. Patience and persistence in the expressions of good will.
  E. Modesty — neither boasting nor demanding — and gratitude.
  F. Industriousness — the lazy friend is a wear on the patience of others.
  G. No gossip, betraying confidences and embarrassing friends.

CONCLUSION — The eternal friendship.
  A. The qualities of true friendship make it better with age, best in eternity.
  B. Jesus Christ, center of friendship. "What a Friend we Have in Jesus." — Millions are friends of each other because they are friends of Him.

74

NAOMI, THE FAITHFUL
(Ruth 1:19-22; 4:13-17)

INTRODUCTION —

Naomi had been away from home for ten years, and on coming back she found everything changed. (The story from the first verses of the Book.)

I. THE SURROUNDINGS HAD CHANGED.

A. Not so great changes as ten years make now, but observe children grown up; old friends dead; new houses built, etc.

B. See the rapidity of change with us. Found church directory 20 years old:
1. One fourth of former members are still active.
2. One person in seven still lives in the same place.
3. One third of the businesses which advertised in it are still going.

C. Through it all Naomi remained faithful.
1. God was real to her, even when it seemed that His hand was heavy.
2. She was quick to bless Him for the good that came to her.
3. "Love is not love that alters when it alteration finds."
(Transition—Part of the seeming change in things may be change in ourselves.)

II. NAOMI HERSELF HAD CHANGED IN TEN YEARS
—"Is this Naomi?"

A. "Call me not Naomi (pleasant) call me Mara (bitter)."
1. "The hand of Jehovah has been bitter against me."
2. Widowhood, childlessness, poverty—what other affliction is there?

B. We go back to the Old Place. Things are not as we remember them; *we* have changed.
1. The changes we see in places and people are often the reflections of the changes that have occurred in ourselves.

75

2. Thus the worship in church is either richer or less helpful; reflecting self.

C. Through the changes in herself, Naomi remained faithful. —Her prayers might now be offered through tears, but they were offered (See 1:20, 21).

III. NAOMI'S FAITH HAD CHANGED—(If it had not she probably would not have kept it.)

A. There was not any change in the revealed truth on which her faith was based. Her God was still the one who gave the Law at Sinai. The change was in her understanding of Him.

B. She had thought of Him as the defender of Israel and the giver of good.
—Now she sees His hand also chastening those whom He loves.

C. Her people thought of Him as the God of Israel only.
1. Hear Boaz, "Jehovah, under whose wing you have come . . ."
2. But Naomi said in a strange land, "May Jehovah deal kindly with you . . ."
3. Thus her faith could survive ten years in a strange land, mid strange worship.

D. It was a triumphant and attractive faith in the midst of difficulty—"Thy God shall be my God," said Ruth.

E. Observe among us the loss of many whose faith never grows, and is shed like an outgrown garment. A man-sized faith needed for the life of a man.

F. The Gospel can not and must not be changed, but our understanding must grow.
—"Now that I am become a man, I have put away childish things" (I Cor. 13:11).

CONCLUSION —

The Apostle who said, "My little children, . . . love one another" was a changed man in changed circumstances and bigger faith than he who said, "Shall we call down fire from heaven?" to burn the unfriendly village.

76

PREACHING THROUGH I SAMUEL

A Book of History, this record tells the story of Israel for a period of three generations, approximtely 1100 to 1000 B.C. It marks several important changes. Before this the tribes of Israel had been united only in God, their King; now they seek a human ruler. God's ministers had been the priests and Levites; beginning with Samuel the order of the prophets, or God's special messengers to men, arose.

Here the Philistines first come into prominence as enemies of Israel. They were the inhabitants of the plains along the Mediterranean Sea, especially in Southwestern Palestine. The Canaanite god, Dagon, was their principal deity. Perhaps more than other pagans, they rejected and reviled Jehovah (Num. 33:55).

For the Christian the Book has special interest as it shows how the kingly line of David, from which Christ came, was established. Note also the emphasis upon righteousness as an element of acceptable worship, trust in God as essential to the life of the nation, and obedience to God's commands as of more value than sacrifice.

A BRIEF OUTLINE OF I SAMUEL

Chapters 1-3   Samuel is born, serves in the tabernacle, and is called to be prophet.

4-7   The Ark of the Covenant is captured in battle and finally returned.

8-10   The Kingdom of Israel is organized, and Saul made king.

11-15   Saul reigns, disobeys God, and is rejected.

16-17   David is secretly anointed king, and comes into prominence.

18-27   David flees the jealous wrath of Saul.

28-31   Saul declines in power, is defeated, and dies.

Sermon Outlines Provided:

"Boys at Home" (I Sam. 2:12-26)
"The Ark That Saved No One" (I Sam. 4:1-11)

"A New Administration" (I Sam. 12:12-25)
"Obedience Better Than Sacrifice" (I Samuel 15:10-23)

Other Suggested Sermon Topics:
"Like All the Nations" (I Sam. 8:1-9, 19-22)
"The Lord Will Not Forsake" (I Sam. 12:12-25)
"God Looks on the Heart" (I Sam. 16:1-13)
"There Is a Friend" (I Sam. 18:1-4; 23:14-18)
"When He Was Hungry" (I Sam. 21:1-10)

QUESTIONS OVER I SAMUEL

1. Who was Samuel's mother? (1:20)
2. Name the priest whose sons were worthless and did not know the Lord. (2:12)
3. God revealed to whom His judgment against Eli's house? (3:11-14)
4. What news caused Eli to fall and be killed? (4:18)
5. Why did Israel desire to have a king? (8:5)
6. Who was the first king of Israel? (9:17)
7. Who anointed the first two kings of Israel? (10:1; 16:13)
8. Why did the Philistines not want the Israelites to have blacksmiths? (13:19, 20)
9. What man and his armor bearer led in surprising and routing the Philistines at Michmash? (14:1-23)
10. Samuel told Saul that obedience was better than what? (15:22)
11. How does I Samuel describe the youngest son of Jesse? (16:11, 12).
12. Goliath, the giant killed by David, was from what army? (17:4)
13. Why did Saul try to kill David? (18:6-11)
14. Who was David's first wife? (18:20, 27)
15. How did she save David's life? (19:12, 13)
16. Who was David's second wife? (25:14, 42)
17. Saul went to a witch at what place in an effort to talk with Samuel who was dead? (28:7, 8)
18. Saul killed himself after who refused to kill him? (31:4)

BOYS AT HOME
(I Samuel 2:12-26)

INTRODUCTION —

Nothing more important in this fate-filled time than children.

A. In the year 1809, Napoleon's battles made news, but babies of 1809 made history:
   - William E. Gladstone, born that year in Liverpool.
   - Abraham Lincoln born in a Kentucky log cabin.
   - Oliver Wendell Holmes born in Massachusetts.
   - Alfred Tennyson born in a Somerset rectory.
   - Felix Mendelssohn at Hamburg; Frederick Chopin at Warsaw.

B. If we lose out with the children we can't recover.
   - Better to form character than try to reform what is deformed.

C. Focus of attention to this matter.
   1. From FBI on down, finger is being pointed to the home.
   2. State law makes parents financially responsible for children's deeds.

D. In our Scripture, we have a story of Eli's success with Samuel, and failure with his own two sons—why?

I. SAMUEL'S COURSE WAS LAID OUT TOWARD GOD: ELI'S SONS' WAS NOT.

A. See names: Samuel (Name of God); Hophni (Fighter); Phinehas (Brazen mouthed).

B. With the coming of a child, one accepts responsibility of determining his course.
   1. In physical matters, as food and health.
   2. In education, that he may have opportunity.
   3. In spiritual matters. If one seeks to withhold training, the very silence trains one to think that God is not important.

C. The child may rebel at discipline as a river rebels at

79

dikes, but he will despise and be made insecure by the lack of it.

D. See Timothy: "From a child thou hast known the Scriptures" (II Tim. 3:15). So each needs church, prayer, Scripture memory; part in home worship.

II. SAMUEL HAD RESPONSIBILITIES; ELI'S SONS HAD PRIVILEGES.

A. For his own sons, Eli seemed to think that life's goal is pleasant fortune; it is really spiritual growth.

B. A mark of manhood is the acceptance of responsibility.
   1. Employers note the lack of it among employees.
   2. Churches suffer for lack of it among members.
   3. Criminals make their own wishes the law.

C. The U.S. Senator whose son carries newspapers in Washington has the right idea.

D. In the church, youth is best served when youth is most serving.

III. SAMUEL HAD CLOSE AND ACTIVE ASSOCIATION WITH ELI; HIS OWN SONS DID NOT.

A. That sort of association produced Elisha with Elijah; Timothy with Paul—and even the Son of God on earth, through contact with His Father.

B. One reason the farm is a good place to bring up a family.
   1. City workers have to make the associations that come naturally on the farm.
   2. Need to include work as well as play together.

C. (Illus.) Judge, sentencing young criminal, says, "How can you so disgrace a splendid man like your father?" Reply: "Yeah, I hear tell he's an all right guy. I wouldn't know. He never had much time for me."

CONCLUSION —

Philippians 2:19-22—Timothy who also had known—
1. A course turned toward God from the beginning.
2. Responsibilities of service.
3. Association "as a son with his father."

THE ARK THAT SAVED NO ONE
(I Samuel 4:1-11)

INTRODUCTION —

There is religion-abuse just as deadly as drug abuse.

    A. The Bible used as a good luck piece. One says, "If you have bleeding, there's a certain verse in Ezekiel you can read and the bleeding will stop."

    B. Religion used to benefit business or politics.

    C. Church used to enhance social status.

    D. So Israel sinned in using the Ark of the Covenant to protect them in war.

        1. Early in Samuel's prophetic career, Philistines were oppressors.

        2. Scene opens with battle at Aphek.

I. ISRAEL LEFT THE ARK AT SHILOH (vv. 1, 2).

    A. The tabernacle with the Ark of the Covenant rested at Shiloh in the central highlands.

    B. In battle near Ebenezer Israel suffered 4000 casualties.
      —They called it an act of God and asked why.

    C. The answer had been given already (Numbers 33:50-56).

        1. They had not obeyed God in clearing the land of idolatrous inhabitants.

        2. "To obey is better than sacrifice." (I Sam. 15:22).

II. ISRAEL BROUGHT THE ARK TO EBENEZER (vv. 3, 4).

    A. It was a foolish move.

        1. The very act was an imitation of their pagan enemies.

        2. They had no command of God (as they did at Jericho) to bring the Ark.

        3. They said of the Ark, "*It* may save us." They didn't mention God.

    B. Eli's sons, Hophni and Phinehas, concurred in the folly.

        1. As priests, they had the care of the Ark.

        2. They came along, following, the military men.

        3. Tragedy follows when men try to use God for men's purposes.

III. ISRAEL TRUSTED THE ARK TO WIN THE BATTLE (vv. 5-9).
   A. They rejoiced loudly in their false hopes of victory.
      1. Some people still rest on such assurances as "once in grace, always . . ."
      2. Others depend foolishly on the symbols of religion.
   B. The Philistines also were impressed.
      1. They were frightened, remembering Jericho and Egypt.
      2. They thought that God was present in the Ark.
      3. They exhorted one another to desperate courage (touch of nobility here).
      4. They feared slavery more than they feared the dangers of battle.

IV. ISRAEL LOST THE ARK, THE BATTLE, AND THEIR ARMY (vv. 10, 11).
   A. The Philistines fought with desperate human courage, and won.
   B. The Israelites —
      1. Lacked God's help; the enterprise was their own.
      2. Lacked human force because they pinned false hopes on the Ark.
      3. Such is the tragic situation of those who believe in faith, rather than believing in and obeying God.
   C. Disaster for Israel was complete.
      1. Casualties numbered 30,000 — seven times greater than former defeat.
      2. The presumptuous priests died. Phinehas' posthumously born son was "Ichabod" (glory has departed).
      3. The Ark in which they trusted was taken from them.

CONCLUSION —
   Observe contrast of two thieves on crosses with Christ.
      A. One, like the foolish Israelites, demanded magic from religion: "Save thyself and us!" (Luke 23:39).
      B. The other acknowledged Christ as King and pled His mercy (Luke 23:40-43). "Seek first the kingdom of God and His righteousness!" (Matt. 6:33).

A NEW ADMINISTRATION
(I Samuel 12:12-25)

INTRODUCTION —

A farewell address from a retiring administrator.

    A. Notable is Washington's Farewell Address. He expressed himself at length and laid down sound principles for the ongoing of the U.S.A.

    B. So I Samuel 12 records Samuel's farewell address.
        1. Samuel felt himself rejected in Israel's demand for a king.
        2. Saul chosen, anointed, and established as king.
        3. Samuel announces his retirement from administration as a judge in Israel, but assures his continuing concern.

I. WHAT SHALL THE NATION DO? ("You and your king" appear as one entity.)

    A. They shall confess their sin of rebellion against God.
        1. That sin was noted in Samuel's recital of history.
        2. That sin was called to attention by a miracle of summer storm (vv. 16-19). — Rain just didn't happen at harvest time (Proverbs 26:1).

    B. They shall accept God's cleansing and go on.
        1. They are to fear God (vv. 14, 24), but not fear the consequences of repented and forgiven sin (v. 20).
        2. The judgments and blessings of God depend on their future actions.

    C. They shall live righteously before God (vv. 14, 24).
        1. Thanks for God's blessing will motivate their service.
        2. Awareness of God's judgment will warn them against idolatry.

II. WHAT SHALL THE MAN OF GOD DO IN RETIREMENT?

    A. He shall face the evil for what it is (v. 20).
        1. Love for his people does not blind him to their faults.
        2. Hatred for sin does not destroy his care for the people.

B. He shall continue to pray for them, people and leader (v. 23). —The admonition in I Timothy 2:1-4.
C. He shall instruct the people "in the good and right way."
　1. The knowledge of right and wrong is a treasure to be cherished and conveyed (I Kings 3:9).
　2. The learner never outgrows need for refresher courses.
　3. The teacher never outgrows opportunities to admonish. —Observe that Samuel remained an unofficial counselor to Saul.

III. WHAT WILL GOD DO?
A. He will remain the constant element amid all changing circumstances.
B. He will leave mankind free to choose his own course.
　1. God had been Israel's King (v. 12), but gave them Saul at their demand (14).
　2. He will judge on basis of their choices, but will not compel.
C. He will reward and punish according to men's relationship to Him.
　1. Both king and people are responsible to God.
　2. God's judgments demonstrated in history, and certain for the future.
D. He will accept the penitent sinner (v. 22).
　1. Punishment does not mean utter abandonment: "He will not forsake."
　2. His identification with His people is part of His unchanging nature.
　3. In Christ He has chosen a "peculiar people" (I Peter 2:9, 10).

CONCLUSION —

In 1865 the news of Abraham Lincoln's assassination brought near riot in New York City. The seething multitude near the stock exchange was quieted when James A. Garfield stepped to a balcony and shouted a brief assurance, concluding, "God still reigns, and the Government in Washington still stands!" —Among all changes in administration, and if government falls, God still reigns.

OBEDIENCE BETTER THAN SACRIFICE
(I Samuel 15:10-23)

INTRODUCTION —

The story of self-satisfied partial obedience to God's command leaving God dissatisfied and Saul rejected.

The Amalekites—Israel's first enemy out of Egypt; Joshua defeated them. They sniped at the helpless in Israel's rear columns. God now commanded that they be "devoted"; destroyed utterly. Saul fought and conquered; but kept Agag and choice beasts.

I. SAUL'S FAILURE.
   A. He obeyed partially—conquered but did not destroy.
   B. He listened to others to disobey; God made him responsible as king.
   C. He offered sacrifice instead of obedience. —Failed to realize that the value of sacrifice is only in obedience.
   D. He claimed to have obeyed (his own interpretation).
   E. He blamed others for his failure.
   F. He was rejected—Compare Amos 5:21-24; Micah 6:6-8; "I desire mercy and not sacrifice; and the knowledge of God more than burnt offerings" (Hosea 6:6).

II. CONTRAST CHRIST.
   A. He obeyed fully—"I have finished the work that thou gavest me to do" (John 17:4).
   B. He refused to be deterred by temptation. "Thou shalt worship the Lord thy God, and Him only shalt thou serve" (Deut. 6:13). Rebuked Peter when he would have forbidden the crucifixion (Matt. 16:21ff.).
   C. Offered obedience rather than sacrifice—His only sacrifice was Himself.
   D. Gave deeds, not words, in evidence of His obedience. "The works that I do bear witness of me" (John 5:36).
   E. Instead of blaming others for His failure, He prayed forgiveness of *their* sin, as He hung on the cross.
   F. He was exalted by the Father—"Became obedient unto death . . . wherefore God also highly exalted Him" (Phil. 2:9-11).

85

III. APPLY TO PEOPLE IN OUR OWN TIME.

A. Nearly every one obeys *some* of the commands of Christ. "These ye ought to have done, and not to have left the other undone" (Matt. 23:23).
   1. There are the formal commands seen in the plan of salvation.
   2. There are the continuing commands of faithfulness to the church.
   3. There are the commands to righteousness, purity, love, generosity.
B. Partial "obedience" is not obedience to Him, but to one's own will (James 2:10, 11). He who obeys the law only where he approves of it obeys only his own judgment.
C. The voice of the multitude must give way to the voice of God.
   1. Saul finally acknowledged his sin in listening to it.
   2. Jesus claimed all authority, leaving no place to hearken to men.
   3. Peter rightly said, "We must obey God rather than men" (Acts 5:29).
D. Sacrifice cannot replace obedience. (Matt. 7:22, 23.)
E. Many, like Saul, claim to have obeyed—to have done the "important things," and to have been negligent only in those things that don't count anyway.
F. Many blame others for their disobedience.
   1. "Hypocrites kept me out of the church."
   2. "Friends led me astray." "Had too much religion as a child."
G. The disobedient rejected—"Depart from me, I never knew you" (Matt. 7:23).

CONCLUSION —

Moody's illustration of the father who asked for a drink of water, and refused to be satisfied when the child brought fruit, candy, and other things thought to be more acceptable than water.

PREACHING FROM II SAMUEL

INTRODUCTION —

This book is the story of approximately forty years, shortly before 1000 B.C. covering the reign of King David, first over the tribe of Judah, then over all Israel. It tells unfalteringly the truth, unpleasant as well as favorable, concerning the person and deeds of Israel's great hero.

VALUE OF THE BOOK FOR CHRISTIANS

It gives God's promise of the eternal reign committed to David's descendants. This promise was fulfilled in Christ.

It shows the hand of God at work in the history of His people, bringing blessing for faithfulness and unfailing judgment for sin.

It demonstrates that God is no respecter of persons, but has the same standards of righteousness and judgment for king and subject alike.

SUMMARY OF CONTENTS OF THE BOOK

1:1 — 4:12 David, reigning in Hebron, deals with the de-Descendants and followers of Saul.

5:1- 25 David is established as king over all Israel.

6:1 — 7:29 He returns the Ark of the Covenant to Jerusalem and plans for the building of the Temple.

8:1 —10:19 He extends his kingdom by further victories, but also keeps his promise concerning Jonathan's son.
12:26-31

11:1 —12:25 He sins in the matter of Bathsheba, and is brought to repentance.

13:1 —20:26 His later reign is troubled by family strife and revolts.

21:1 —25:24 Various records, censuses, and songs conclude the book.

Sermon Outlines Provided:

"Punished for a Good Deed" (II Sam. 6:1-11)
"Thanks to God in Tent and Temple" (II Sam. 7:1-11)
"The Greatness of a Man" (II Sam. 8:13-15; 9:9-11)
"Dark Pages in David's Record" (II Sam. 12:1-14)

Other Suggested Sermon Topics:

"How Are the Mighty Fallen!" (II Sam. 1:1-27)
"Tears for a Rebellious Son" (II Sam. 18:24-33)
"A Warrior's Psalm" (II Sam. 22)

QUESTIONS OVER II SAMUEL

1. Upon what mountain did Saul die? (1:6)
2. David felt a greater loss at Saul's death because of the death of what other person? (1:11, 12)
3. Why did David promise kindness to the men of Jabesh-gilead? (2:4-6)
4. Who killed Abner? (3:27)
5. Name Jonathan's crippled son. (4:4; 9:6, 7)
6. David ruled as king at what town before he moved to Jerusalem? (5:3-5)
7. Why did God strike Uzzah dead? (6:6, 7)
8. Who was Uriah? (11:3)
9. What two great sins did David commit? (11:4, 15)
10. What story did Nathan tell which caused David to acknowledge his sin? (12:1-4)
11. What happened to the first son born to David and Bathsheba? (12:15,18)
12. What statement of David's in II Samuel indicates he believed in life after death? (12:23)
13. Who ordered Ammon killed? (13:28, 29)
14. Which son of David led a rebellion against his father? (15:1-12)
15. Name the man from the house of Saul who cursed David. (16:5-7)
16. How did Absalom die? (18:9-15)
17. How did David respond to his death? (18:33)
18. David craved a drink from what well? (23:15)
19. What sin of David brought a pestilence on the land? (24:10, 15)

PUNISHED FOR A GOOD DEED
(II Samuel 6:1-11)

INTRODUCTION —

The story puzzles us, perhaps making us say with the people of Ezekiel's time, "The way of the Lord is not equal" (Ezek. 18:25). The event puzzled and displeased David. But let us understand the work of the Lord.

I. THE RULES CONCERNING THE ARK WERE SUCH AS TO INSIST ON HOLINESS OF IT.
   A. Made under the direction of God through Moses. Two and a half cubits ($3\frac{3}{4}$ feet) long. One and a half cubits ($2\frac{1}{4}$ feet) deep and wide of tough native wood.
   B. Called "Ark of the Covenant," "Ark of the Testimony," "propitiatory" and "throne of God" (Jer. 3:16).
   C. Contained tables of stone, pot of manna, Aaron's rod that budded.
   D. Overlaid with gold, covered with "mercy seat" and cherubim.
   E. Provided with rings, for carrying without touching, and to be carried by the consecrated priests.

II. THE HISTORY OF THE ARK WAS SUCH AS TO IMPRESS ALL WITH ITS SACRED CHARACTER.
   A. Brought with the tabernacle to Shiloh in the time of Samuel.
   B. Carried into battle against the Philistines, and lost to them.
   C. Housed in the temple of Dagon, it became a plague to them.
   D. Returned to Israel, received at Bethshemesh, became a cause of death to the men who looked into it.
   E. Kept at Kiriath Jearim, in the house of Abinadab about twenty years, became a source of blessing to the house.
   F. Now David desired to establish it in a great place in Jerusalem. — It was a public event, to which people came from all Israel.

89

III. THE MANNER OF THE REMOVAL WAS SUCH AS TO PREPARE FOR WHAT HAPPENED.

    A. Putting it on a new cart drawn by oxen was a copy of the way the Philistines had returned it to Israel.

    B. Having it accompanied by the sons of Abinadab was natural, but they were not priests, such as instructed to carry it. — If it had been carried, there would have been no such danger of falling, as occurred.

    C. Uzzah had been for twenty years in the house where it was kept. He should have known its history. He perhaps felt the liberty of long familiarity.

    D. In several details there had been moderate adjustment of the provisions of God. These moderate adjustments prepared the way for outright disobedience.

IV. WHAT THAT HAPPENED WAS THE NATURAL OUTCOME OF ALL THAT WENT BEFORE.

    A. The oxen stumbled and jostled the cart, as might be expected.

    B. Uzzah reached to steady the ark, as was most natural.

    C. God acted to rebuke the disobedience, as He had in time past, and as was necessary to teach the young nation regard for His law.

V. RESPONSE OF MEN TO THE ACT OF GOD.

    A. David frightened, puzzled, displeased.

    B. Causes the ark to be taken aside to the house of Obed Edom—blessing comes.

    C. Three months later, David provides the proper means, and the ark is carried to Jerusalem.

CONCLUSION —

"Now these things happened unto them by way of example; and they were written for our admonition . . ." (I Cor. 10:11).

    A. We have instructions from God concerning salvation, the church, living.

    B. Tempted to made adjustments to "new circumstances."

    C. Tempted to put forth disobedient hands to steady the shaking things of our own doing.

THANKS TO GOD IN TENT AND TEMPLE
(II Samuel 7:1-11)

INTRODUCTION —

This chapter answers the questions which are raised elsewhere in II Samuel. What was the essential greatness of David? — He did not forget source of blessing. How could God deal with such a man? He was constantly humble. What is the great power of his worship? It centers in thanks and praise — not self-interested petition.

I. DAVID'S CONCERN FOR THE BUILDING OF THE TEMPLE.

    A. It sprang out of gratitude — "Blessed art thou, O Lord" (See Phil. 4:6).

    B. It was expressed in material ways. (Illus. — Darrow, asked "How can I ever thank you?" said, "Madam, there has been only one answer to that question since that ancient time when the Phoenicians invented money.") The human mind sees material things — "The things which are seen are temporal."

    C. His plan accorded with his sense of the fitness of things. He should not live in luxury, while God was worshiped in squalor.

    D. Nathan was impressed with David's plan. (If we can persuade the preacher that we are all right, all is fine.) (Transition) — But Nathan recognized that there was a difference between him and God. He was not too proud to admit that he was wrong, nor to change his mind.

II. GOD'S REPLY TO DAVID'S PLAN.

    A. This is your plan, David, and not mine.

        1. "My thoughts are not your thoughts, neither are my ways your ways, saith the Lord. For as the heavens are higher than the earth, so are my ways higher than your ways, and my thoughts than your thoughts" (Isa. 55:8, 9).

        2. Showed kindness because of David's gratitude.

91

B. Do not consider that the material house is the thing of first importance, nor that God has need of man's material service.

  1. "The most High dwelleth not in temples made with hands; as saith the prophet: Heaven is my throne, and earth is my footstool: what house will ye build me, saith the Lord: Or what is the place of my rest? Hath not my hand made all these things? (Acts 7:47-50).

  2. "God that made the world and all things therein, seeing that he is Lord of heaven and earth, dwelleth not in temples made with hands; neither is worshiped with men's hands as though he had need of anything, seeing he giveth to all life, and breath, and all things" (Acts 17:24, 25). "Bethel"—"This is the house of God, the gate of heaven" (a stone set on end beside a lonely road).

C. Man's sense of what is fit, often fails. (See I Cor. 1:27-29, Cf. Gideon and "Unlearned and ignorant men.") How then shall a man be pleasing to God? How shall he express thanks?

D. In My own time and My own way I will provide for Me a house.

  1. The Temple built by Solomon.

  2. See also Haggai 1:2-8 and Zechariah 8:9.

  3. What sort of building is required in the present day? Decent adequacy, proportionate to your homes, perhaps, but especially faithfulness to Christ by His word, and consistent living. Forsake not the assembling; care to spread the Gospel.

E. *I will establish you a house*—The end of Thanksgiving finds us more indebted. Like trying to return water to the spring.

CONCLUSION —

Holy, acceptable unto God (Rom. 12:1).

THE GREATNESS OF A MAN
(II Samuel 8:13-15; 9:9-11)

INTRODUCTION —

A class in school was asked to write what they knew about David. One boy wrote two short sentences: "David was a boy. He became king." That is David: hero of boys; ideal of young men; leader of men; king of his nation; forefather of the Messiah; "king after God's own heart." He never lost the grace and charm of the boy, but added the strength and skill of a man in heroic measure.

I. SIMPLICITY, DIRECTNESS, HONESTY.
   A. To Goliath (I Sam. 17:45, 46) "This day will Jehovah deliver thee into my hand; and I will smite thee, and take thy head from off thee."
   B. His one attempt at subtlety, in the case of Uriah, appears clumsy, amateurish. He was not used to being deceitful: he was a bad liar.
   C. He had no part in the intrigues of the court that went on around him.
   D. Faced the facts honestly when accused by Nathan—"I have sinned against the Lord."
   E. See incident of Shimei's cursing him: "Let him alone and let him curse, for Jehovah hath bidden him." Later explanation, "For do not I know that I am this day king over Israel?"

II. ENTHUSIASM, FOR ISRAEL AND FOR THE LORD.
   A. In youth he refused to think that the armies of the Lord's people should be defied by an unbeliever.
   B. In age, he sought to build, then prepared for the building of the Temple.

III. RESPECT FOR COMMON THINGS AND COMMON PEOPLE.
   A. See incident of the water from the well at Bethlehem's gate. He refused to take to himself what had been brought at risk to others.

B. He had learned that:
1. The basis of all wealth is toil.
2. The basis of all power is sacrificial service.

IV. LOYALTY.

Observe how he kept his vow to the house of Jonathan; inci-cent of Ishbosheth.

V. GENEROSITY.

A. Always appreciative of the generosity of God and his friends.
B. Incident of Araunah—refused to offer in sacrifice what had cost him nothing.

VI. RESPECT FOR THINGS SACRED.

A. Thus refused to lay hands on Saul, the Lord's anointed.
B. Provided for the reverent return of the Ark of the Covenant, bringing it to Jerusalem.

VII. FAITH IN GOD.

A. The Shepherd's Psalm (Psalm 23).
B. To Goliath—"Thou comest to me with a sword, and with a spear and with a javelin; but I come to thee in the name of Jehovah of hosts, the God of the armies of Israel, whom thou hast defied."
C. See his farewell admonition to Solomon, still confident of God's promise.

CONCLUSION —

We admire David, and learn much from his boyish charm and heroism. We worship David's greater Son, and gain eternal life from His perfect sacrifice on our behalf.

DARK PAGES IN DAVID'S RECORD
(II Samuel 12:1-14)

INTRODUCTION —
  A. This is the kind of story one might wish need not be in the Bible; but if this kind of story were not necessary we would not need the Bible.
  B. It proves the divine quality of the Bible's moral teaching.
    1. Many consider that those who are high can make their own laws; God does not.
    2. The thing is labeled as sin, shown in all its hideous darkness.
  C. David committed adultery and then murdered to try to cover up his sin.

I. SIN'S ADVANCEMENT.
  A. David remained in Jerusalem, idle, worried, seeking release from care.
    1. "Idle mind is the devil's workshop."
    2. Of Jesus, He went about doing good.
  B. One sin committed, David sought clumsily to cover it by another and another.
    1. David was not skilled in intrigue—that is to his credit.
    2. The struggles of a fly in fly-paper, or a spider web.
  C. The crime grows greater—murder, and disregard for the interests of all Israel.
    1. See the progression—Passion, deceit, hypocrisy and intrigue, then murder.
    2. The anxiety is to hide sin, not be rid of it.

II. SIN'S REBUKE.
  A. It displeased Jehovah.
    1. Sin has the same name, in mansion or in hovel.
    2. The king's sin has the greater consequence.
  B. God used a man to carry his message—as always.
    1. You can't afford to be out of earshot of the Word.
    2. Courage of Nathan.

C. Nathan's skill; David was king, set to judge; he was still the shepherd at heart.
   1. The sinner must not only be told, he must see for himself that he has sinned.
   2. "David's anger was kindled against the man"—how wise in affairs of others!
   3. "You are the man."
D. Self-judgment cannot be avoided.
   1. He who considers self above the law is he who must bear heavier judgment (James 3:1).
   2. Great is the responsibility of the religious teacher; law enforcement officer; school man; parent (Compare Romans 2:1).

III. SIN'S RESULTS.

Here promised, they are related in later chapters; sin, intrigue, rebellion in David's own house. He enters the picture a hero, full of faith and carefree; he departs, an old warrior, who knows out of how great troubles deliverance can come.

IV. REPENTANCE AND CONFESSION OF SIN.

A. One of the greatest things David ever did. "He that ruleth his own spirit is greater" (Prov. 16:32).
B. *I* have sinned.
   No blame of others, nor of the temptations that came to him as king. I have *sinned*; he didn't choose a more polite name for his wrong.
C. Have sinned *against Jehovah.*
   1. Against many others, yes—Bathsheba, Uriah, Israel, but
   2. Chiefly against Jehovah
   Who had advanced him to place of king.
   Who had given the law and commandment, and set right way before him. See Psalm 32:1-7.

V. FORGIVENESS OF SIN.

Why can't we be like God? We haven't forgiven David. Can God forgive a great sin; answer is, He has.
"Men and brethren, what shall we do?"

PREACHING THROUGH THE RECORDS OF DAVID'S REIGN (An alternative special month's study)
(II Samuel; I Chronicles; and Psalms)

FROM VARIOUS POINTS OF VIEW

The story of David's life and reign, covering approximately seventy years, approximately 1000 B.C., is told in these records from several points of view. Second Samuel is an unfalteringly truthful history, telling the dark as well as the bright side of David's story. First Chronicles, equally truthful, dwells especially on the religious significance of the history. It records the details of David's political and religious organization of the kingdom. The Psalms—songs from the heart of the "sweet singer of Israel"—are written from David's own point of view, and tell the response of his spirit to many of the events told in the history.

PRESENT-DAY VALUES OF THE RECORDS

They give God's promise of the eternal reign committed to David's descendants. This promise was fulfilled in Christ.

They show the hand of God at work in the history of His people, bringing blessings for faithfulness and unfailing judgment for sin.

They demonstrate that God is no respecter of persons, but has the same standards of righteousness and judgment for king and subject alike.

ANALYSIS OF THE BOOKS

Second Samuel

Chapters	1-4	David, reigning in Hebron, deals with Saul's followers.
	5	He is established as king over all Israel.
	6-7	He establishes the central place of worship in Jerusalem.
	8-10	He extends his kingdom through conquest, and honors the promise made to Jonathan concerning his son.
	11,12	He sins in the matter of Bathsheba, and is brought to repentance.

97

13-20 His later reign is troubled by family strife and revolts.

21-24 Various records, censuses, and songs complete the Book.

First Chronicles

Chapters 1-9 Genealogies from Adam to approximately 400 B.C.

10-12 Stories of the men who helped establish the throne of David.

13-16 Records of David's establishment in Jerusalem.

17 Preparations for building the Temple are begun.

18-21 David's kingdom enlarged by defeat of his enemies.

22-30 Plans for the Temple and for the organization of those who were to serve in it.

Suggested Sermon Topics:

"Search Me, O God" (Psalm 139)
"The Greatness of a Man" (II Sam. 8:13-15)
"The Lord Is My Shepherd" (Psalm 23)
"In Time of Trouble" (Psalm 56)
"Punished for a Good Deed" (II Sam. 6:1-11)
"Dark Pages in David's Record" (II Sam. 12:1-14)
"Thanks to God in Tent and Temple" (II Sam. 7:1-11)
"When the Prophet Was Wrong" (I Chron. 17:1-10)
"The Sin of the Census" (I Chron. 21:1-8)

PREACHING THROUGH I KINGS

IN THIS BOOK WE SEE

How God kept His promise to preserve the kingly line of David to the coming of the Messiah.

Examples of the human qualities of stubbornness, selfishness, pride, and ungodliness on one side, or faithfulness, courage and godliness on the other, with the results of each.

The working of God in the history of the Jews, bringing strength for faithfulness, and withdrawing His favor from the nation when it disobeyed.

WRITING OF THE BOOK

The books of I and II Kings were originally a unit, following directly on the books of Samuel. They were divided for the sake of convenience by those who translated the Old Testament into Greek about 200 years before Christ. The book was completed some time after the events related (See I Kings 10:19.), and it mentions by name at least ten written records of history and prophecy dealing with the same period—especially the "Chronicles of the Kings of Judah" and the "Chronicles of the Kings of Israel." Along with, and perhaps drawing from, these other, now extinct, writings, the inspired writer has preserved that which best serves the religious needs of the Lord's people.

ARCHAEOLOGICAL DISCOVERIES ESTABLISH THE HISTORY

In 1939 the mummy of Shishak, King of Egypt, was discovered at Tanis in a sarcophagus covered with gold not native to Egypt. Was it the gold he took at Jerusalem (I Kings 14:25, 26)? At Megiddo, the stone hitching posts and mangers of Solomon's vast stables (I Kings 9:15, 19) have been found. Their number agrees with the description given in the Bible. At Samaria the Harvard University Expedition found the foundations of Omri's palace (I Kings 16:24) with evidence that no city was there before.

ANALYSIS OF THE BOOK

Chapters	1-4	Solomon is established on the throne.
	5-8	He builds the Temple for which David has prepared.

99

9-11	Solomon's splendor. His introduction of idolatry.
12-14	The kingdom is divided between Rehoboam of Judah and Jeroboam of Israel.
15:1 — 16:28	Less known kings of Israel and Judah.
16:29 — 22:40	Ahab, King of Israel, and Elijah, God's prophet.
22:41-53	Kings Jehoshaphat and Ahaziah.

Sermon Outlines Provided:

"School Days" (I Kings 3:4-15)
"The Nearest Church" (I Kings 12:25-33)
"That Juniper Tree" (I Kings 19:1-14)
"Nothing But the Truth" (I Kings 22:12-24)

Other Suggested Sermon Topics:

"He That Exalteth Himself" (I Kings 1:5-10)
"The Blood of War in Peace" (I Kings 2:1-10)
"The Beginning of Wisdom" (I Kings 3:4-15)
"The House of Prayer" (I Kings 8:22)
"The Peculiar People" (I Kings 9:1-9)
"The King Who Was Diseased in His Feet" (I Kings 15:9-15)

QUESTIONS OVER I KINGS

1. When David was aged what son tried to install himself as king? (1:5)
2. Who did become the king after David? (1:38, 39)
3. Why was David not permitted to build the Temple? (5:3)
4. Solomon overlaid the Temple with what material? (6:21)
5. What queen came to test Solomon with questions? (10:1)
6. Rehoboam succeeded his father. Whose advise did he accept — that of the elders or that of young men? (12:8)
7. Who became the first king of the ten northern tribes? (12:20)
8. Who was the wicked wife of Ahab? (16:31)
9. Who was fed by the ravens by the brook Cherith? (17:1-6)
10. Who was ordered killed by Jezebel so her husband could obtain a vineyard? (21:1)

SCHOOL DAYS
(I Kings 3:4-15)

INTRODUCTION — Solomon and today's young person.

Solomon had only recently come to the throne. The early days of his reign were occupied with carrying out the expressed wishes of his father. Now he must make policies and accept responsibilities himself. The story is the story of his wisdom. "The Lord giveth wisdom, and out of His mouth cometh knowledge and understanding" (Prov. 2:6).

I. SOLOMON GOES TO GIBEON TO SACRIFICE
   —"The fear of the Lord is the beginning of wisdom."
   A. The worship of God has always resulted in the desire to train as many as possible of the people. "When thy son shall ask . . ."
   B. Harvard College (and fifteen of the first sixteen colleges in the U.S.) were for ministers.
   C. Danger in getting away from it—as in Germany, where schools had other purpose. (Gideons examined school books in Vermont. In 1800 to 1850 they were 23% to 100% definitely Christian. Now a few references to God, Christ or the Bible; far more to mythology, and other religions.
   D. We must learn much that the school doesn't teach.
   E. If we don't follow God's wisdom, He will raise up others who will.

II. GOD SAID, "ASK WHAT I SHALL GIVE THEE."
   A. What do you seek in life and in school?
      1. The question must be faced. Refusal to make a choice is itself a choice to follow the downward path of least resistance.
      2. "Ask and ye shall receive, seek and ye shall find, knock and it shall be . . ." (Matt. 7:7).
   B. The worthwhile gift is of God.
      1. Who has the key to the things that God has made?
      2. William Lyon Phelps said that a knowledge of the Bible without college is better than the reverse.

III. SOLOMON GAVE THANKS FOR FORMER BLESSINGS BEFORE MAKING REQUEST.
   A. God is not forgotten in any step.
   B. Thus he was prepared to receive what God would give.

IV. THE CHOICE — UNDERSTANDING OF GOOD AND ILL. 'Wisdom' covers a multitude of sins and virtues.
   A. First a sense of need — without it nothing could be given. "I came not to call the righteous but sinners to repentance" (Luke 5:32).
   B. The gift asked is an eternal gift. Property, honor, and life itself are for time, wisdom for eternity.
   C. It is an unselfish gift — that he may serve God's people.
   D. It is a practical gift. There is purpose in it. Wisdom to be applied.
   E. "That I may discern right and wrong."
      1. He might have asked for political skill, shrewdness — here for truth.
      2. What are our purposes? Lawyer, preacher, workman, manufacturer, engineer, salesman, doctor.
      3. Purposes and habits fixed in school days — Wisdom to get good grades and gain favor — or honesty to learn?

V. THE GIFT IS GRANTED — AND MORE. "Prove me now herewith, saith the Lord . . ." (Mal. 3:10).
   A. Byproducts of education — measured in terms of greater income; rentals; sales.
   B. In America, a land of liberty, meeting better than any other her own needs and those of a suffering world.

VI. SOLOMON SACRIFICES — TRUE WISDOM IS TOWARD GOD, AND NOT AWAY.
   The present age is either one of hopeless, fearful cynicism, or great faith.
   "Come . . . and learn of me" (Matt. 11:28, 29).

THE NEAREST CHURCH
(I Kings 12:25-33)

INTRODUCTION —

Jeroboam was in many ways far ahead of his time.

I. THERE WAS MUCH IN THE INCIDENT FOR WHICH EXCUSE MIGHT BE FOUND.
   A. Worshiping the same God.
      1. "These are the Gods that brought you out of Egypt."
      2. So now, "We are all going to the same place."
   B. Teaching with familiar symbols.
      1. From Egypt, the worship of the ox Apis and the calf Mnevis.
      2. There was heifer worship in Palestine.
      3. In the same manner as the use of images in modern churches (or "worship centers," etc.), it could be argued that they were using familiar symbols to teach the heathen concerning the true God.
   C. Need for national unity.
      1. Jeroboam feared that worship in Jerusalem would divide his kingdom.
      2. This was a prime factor in the establishment of the church of England in the days of Henry VIII.
   D. Convenience.
      Here it could be argued that Jeroboam was showing special kindness to the poor, who could not afford to go to Jerusalem to worship.

In spite of all arguments, Jeroboam was always known as "Jeroboam . . . who made Israel to sin."

II. SOME OBJECTIONS CAN BE PLAINLY SEEN.
   A. Jeroboam destroyed the very quality of worship itself by making it subservient to other interests.
   B. He made religion to serve the state. — But how about bond drives, political campaigns, special days to serve government agencies, all carried on in churches?

C. He made convenience more important than conviction in religion.
  1. Said in effect, "Your comfort is more important than God's command."
  2. Apply to:
    Your friends.
    Your convenience.
    The good feeling of going where you are appreciated.
    The up-and-coming organization, etc.
  3. In all these things the very throne of God is challenged by the "worshiper."

III. One objection is paramount.
  A. He set the authority of his reason above the authority of the will of God as revealed in the Law and the prophets.
  B. This objection seems to fit also—
    1. Those who follow denominational teaching in spite of the Bible.
    2. Those who "don't just believe in their way of doing, but it is better to go there than not to go to church at all."

CONCLUSION —

In every city the Restoration movement is a tribute to those who refused to acknowledge convenience as the most important thing in religion. How shall those who have consulted the easy way find comfort in the presence of Him who took the way of the Cross, simply because it was God's will?

THAT JUNIPER TREE
(I Kings 19:1-14)

INTRODUCTION —

The "juniper tree" has come to mean the place of despondency. An experience not limited to any one group of people. Like the rain, it comes on the just and the unjust, the evil and good, old and young.

I. CAUSE OF DESPONDENCY.

(Put Elijah under the scrutiny of a psychiatrist.) Appearance from nowhere, springing to prominence; promise of drought, experience at Cherith, then at Serepta. Reappearance and the contest at Carmel. Return to Samaria ahead of the rain. Jezebel's threat, and Elijah's flight.

A. Partly a matter of exhaustion. Experience of the years as a fugitive. The heavy drain of Carmel—the flight of at least 100 miles.

B. Emotional reaction from a high and stirring occasion. —Ask yourselves—
Sometimes more dramatic as in a quick score by opposition after a fumbled touchdown. More commonplace as in basketball—you make the basket; other side gets ball. So in things of the spirit—"Let him that thinketh he standeth . . ." (I Cor. 10:12). E.g. Simon Peter after the Confession. Apostles after the Transfiguration. So the necessity for care of the new converts, especially in case of high emotion.

C. Loneliness—the servant was present, but there was not fellowship there.

D. Idleness—the great occasion is over and he has nothing to which to lay hand.

II. NATURE AND RESULT OF DESPONDENCY.

A. God's servant becomes useless. It was near the wind-up of affairs for Elijah.

B. Man of high courage appears as a coward.

105

III. GOD'S CARE FOR THE DESPONDENT.

A. Patience, and nothing of derision.
 1. First no mention of chiding.
 2. Provides food and protection.
B. Take a square look at situation from a long way off— "What are you doing here?"
C. The assurance and reminder of God's presence in little things for every day. The Mount of God, fire, wind, earthquake, "gentle whisper."
D. The assurance of human fellowship. Seven thousand faithful. Companionship of Elisha—thus the church.
E. Work to do—Arise and go. See "Fear not, from hence forth thou shalt catch men" (Luke 5:10). "Feed my lambs" (John 21:15).

CONCLUSION —

> Is life worth living? Yes, so long
>   As there is wrong to right
> Wail of the weak against the strong
>   Or tyranny to fight;
>
> Long as there lingers gloom to chase
>   Or streaming tear to dry;
> One kindred woe, one sorrowing face
>   That smiles as we draw nigh . . .
>   — *Wm. Cullen Bryant*

106

NOTHING BUT THE TRUTH
(I Kings 22:12-24)

INTRODUCTION — The story of Micaiah.

1. Chides Ahab (under guise) for allowing Ben-Hadad to go. Josephus says Ahab put him in prison then.
2. Called to confer with Ahab and Jehoshaphat in regard to Ramoth Gilead. Messenger urges him to speak well. "What God says." "Go and prosper"—an evident mockery of the four hundred. "Sheep without a shepherd." "Who shall convince Ahab that he may go up to Ramoth and be destroyed?"
3. Josephus mentions apparent contradiction between Elijah and Micaiah, for Elijah had said that dogs would lick Ahab's blood in Naboth's vineyard.
4. Fulfillment in every detail.
5. "If you return in peace at all, then God has not spoken by me."

I. UNPLEASANT TRUTH HATED.
   1. "If the world hath hated you . . ." (John 15:18).
   2. "Because their deeds were evil" (John 3:19).
   Love of lies—
   "No matter what you believe."
   "All will be saved."
   "No such thing as evil."
   "Go to church best suited."
   "Choose own baptism."
   "Once in grace, always in grace."

II. UNPLEASANT TRUTH RESPECTED.
   1. "What man convicteth me of sin?" (John 8:46).
   2. Spiritualism's self-condemning salve.

III. UNPLEASANT TRUTH PRESENTED.
   1. Difficulties to the one presenting it. Lack of favor. Gallery of heroes—Hebrews 11:35 ff.
   2. Who follows in their train?

How may we know the truth?
 By their fruits.
 Search the Scriptures daily.
 Truth above policy.
 Stand, or blown with every wind.

IV. UNPLEASANT TRUTH REJECTED.
1. Ahab rejects because it is unpleasant. So Agrippa rejected Paul. Herod, John the Baptist.
2. So the doctrine of hell is widely rejected, with need of Christian conversion for salvation. "Heap to themselves teachers, having itching ears."
3. Jehoshaphat rejected it because he was already committed to false course. How many others like him . . .

V. UNPLEASANT TRUTH FULFILLED.
1. Truth is not broken—men break themselves on it.
2. Josephus: "And as what things were foretold should happen to Ahab by the two prophets came to pass, we ought thence to have high notions of God, and everywhere to honor and worship him, and never to suppose that what is pleasant and agreeable is worthy of belief before what is true."

CONCLUSION —

"Truth forever on the scaffold."
 Truth, crushed to earth, shall rise again—
  The eternal years of God are hers;
 But error, wounded, writhes in pain,
  And dies among his worshipers.
             — *Wm. Cullen Bryant*

108

PREACHING THROUGH II KINGS

IN THIS BOOK WE SEE

Continuance of the history recounted in the books of Samuel and First Kings, providing parallel accounts of two kingdoms — Israel with its capital at Samaria, and Judah with its capital at Jerusalem. The period covered is roughly three hundred years, leading to Judah's captivity in Babylon. Judah was ruled by the descendants of David, according to God's promise. Israel was ruled by many kings from many families, with brief reigns and frequent assassinations.

The historic background for the prophetic ministries of most of the Old Testament prophets.

A contrast between Elijah, the rough-hewn prophet from the open country, and Elisha, the gentler prophet in the cities, with a program of teaching and with manifold miracles of healing, provision, and even raising of the dead. It foreshadows the contrast between John the Baptist, who came in the spirit and power of Elijah, and Jesus, who came with teaching and with miracles of life and healing.

WRITING OF THE BOOK

It is a part of the Samuel-Kings history of kings and kingdoms among the children of Israel. Combining research and inspiration it shows that God is the ultimate judge and ruler of His people.

ARCHAEOLOGY CONFIRMS THE HISTORY

The "Moabite Stone," found in 1868 at Dibon, east of the Dead Sea, and now in the Louvre Museum in Paris, is inscribed with an account of Moab's rebellion against Israel (II Kings 3), in the words of Mesha, king of Moab. This is only one of many inscriptions found to corroborate names, places, and relationships among nations, as they appear in the inspired record.

Most important are discoveries at the sites of Nineveh and Babylon, major cities long lost but recently found to have been as the Bible indicated them to be. These were capitals of the nations that took captive Israel and Judah.

ANALYSIS OF THE BOOK

Chapters 1,2   Last days of Elijah.

3-8   Doings of Elisha.

9,10   Jehu destroys the house of Ahab and Baalism.

11,12   Reign of Joash in Judah, repair of the Temple.

13   Death of Elisha.

14-16   Brief records of 60 years; 6 kings of Israel, 2 in Judah (Time of Joel, Jonah, Amos, Hosea, Isaiah).

17   Hoshea, and Israel's destruction by Assyria.

18-20   Hezekiah's good reign in Judah (Isaiah and Micah).

21   Manasseh's evil reign.

22,23   Josiah's reforms (Nahum, Jeremiah, Zephaniah, Habakkuk).

24,25   Last twenty years, captivity (Ezekiel, Daniel, Obadiah).

Sermon Outlines Provided:

"Silent in a Day of Good News" (II Kings 7:13-17)
"The Wrong Wife" (II Kings 8:16-19, 25-27)
"Come and See My Zeal" (II Kings 10:15-31)
"They Feared Jehovah and Served Other Gods" (II Kings 17:23-33)

Other Suggested Sermon Topics:

"Given to Hospitality" (II Kings 4:8-13)
"A Mighty Leper" (II Kings 5:1-4, 10-14)
"Severity and Mercy" (II Kings 13:14-19)
"We Have Found a Book" (II Kings 22, 23)

QUESTIONS OVER II KINGS

1. First Ahaziah sent messengers to inquire of whom to see if Ahaziah would recover? (1:2)
2. Who was the captain of the army of the King of Syria? (5:1)
3. Who had 70 sons in Samaria? (10:1)
4. In what city did God place His name? (21:4)

SILENT IN A DAY OF GOOD NEWS
(II Kings 7:3-17)

INTRODUCTION — The story:

Seige of Samaria, with indescribable suffering and hunger. King sends to destroy Elisha; he replies to captain that a measure of fine flour shall sell for a shekel tomorrow. Disbelief. The lepers venture out, and find the camp deserted. (The Lord sent sound.) The king suspects a trap, investigates and finds Syrians gone. The people feast; the captain dies.

I. THE WORLD IN DYING NEED WITHOUT CHRIST, AS ISRAEL IN SAMARIA.

    A. John R. Mott said: "In all my many years of service, never have I been called upon to enter into fellowship with so much of tragedy. I find it impossible to decide where the area of starvation, of disease, and of despair is the greater—in Europe and the Near East or in Asia from India to North China and Japan. It still haunts me in the watches of the night." The "have" nations are in a sense but little better off, for fear and distrust.

    B. Gen. MacArthur: "Military alliances, balances of power, the League of Nations, all in their turn have failed. We have had our last chance. If we do not now devise some greater and more equitable system, Armegeddon will be at our door. The problem basically is theological and involves a spiritual recrudescence and improvement of human character that will synchronize with our almost matchless advance in science, art, literature, and all the material and cultural developments of the past two thousand years. It must be of the spirit if we are to save the flesh."

II. THERE IS RELIEF PREPARED BY GOD AND PROVIDED BY HIM.

    A. Satan has beseiged the souls of men with:

        1. The weight of dead past hanging about their necks.

2. Sin and the power of it.
3. Selfishness that enslaves me and puts me at my neighbor's throat.
4. Death.

B. Christ has provided relief. "Who shall free me from the body of this death? I thank God through . . ." (Rom. 7:24, 25). —Come out and be free.

C. Christianity works.

III. HAVING FOUND THE GOOD NEWS WE MUST TELL IT.

A. "Into a tent where a gypsy boy lay, dying alone at the close of the day

News of salvation we carried, said he, "Nobody ever has told it to me."

Smiling he said, as his last sigh he spent, 'I am so glad that for me He was sent.'

Whispered while low sank the sun in the west, 'Lord, I believe; tell it now to the rest.'

Tell it again, tell it again. Salvation's story repeat o'er and o'er,

Till none can say of the children of men, 'Nobody ever has told me before.'

B. We must tell it for our own sakes. When Jerusalem stayed home, Jerusalem died.

C. But the greatest need is for men rather than money.

CONCLUSION —

Go ye! *Then* I am with you.
Shall the days find us feasting, while our brothers starve?

112

THE WRONG WIFE
(II Kings 8:16-19, 25-27)

INTRODUCTION —

The story of a tragic and busy forty years in the history of Judah.

I. THE STORY:

A. Started when Jehoram was seven years old, and his father came to throne. Jehoram remembered Asa, his godly grandfather; perhaps Jehoshaphat taught of God. Now there was not time for that; Jehoshaphat was busy shaping a strong kingdom. Jehoshaphat visited Samaria, and King Ahab; joined in treaties and battles. Did Jehoram go along, and and play with little Athaliah, daughter of Ahab?

B. The marriage took place when Jehoram was not more than seventeen . . . Probably a great state occasion; the couple were in both courts. A year later little Ahaziah was born, "Jehovah preserves"—(Named for uncle in Israel) Jehoram became steeped in the idolatry and wickedness of Jezebel's court.

C. Jehoram comes to the throne at age 32. His brothers are given charge of cities. He kills his six brothers. Brings the worship of Baal to Judah, with all the wickedness attached.

D. Troubles in the kingdom. (Men would rather have happy home than congenial work.) Edom, east of Jordan revolts; Jehoram makes a fruitless foray against them. The Philistines rise up and take the cities southwestward. Elijah, in his last days sends a letter, telling that Jehoram will die of bowel consumption. Later days in complete misery; dies at age forty. "Died without being desired."

E. Ahaziah reigns one year (age 22). "His mother was his counsellor to do wickedly" (II Chron. 22:3) He made league with the idolatrous king of Israel, and when Jehu destroyed the family of Ahab, he killed Ahaziah also (on visit to Samaria).

    F. Athaliah destroys the seed royal, i.e. her own children and grandchildren. Reigns for six years — no indication it was a weak rule, but cruel. Joash, Ahaziah's baby boy, born about time Jehoram died, saved.

    G. Joash placed on throne, and Athaliah, aged about 45, destroyed at Kidron.

Here is the story of domestic tragedy that became national tragedy. It is the story of the wrong marriage, chosen apparently by a good man, Jehoshaphat.

II. WHAT WAS WRONG?

    A. The over-privileged son. "To get the right partner, be the right partner." (Woodrow Wilson, at Princeton, was asked "Why do you not make more out of our sons?" Answered, "Because they are *your* sons."

    B. The match was one of policy, for political advantage. Set the sense of values all wrong to start.

    C. Like it or not, Jehoram *did* marry Athaliah's family. He probably thought Athaliah would have all Jezebel's charm and looks, but none of her devilish temper and disposition.

    D. There may have been a real romance; that didn't save the marriage or home. cf. Samson and Delilah.

    E. The marriage was made too soon; maturity of judgment had not been reached by either. (Successful homes come from more mature personalities; some succeed.) Their home was dominated by the in-laws' influence — "Leaving and cleaving."

    F. God and His law were not at all consulted . . .
(Minister, going to visit prison, was asked by elderly woman to take a small package to her son. He did. It was her picture. Boy looked at it, said "Take it back; I don't want it." Later told story. Mother had social ambitions, required of him that he learn the "social graces." Wanted to join church, and delayed, that she might be present. She couldn't; he learned that she had a bridge date. He drifted; finally killed a man in a fight over a poker game.)

114

COME AND SEE MY ZEAL
(II Kings 10:15-31)

INTRODUCTION —

    A. There is lack-luster and lack-power in a life with no zeal.

    B. Zeal is the motor in the car. It makes it go. But sometimes "hooked to nothin'." Every life must have the drive of some great enthusiasm. Every other enthusiasm than Christ is bound to disappointment.

    C. Zeal gets a bad name from the excesses of such as Jehu. His story. Annointed by the messenger of Elisha, goes at once to Jezreel, slays Joram and his guest, Ahaziah. Causes death of Jezebel. Leads in destruction of Ahab's seventy sons. Tricks the worshipers of Baal into gathering, and slays all. Twenty-eight years' reign.

  I. BEWARE OF A ZEAL FOR GOD THAT ADVERTISES ITSELF.

    A. "When thou prayest, be not as the hypocrites are . . . (Matt. 6:5). "When thou givest alms, be not as the hypocrites . . . (Matt. 6:2).

    B. There is evidence that it is actually a zeal for self, finding expression in acts that are associated with the service of God.

    C. Can one imagine Christ calling conscious attention to His acts of zeal?

 II. BEWARE OF ZEAL THAT DESTROYS MORE THAN IT BUILDS UP.

    A. There is sometimes need for the wrecking crew, but weed-grown vacant lots add nothing to beauty of a city —one must also build.

    B. No evidence of a consistent constructive policy on part of Jehu. "I prove that I love God by hating everybody else."

    C. See the policy of Christ: Twice cleansed the Temple, faced the hypocrisy of the Pharisees (but how many acts

of mercy more than can be counted) twice fed the multitude. His was the feeding, healing, helping touch.
D. Let ours be a blazing, constructive zeal.

III. BEWARE OF A ZEAL THAT DOESN'T ACCEPT RESPONSIBILITY FOR CONSISTENT CHRISTIAN LIVING.
A. Jehu "departed not from the sins of Jereboam." Took no heed to "walk in the way of Jehovah with all his heart."
B. A certain preacher and his black cigars. "First take the beam out of thine own eye; then shalt thou see clearly to take the mote out of thy brother's eye" (Matt. 7:5).
C. Much better is the fiery passion of an Isaiah or a Jeremiah, or an Amos.

CONCLUSION —

First beware of these things within ourselves! Paul, the "Christ intoxicated man" said "Be not drunk with wine, wherein is excess, but be filled with the Spirit" (Eph. 5:18).

THEY FEARED JEHOVAH AND SERVED OTHER GODS

(II Kings 17:23-33)

INTRODUCTION —

In this passage: (1.) Explanation of "The Jews have no dealings with Samaritans." (2.) Insight into one of greatest difficulties of the Christian life.

HISTORY

The victorious Assyrians do a resettlement project in Samaria, bringing to replace absent Israel the citizens of four conquered cities of Babylonia. They in turn introduce their own gods.

Babylon — Succoth Benoth — guardian goddess of Babylon,
Cuthah — Nergal — *Assyrian* god of war,
Ava — Nibhaz and Tartak,
Hamath — Ashima,
Sepharvaim — Adarmelech and Annumelech.

I. THEY FEARED JEHOVAH — BUT FEAR IS NOT A SUFFICIENT MOTIVE IN RELIGION.

   A. It drives to negative, empty life, rather than real service.

   B. It drives to a minimum sort of religion — "How far must I go?" (Illus. with the pigeon on the city street, moving just a step to avoid auto.)

   C. Presently, it causes many to join the church, but that is all. (Conversation with Charles Williams, once active, long inactive "What is greatest motive in Christian life?" "Fear and desire.")

   D. The Christian motive is love. "Thou shalt love the Lord thy God" (Matt. 22:37). "If you *love me* ye will *keep my* commandments" (John 14:15). "He that loveth father or mother more than me is not worthy of me" (Matt. 10:37). "The love of Christ constraineth us" (II Cor. 5:14). This is the motive that draws people all the way. "Perfect love casteth out fear" (I John 4:18).

117

(But lacking this motive, the Samaritans gave a good example of what others have done.

II. THEY SERVED THEIR OWN GODS. TOOK THE FORM AND NAME OF JEHOVAH, BUT *DID* AS ALWAYS HAD.

A. In religion.
1. Family tradition—"My parents were thus, that is what I will be." "If you were shown by New Testament that your program is wrong—"?
2. Denominational authority.
   a. Campbell says of many religionists, "The Bible is on their lips, but the creeds are in their heart."
   b. Closer home "That church representative should be recalled—but we must stay with the organization."
3. The memory of a preacher. How about the memory of Christ?
4. The church back home. How about the church in Heaven?

B. In life.
1. Business success: "No man can serve two masters, for either he will love the one and hate the other or he will hold to the one and despise the other. Ye cannot serve God and mammon" (Matt. 6:24).
2. The thing that is being done, socially. What sets the standards for your conduct? and your family?

3. Self interest—promotion of the ego—this enters religion. "Pride of life."
4. Lusts of the flesh.

If you love Him, why not serve Him?

PREACHING THROUGH I CHRONICLES

"A chronicle" is a story of the time. The Biblical Chronicles form a story of the Kingdom of Judah, telling first the genealogical background of its kings, and then following them through their reigns, from David to the time of the captivity and return. Jewish tradition says that Ezra is the writer. In I Chronicles 30:29, 30 he names some of the earlier records to which he had access in preparing his work.

The story is parallel to much that is in II Samuel and the books of Kings. Even more than those books, it points out the religious significance of the historical events.

ANALYSIS OF THE BOOK

Chapters 1-9 Genealogies from Adam to the return from captivity.

10-12 Stories of the men who helped to establish David on the throne.

13-16 Record of the establishment of David in Jerusalem.

17 Preparations for the Temple are begun.

18-21 The enlargement of David's kingdom by defeat of his enemies.

22-30 Plans for the Temple and for the organization of those who should serve in it.

FOR THE CHRISTIAN READER

There is much of value behind the catalog of names which make up much of the book. We trace the line of fulfillment in God's promise to establish Messiah on the throne of David. We find the careful preparation for public worship—a matter too much neglected by church members. We trace the hand of God in the political fortunes of His people; "Righteousness exalteth a nation, but sin is reproach to any people."

Sermon Outlines Provided:

"The End of Mother's Sorrow" (I Chron. 4:8, 9)
"Song of Praise" (I Chron. 16:7-15, 29-36)
"When the Prophet Was Wrong" (I Chron. 17:1-10)
"The Sin of the Census" (I Chron. 21:1-8)

119

Other Suggested Sermon Topics:

"The Family Record" (I Chron. 1)
"The Mighty Men" (I Chron. 11, 12)
"What Shall We Give to God?" (I Chron. 16:25-36)
"The Nation's Offering" (I Chron. 26:6-19)

QUESTIONS OVER I CHRONICLES

1. Who was the father of David? (2:13-15)
2. Who was the first born of Israel (Jacob)? (2:1; 5:1)
3. Who was Solomon's father? (3:1-5)
4. I Chronicles 9:1 says Judah was carried into exile in Baylon because of what?
5. The four chief gate keepers kept watch over the chambers and treasuries in the house of God were from what tribe? (9:26)
6. What group of people killed Jonathan? (10:1)
7. Upon what mountain did Saul die? (10:1-5, 8)
8. What was Jerusalem called when David went up to the city? (11:4)
9. What was David's response when God struck Uzza dead for touching the ark? (13:11)
10. Who gave David the instructions for defeating the Philistines between Gibeon and Gezer? (14:14-17)
11. Men of what tribe could carry the ark? (15:2)
12. After the ark was brought to Jerusalem David appointed what man as chief minister before the ark to thank and praise God? (16:4, 5)
13. God revealed to whom first that David could not build the house for God to dwell in? (17:3, 4)
14. The giant of Gath had how many fingers and toes? (20:6)
15. God sent a pestilence on Israel because David sinned by doing what to the people? (21:1-14)
16. Even though David could not build the Temple he did what to help Solomon? (22:1-5; 28:11-19; 29:2-7)
17. When David was old he made whom king over Israel? (23:1)
18. How long did David reign over Israel? (29, 27)

THE END OF MOTHER'S SORROW
(I Chronicles 4:8, 9)

INTRODUCTION —

This is indeed a thumbnail sketch—there is no background. Who was Jabez? Apparently of the tribe of Judah. Who were his brothers? Who was his mother? What was her sorrow? What was his nobility? None of these things is known. He is therefore reduced to the common state with all, and not evidently different from any.

I. "I BARE HIM WITH SORROW"—Perhaps because of unworthiness of brothers, perhaps other.
  A. Sorrow is the first promise to womankind, with the promise of a Savior (Gen. 3:16).
  B. There is the sorrow of the "rule over"—women have tried to shake it.
    1. "Liberated" to equality, and doesn't like it (woman tries to get seat on crowded bus, expresses opinion in strong language; one workman says, "I was right in my first opinion; she isn't a lady.")
    2. "Liberated" from husband to oversight of doctor, psychiatrist, or priest.
    3. (The hands got tired of the feet carrying them around, and decided they could go by themselves; so they did, and were no longer able to sew the garments, write, or mold the fine thing.)
    4. ("Forever trying to dominate their men, and forever afraid they will succeed.")
  C. There is sorrow in motherhood.
    1. Pain of *childbearing*, confinement of *childrearing*.
    2. Extension of sensitiveness to all the sufferings of the child.
    3. Distress in ingratitude and unworthiness.
    4. Some would be "liberated": To following after pets, hobbies, business; clubs, lodges (who is not driven?) or drinks, drugs, and dance halls.

There are still some who don't dodge the sorrow—and the joy!

II. THE JOY OF MOTHERHOOD IS VERY CLOSE TO THE SORROW (John 16:21).

Note how close together—"Blessed art thou among women" (Luke 1:28). "Yea and a sword shall pierce thine own soul" (Luke 2:35). (It is noted that unmarried women are as beautiful and intelligent as their married sisters, but smile less.) There is in the very sorrow a source of serenity and a sense of values.

III. JABEZ BRINGS THE END OF SORROW; I HOPE SHE LIVED TO SEE IT.

A. His name brought a sense of need, and he went to the right place for help.

B. "Keep me from the evil" cf. "Deliver us from evil" (Matt. 6:13).

C. Jabez' *nobility*—of what sort was it? Considerate at home? Brought good reports from school? Friends? Were there grateful employers? A grateful daughter-in-law? Were there great days? Graduation, election, a hero's medal? At any rate, "It's been worth it, a thousand times."

I do not ask that you repay the hours of toil and pain.
The sacrifice of youth and strength shall not have been in vain.
I do not ask for gratitude, but only this, my child,
That you shall live your life so well my gifts be not defiled.

The nights I watched beside your crib, the years of love and care
Will amply be repaid if once I see you standing there—
An upright and an honest soul on whom success has smiled,
That I may say with humble pride "That is my child!"

— *Oma Freeman Lathrop*

122

SONG OF PRAISE
(I Chronicles 16:7-15, 29-36)

INTRODUCTION —

The occasion of bringing the Ark of the Covenant to Jerusalem. The establishment of the worship of God in the capital city. The Psalm becomes a sort of manual of worship — examine it. (We make our own order of its elements.)

I. REMEMBER THE WORKS OF GOD — CONSIDER — MEDITATE
   A. Consider what He has done —
      1. He has made the earth (Psalm 8).
      2. He has blessed and kept covenant with Israel through centuries.
      3. To us He has sent His Son as Savior.
      4. He has visited judgment upon the earth.
   B. Consider who is behind the doing. He is great and just and to be reverenced. Holy and reverend is His name.
      1. See Psalm 90. "Even from everlasting to everlasting."
      2. The "Mysterium" and the "Tremendum."

II. GIVE GLORY — WORSHIP — TREMBLE BEFORE HIM.
   The response of the normal man to the goodness of God — Hallelujah!
   A. Praise — the fullness of the psalms.
      "For the beauty of the earth, for the glory of the skies,
         For the love which from our birth over and around us lies,
            Lord of all, to Thee we raise this our hymn of grateful praise."
   B. Give thanks — be glad — "rejoice in the Lord always."
   C. Sing unto Him; sing psalms unto Him (v. 9).
      1. "Let the word of Christ dwell in you richly in all wisdom; teaching and admonishing one another in psalms and hymns and spiritual songs, singing with grace in your hearts to the Lord" (Col. 3:16).

123

"Be not drunk with wine, wherein is excess; but be filled with the spirit; speaking to yourselves in psalms and hymns and spiritual songs, singing and making melody in your heart to the Lord"(Eph. 5:19).

    2. The church which will let the choir do the singing will let the preacher do all the rest. Why not sing? Preoccupied? Don't care to take part in worship?

D. Bring an offering and come before him (v. 29). "Where your treasure is there will your heart be also" (Luke 12:34). (Where your heart is, there will your treasure be also.) ("When did you last write to John?" "I'll look in my check book and find out.")

E. "Talk ye of all his wondrous works." "Make known his deeds among the people." (One shares with others according to his greatest enthusiasm.)

III. SEEK THE LORD AND HIS STRENGTH.

A. "Say ye, save us, O God of our salvation, and gather us together, and deliver us from the heathen, that we may give thanks to thy holy name and glory in thy praise."

B. Words of praise without dependence and trust are but empty.

C. Words of thanks without receiving are impossible.

CONCLUSION —

"I need thee every hour, most gracious Lord;
No tender voice like thine can peace afford.
I need, thee, O I need Thee, every hour I need Thee;
O bless me now my Savior, I come to Thee."

WHEN THE PROPHET WAS WRONG
(I Chronicles 17:1-10)

I. THE STORY OF NATHAN'S REPLY AND GOD'S GOD'S AMENDMENT.

    A. David suggests the building of the Temple.

        1. Nathan accepts.

        2. God interposes and makes His own plans as to time, the builder, and the plans.

        3. It becomes the pattern for worship until the time of Christ.

    B. Nathan's error.

        1. Having received God's Word, he came to assume that he could speak in God's place.

        2. "Thou savorest not of the things of God, but of men" (Jesus to Peter). Physical beauty of place of worship. Likeness to the nations round about. Good intentions of the builder.

    C. Nathan's merit.

        1. He was willing to be corrected by the word of God.

        2. He admitted his mistake, and conveyed the correction to David.

        3. Had courage to face a hurt and disappointed monarch.

II. PETER, PENTECOST, AND THE CHURCH, AS PARALLEL.

    A. The Lord's plan—"I will build My church" (Matt. 16:18).

    B. Peter's haste (at transfiguration) "Let us build three tabernacles"—"Hear Him."

    C. "Tarry ye in Jerusalem until ye be endued with power" (Luke 24:44-49). —See Acts 1, and the choosing of Matthias, as apostles' hasty move.

    D. God makes His own plans. Evidence of His hand in Pentecost. The Holy Spirit begot the church on that day. "The Lord added to the church such as should be saved" (Acts 2:47).

E. Thus, as in case of the Temple, God's are the time, the builder, and the plans. These become the pattern for acceptable worship in the Christian era.

III. PRESENT APPLICATION.
   A. Even the prophet may be wrong—great danger to the Christian leader.
      1. That he assume to speak that which the Lord has not spoken. "Mourner's bench" conversion plan based on experience. "The Bible is all right, but you have to use common sense, too." "I think that Jesus, if He were in the world today, would . . ."
      2. Greater danger if he refused to be corrected by the Word, as Nathan was.
   B. Good intentions and reasonable assumptions do not make acceptable worship.
   C. What of the church in which you are:—Is it the one of which He said, "I will build my church"? It is a matter of identity. (The person who would establish inheritance proves by his birth certificate that he is the person who was born at a given time and place to given parents.)

CONCLUSION —

"Take time to be holy, Let Him be thy Guide,
   And run not before Him, whatever betide.
In joy or in sorrow, still follow thy Lord,
   And looking to Jesus, still trust in His Word."

THE SIN OF THE CENSUS
(I Chronicles 21:1-8)

INTRODUCTION —

The story and the puzzle of it (Cf. II Sam. 24).

    A. David commands Joab and the others of the army to make the census.

    B. Joab objects, but goes reluctantly; the census is completed in 9 months, 20 days.

    C. Result finds in Israel 800,000 "valiant men that drew the sword." In Judah 500,000 "valiant men that drew the sword." (This is the tip-off that it was purely a military census.)

    D. God arranges punishment by choice: Seven years of famine, or "three months before thy foes," or three days' pestilence. (This was chosen and 70,000 of the valiant men died.)

I. DAVID'S SIN.

    A. Rejects God's rule for independent course of action.

    B. Comes to rely on material numbers rather than on God (I Sam. 17:45, 46).

    C. Nature of the census considers the people of God to be but units in a military machine.

    D. Such a census in a time of peace could mean only a plan for aggressive war. God's people were to have a home, but not to be marauders.

    E. See the punishment—David's pride was in his army—that is where he was hit.

II. THERE IS A CERTAIN APPLICATION TO AMERICA IN THIS PRESENT DAY.

    A. Her finest hours have been when her reliance was greatest on the right, rather than on might. (Was there a military census before 1776?)

    B. What is America today? Only a disproportionate share of the world's autos, TV's, telephones, and bathtubs? What is the American way of life? —A stockpile of atomic bombs, huge planes, and big armies?

C. "Soul, take thine ease, thou hast much goods laid up for many days.

Thou fool, this night shall thy soul be required of thee; then whose shall the things be?

So is he that layeth up treasure for himself, and is not rich toward God" (Luke 12:21).

III. THERE IS APPLICATION TO THE CHURCH

A. Great power in the days of numerical weakness— eleven men against the world.

B. Lost out when she proudly counted emperors and armies in her ranks. Darkest days when she had armies and great political power.

C. There are those who would repeat the experiment by insistence on over-ruling organization to exert pressure on governments, etc.

IV. DAVID'S EXPERIENCE HAS SPECIAL APPLICA-TION TO US WHO CLAIM NONE BUT CHRIST AS THE HEAD OF HIS CHURCH—

As Israel was a theocracy, so we a Christocracy.

A. In early days of the restoration we had no power in numbers, and must depend on the power of the Word —we had to know it, believe it, teach it.

B. Numbers grew rapidly—we counted them and admired selves in 1909.

C. Built up organizations, as necessary to accomplishment, and depended on them. Counted numbers "a great Brotherhood." —The centers of pride became a plague. Boasted organizations cankered and became a bone of contention. Boasted numbers become a weakness, and growth ceased.

CONCLUSION —

What is our power locally? Numbers, wealth, influence, building? Or the Word known, loved, and lived (Cf. I Cor. 1:26-31)?

PREACHING THROUGH II CHRONICLES

This book continues the narrative of First Chronicles, with which it forms a unit. It begins with the reign of Solomon, about 1000 B.C., and concludes with the close of the Captivity in Babylon, about 500 B.C. The Book of Ezra follows it directly, telling of the return from Babylon.

"The memory of the righteous is blessed,
But the name of the wicked shall rot"
(Proverbs 10:7).

Great emphasis is placed upon the historical outworking of God's promise that His people would prosper if they remained true to Him, but if they wandered in sin and idolatry, they would suffer. Note that the record dwells at length on the reigns of the better kings and pays a much briefer notice to the wicked and idolatrous kings.

Second Chronicles is definitely a history of the kings in David's line. There is no record of the Kingdom of Israel, the ten northern tribes, after their revolt from Judah.

Archaeological discoveries have borne out, in a most interesting fashion, the history recorded in this book. The wars of Judah's kings are recorded from the enemies' point of view on tablets, arches, and walls discovered in Mesopotamia. The events of Hezekiah's reign are most generously established. The tunnel by which he brought water into Jerusalem (32:3, 4) still exists. His defensive walls (32:5) have been traced as described. Sennacherib's invasion, the failure of his siege of Jerusalem, and his assassination by members of his own family (32:1-23), are all recorded in Assyrian inscriptions.

ANALYSIS OF SECOND CHRONICLES

Chapters	1-9	Reign of Solomon and building of the Temple.
	10-13	Reign of Rehoboam and division of the kingdom. Abijah's reign.
	14-20	The good kings Asa and Jehoshaphat.
	21,22	The evil reigns of Jehoram, Ahaziah, and Athaliah.
	24-26	The reigns of Joash, Amaziah, and Uzziah mix evil with good.

129

27,28 The evil reigns of Jotham and Ahaz.
29-32 The great reign of Hezekiah.
33 The evil reigns of Menasseh and Amon— 57 years.
34-35 The good reign of Josiah.
36 The four last kings of a dying realm; captivity; Cyrus' decree for release.

Sermon Outlines Provided:

"House of Prayer" (II Chron. 6:12-21)
"The King and the Teachers" (II Chron. 17:1-9)
"Evil Companions Corrupt Good Manners" (II Chron. 18:1-3; 19:1-3; 20:35-37)
"Humble Judgment" (II Chron. 28:8-15)

Other Suggested Sermon Topics:

"The Big 'If'" (II Chron. 7:11-22)
"The Passing of the Prophet" (II Chron. 24:15-22)
"The Great Deliverance" (II Chron. 32:9-23)
"Honor Thy Father" (II Chron. 34:1-3)

QUESTIONS OVER II CHRONICLES

1. What did Solomon ask God to give him? (1:10)
2. Where in Jerusalem did Solomon build the House of the Lord? (3:1)
3. What was in the Ark of the Covenant when Solomon had it brought into the Temple? (5:10)
4. Who was the next king after Solomon? (9:31)
5. In comparison to his father, how did Rehoboam describe his type of discipline? (10:14)
6. What did Azariah tell Asa about one's relationship with the Lord? (15:2)
7. Why was the Lord with Jehoshaphat? (17:3-4)
8. Whom did Joash murder? (24:22)
9. When Hezekiah commanded the people to give, what was their response? (31:4-12)
10. What did Amon multiply? (33:23)

HOUSE OF PRAYER
(II Chronicles 6:12-21)

INTRODUCTION —

The Temple was complete and the time of dedication had come. Last stone set in place and made fast. Last gorgeous pillar set and covered with its gold leaf. Tapestries and hangings in place. Altar and brazen sea ready to be used. Now the king goes to his knees before God in the presence of all the people. "My house shall be called a house of prayer." "When they shall pray toward this place, then hear Thou in heaven."

I. THE SYMBOL OF GOD'S PRESENCE, AND THE CENTER OF PRAYER.

   A. The Temple was such a symbol in Israel, replacing the tabernacle.

   B. Christ is our Temple, "God with us" — "if ye shall ask anything in My name."

      1. "In him dwelleth all the fullness of the Godhead bodily" (Col. 2:9).

      2. The place of prayer is where we turn to Him.

   C. The house of worship is a house of prayer. We come together to Him.

      1. Acts 2:42. ". . . and in prayer."

      2. It is the place of gathering on His Day.

      3. Here is *His Table*.

      4. It is the place of bringing offerings in His name (I Cor. 16:2).

      5. His word is here spoken and heard.

II. ADMONITION, "ENTER INTO HIS GATES WITH THANKSGIVING AND INTO HIS COURTS WITH PRAISE."

   A. There are dangers in church-going which cannot harm the prayerful.

      1. If there is "see how good I am," God knows exactly how good we are not. Pharisee prayed *with himself*, "I thank thee that I am not as others."

131

2. If there is display, "God looketh on the heart" and not on garments.
3. If there is tendency to empty form, the presence of God gives sincere meaning.
4. Fault finding—we stand before our own judge. You can't pray for one and find fault at the same time.

B. Have we lost the sense of "House of Prayer," that the special services of prayer should be so poorly attended?
1. Prayer meeting for teachers and officers before Bible School.
2. Wednesday evening prayer and study hour.

C. Opportunities for prayer in public worship.
1. "Say amen at the giving of thanks" (I Cor. 14:16). (Share in public prayer.)
2. Upon entering, "Create in me a clean heart, O God, and renew a right spirit"—prayers for others.
3. At time of communion; let Him walk again among us, and carry to Him our praise.
4. At the invitation.

III. SUBJECTS OF PRAYER IN THE HOUSE OF GOD.
A. Among Israelites.
1. Repentance—"forgive."
2. Neighbor and neighbor, nation and nation, drought, pestilence. The foreigner's prayer, the warrior's prayer, prayer in captivity.

B. Subjects for Christian prayer.
1. Likewise humble repentance, prayer for forgiveness.
2. Thanks for salvation.
3. "Casting all your care on Him, for He careth for you."
4. Especially prayers including others of the church.

CONCLUSION —

He is our Temple; to Him we invite.

THE KING AND THE TEACHERS
(II Chronicles 17:1-9)

INTRODUCTION –

We dare to tell a story of what happened more than 2800 years ago, and that of a man who used a book, more than 500 years old already, as the basis of his instruction. Jehoshaphat, (Jehovah judges), son of Asa (physician), comes to throne at age of 35. Characterized by industry, intelligence, faith. Reigned 25 years.

I. HE SOUGHT A *PERMANENT* POLICY OF IMPROVEMENT FOR JUDAH.

   A. Asa had destroyed heathen idols, even deposed own mother (weeds came up again). "He that governs well, leads the blind; but he that teaches, gives him eyes" (South).

   B. Jehoshaphat sends teachers throughout the land.

   C. There is a permanent nature to what you have learned.
      1. You know reasons; they will be good forever.
      2. You have gained lasting characteristics:
         a. Has it given sympathy and caused you to espouse good causes? Has it made you public-spirited? A brother to the weak?
         b. Have you learned to make and keep friends?
         c. Can you look an honest man or woman straight in the eye?
         d. Can you see something to love in a little child? Will a lonely dog follow you in the street?
      3. True education trains not only to make a living, but to make a *life*.

II. JEHOSHAPHAT SENT *PRINCES*. (Alexander the Great: "I owe my father for living; teachers for living *well*.)

   A. The best in the country, and the noblest, were none too good.

   B. You will come more and more to appreciate your own teachers.

   C. They mark one of the noblest groups in the country.

133

1. None other would have stuck through, with poor pay, etc. as they have. A Grade School teacher says, "I wouldn't be happy doing anything else because I feel I am rendering a worthwhile service to humanity—and the Lord knows they need it."
2. Make teacher's pay worthy, but don't make it tempting.
3. Pride in teachers who are members of this congregation.

D. *More princes needed.*

III. JEHOSHAPHAT'S POLICY WAS SUCCESSFUL.

A. It brought a strong nation, respected by neighbors, who paid tribute.
B. America's power is due to her placing value on people —education.
C. Values less easily counted. Citizenship—"Improve your schools or enlarge your prisons" (Horace Mann).
D. To continue success, the work must go on.
1. Cry for better schools, but spend more on liquor than on education. Keeping criminal 2% of population costs five times more than to educate 100%.
E. What schools need more than money:
1. Teachers who love their pupils and their job.
2. Pupils taught to respect people and property.
3. Parents who are really interested in the right kind of education.
4. Citizens who will free schools from politics.

IV. JEHOSHAPHAT'S PROGRAM WAS *RELIGIOUS* EDUCATION.

A. "The fear of the Lord is the beginning of knowledge."
B. This makes a life more than a living.
C. While the classroom discussed airy theories, Christianity demands a commitment to the best.
D. How does the religious element in your education stack up?

"Come and learn of Me" (Matt. 11:29). "I am the Way, the Truth, and the Life." (John 14:6).

EVIL COMPANIONS CORRUPT GOOD MANNERS
(II Chronicles 18:1-3; 19:1-3; 20:35-37)

INTRODUCTION —

Well-known lessons from little-known characters. Jehoshaphat —King of Judah, 877-852, fifth generation from David (son of Asa). 150 years and 9 kings before Hezekiah. Sent religious teachers about Israel. Organizer. Won war over Moab and Ammon by help of the Lord. We look into his unfortunate alliances.

I. NOT WILLING TO STAND ALONE, HE SOUGHT ALLIANCES.

   A. Our own day needs to learn the value of being and standing alone.

      1. Moses on the mount; Amos following the sheep; Elijah in the wilderness; John the Baptist; Paul in Arabia.

      2. Paul in prison; Milton, the blind; John Bunyan in prison, produced alone.

      3. "Jesus went into a mountain apart to pray" (Matt. 14:23).

   B. He who can be content alone is the one worth following in the crowd. — Each of the men whom we have named was a leader of men.

   C. "I have to live with myself, and so I want to be fit for myself to know."

II. WHEN JEHOSHAPHAT AND AHAB BECAME ALLIES, THEY WENT ON *AHAB'S* MISSION. — (Can two walk together, except they be agreed?)

   A. The tendency is downward, as each will do in company what he would not alone. (American Legion convention breaks up the furniture.)

   B. The story of every criminal—"He fell into bad company."

   C. Partnerships and marriages often have deleterious effect on religion. Both go the easiest way.

D. By contrast, Jesus, "wine-bibber and glutton" (?) was Master and Teacher at every banquet.

III. THE ALLIANCES RESULTED IN DEFEAT AND DISGRACE.

A. The better partner may not be affected morally, but his witness is lost. Such alliances do not command the respect of very men for whose favor they are formed.

B. This is the direction of friendships and partnerships formed for the sake of present advantage. (Charlton learns to drink for the sake of his business.)

C. "My son, consent thou not" (Prov. 1:10). (No wine on the table in William Jennings Bryan's affairs.)

IV. THE GREATER EVIL WAS RESERVED TO JEHOSHAPHAT'S SON, JEHORAM.

A. "He walked in the ways of the kings of Israel, as did the house of Ahab; for he had the daughter of Ahab to wife; and he did that which was evil in the sight of Jehovah . . . and he departed without being desired" (II Chronicles 21:6, 20).

B. The sins of the fathers are, in this sense, visited upon the children.

1. Contracts with Rome, in mixed marriage: Think of the children!

2. When the boys begin to talk and act like Dad's partners, then what?

3. A youngster dies of acute alcoholism, having "entertained," as Dad and Mother.

C. Some friendships cost too much. "Friendship with the world is enmity against God" (James 4:4).

CONCLUSION —

A safe rule; make Christ your first partner, then join in friendship with those who can share that partnership.

136

HUMBLE JUDGMENT
(II Chronicles 28:8-15)

INTRODUCTION — the story of Ahaz.

Weakling king of Judah, admirer of things Assyrian, worshiper of whatever gods were at the moment in favor. Constantly warned by Isaiah, but to no avail. Disrespected by neighbors round about, who recovered cities. Defeated by Syria and Israel in combination. The message of Oded . . .

I. GOD BRINGS JUDGMENT UPON THE SINNER; DEFEAT WAS FOR THE SINS OF JUDAH.
   A. Perfect justice is never seen in the earth; not all events are judgment.
      1. "Who sinned, this man or his parents, that he was born blind?" (John 9:2).
      2. "Suppose ye that the eighteen men on whom the tower of Siloam fell were sinners above all that are in Israel?" (Luke 13:4).
   B. Some evils, both to guilty and innocent, are direct result of sin.
      1. Present wave of violent crimes—lack of home training, materialism, alcohol and drugs.
      2. Accidents—over one-fourth are alcohol-related.
   C. General warnings in catastrophe?
      1. Air crashes—too big a hurry to think of eternal.
      2. Weather-crop failures, storms, etc.: "Still not all in your hands."

II. GOD SAYS, "THOU DOEST THE SAME THINGS THYSELF" (See Rom. 2:1, 17-24).
   A. Thus no human judge has the right to be harsh with his brother.
   B. "Condemn not that ye be not condemned" (Matt. 7:1).
      "Let each one know himself.
      To gain that knowledge let him labor,
      Improve those failings in himself

137

He condemns so in his neighbor.
O how lenient our own faults we view,
And conscience voice adroitly smother:
But O how harshly we review
The selfsame failings in another!"

C. Dare we condemn atheistic cultures? What do we do with the Lord's Day? What with God's Word? What do we read, laugh at, be entertained by? Gambling, profanity, obscenity . . .

III. ODED'S HEARERS CAUGHT THE POINT— MERCY IN RESTITUTION.

"Ye that are spiritual, restore such a one in a spirit of meekenss . . ." (Gal. 6:1, 2). "Blessed are the merciful . . ." (Matt 5:7).

A. We need God's view—"The mighty he hath brought low, and exalted them of low degree" (Luke 1:52). —easy to have respect to the proud, uncaught criminal, and to shy away from the man with a prison record.

B. Mercy to the punished and penitent.

C. The Christian has mercy to give, better than clothing and gifts. He has the story of a loving Savior.

CONCLUSION —

See Rom. 3:21-25. "But the scripture hath concluded all under sin, that the promise by faith of Jesus Christ might be given to them that believe" (Gal. 3:22).

PREACHING THROUGH EZRA, NEHEMIAH AND ESTHER

These three books, containing a total of 33 chapters, close the Old Testament historical record. They tell of the Jews' return from captivity in Babylon, the rebuilding of the city of Jerusalem and the Temple within it, and the reorganization of their national life in their own land. The three last of the Prophets — Haggai, Zechariah and Malachi — minister during the period.

Ezra was a priest, who returned from Babylon to Jerusalem with a large company of people in 457 B.C. He records also the story of a group who returned eighty years before that. Ezra's work was designed to keep the national and religious life of his people free from the heathen influences about them.

Chapters 1,2   The return of the first refugees permitted by Cyrus.

       3-6   The building again of the temple.

       7,8   Ezra's return to Jerusalem.

       9,10   His action to avoid intermarriages with the heathen.

Nehemiah was a trusted servant of the Persian king. He requested, and received, permission to take a company to Jerusalem in 444 B.C. and to rebuild the walls of Jerusalem. He remained as governor of Judea.

Chapters 1,2   Nehemiah journeys to Jerusalem.

       3-6   The walls are rebuilt in spite of many difficulties.

       7   Records of a former company returning to Jerusalem.

       8-10   Reading of the Law and renewing of the covenant.

       11,12   Dedication of the wall.

       13   Correction of abuses.

Esther, a Jewess, became queen of Persia in 478 B.C., at a time when her influence was providentially used to avoid the complete destruction of the Jewish people by their enemies. She was probably still living when her stepson, Artaxerxes, sent Nehemiah to Jerusalem.

Chapters   1,2   Esther becomes queen of Persia.
           3-7   She is able to defeat Haman's attempt to secure
                  the death of all the Jews.
           8-10   The Jews celebrate a great triumph and Mordecai
                  is exalted.

Importance For The Christian: In addition to their plain moral and religious teachings and examples, these books tell how God acted through the history of His people to preserve a nation through whom he could send His Son. Ezra tells of their religious preservation; Nehemiah of their political establishment; and Esther of their preservation from physical destruction.

Sermon Outlines Provided:

"The King's Decree" (Ezra 5)
"Rise Up and Build" (Neh. 2:17-20)
"Enemies of the Builder" (Neh. 4)
"How to Get a Raise" (Esther 6:1-13)

Other Suggested Sermon Topics:

"Assistant Builders" (Ezra 1:1-6)
"A Statesman Prays" (Neh. 1:4-11)
"The Family's Business" (Neh. 5:1-13)
"The Old Word for a New Day" (Neh. 8:1-8)
"For Such a Time as This" (Esther 4:13-17)
"Pride's Suicide" (Esther 7)

QUESTIONS OVER EZRA, NEHEMIAH, ESTHER

1. Who was the prince of Judah in Ezra's day? (Ezra 1:8)
2. How many Jews returned to Jerusalem with Ezra after the Babylonian captivity? (2:64-65)
3. What motivated the people to build the wall? (Neh. 4:6)
4. What did the people ask Ezra to do? (8:1)
5. When did Nehemiah return to Babylon? (13:6)
6. What did Nehemiah do when he discovered that the Jews had married foreigners? (13:23-27)
7. What did the sleepless king remember? (Esther 6:1-3)
8. What position was Mordecai elevated to? (10:3)

THE KING'S DECREE
(Ezra 5)

INTRODUCTION —

The story of the rebuilding as parallel to the Restoration Movement.

- A. Cyrus gives the command and provisions for building (Commission).
- B. Samaritans and others send letters to Ahasuerus and Artaxerxes, condemning Jerusalem for insubordination (Paganism vs. the church).
- C. Artaxerxes commands the building to stop (Paganism takes over).
- D. Haggai and Zechariah urge and secure rebuilding (Reformers and restorers).
- E. Tatnai, the governor, challenges authority (human attempts to regulate the church in present time).
- F. Reply of the builders — old foundation and former authority. (We build where the apostles and prophets built.)
- G. Inquiry to Darius and his reply. ("I found the former writing.")

I. WE BUILD ON THE PATTERN GIVEN BY THE AUTHORITY OF CHRIST.
- A. We know what it is to restore according to a former plan — story of Ft. Niagara, N.Y., and the well that had been forgotten.
- B. The plan of the New Testament church (as though a set of by-laws).
  1. Its name. The church, "The churches of Christ."
  2. Its make-up. Bridegroom's bride. Building on foundation. Body with head.
  3. Its members. Saints, disciples, brethren, Christians.
  4. Its officers. Elders, bishops. Deacons, servants, ministers.
  5. Its creed. "Thou art the Christ."

6. Its ordinances. Baptism and the Lord's Supper.
7. Its activities. Teaching, fellowship, breaking bread, prayers.

(There is no provision for amendment to these by-laws.)

II. THE AUTHORITY MUST BE UNCHALLENGED (Matt. 28:18-20).

 A. Josephus says that: "King Darius to Sisinnes the governor, and to Sathrabuzanes, sendeth greeting. Having found a copy of this epistle among the records of Cyrus, I have sent it to you; and I will that all things be done as therein written. Farewell."

 B. Having found these things written in the New Testament by the hand of the inspired apostles, we deliver them to all men; and we will that all things be done as written therein.

III. WHAT DO YE MORE THAN OTHERS?

 A. Elijah Goodwin: "Brethren, this reformation in which we are engaged has not done its work until the people of God who occupy Bible ground in theory have become so upright, so pious, so devout, so heavenly minded, that all who revere the Bible will be constrained to say, 'These people are not only Christians in name, but they are Christians in deed and in truth.'"

 B. We have not done it—shall we then abandon the plea? "These things ought ye to have done, and not to have left the other undone." It is easy to pare the program down to fit the man, but we must build the man up to fit the pattern.

142

RISE UP AND BUILD
(Nehemiah 2:17-20)

INTRODUCTION — The story

Nehemiah's tour of the walls at night — a description of their condition. His meeting with the people, making clear to him the aim. The allotment of portions of the building — guilds, cities, families. Difficulties and success. Double application — to the personal Christian life, and to the church.

I. GIVING A CLEAR IDEA OF WHAT IS EXPECTED —A BLUE-PRINT FOR THE BUILDING.
   A. For the Christian life.
      1. Must get away from vague idea of "join the church and be good."
      2. The pattern is given in the person of Christ. Illustrated by the lives of many heroes. Described in the epistles.
      3. "Love, joy, peace, longsuffering, gentleness, goodness, faith, meekness, temperance" (Gal. 5:22, 23).
      4. "Faith, virtue, knowledge, temperance, patience, godliness, brotherly kindness, love" (II Pet. 1:5-7).
      5. Who is a Christian?
   B. For the Church — what is the purpose of its existence?
      1. Have we a pattern for the Church? Government, polity, life, etc.
      2. One says, "Anything good is the church's business." That is wrong!
      3. Briefly, the Commission.

II. THE AUTHORITY BEHIND THE BUILDER — NEHEMIAH'S LETTER FROM THE KING.
   A. We have a letter from the King.
   B. "All authority hath been given unto me" (Matt. 28:18).
   C. Promises of success.
      1. "The gates of hell shall not prevail" (Matt. 16:18).
      2. "I am with you always" (Matt. 28:20).

3. "With every temptation there will be provided a way of escape" (I Cor. 10:13).
4. "Be thou faithful unto death and I will give unto thee the crown of life" (Rev. 2:10).

III. THE ASSIGNMENT OF WORK TO INDIVIDUALS AND GROUPS—APPLY ESPECIALLY TO CHURCH.
   A. The assignment is that nearest home.
   B. "Their nobles put not their necks to the work."—some object to obscure place.
   C. Discouragement in the carrying out of the work.
   D. Assignments in the church—
      1. Special—teaching, calling, ushering, office work.
      2. General—presence, welcome, enthusiasm made known, calling in case of need, finance, invitation.

IV. ACCOMPLISHMENT—THE PEOPLE HAD A MIND TO WORK.
   A. Lack of dependability is partner to the lack of willingness, in discouraging Christian leaders and paralyzing the church.
   B. In the personal life—"To him that knoweth to do good . . ." (James 4:17).

V. THE VICTORY IN THE COMPLETION OF THE TASK.
   A. —"That the man of God may be complete, throughly furnished" (II Tim. 3:17).
   B. "Till we all come to the stature of a full grown man in Christ" (Eph. 4:13).
   C. "That He might present it to himself a glorious church, without spot or wrinkle or any such thing" (Eph. 5:27).
   D. This is a task that is completed only when the builder is called home.

ENEMIES OF THE BUILDER
(Nehemiah 4)

INTRODUCTION —

Consider the need of Christians in building faith, character, and service, according to Galatians 5:22.

    A. For new Christians it is construction of something new, requiring work.

    B. For most of us, it is a matter of repair and addition.

    C. We learn from Nehemiah, who returned to Jerusalem and rebuilt the walls.

I. THE ENEMIES.

    A. To Nehemiah.

        1. Himself — but by prayer and energetic discipline he conquered himself.

        2. Tobiah — a slave who became ruler of Ammon, eastward across the Jordan. He kept up correspondence with spies in Jerusalem.

        3. Gashma the Arabian, from the land south of Judea.

        4. The enemies were persons, and they were in and around Jerusalem.

    B. To yourself as a Christian. No enemy can destroy you as long as you stay faithful.

        1. Yourself must be conquered as the first accomplishment (I Cor. 9:24-27).

        2. Folk who stand to make gain by your moral failure, persuading you to smoke, drink, use other drugs, gamble, etc.

        3. Folk who are uncomfortable in the presence of a life better than theirs and so try to pull you down.

        4. Folk who see no purpose in standards higher than those of general decency, and so decry "Puritanism" and "religious fanaticism."

        5. Careless folk who mislead by weak example, e.g. parents who "want their children to go to Sunday School."

6. Folk who undermine the faith by "religious teaching" whose ultimate authority is "scientific scholarship."

II. METHODS OF THE ENEMY. (Here we note the example of Nehemiah's enemies.)

A. Ridicule—"Will they build in a day?" "Will the rubble rise into a wall?" "A fox running over it will knock it down!"
   1. Aim to discourage and cause one to quit trying.
   2. Result in defeated one's saying, "That is what everyone expected, so I'd hate to disappoint them."

B. Serious attacks, when ridicule failed.
   1. Nehemiah's enemies made a league with Samaritans, Arabs, Ammonites, and Philistines to discredit and destroy his work.
   2. Enemies of Christ sometimes resort to persecution and pressure.
   3. Enemies of Christ use "intellectual" attack, denying the Gospel.

C. Conference and compromise.
   1. Nehemiah invited to conference on plains of Ono, thirty miles northwest in the maritime plain. He saw invitation as disruptive of his purpose.
   2. Nehemiah was threatened by pretended friendship of those who would "put to rest the evil reports against Nehemiah."
   3. So the church is robbed of its evangelistic vigor at home and abroad by time spent in conferring rather than in doing its own work.

CONCLUSION —

Victory came to Nehemiah, and is available to us, through constant watchfulness and the help of God.

146

HOW TO GET A RAISE
(Esther 6:1-13)

INTRODUCTION –

The story of Mordecai, uncle and protector of Esther, who came to palace at Shushan with her.

   A. Heard of plot versus life of king and let it be known.
   B. Refused obeisance to Haman, and was cause of his wrath versus Jews.
   C. Heard of Haman's decree for the destruction of Jews; fasted; directed Esther's plea to Ahasuerus.
   D. Was belatedly honored, as here described, for discovery of plot. (Josephus fills in details of the night and day.)
   E. Placed over the house of Haman after his death; later made "next to king."

His example speaks to point of how to gain advancement.

   I. DO THE THING YOU LOVE TO DO, OR LOVE THE THING YOU HAVE TO DO.

   A. Mordecai cares for his niece and his people.
   B. Farmer says, "How did I happen to be a farmer? Just lucky, I guess." – Edison has prospective employes go over the whole plant and make remarks and suggestions.
   C. "Greatest field for success is probably right where you are."
   D. See the story of Jesus, the shepherd and the hireling (John 10:11-14).

   II. BE HONEST WITH YOURSELF, AS MORDECAI'S REFUSAL TO BOW TO HAMAN.

   A. Complete honesty and faithfulness are not for sale. Henry Ford II, says "All of us will be better off when we can pay a man $5 an hour because he produces $5 worth of effort than when we try to pay him $1.50 as hour for 75¢ worth of effort."

147

B. Advantage gained by violation of one's conscience isn't worth it. "What shall it profit a man if he gain the whole world . . .?" (Matt. 16:26).

III. CONSIDER THE INTERESTS OF YOUR EMPLOYER.

A. "With what measure ye mete, it shall be measured to you again" (Matt. 7:2). "Give, and it shall be given unto you" (Luke 6:38).

B. Consider value to him, not demands for yourself. (Employer kept goldfish on the desk: "something that can open its mouth without asking for more money.")

IV. TAKE RESPONSIBILITIES.

A. Quelling the plot was the work of the palace guard, but Mordecai took it.

B. (If the giraffe did not stick out his neck, he wouldn't eat.)

V. EXERCISE INITIATIVE. MORDECAI THINKS, PLANS, PERSISTS IN HIS WORK.

A. Perhaps his was a stroke of good fortune, but he was ready to take advantage of it.

B. A secretary wins a trip to Bermuda by a suggestion to steamship line.

CONCLUSION –

The rewards–

A. First, the hollow display desired by Haman.

B. Then the advancement which measured to his own abilities. "Well done, thou good and faithful servant: thou hast been faithful in a few things, I will make thee ruler over many things" (Matt. 25:21).

PREACHING THROUGH THE BOOK OF JOB

"I call this book, apart from all theories about it, one of the grandest things ever written. Our first, oldest statement of the never-ending problem — Man's destiny, and God's ways with him in the earth. There is nothing written, I think, of equal literary merit." — *Thomas Carlyle.*

If you are a lazy reader, you will pass up Job, and thereby miss some of the most beautiful and helpful material in the entire Old Testament. Its form as Hebrew poetry, its dramatic arrangement, and the depth of the problem it faces, all combine to place Job very far out of the class of light reading. You must give it more than ten minutes at a time, and you must give it thought. You will be glad you did.

The Book of Job is the poetic, dramatic presentation of the problem of suffering faced by a real person under real circumstances. While the children of Israel were toiling in Egypt, between the time of Joseph and that of Moses, Job lived among the descendants of Esau in the edge of the Arabian desert. The problem he faced is one that comes to everyone in some measure: why do the righteous suffer?

ANALYSIS OF THE BOOK

Chapters 1-2 Prologue in prose. The characters are introduced, and the nature of Job's affliction is told.

3-31 The body of the drama in poetic form.

32-37 Elihu concludes the friends' arguments.

38-41 God speaks. Is this problem the only thing in all God's doings which Job cannot understand?

42 Epilogue in prose. Job humbles himself in worship and is restored.

Each of Job's friends speaks in turn. They argue that suffering is always a result of sin. Job must repent, they say, and he will be healed.

Job replies to each address. He protests that he is innocent. This cycle is repeated three times.

Sermon Outlines Provided:

"Between God and Man" (Job 9:1-4, 10-12, 16-20, 31-35)
"If My Soul Were in Your Soul's Stead" (Job 16:1-5)
"I Know That My Redeemer Liveth" (Job 19:25-27)
"Mine Eye Hath Seen Thee" (Job 42:1-10)

Other Suggested Sermon Topics:

"Hasty Fruit" (Job 15:31-33)
"Can a Man Be Profitable to God?" (Job 22:1-5)

QUESTIONS OVER JOB

1. How did the Lord describe Job's character? (1:8)
2. Who were Job's three friends? (2:11)
3. According to Eliphaz, what is man born for? (5:7)
4. What did Job call God in 7:20? (7:20)
5. How did Job view his length of life? (9:25-26)
6. What did Zophar think was the cause of all of Job's problems? (11:13-20)
7. How totally did Job trust God? (13:15)
8. What did Job ask about life after death? (14:14)
9. What was Job's belief about his Redeemer? (19:25)
10. What did Zophar say about the wicked and the Godless? (20:5)
11. What did Job say that he had observed about the wicked? (21:7)
12. How did Job point out that sinfulness was not the cause of his troubles? (23:10-12)
13. What did Job say concerning his truthfulness and righteousnes? (27:5-6)
14. According to Job, what is the value of wisdom? (28:12-22)
15. What did Job expect but then receive? (30:26)
16. What was the covenant Job made with his eyes? (31:1)
17. According to Elihu, what is God's action toward man based upon? (34:10-12)
18. Out of what did the Lord answer Job? (38:1)
19. Describe Job's last days. (42:12)

150

BETWEEN GOD AND MAN
(Job 9:1-4, 10-12, 16-20, 31-35)

INTRODUCTION —

There is no finer prophecy of the things that Christ brings to man than the longings of the Patriarch Job. The shape of Job's emptiness is the shape of Jesus! (Illus. — Archaeologists at Pompeii found hollow places in the lava. They poured plaster of Paris in some of the hollows, and the plaster took the form of human figures that had been covered and then leached away.)

I. THE UNIVERSAL LONGING FOR A MEDIATOR.
   A. Job 9:33 "Neither is there any daysman betwixt us."
   B. Moses was asked to speak for God to Israel, lest they die in God's presence.
   C. God provided the priesthood to represent men to God, and the order of prophets to represent God to men.

II. THE GAP BETWEEN GOD'S JUSTICE AND MAN'S FRAILTY.
   A. Job 9:2 — "How should man be just with God?"
   B. Romans 3:20 — "By the deeds of the law shall no flesh be justified."
   C. I Corinthians 6:11 — "Such (sinners) were some of you, but ye were washed, ye were sanctified, but ye were justified in the name of the Lord Jesus Christ, and in the spirit of our God."

III. THE GAP BETWEEN GOD'S STRENGTH AND MAN'S WEAKNESS.
   A. Job 9:4, 10 — "He is wise in heart and mighty in strength: who hath hardened himself against him, and hath prospered? . . . Which doeth great things past finding out."
   B. Philippians 4:13 — "I can do all things in him that strengtheneth me."

IV. THE GAP BETWEEN GOD'S BEING AND MAN'S UNDERSTANDING.
   A. Job 9:11 — "Lo, he goeth by me, and I see him not:

he passeth on also, but I perceive him not."
B. Christ came as the revelation, visible and tangible, of God who is love.
C. Man's perception of God is seen, not in describing Him, but in reflecting His nature, love for love.

V. THE GAP BETWEEN GOD'S CALLING AND MAN'S HEARING.
A. Job 9:16 — "If I had called, and he had answered me; yet would I not believe that he had hearkened unto my voice."
B. II Corinthians 5:19 — "God was in Christ, reconciling the world unto himself, not imputing their trespasses unto them, and has committed unto us the ministry of reconciliation."
C. There are many evidences that God is, but the greatest possible evidence is the person of Jesus Christ.

IV. THE GAP BETWEEN GOD AND MAN IN JUDGMENT.
A. Job 9:32 — "He is not a man, as I am, that I should answer him, and we should come together in judgment."
B. I John 2:1 — "We have an advocate with the Father, Jesus Christ the righteous."
C. Romans 8:34 — "Who is he that condemneth? It is Christ that died, yea rather, that is risen again, who is even at the right hand of God, who also maketh intercession for us."

CONCLUSION —

I Timothy 2:5-6 — "There is one God, and one mediator between God and men, the man Christ Jesus; who gave himself a ransom for all."

The umpire ("daysman" for whom Job longed) mercifully favors the weak.

IF MY SOUL WERE IN YOUR SOUL'S STEAD
(Job 16:1-5)

INTRODUCTION –

Job puts his finger on the pulse of the world's troubles.

I. "MISERABLE COMFORTERS."

  A. In his suffering he longed for sympathy – "Rejoice with them that do rejoice, and weep with them that weep."

   "The touch of human hands – that is the boon we ask;
   For groping day by day along the stony way,
   We need the comrade heart that understands,
   And the warmth, the living warmth of human hands."

   – T. Curtis Clark

  B. Instead he was given unfeeling moralizing and philosophizing. They made him exhibit A in a philosophical discussion.

  C. Miserable comforters in the earth – Labor to capital, and vice versa – each a "problem" to the other. The racial problem. Youth problem. Returned veteran. Juvenile delinquent.

II. "I ALSO COULD SPEAK AS YOU DO."
CONDEMNING WORDS WITHOUT FEELING.

  A. Words are cheap when one doesn't understand. The petty thief flares up, "Have you ever been hungry?"

  B. Scotch professor Blackie chides lad for not holding paper in right hand, then learns he has none.

  Thus is introduced:

III. "I WOULD STRENGTHEN YOU WITH MY MOUTH."

  A. Perhaps partly the usual conceit that oneself would do better than other.

  B. Mostly, sympathy would be born of suffering. "There is, in the experience of sorrow, a power to help others which can be bought at no lesser cost."

153

1. Illus.: The paralytic in Canton says, "If I ever get out, I'll call on them, for I know what it means."
2. Of it there is born tenderness and strength.
3. "Before I brand a brother with envy or with shame, I'll whisper to my heart, 'He comes the road I came.' If any sue for pity—Though friend he be or foe— I'll whisper to my soul, 'He goes the road I go.'"

C. He has not only traveled the path, but traveled it well.
   1. False idea that much experience makes a sound adviser. Five-time divorcee offers to write on "How to keep a husband."
   2. Suffering leaves some embittered and incapable of spiritual good. (Job's wife.)

IV. I WOULD SPEAK TO YOU OF CHRIST.

A. Others are miserable comforters—"Thieves and robbers." Confucius moralized, Buddha spiritualized, Socrates philosophised. None could sympathize—carry the load for us.
B. Christ could condemn. "Let him that is without sin cast the first stone" (John 8:7).
C. Instead He invites, comforts, strengthens.
   1. "We have not a high priest that is not touched with a feeling . . . (Heb. 4:15).
   2. He has not only gone the way before, but He has gone successfully. "I have overcome the world" (John 16:33).

CONCLUSION —

Accept His comforting, sustaining power today.

I KNOW THAT MY REDEEMER LIVETH
(Job 19:25-27)

INTRODUCTION — Bold faith speaks for itself.

   A. "Who is this that hideth counsel without knowledge?"

   B. "Therefore have I uttered that which I understood not. Things too wonderful for me, which I understood not."

I. JOB MADE HIS OWN PLEA.

   A. The need of a redeemer.

      1. He is a vindicator (describe).

      2. Otherwise one becomes free only by avenging or repaying.

      3. None else understands—all lay false charges of conscious evil.

      4. None else believes—he cries for the opportunity to speak permanently.

   B. The Redeemer lives.

      1. Faith leaps out of the darkness.

      2. It appeals to God—there is none other to help.

      3. It sees personal quality of God in His self-revelation.

   C. He will stand at last upon the earth.

      1. The longing for immediate fellowship with Him is not to be denied.

      2. Since man cannot achieve Heaven, God condescends to earth.

   D. I shall see Him and not as a stranger.

      1. God has seemed to be far and aloof.

      2. His love and man's longing will find a meeting place.

II. THE SPIRIT HAS WRITTEN HIS OWN MESSAGE.

   A. It appears in the revelation to patriarchs and prophets.

   B. Christ is accurately described in the longings of those who know Him not.

III. THE MESSAGE OF THE REDEEMER IS FOUND IN CHRIST.

   A. The need of the redeemer.

1. The reasons assigned to Job, plus the burden of accumulated sin.
2. Cleansing from the burden of known sin.
3. Fellowship in spite of sins not known in ourselves.

B. The Redeemer lives.
   1. Before Abraham was, I am" (John 8:58).
   2. "Lo, I am with you always" (Matt. 28:20).

C. He did—and will—stand upon the earth.
   1. "The Word became flesh and dwelt among us" (John 1:14, see 1:1-18).
   2. He emptied Himself, taking the form of a servant, being made in the likeness of men; and being found in fashion as a man, he humbled himself, becoming obedient even unto death, yea, the death of the cross" (Phil. 2:5-11).

D. I shall see Him.
   1. The seeing is both personal and universal: "Every eye shall see him" (Rev. 1:7).
   2. It will be a time either of supreme joy or supreme anguish.

MINE EYE HATH SEEN THEE
(Job 42:1-10)

INTRODUCTION —

    A. The age-old quest: "Show us the Father and it sufficeth us" (John 14:8).

    B. "No man hath seen God at any time" (John 1:18).

    C. God has given many partial revelations of Himself.

I. "MINE EYE HATH SEEN THEE."

    A. Job saw God partly in his own suffering—The purposes of God are not exhausted in material things.

    B. Others saw God—partly in Job's response to his suffering.

        1. He insisted on the being of God, who seemed far away.

        2. He declared the goodness and justice of God, despite experience.

    C. All men can see the overweening power of the Creator. Seven reasons why a scientist believes in God:

        1. By unwavering mathematical law we can prove that our universe was designed and executed by a great engineering Intelligence.

        2. The resourcefulness of life to accomplish its purpose is a manifestation of all-pervading intelligence.

        3. Animal wisdom speaks irresistibly of a good Creator who infused instinct into otherwise helpless little creatures.

        4. Man has something more than animal instinct— the power of reason.

        5. Provision for all living is revealed in phenomena which we know today but which Darwin did not know—such as the wonders of genes.

        6. By the economy of nature, we are forced to realize that only infinite Wisdom could have foreseen and prepared with such astute husbandry.

7. The fact that man can conceive the idea of God is in itself a unique proof.

(Build on the greatness of God.)

II. THE RESULT OF SEEING GOD IS THE END OF PRIDE IN ONE'S OWN INTELLIGENCE AND GOODNESS.

A. Job—
  1. Comparing himself with himself he could be pleased with himself.
  2. Not so, having seen God.
B. Ourselves, becoming acquainted with Christ
  1. Ends the pride that makes difficulty in the church. "Let this mind be in you, which was also in Christ Jesus" (Phil. 2:5).
  2. Ends the self-satisfaction that keeps one out of the church.
C. Some, seeing themselves, are despondent.
  1. They likewise need to "see God."
    a. Moses thought he could not do the thing that God required. God responded, "I AM that I AM. I Am hath sent thee" (Exod. 3:14).
    b. Jeremiah—"Blessed is the man that trusteth in the Lord" (Jer. 17:7). Smile of faith amidst the tears of sorrow.
  2. Some withhold self from Christ because of lack of faith in self. He asks us to have faith not in self, but in Him.

CONCLUSION —

Result of Job's self-abnegation was acceptance and restoration.

PREACHING THROUGH PSALMS (1 to 72)

The book of Psalms, "Israel's Hymn Book," has been from very ancient times divided into five parts, as follows: Psalms 1-41; 42-72; 73-89; 90-106; 107-150. Each part closes with a song of praise to God. For convenience, we study the first two divisions this month, returning to complete the Psalms in a future month.

The word "psalm" indicates a song composed especially to be sung to the accompaniment of a stringed instrument. Thus the Psalms are songs, expressing the deepest and highest feelings of the writers in their worship, praise, and dependence upon God. In Hebrew they are the highest form of poetry, depending not upon rhyme and meter as English poetry does, but rather depending upon strength and beauty of expression, and upon rhythm and balance of thought and form. The power of this form of verse is carried over into the translations appearing greatly different from ordinary prose.

Writers of the Psalms are numerous and varied, as are the writers of modern songs. David is named as the author of very many of them; they express well his faith, his character, his experiences, and his skill as a musician. Moses is named as a writer of at least one. Others bear the names of Asaph, the "sons of Korah," Solomon, and Ethan. Many are anonymous; some of them no doubt coming from David.

The Psalms were loved by Jesus. His speech shows that He knew them well, and treasured their message. His words of agony on the cross fall into the expressions of Psalm 22, which tells of Messiah's suffering.

Principal thoughts of the Psalms are (1) trust in God, (2) praise to Him, (3) rejoicing in His goodness, (4) reminders of His loving kindness or mercy, and (5) pleas or thanks for His protection against the wicked enemies of the righteous.

There is much in the book and these messages which will be helpful to you. Share with us in the reading and in the worship of this month. Bring your friends.

159

Sermon Outlines Provided:

"To Have Dominion" (Psalm 8)
"The World and the Word" (Psalm 19)
"I Will Confess My Transgressions Unto the Lord" (Psalm 32)
"Where Is Thy God?" (Psalm 42)

Other Suggested Sermon Topics:

"Thou Art My Son" (Psalm 2)
"Song of the Suffering Savior" (Psalm 22)
"Hallowed Be Thy Name" (Psalm 34)
"Fall House Cleaning" (Psalm 51)
"What to Do With Trouble (Psalm 56)

QUESTIONS OVER PSALMS 1 to 72

1. What is the delight of the blessed man? (1:2)
2. How does David state his amazement over God's attention to man? (8:3-4)
3. Whom does God's soul hate? (11:5)
4. What has the fool said? (14:1)
5. How worthwhile is the Word of God? (19:7-11)
6. How does Psalm 22 describe the crucifixion? (22)
7. What reason does David give for fearing no evil? (23:4)
8. How did David handle sin in his life? (32:1-5)
9. In whom did David's soul boast? (34:2)
10. How does David compare the righteous and the wicked? (37:16-22)
11. How greatly did David's soul desire God? (42:1)
12. Who is our refuge, strength, and help? (46:1)
13. What will God do with David's soul? (49:15)
14. In what manner does David say he will sacrifice to God? (54:6)
15. How great are God's lovingkindness and truth? (57:10)
16. Why does David say he will not get greatly shaken? (62:1-2)
17. What should all the earth say to God? (66:1-3)
18. Who daily bears our burden? (68:19)
19. How strong was David's hope? (71:14)

TO HAVE DOMINION (Labor Day Sermon)
(Psalm 8)

INTRODUCTION — Labor Day.

"Knights of Labor" paraded in New York in 1882 and again in 1884. Other workers began action to have a legal holiday created. First law in Oregon on February 21, 1887; other states followed soon after.

> To those who labor with their calloused hands;
> Who mine the coal and make the clanging steel;
> Who from the forest wrest new, fertile lands;
> Who build tall towers where the planets reel;
> Who fashion houses, factories, and ships;
> Who work with wrench and bar, with plow and hoe;
> Who joying in their strength come to glad grips
> With mighty forces that the ages know,
> We give high praise and humbly bow the knee
> Before the glory of their lasting worth
> That shapes their dreams into reality
> And mystically blesses all the earth,
> Because through toil and sweat the seeking clod
> Gropes back through Eden to discover God.

(The writer recognized that God is in labor, but he has the reverse on who seeks whom.)

Read Psalm 8.

I. "THE WORK OF THY FINGERS"—GOD THE ARTISAN

A. God labors; labor is of God. "My Father worketh hitherto and I work."

B. Labor is worthy of respect: Says U. S. Grant, "Labor disgraces no man; unfortunately you occasionally find a man who disgraces labor."

C. The true laborer becomes a fellow artisan with God.

  1. God's purpose becomes his—to bring beauty and usefulness out of things.

  2. Labor becomes an expression of love and respect to

161

the men God made. See Ephesians 6:5-9. Leviticus 25:43 "Thou shalt not rule over him with rigor, but shalt fear thy God."

(This sort of relationship is not made by asking for it — there must be a motive.)

II. "WHAT IS MAN, THAT THOU ART MINDFUL OF HIM?"

  A. The cry of amazement. God is so great: how is He concerned with man? Man is so small in the scale of God's creation — how is he noticed?

  B. Man is nothing, except as God makes him something.

  C. The very being of man, his nature, his activities, must be understood in relationship to the question: For what purpose did God create him?

III. "THOU MAKEST HIM TO HAVE DOMINION" "Thou hast made him but a little lower than God."

  A. Dominion wrongly used is a curse to the creation. See Romans 8:19-22. The land, the streams, the forests, the creatures, suffer man's cruel greed.

  B. Does man have dominion over things or do they have dominion over him? (On the wind gadget was the farmer chasing the calf, or vice versa?)

  C. Dominion over things takes labor — and self-control. The plan of God is in Genesis 1:26 ff.

IV. THE WAY OF CHRIST.

  A. Work is dignified, since He was a carpenter.

  B. His purpose was not to make houses, but to make men. "I must work the works of Him who sent me while it is yet day, for the night cometh when no man can work" (John 9:4).

CONCLUSION —

At Ludlow, Okla., Henry Ferris, rancher, non-churchman, saw a small group of faithful — mostly women — trying to build a church. He left his own work and built the church. At the first invitation given in the new building he accepted Christ.

THE WORLD AND THE WORD
(Psalm 19)

INTRODUCTION —

Since the day when Adam's sin put a veil between him and God, man has sought to know again his Maker (Show us the Father), and God has sought to make himself known. Psalm 19 is one of the great and noble passages on revelation: "The glory of God's works and the perfection of God's word."

I. THE HEAVENS DECLARE

    A. Man has always stood in awe as he contemplated creation. Psalm 8:3 "When I consider thy heavens, the work of thy fingers, the moon and the stars which thou has ordained."

        1. "The spacious firmament on high, with all the blue ethereal sky,

           And spangled heavens, a shining frame, their Great Original proclaim;

           The unwearied sun, from day to day, Does his creator's power display,

           And publishes to every land the work of an almighty Hand.

           What though in solemn silence all move round this dark terrestrial ball?

           What though no real voice nor sound amid the radiant orbs be found?

           In reason's ear they all rejoice and utter forth a glorious voice;

           Forever singing as they shine, "The hand that made us is divine."
           —*Joseph Addison.*

        2. Well the awe may be—the knowledge of scientist enhances it: (There can be no scale model of the universe; world 1 inch diameter calls for nearest fixed star forty thousand miles away.)

        Its silent testimony everywhere known.

    B. But some worship the creation more than the Creator.

163

1. For they exchanged the truth of God for a lie, and worshiped and served the creature rather than the Creator, who is blessed for ever" (Rom. 1:25).
2. So we have days named for pagan gods — Saturday Sunday, Monday. The firmament showeth *His* handiwork, but God knew something more was needed.

II. THE *LAW OF THE LORD* IS PERFECT, RESTORING THE SOUL — a quick turn to fuller revelation.
   A. The completeness of revelation in the Word.
      1. The law — "Thou shalt not" — cannot be broken, but broken upon.
      2. The testimony is sure. "Hear, O Israel" — "Thou hast hid these things from the wise and prudent and hast revealed them unto babes" (Matt. 11:25).
      3. The precepts are right, rejoicing the heart — stewardship, partnership, sacrifice.
      4. Commandment is pure, enlightening — "Thou shalt love the Lord."
      5. Fear of the Lord is clean — reverence (coal from the altar).
      6. Ordinances of the Lord are true — "What doth God require of a man but to do justice, and love mercy, and walk humbly with his God? (Micah 6:8).
   B. Here again there were those who worshiped the message, and not God.
      1. Pharisees spent lives in hair-splitting, and forgot justice and mercy.
      2. "The sabbath is made for man, and not man for the sabbath" (Mark 2:27).

III. FINAL REVELATION IN THE LIVING WORD.
      1. He was partner in the creation, "Without him was not anything made that hath been made" (John 1:3).
      2. He was the fulfillment of the Law. "They are they which testify of me" (John 5:39).
      3. When the question comes, show us the Father. "He that hath seen the Father" (John 14:9).
      4. He is to all creation, as the sun to the heavens. Verses 4-6 a description of His coming again.

I WILL CONFESS MY TRANSGRESSIONS UNTO THE LORD

(Psalm 32)

INTRODUCTION —

The basic brotherhood of men no better attested than here. The background is apparently the story of David and Bathsheba. The events leading up — the thing is done.

I. "WHEN I KEPT SILENCE" — MENTAL ANGUISH AND BODILY ILLNESS.

   A. Pride says, "It is not a sin" — an affair of war and idleness. Conscience knows better.

   B. Pride says, "A king has a right to do these things; all do same." Conscience says a man is a man.

   C. Pride says, "Keep the thing quiet; no one will find it out." Conscience says God knows it, and guilt is great.

   D. (Illus.) A young man in Canton who struck and killed a lad, went home and hid. Police traced from piece of headlight. He came in, having lost twenty pounds in four days.

   E. The coverage of *sin* — missing the mark "of the high calling"
     1. Transgression — getting out of bounds.
     2. Iniquity — Moral deformity or perversity.

   F. "All have sinned and come short of the glory of God" (Rom. 3:23). "If we say we have not sinned, we make Him a liar" (I John 1:10).

II. "I ACKNOWLEDGED MY TRANSGRESSION, AND SAID, I WILL CONFESS MY TRANSGRESSION TO GOD."

   A. Historical — Nathan's story and accusation (II Sam. 12).
     — Like a sharp lance to a festering boil.

   B. Is the feeling and acknowledgement of guilt a wholesome thing? How is it with the criminal? Confession the one hope of reformation.

165

C. To whom shall we confess?
  1. To the one whom we have wronged. "I have sinned against heaven and in thy sight."
  2. To a real person—and God is that. Those who can't find reality in Him need another.

III. "THOU FORGAVEST."
  A. Completeness of forgiveness—
    1. Forgive—lift the burden of guilt.
    2. Cover—hide from the eyes and memory of man and God.
    3. Not imputing—Remove from the record of dealings. "A perfect and upright man"—King after God's own heart."
  B. "If we confess our sins, he is faithful and righteous to forgive us our sins, and to cleanse us from all unrighteousness" (I John 1:9).
  C. This is true before baptism in the confession of Christ as Savior.
  D. After baptism—"Repent and pray God, if perhaps the sin of thine heart may be forgiven" (Acts 8:22).

CONCLUSION —

"Thou art my hiding place."
  A. A friend is one who knows the worst and still loves us.
  B. "Gracious hiding place; Gracious hiding place,
      in the shelter of His love;
    Not a doubt, nor fear, since my Lord is near,
    And I'm sheltered in His love."

WHERE IS THY GOD?
(Psalm 42)

INTRODUCTION — "Singing hymns at midnight."
- A. Where has ease and brittle laughter produced a song like "Home, Sweet, Home"?
- B. This is one of the Psalms not attributed to David, but by the locations named, is the song of an exile in the north of Palestine.
- C. It speaks the same truth. The "home" is God's house.

I. THE SOUL'S NEED FOR GOD.
"Connection between the human soul and the living God, and the thirst of the soul for God's presence form the first principle of the Book of Psalms."
- A. A part of the natural need of man, as water for the body. "I spread forth my hands unto thee, My soul thirsteth for thee, as a weary land" (Psalm 143:6). "My soul longeth, yea, even fainteth for the courts of the Lord. My heart and my flesh cry out unto the living God."
- B. "When God makes man with longings it is a prophecy that these longings will be supplied."
- C. Thirst is for the living God, as opposed to a Force, Principle, or idol.
- D. The need is more noticeable in sorrow.
  1. Here the failure of false gods is most apparent.
  2. Can any supply contentment? Spiritual growth? Human love and fellowship? Help in sorrows? Eternal life?

II. SPIRITUAL DEPRESSION—LONELINESS IN TROUBLE: "WHERE IS THY GOD?
- A. Memory of better days, when one was in the house of God.
  1. This is reflected in the experience of many moderns.
  2. Many who worship other gods were once in the house of the Lord.

B. The tears of hopelessness ask the question.

C. The enemies in derision ask it.

III. PERSISTENT HOPE IN GOD—"I WILL YET PRAISE HIM."

A. His presence cannot be dimmed by trouble—His care is with the suffering.

    1. (Illus.—Convoy stops in submarine-infested waters to form breakwater for destroyer while doctor takes appendix of a sailor.)

    2. This is the expression of God's care for one.

B. He has not promised ease—that might be to destroy the soul.

C. His perfect gifts cannot be given in the present—they are yet to come.—"When shall I appear before the living God?"

CONCLUSION —

The question for us:

A. Where is thy God?—Where have you made, or found your center of life and worship?

B. As to the living God, He has made Himself approachable to you in Christ. No longer, Where is He?

C. Are you approachable to Him? Where are *you*?

168

PREACHING THROUGH PSALMS (73-150)

Israel's hymn book occupied our attention two months ago, but there is more to it. See again the general introductory matter which was distributed then. Psalms 73-150 include the last three of the five general divisions of the book.

GREAT PSALMS IN THIS GROUP. Notice especially:

Psalm 90	The eternal majesty of God.
Psalm 91	Hymn of devotion and trust.
Psalm 103	God's care for His children.
Psalm 113-118	Psalms of Thanksgiving, which were sung at the Jewish Passover, and probably include the "hymn" which Jesus and His apostles sang as they departed from the Upper Room toward Gethsemane (Matt. 26:30).
Psalm 119	Concerning the Bible, God's Word.
Psalm 127	On building the house; basis of substantial family life.
Psalm 139	God's complete knowledge.
Psalm 146-150	Hallelujah Psalms.

MESSAGE FOR THE CHRISTIAN

The Christian will be especially interested in the Messianic Psalms, many of which are quoted in the New Testament, and in the glorious messages of trust and praise which are timeless, not depending at all upon the dispensation under which they were written.

Sermon Outlines Provided:

"Number Our Days" (Psalm 90)
"Reason Enough to Sing" (Psalm 98)
"Thy Word Is a Lamp" (Psalm 119:9-15, 105)
"Search Me, O God" (Psalm 139:23, 24)

Other Suggested Sermon Topics:

"The Security of the Righteous" (Psalm 73)
"His Mercy Endureth Forever" (Psalm 118)

169

QUESTIONS OVER PSALMS 73-150

1. What did Asaph desire on earth? (73:25)
2. Who is feared by the kings of the earth? (76:11-12)
3. What is the bread of angels? (78:24-25)
4. To whom is God's salvation near? (85:9)
5. What is God's covenant with David? (89:28-37)
6. How long is a man's life? (90:10)
7. What is to be told about God? (96:2, 3, 10)
8. How should we serve the Lord? (100:2)
9. What is it that David said he would not set before his eyes? (101:3)
10. How far does God remove our sins from us? (103:12)
11. Why is the Lord good? (106:1)
12. Whose name is holy and reverend? (111:9)
13. What is an idol like? (115:4-8)
14. "How can a young man keep his way pure?" (119:9)
15. Where does help come from? (121:2)
16. How desirable is unity? (Psalm 133)
17. What does the Lord do? (135:6)
18. How vast is the sum of God's thoughts? (139:17)
19. How enduring is God's kingdom? (145:13)
20. With what three words do the last five Psalms begin?

NUMBER OUR DAYS (Anniversary Sermon)
(Psalm 90)

INTRODUCTION —

The time seems much shorter afterward than before: Jacob to Pharaoh: "The days of the years of my pilgrimage are 130 years: few and evil have been the days of the years of my life, and they have not attained unto the days of the years of the life of my fathers in the days of their pilgrimage" (Gen. 47:9).

So Moses *meditated and prayed*, during the wilderness wanderings, as death decimated the generation that had come out of Egypt. None, except Caleb and Joshua, that were of voting age at Sinai went into Canaan. Older ones might have lived to a hundred in the wilderness, but the seniors were disappearing! Moses' prayer contrasts God and man, with reference to time.

I. GOD IS; MAN IS TRANSIENT (vv. 1-6).

    A. Dwelling place—From basket to palace to tents, Moses knew the difference between transition and permanence. God is our sole security and shelter. "The eternal God is thy dwelling place, and underneath are the everlasting arms" (Deut. 33:27).

    B. Fills time and extends beyond it: All generations; everlasting to everlasting. "Before the mountains were born"; but even that doesn't cover it.

    C. "Thou *art* God" "I AM that I AM" Changeless, eternal present. A thousand years as yesterday—No, as one-third of a night! Things of men as transient as a desert torrent. "Don't regret growing old; it's a privilege denied to many." So we rejoice in old age, knowing its limitations. "Change and decay in all around I see; O Thou who changest not, abide with me!"—What is 75 years? Just enough to remind us that God transcends the years!

II. GOD JUDGES; MAN LANGUISHES (vv. 7-12).

    A. Death and mortality because of sin. The smells of sin and death have always mingled in the nostrils of mankind. Sin makes him a suicide and/or murderer, suddenly or by slow degrees.

B. God—outraged holiness. "Anger"—The flared nostrils. Wrath—Judicial execution.

C. God—totally and accurately aware—"Our secret sins in the light of thy countenance." (Murdered Egyptian or a golden calf.)

D. Sentence—Our days are passed away in thy wrath—"our years as a sigh." Kadesh and the sentence of death; so there were fewer and fewer senior citizens among the children of Israel.

E. Need we count the high cost of low living? How much better and easier we could live if workmen were trustworthy, and customers were honest!

 1. Sin is a matter of life and death; life being held with a slipping grasp, and with death victorious.

 2. Much that we do is transient because of sin's decay: cleaning, paint, building, influence.

III. GOD FORGIVES, MAN REVIVES (vv. 13-17).

A. Moses pleads mercy, glory, beauty, establishment. Futilly wishful?

B. Not in Christ! "I will raise up a prophet from among thy brethren, like unto thee; and I will put my words in his mouth, and he shall speak unto them all that I shall command him. And it shall come to pass that whosoever will not hearken unto my words which he shall speak in my name, I will require it of him" (Deut. 18:18, 19).

C. In Him it becomes a matter of death and life, with life victorious! "If we be dead with Him we shall also live with Him" (II Tim. 2:11).

D. In Him all our assets are converted into eternal values —"now we live."

CONCLUSION —

I Corinthians 15:55-58. "A thousand years . . ." "So teach us to number our days!" "Establish thou . . ."

REASON ENOUGH TO SING
(Psalm 98)

INTRODUCTION — From "Joy to the World"

A. England at the time of Isaac Watts (1674-1745) is reflected in this: "Inside the churches fervor was frowned upon, and the preaching was frigid, formal, and argumentative."

B. Watts responded by writing the hymns that set English church folk to singing. No hymn is more meaningful than "Joy to the World," based on Psalm 98.

I. GOD HAS DONE MARVELOUS WORKS (vv. 1-3).

A. The psalmist speaks of a national deliverance to Israel, known to all.
   1. His message is best fulfilled in deliverance through Christ to all men.
   2. His words describe God's timeless character.

B. Salvation (literally, "safety," from Hebrew *jeshua*)
   1. The power of God is exerted to man's benefit. (We misrepresent God by referring to flood, storm, and earthquake as "acts of God," and putting no such legal label on sunshine and gentle rain.)
   2. "God sent not his Son into the world to condemn the world; but that the world through him might be saved" (John 3:17).
   3. "Salvation"—*Jeshua*—becomes the name of Joshua and Jesus.

C. RIGHTEOUSNESS (Literally "rightness" or "justice").
   1. Not always, but generally, God's rightness is established in human events. "One does not break God's law; he breaks himself upon God's law!"
   2. Still God does not settle all His accounts on the first of the month or the end of the fiscal year.

D. Mercy and truth (otherwise translated "lovingkindness and faithfulness").
   1. God is love, and unchanging.

173

2. His persistent goodwill to Israel was seen in national deliverance.

3. His eternal purpose to mankind has been seen in the Gospel of Christ.

II. REJOICE, AND BE HEARD IN REJOICING (vv. 4-8).

—As God's goodness to His people is seen even by the heathen, so His people's praise should be heard even by unbelievers.

A. Let mankind praise! (vv. 4-6).

1. With the voice, loudly and joyously. — The army of Christ is a singing army!

2. With instruments accompanying.

a. The harp and the psaltery are suited to accompany the voice.

b. The trumpet and cornet have their own stirring sound.

B. Let the natural world be heard praising God (vv. 7, 8).

1. The perceptive observer hears natural sounds as honor to the Creator.

2. Compare Luke 19:40: "If these [who welcomed Jesus to Jerusalem] should hold their peace, the stones would immediately cry out."

III. GOD IS COMING IN JUDGMENT (v. 9).

A. To the unbeliever and rebel this is no cause for rejoicing, but for His own it is the basis for greatest assurance.

B. His rightness will be finally established, and all resisters proved wrong.

C. His "equity" will correct all the inequities in human relationship.

CONCLUSION —

God's coming in Christ reveals a love that goes far beyond justice; it establishes His mercy! Hallelujah!

THY WORD IS A LAMP
(Psalm 119:9-15; 105)

INTRODUCTION —

Many blessings are most appreciated in the lack of them. So with a light upon the path:

I. TO CLEANSE THE ERRING WAY. "WHERE-WITH SHALL A YOUNG MAN CLEANSE . . . ?"
   A. The tendency to wander.
      1. (Scouts learned that we walked circles in the dark or when lost.)
      2. Without a spiritual guide we are hopelessly lost. "How can I, except some man should guide me?" (Acts 8:31).
   B. The use of the Word: Profitable for doctrine, for reproof, for correction (II Tim. 3:16). — What do we do when we learn that we are off the track? Insist that the track must conform to our way? Refuse to correct, and go on?

II. TO HOLD TO THE TRUE WAY: "LET ME NOT WANDER . . ."
   A. Besides doctrine, reproof, correction there is instruction in righteousness.
   B. So the instructed should be very thankful for the instruction. Use it to avoid the wrecks.

III. HOW — THE EXISTENCE OF THE LAMP DOES NOT GUARANTEE SAFETY — (Compare the foolish virgins).
   A. Thy word have I laid up in my heart (v. 11). — The process of transferring from paper on the shelf to truth in the heart.
   B. Teach me thy statutes (v. 12). The humble acknowledgement that these are from God, and the prayerful approach to learning.
   C. With my lips have I declared (v. 13).

      1. Learn to teach, and thus is the greatest learning.
      2. Missionary Frank Laubach's program—"Each one, teach one."

D. I have rejoiced—I will delight (vv. 14-16).
      1. The attitude speeds the process of learning, and fixes what is learned.
      2. It more easily becomes a part of life.
      3. That which is best known is most loved.

E. I will meditate (v. 15).
      1. "In his law doth he meditate day and night" (Psalm 1:2).
      2. This is an art well on the way to being lost—hence hurry and loneliness.
      3. Recall, review, apply, consider, repeat.

F. I will have respect (v. 15). "Ye received it as it is, not the word of man, but the word of God, which worketh in you that believe" (I Thess. 2:13).

G. I will not forget (v. 15).
      1. It has become a permanent, usable part of one's experience.
      2. Review, repetition, practice, application necessary to avoid forgetting.

CONCLUSION — Peroration on the Bible.

But salvation is in Christ, the Living Word: "Search the scriptures; for in them ye think ye have eternal life: and they are they which testify of me" (John 5:39).

SEARCH ME, O GOD (A New Year Sermon)
(Psalm 139:23, 24)

INTRODUCTION — What of the coming year?

    A. The entrance to the New Year is the exit from the old. If we are content with what we were in the year past, the next will probably show no improvement.

    B. Resolutions are still valuable; some still make them.

    C. Any resolution, to be effective must be often renewed; otherwise it is as powerless as Easter religion.

        1. God's mercies are new every day; so must be our response.

        2. The inward man is renewed day by day (II Cor. 4:16).

        3. We must have today's faith and today's purpose for today's living.

    D. Psalm 139, especially verses 23, 24, provide basis for renewal. — We may contrast it step by step with the easy, prideful, self-satisfied way.

  I. SEARCH ME, O GOD

(What a request! "Have mercy on me"; "forgive me"; "bless me"; yes! But "Search me"?)

    A. This is not self-examination, but examination by the "all-seeing eye."

        1. Self examination may excuse self; or it may refuse to forgive self.

        2. How is divine examination accomplished? "Wherewithal shall a young man cleanse his way? By taking heed thereto according to thy word" (Psalm 119:9).

        3. This is the plea of complete sincerity; God's awareness is total and without limit (Psalm 139:1-13).

 II. KNOW MY HEART

(You can't put a man in jail for what he is thinking. How about, "Hear my boast of goodness and right belief"? —See Luke 18:10-12.)

    A. This is where any effective understanding and improvement must start.

B. "Keep thy heart with all diligence; for out of it are the issues of life" (Prov. 4:23).

C. The innermost being cannot be hid from God.

III. TRY ME AND KNOW MY THOUGHTS
(Why not be satisfied with, "Accept my profession of faith"?)

A. This "trying" can be rugged, as the testing of precious metal in refiner's fire (I Peter 1:7).

B. The testing of public officials has sometimes taken the form of offering them bribes, testing whether they are subject to influence.

C. The "ways" grow out of the thoughts, and they are the basis of man's judgment.

1. "By their fruits ye shall know them" (Matt. 7:20).

2. "Even a child is known by his doings, whether his work be pure, and whether it be right" (Prov. 20:11).

IV. SEE IF THERE BE ANY WICKED WAY IN ME.
(Isn't it enough that I do more good than evil?)

A. We ask the physician or the dentist to discover any damaging flaw so it may be corrected before it does major harm; why not also God?

B. We may be sure that an honest examination will discover a fault; are we ready for the discovery?

C. The wicked way may be failure to do the good we know (James 4:17).

D. The wicked way may poison all the relationship with God. —One says, "I don't enjoy the Bible . . . I'm not living as I ought."

V. LEAD ME IN THE WAY EVERLASTING
(No place for "Forgive me again, and let me go on sinning.")

A. True repentance found in the genuine desire to change.

B. The prayer does not even ask forgiveness, but it goes the way in which sins are forgiven.

C. The way everlasting is found ultimately only in Christ (John 14:6). —"Lord, to whom shall we go? Thou hast the words of eternal life" (John 6:68).

CONCLUSION —

The "way everlasting" is the right way of the NEW YEAR!

178

PREACHING THROUGH PROVERBS

"A proverb is a short sentence based on long experience," according to a recent definition. The book of Proverbs is basically a collection of such sentences, although it includes several more extended poems praising the virtues of wisdom and its practical applications in the life of man. The proverbs find their power in repetition, comparison, and contrast. Many of them sparkle with wit.

The form of teaching in Proverbs is different from that in any other book in the Bible. It speaks in the terms of a father instructing his son. The book urges the same virtues which the prophets did—honesty, chastity, thrift, justice, reverence, and self-control, especially in the use of the tongue—but it approaches the matter from a different angle. Viewing the same breach of the commandments, the teacher in Proverbs would say, "It is folly," whereas the prophet would say, "It is sin." Both agree that reverence for God is the "beginning of wisdom."

ANALYSIS OF THE BOOK

There are five titles in the book, indicating a general division into five sections, beginning at Chapters 1, 10, 25, 30, and 31. The first three are ascribed to Solomon, the third being the "proverbs of Solomon, which the men of Hezekiah king of Judah copied out." The final two chapters are from Agur and King Lemuel, men who are otherwise unknown. The first part (chs. 1-9) forms a general introduction to the collections of brief, disconnected proverbs which make up the main body of the book. The whole bears out the reputation for wisdom and the love of wise sayings for which King Solomon was known (see I Kings 4:29-34).

The book of Proverbs is one of the easiest and most entertaining to read in the entire Bible. If you have not joined us in the Book-of-the-Month readings before, this is a good place to start. You will be glad you did.

Sermon Outlines Provided:

"God's Way to Plenty" (Proverbs 3:9, 10; Philippians 4:10-20)

179

"The Way of Man" (Proverbs 14:12)
"The Eyes of the Lord" (Proverbs 15:3)
"The Law of Kindness on the Tongue" (Proverbs 26:18 — 27:2; 31:8, 9, 26)

Other Suggested Sermon Topics:

"Of Sparing and Spoiling" (Proverbs 3:11, 12)
"Withhold Not Good" (Proverbs 3:27-35)
"Better Than Temperance" (Proverbs 16:16-32)
"The Cheerful Heart" (Proverbs 17:22)
"Things" (27:23-27)

QUESTIONS OVER PROVERBS

1. What is the beginning of knowledge? (1:7)
2. How valuable is wisdom? (3:13-18)
3. What is the beginning of wisdom? (4:7)
4. What insect is used as an example of industry? (6:6)
5. What did the Lord possess at the beginning of things? (8:22)
6. Who is on the path of life? (10:17)
7. What does a wise son do? (13:1)
8. What exalts a nation? (14:34)
9. What will the Lord do to the house of the proud? (15:25)
10. How can one's plans be established? (16:3)
11. What is the extent of a friend's love? (17:17)
12. What does he who finds a wife find and obtain? (18:22)
13. What preserves the king? (20:28)
14. What is named as being better than living in a house with a contentious woman? (21:9)
15. What will remove foolishness from the heart of a child? (22:15)
16. What happens to those who drink much wine? (23:29-35)
17. What is a word fitly spoken like? (25:11)
18. What happens to a child who gets his own way? (29:15)
19. What is the value of an excellent wife? (31:10)

GOD'S WAY TO PLENTY
(Proverbs 3:9, 10; Philippians 4:10-20)

INTRODUCTION — A matter of attitude.

A farmer was once asked how much milk a certain cow in his prize herd would give. He answered, "She will give nothing voluntarily, but if you can get her in a corner, hitch her fast so that she can neither kick nor hook, she will let go eleven quarts." That is not the attitude we wish to take in church finance, for: "Though I bestow all my goods to feed the poor, and though I give my body to be burned, and have not charity, it profiteth me nothing" (I Cor. 13:3). We seek the profit to the giver: "Not that I seek for the gift, but I seek for the fruit that increaseth to your account" (Phil. 4:17).

I. UNGENEROSITY IS AN INSIDIOUS EVIL—TO OURSELVES.

   A. The wealth of the rich young ruler stood between him and Christ, for he refused to give it to the poor (Matt. 19:16-26).

   B. We seldom recognize this sin in ourselves. St. Xavier said, "I have had many people resort to me for confession. The confession of every sin that I ever heard of, and of sins so foul that I never dreamed of them, have been poured into my ears, but no one person has ever confessed to me the sin of covetousness."

II. ITS TREATMENT CONSISTS IN BECOMING BETTER ACQUAINTED WITH CHRIST.

   A. His love and generosity to us were not measured. (Illus.—A young woman needed help. The other was sorry, but could do nothing, for her budget for charities was already spent!)

   B. Contrast the feeding of the five thousand, to church bazaars and ice cream suppers.

   C. Contrast "Naked, and ye clothed me" (Matt. 25:36), with church women haggling for pennies at a rummage sale.

181

D. So Paul urges generosity, "For ye know the grace of our Lord Jesus Christ, that, though he was rich, yet for your sakes he became poor, that ye through his poverty might become rich" (II Cor. 8:9).

III. THE RICHES OF GOD'S BLESSING COME TO THE GIVER.

A. The Jew was promised material blessings.
  1. In all ages the bounties of God's finest gifts are promised to the generous. (Compare Mal. 3:10).
B. There is something better reserved to Christians. "My God shall supply all your need" (Phil. 4:19).
  1. Fellowship—this is the real heart of Christian fellowship, and there is no scriptural evidence that there is Christian fellowship without it.
  2. Satisfaction in Christianity. It is not the worker and contributor who are dissatisfied. (A man came to a missionary society head and complained of the way its funds were managed. The society head thereupon offered to return to him all he had put into the project. He had given nothing.)
  3. The perfect stature of Christ (II Cor. 9:8):
     Spiritual power like His who gave:
       To overcome temptation
       To gain a serene nearness to God
       To accomplish the work whereunto we were sent.
     A genuine prayer life:
       "Give us this day our daily bread" can mean little to him who spends most of his time taking care of No. 1.

CONCLUSION —

The ultimate blessing: "Come ye blessed . . . ye gave me . . ." (Matthew 25:34-40).

182

THE WAY OF MAN
(Proverbs 14:12)

INTRODUCTION — A pair of doubles:
- A. Our text is repeated in Proverbs 16:25.
- B. Another double—Judges 17:6 and 21:25. "And there was no king in Israel in those days, and every man did that which was right in his own eyes." The two appearances of this verse serve as a frame between which is set the history of Israel's darkest days: idolatry, theft, murder, rapine, inter-tribal warfare, treachery, wife-stealing, etc.

I. "THE WAY OF A FOOL IS RIGHT IN HIS OWN EYES, BUT HE THAT HEARKENETH UNTO COUNSEL IS WISE" (Prov. 12:15).
- A. We have our own proverbs for it: "He who is his own lawyer has a fool for a client," and "He who is his own doctor has a fool for a patient." —Thus, what would we say of him who would be his own savior?
- B. There is the story of the one who declared loudly for a religion in which every man chooses that which is best for himself, following his own conscience; and then almost at once, as he missed a turn in the road through failure of another to direct him, complained, "I've never been here before; how can I know where to go, if you don't tell me?" We have never been the road of this life before, and hence are given as Guide Him who has trod it without stumbling.

II. CONSCIENCE A COMPASS FOR MAN'S DIRECTION.
- A. There are many who set their faith in it. (Herbie Vaught, who boasted in one breath of being as tough a man as there was in the community, and then in the other expected to get to heaven because he had not defrauded his neighbor and had followed his conscience.)

B. But the compass must be set properly. (Doug Corrigan claimed that a mis-set compass directed him from New York to Dublin, Ireland, when he intended to go to Los Angeles, but men didn't believe him, because a mis-set compass leads far more often to destruction than to any sort of victory, even by chance.)

C. The true compass is squared with the north pole as its guiding ideal, and points to it faithfully.
   1. We have one true Christ on which the compass of our conscience must be set as an ideal, that we shall not be content to point inward, but toward Him.
   2. The compass must be squared with God's Word, for there alone is revealed the perfect Christ.

III. THE WAY OF MAN

A. The way of self indulgence seemed right to those to whom Proverbs was written.
   1. But Solomon tried the way of self indulgence to the end, and concluded that it was all vanity.
   2. That was the fault of the rich fool, who committed no sin in the eyes of man when he said, "Soul, take thine ease," but before God he was worthy of death (Luke 12:16-21).

B. Closely akin to it is the way of riches. The parable of the rich man and Lazarus is brief commentary on the value of riches. We know of no sin the rich man committed except that he was rich, and did not minister to the beggar at his gate. He awoke in hell. (Luke 16:19-25).

C. The way of the Law. Saul of Tarsus tried it and found that he had to listen to a guide. "By deeds of the law shall no flesh be justified" (Gal. 2:16).

D. The way of religion. The Athenians—"I perceive that in all things ye are very religious." Then Paul preached that God had raised up a Son to judge (Acts 17:22-31).

CONCLUSION —

The way of the *Son of Man* is the way of life!

THE EYES OF THE LORD
(Proverbs 15:3)

INTRODUCTION —

The Greeks have a word for secrecy: e.g. "He *escaped notice,* approaching the city." The Hebrews do not use it so blithely; they know that nothing completely escapes notice. God sees!

I. THE EYES OF THE LORD ARE IN EVERY PLACE.

A realization of the children of God from first till last! Hagar—"Thou God seest me" (Gen. 16:13). Revelation 6:16: They shall call for the rocks and mountains to fall and hide them from God. The middle book of the Bible, we find Psalm 139. See Proverbs 15:11.

II. BEHOLDING THE EVIL.

This is most often emphasized, because that is what we most often try to hide. —"The seamy side," hidden from view.

A. Therefore, fear judgment, when every secret thing shall be made known. —Many are more afraid of their neighbors' finding out than they are of God's present knowledge.

B. Therefore, respect His will, for He loves, and seeks the best for us. —His purpose is to save us *from* that sin.

C. Therefore, seek not revenge: God will take care of the matter. "Dearly beloved, avenge not yourselves, but rather give place unto wrath" (Rom. 12:19). "Wherefore judgest thou another man's servant? To his own master . . ." (Rom. 14:4).

III. BEHOLDING THE GOOD.

A. Therefore, boast not (God can see the good; you need not tell of it). "Where is glorying then? it is excluded" (Rom. 3:27).

B. Therefore, don't worry about man's praise or gratitude. For whom do you do the good?

C. Therefore—"when thou prayest"—"when thou doest thine alms" be content with God's—not man's—seeing and knowing (Matt. 6:1-6).

D. Therefore, God can see good in the other man when you cannot. Let not a man "think of thimself more highly than he ought to think; but . . . think soberly, according as God hath dealt to every man the measure of faith" (Rom. 12:3).

IV. "KEEPING WATCH OVER" (ASV)—"keeping watch over their flocks by night" (Luke 2:8).

A. What is the purpose of God's beholding the evil and the good (people)?

B. What kind of sheep were in the flocks? Black as well as white? What was the purpose of the shepherds in keeping watch?

C. God commended his love toward us, that while we were yet sinners, Christ died for us (Rom. 5:8).

CONCLUSION —

Story of two watching the world's mightiest tide, in the Bay of Fundy. Seeing its mighty power, "Why, in the face of such might as is His, should God care for such insignificant creatures as we"? "Because He is God."

THE LAW OF KINDNESS ON THE TONGUE
(Proverbs 26:18 — 27:2; 31:8, 9, 26)

INTRODUCTION —

A special responsibility has come to mankind with the special power of speech. Proverbs' 31 chapters contain more than 130 verses, more than four per chapter, on the subject. It is in every chapter, except possibly two.

I. FOLLY IN SPEECH OF THE "FOOL," "WICKED," AND "SCOFFER."

    A. Falsehood, slander, false witness. (This one thing is most often mentioned.) Six things which Jehovah hateth (6:16-19). (See the company in which the liar and false witness keep.) "Remove far from me falsehood and lies" (30:8). "A false witness shall not be unpunished: and he that utters lies not escape" (19:5).

    B. Whispering, talebearing. (If you can't be heard in a shout, try whispering.) "A talebearer revealeth secrets; But he that is of a faithful spirit concealeth the matter" (11:13).

> "A worthless man deviseth mischief,
> And in his lips there is a scorching fire.
> A perverse man scattereth abroad strife;
> And a whisperer separateth chief friends"
> (16:27, 28). (ASV)

    C. Violent words. "A soft answer turneth away wrath; but grievous words stir up anger" (15:1). "In the mouth of the foolish is a rod of pride; but the lips of the wise shall preserve them" (14:3).

    D. Clamorous, contentious. Of the wicked woman—"She is loud and stubborn" (7:11). "A continual dropping in a very rainy day and a contentious woman are alike" (27:15).

    E. Flattering and boasting. "A man that flattereth his neighbor spreadeth a net for his feet" (29:5). "The lips of a strange woman drop as an honeycomb and her mouth is smoother than oil, but her end is bitter as wormwood, sharp as a twoedged sword" (5:3, 4). "Let another man praise thee, and not thine own mouth" (27:2).

F. Thoughtless words. "Seeth thou a man that is hasty in his words? There is more hope of a fool than of him" (29:20). "The heart of the righteous studieth to answer: but the mouth of the wicked poureth out evil things" (15:28).

G. Too much talk. "In the multitude of words there wanteth not sin: but he that refraineth his lips is wise" (10:19). "Even a fool when he holdeth his peace is counted wise" (17:28). But the power of speech was given to be used.

II. WISDOM IN SPEECH.

A. Speak up for the afflicted: "Open thy mouth for the dumb in the cause of all such as are appointed to destruction" (31:8).

B. Teach or rebuke. "He that rebuketh a man afterward shall find more favor than he that flattereth with the tongue" (28:23). "As an earring of gold, and an ornament of fine gold, so is a wise reprover upon an obedient ear" (25:12).

C. Encourage. "Heaviness in the heart of a man maketh it stoop: but a good word maketh it glad" (12:25). "Pleasant words are as a honeycomb, sweet to the soul, and health to the bones" (16:24).

D. Pray and praise. "The sacrifice of the wicked is an abomination to the Lord: but the prayer of the upright is his delight" (15:8).

CONCLUSION —

"Every tongue shall confess that Jesus Christ is Lord" (Phil. 2:11). "With the heart man believeth unto righteousness, and with the mouth confession is made unto salvation" (Rom. 10:10).

PREACHING THROUGH ECCLESIASTES AND SONG OF SOLOMON

The word "Ecclesiastes" is the Latin translation of the Hebrew *Koheleth*, meaning "preacher" or "Convener of the assembly." The title appears in the first verse of the book. Based on the experience of Solomon, son of David, King of Israel, it gives his observations concerning the futility of all that men count worthy in this present life, and concludes, "Fear God, and keep his commandments, for this is the whole duty of men" (12:13).

You will find in the book many wise sayings, some of which have found their way into the common speech of men.

A deep uncertainty about that which lies beyond the grave is felt when God is left out of the picture. This results in a pessimistic attitude which contrasts sharply with the confidence that Christians have because of Christ's victory over death.

The book reminds us of the ultimate power of God, and the frailty of all things which do not have their foundation in Him.

ANALYSIS OF THE BOOK

Chapters 1-3   The indulgences of the flesh in pleasure, and of the mind in wisdom, are a "striving after wind."

4-10   Solomon's experience shows certain evils to be avoided, and guides toward a more meaningful and happy life.

11,12   Ultimate trust in God and obedience to Him is the only sure way.

The Song of Solomon, is titled in Hebrew "The Song of Songs, which is Solomon's." It appears to have been used in celebration of the marriage of Solomon with his favorite wife, "The Shulamite." It is a series of long songs, alternating parts sung by the bridegroom to his bride, by the bride to her husband, and by an attendant chorus of maidens. This is the Bible's tenderest romantic literature. It has been used by the Jewish nation to sing of God's tenderness toward His chosen people, Israel, and it is used by Christians to speak of Christ's love for His bride, the Church (compare Ephesians 5:23-24). In the time of Christ the Song of Solomon was read at the Passover season, to remind

189

them of God's tenderness to Israel, and Ecclesiastes was read at the Feast of Tabernacles, its somber reminders giving balance to the otherwise merry observances of this most joyous of Jewish festal seasons.

Solomon's youthful love for his bride is reflected in the Song; the practical wisdom of his mature years in the Book of Proverbs; and the somber conclusions of his old age in Ecclesiastes.

Sermon Outlines Provided:

"The Preacher" (Eccl. 1:1; 12:9-14)
"Solomon and Jesus: Vanity and Victory" (Eccl. 2:1-11)
"Of Sowing and Reaping" (Eccl. 11:1-7)
"The Shade of the (Apple) Tree" (Song of Solomon 2:3-6)

Other Suggested Sermon Topics:

"The Cord Not Quickly Broken" (Eccl. 4:7-12)
"Wisdom in the House of God" (Eccl. 5:1-7)
"The Crackling of Thorns" (Eccl. 7:1-10)
"Life's Answer to Death" (Eccl. 9:4-10; I John 3:1-3)
"The Days of Thy Youth" (Eccl. 11:9-12:8)

QUESTIONS OVER ECCLESIASTES AND SONG OF SOLOMON

1. What did the writer of the Book of Ecclesiastes set his mind to do? (1:13, 17)
2. What was Solomon's conclusion about all the activities his hands had done? (2:11, 17)
3. What problems will he who loves money have? (5:10-17)
4. What is better than the shouting of a ruler? (9:17)
5. How difficult is it to know the activity of God? (11:5)
6. Who wrote the Song of Songs? (1:1)
7. How did Solomon arrive on his wedding day? (3:6-11)
8. How did Solomon describe the beauty of his beloved? (4:1-7)
9. How did Solomon's beloved describe him? (5:10-16)
10. Of what people was Solomon's beloved? (6:13)
11. Whom did Solomon desire and why? (7:10)
12. How strong is love? (8:6-7)

THE PREACHER

(Ecclesiastes 1:1; 12:9-14)

INTRODUCTION — A strange kind of preacher.

    A. *Koheleth* — "caller, congregator, preacher" — becomes the name of the book.

    B. Not used elsewhere in the Bible.

        1. Does not offer sacrifices as a priest.

        2. Does not approach the prophet's office. Speaks of God from experience; not as preacher of the Gospel.

    C. The peculiar connection with Solomon.

I. WHAT MAKES A PREACHER? Must not limit to pulpit orators.

    A. A heart full of something that needs to be said — a great conviction. "Woe is unto me if I preach not the gospel" (I Cor. 9:16).

        1. Not necessarily great ability — "Too many authors; too few preachers." The new generation of preachers comes frequently from the work of men having moderate ability.

        2. "In the hundred years after the New Testament was written, there is no record of a single outstanding preacher. But Christianity was spread by ordinary people, telling the story of the love of Christ to those whom they met in the circle of their friends and acquaintances."

    B. Desire to share one's conviction with others.

        1. The "every man to his own taste" person will never make a preacher.

        2. With Solomon, it may have been a desire to leave a lasting impression. If so, he succeeded here better than anywhere else.

        3. In the Christian: a love of his fellow man, and interest in his welfare.

II. THE ACTIVITY OF THE PREACHER.

    A. He still taught wisdom — Nothing else needs to be done so persistently.

191

1. Those who have heard have not understood.
2. There are others who have not heard.
3. Those who have heard and understood have forgotten—it comes undone.

B. He still studied.
   1. "Pondered, and sought out, and set in order many proverbs"—(Methods).
   2. Sought to find out words of truth—acceptable words —(Material).

C. The words of the wise are as goads—he will not seek to please men.
   1. If he speaks only good, it does not mean that evil is not present. (A. Campbell, accused of being unkind in excoriation of denominationalism: "The physician is not less benevolent when as a surgeon he amputates a limb than when he administers an anodyne—yet there would be a manifest difference in his spirit and temper in the judgment of a spectator who did not enter into his views and motives in these two actions.")
   2. If all things were right, there would be no need of preaching (Acts 2:37).
   3. "No salvation without condemnation."

III. THE MESSAGE OF THE PREACHER.
  A. Fear God—reverence, respect, awe, worship.
   1. Of the lion-torn corpse beside the road, "It is the man of God who was disobedient to the word of the Lord" (I Kings 13:26).
   2. For Christians this is a hymn of praise for His love.
  B. Keep His commandments—for Christians "All authority hath been given unto Me" (Matt. 28:18).

CONCLUSION —

Judgment will reveal obedience and disobedience. "The Father hath committed all judgment unto the Son" (John 5:22).

SOLOMON AND JESUS: VANITY AND VICTORY

(Ecclesiastes 2:1-11)

INTRODUCTION —

Life a labyrinth, or maze—what path will bring us out right? Solomon made deliberate scientific experiments in many ways. As Edison, he "knew a hundred things that wouldn't work." Men profit by Edison's experience, not repeating his false starts— but many are repeating Solomon's experiments daily.

I. THE CONTRAST OF CONCLUSIONS.

  A. Solomon—"All is vanity"—emptiness—futility—"chasing after wind."

  B. Jesus: "For of His fulness we all received, and grace for grace" (John 1:16). Growing up in Christ. "Till we all attain unto the unity of faith, and of the knowledge of the Son of God, unto a fullgrown man, unto the measure of the stature of the fulness of Christ" (Eph. 4:13, ASV).

II. THE CONTRAST OF THE METHODS.

  A. Solomon—self centered—seeking to have. "I will prove thee" "I made ME great works" "I gather ME silver."

   1. "Whatsoever mine eyes desired I kept not from them." Self indulgent, deliberately seeking happiness. —He did at last conclude, "Fear God and keep his commandments, for this is the whole duty of man" (12:13).

  B. Jesus started where Solomon left off: "I must be about my Father's business" (Luke 2:4). "I came not to do mine own will, but the will of him that sent me."

   1. God-conscious rather than self-conscious.

   2. Set a new pattern for life:

     Not what we have, but what we are;
     Not what we receive, but what we give;
     Not what enters in, but what proceeds out;
     Not how we are served, but how we serve.

III. THE SPECIFIC CONTRASTS.
  A. Mirth.
    1. Solomon sought laughter — pleasure — wine — folly. (The experiment is being repeated daily and nightly in every house of entertainment.) They are sad places next morning.
    2. Jesus was a man of sorrows, and acquainted with grief. "Blessed are ye that weep now, for ye shall laugh" (Luke 6:21). "Woe unto you, ye that laugh now! For ye shall mourn and weep" (Luke 6:25). "Verily, verily, I say unto you, that ye shall weep and lament, but the world shall rejoice; ye shall be sorrowful, but your sorrow shall be turned to joy" (John 16:20). (He knew tears, but never remorse.)
  B. Material accumulation.
    1. Solomon said, "I made me great works" — houses, vineyards, gardens, parks, pools. (Among the worthier efforts of man, but definitely limited in scope.)
    2. Jesus said, "A man's life consisteth not in the abundance of the things which he possesseth" (Luke 12:15). "The foxes have holes, and the birds of the heaven have nests, but the Son of man hath not where to lay his head" (Luke 9:58). "Lay up for yourselves treasures in heaven where neither moth nor rust doth corrupt" (Matt. 6:20).
  C. Servants.
    1. Solomon had men — maids — servants born in the house (Matt. 20:25-28).
  D. Wisdom.
    1. "I applied my heart to know wisdom —"(1:17) "My wisdom remained" (I Cor. 1:26-31).
    2. (Christ's wisdom known for its depth and height, not breadth.)

CONCLUSION —

"To whom shall we go? Thou hast the words of eternal life" (John 6:68).

OF SOWING AND REAPING
(Ecclesiastes 11:1-7)

INTRODUCTION —

The changing point in the sonnet of Ecclesiastes. That which goes before is introduction — the unaided work of men's hands is vain. There follows the conclusion — that in the providence of God life is still worthwhile. Thesis: Be diligent — you don't know which part of your diligence will be rewarded. Give — not every gift will bring joy; some will, and you don't know which. Plant — not every seed will grow; some will, and you don't know which.

"He that observeth the wind shall not sow; and he that regardeth the clouds shall not reap." Agricultural terms — Those who are overly afraid of doing something wrong will not do anything at all.

I. IN BUSINESS AFFAIRS.
   "It may get too hot to work; think I'll wait and see."
   A. Cast your bread upon the waters — sow grain on the water that irrigates the field.
   B. Parable of the talents — It has a spiritual meaning but it is a business parable. The man's only sin was that he did nothing (Matt. 25:14-30).

II. IN BENEVOLENCE.
   A. Red Cross drive — some will not support it, fearing some money may be misused — What are you *supporting*? Not, what are you avoiding?
   B. Scene of the judgment (Matt. 25:31-46). "I was hungry and ye gave me no meat": "What have we done to deserve to be cast into outer darkness?" "Nothing — and by doing nothing you deserve it!"

III. IN CITIZENSHIP.
   A. The breakdown of law enforcement. Officers discouraged by lack of co-operation. Citizens discouraged by lack of success. Where a principle is at issue, those who weakly watch and offer no assistance to either side have

195

no part with the valiant. "To be indifferent to error or to any evil is to give great comfort and encouragement to error and evil. And in such circumstances, indifference is not neutrality. In such circumstances, indifference is an active evil." — *Richard L. Evans.* "The probability that we may fail in the struggle ought not to deter us from the support of a cause we believe to be just." — *A. Lincoln.*

IV. IN CHURCH WORK — SPIRITUAL APPLICATION OF THE TALENTS.
   A. One won't speak or lead in prayer for fear of being laughed at. Better the man who replied, "With my meager ability and training I am serving God the best I can; how about you?"
   B. The apostle Peter spoke up — he said many wrong things — but we're glad he spoke.
   C. So sin goes unrebuked. The sorrowing go uncomforted; The wandering continue to wander; because Christians, afraid they'll say the wrong thing, say nothing.

V. MOST DAMAGE IN MATTER OF EVANGELISM.
   A. Who is successful? Not those of great training, but those with a holy boldness.
   B. Fear of driving away —
      1. But how about the multiplied thousands who perish in the fearful silence?
      2. Pray to speak as we ought to speak.

VI. THE BELIEVER WHO WILL NOT ACCEPT CHRIST FOR FEAR HE CAN'T HOLD OUT.
   A. You can never hold on to what you don't take hold of.
   B. Two things we will guarantee —
      1. You will do some things wrong.
      2. With diligence you will plant what God can bring to fruition.

CONCLUSION — Revelation 21:8.

> Greatly begin! though thou have time
> But for a line, be that sublime —
> Not failure, but low aim, is crime. — *Lowell.*

THE SHADE OF THE (APPLE) TREE
(For Senior Citizens Day)
(Song of Solomon 2:3-6)

INTRODUCTION — We enjoy refreshment in the shade.

A. The bride in Solomon's Song speaks of both shade and nourishment in praising her beloved as like "the apple tree among the trees of the wood."

B. The reference suggests the experience of other Biblical characters in the shade of various trees.

I. ADAM'S TREES IN THE GARDEN OF EDEN. (Gen. 3:6-11)—A PLACE OF HIDING.

A. Having eaten of the forbidden fruit, he knew guilt.

B. Shade and darkness beckoned to attempted escape.

C. He learned the futility of hiding from God (See Psalm 139:7, 11, 12).

II. ABRAHAM'S OAKS OF MAMRE. (Gen. 18:1-15)— PLACE OF HOSPITALITY.

A. He welcomed to the comfort of shade.

B. He offered the companionship of friends.

C. He provided the best of food for his guests.

D. He received honor and reward from God himself.

III. ELIJAH'S JUNIPER TREE. (I Kings 19:1-8)— PLACE OF REST AND REFRESHMENT

A. Depression and exhaustion sent him there.

1. He suffered the backwash of high victory at Mt. Carmel, like the undertow of a great wave.

2. He suffered the physical exhaustion of a long journey in flight from Jezebel.

B. Rest and refreshment sent him on his way.

1. Sleep worked its own measure of restoration.

2. Food, divinely given, provided strength.

3. Renewed assignment sent him on God's business.

4. These values are presently available in a shady place among friends.

IV. THE GREEN TREES OF IDOLATRY. (II Kings 16:4)—PLACE OF WORSHIPING THE CREATION WORLD MORE THAN THE CREATOR.
  A. Danger of prizing the gift more than the Giver.
    1. Shade trees treasured in a parched land.
    2. The association with Father Abraham and Mamre may have been tempting.
    3. In any case idols were worshiped "under every green tree."
  B. False worship (false sense of values) brought condemnation. —Esp. of prophets Isaiah and Jeremiah.

V. JONAH'S BRUSH ARBOR AND VINE. (Jonah 4) PLACE OF FRUSTRATION AND INSTRUCTION.
  A. Disappointed that his prediction of Nineveh's fall had not been fulfilled, Jonah felt personally rejected.
  B. He erected a brush arbor for shade, and God raised a vine to assist.
  C. The vine destroyed, Jonah's depression intensified.
  D. God gave a suntanned Jonah instruction in God's way.

VI. NATHANAEL'S FIG TREE. (John 1:43-51)— PLACE OF DISCOVERY.
  A. As God had discovered Adam hiding among the trees, so Jesus "saw" Nathanael in his place of relaxation.
  B. That discovery keyed Nathanael's discovery of Jesus as Messiah.

VII. GOD, NOT TREES, IS THE ULTIMATE PROTECTIVE SHADE.
  This, in prophetic figure, says Song of Solomon 2:3-6.
    1. "The Lord is thy keeper: The Lord is thy shade upon thy right hand. The sun shall not smite thee by day, nor the moon by night" (Psalm 121:5).
    2. The Lord's presence sustains and nourishes. ("Jesus, Lover of My Soul")

CONCLUSION —

Prophecy fulfilled in the Tree of Life (Rev. 22:1-5). Fruit every month, and leaves for healing. Thus sustained, His people "shall reign for ever and ever" (v. 5).

PREACHING THROUGH ISAIAH

Isaiah, the son of Amoz, (and according to one tradition the nephew of King Uzziah of Judah,) lived and prophesied in Jerusalem 749-690 B.C. during the reign of Uzziah, Jotham, Ahaz, and Hezekiah. He was the familiar friend and advisor of the latter two kings. He is often called the Gospel Prophet because of his many predictions about the coming Messiah.

THE MESSAGE OF ISAIAH

The people of Judah have been untrue to Jehovah, both in their worship and in their manner of life. God will punish their wickedness by the destruction of their nation at the hands of the Assyrians. Their punishment complete, God will restore a remnant, who will rebuild the nation in greater glory. Jehovah, known as the God of Israel, will come to be known as the one God of all the earth. His Messiah will come to establish His perfect reign.

ISAIAH IS KNOWN FOR

(1) The surpassing beauty of his discourses. Many of them have been woven into the best-loved anthems of the church.

(2) His prophecies of the Messiah. Speaking by inspiration things he could not have known naturally, he wove into the messages of ancient Judah the story of Christ's coming, being born of a virgin, in the line of David; His ministry in Galilee; His suffering and death; and the manner of His burial.

For the Christian, this is one of the most important of Old Testament books. The reader will find himself charmed by its beauty, inspired by its message, humbled by its warnings, and strengthened by its assurances. The Sunday evening sermons will form a series on "The Gospel in Isaiah."

ANALYSIS OF THE BOOK

Chapters 1   General introduction—the burden of Isaiah.
2-4   Pre-vision of the Christian Age.
5-6   The call of Isaiah to prophesy.
7-12   Events of the league of Israel and Syria against Judah, and of the later Assyrian invasions.

199

13-23 Prophecies of God's judgment against nations nearby.

24-27 God's judgment of the whole earth and establishment of His kingdom.

28-39 Prophecies in the reign of Hezekiah; warnings, assurances, and their fulfillment.

40-66 Israel's Restoration:
        The supremacy of God as Lord of all. (40-48)
        The work of God's faithful Servant. (49-56)
        Glorious future of the Jewish race. (57-66)

Sermon Outlines Provided:

"The Burden of Isaiah" (Isa. 1)
"Who Will Go?" (Isa. 6)
"The Perfect Government" (Isa. 11:1-9)
"Prepare Ye The Way of the Lord (Isa. 40:1-5)
"God's Servant Serves God" (Isa. 53)

Other Suggested Sermon Topics:

"Immanuel" (Isa. 7:10-17)
"The Axe That Boasted" (Isa. 10:5-19)
"Strength for the Journey" (Isa. 40:27-31)
"He Will Not Fail" (Isa. 42:1-9)
"Put on Thy Strength" (Isa. 52:1-4)
"Of Whom Speaketh the Prophet?" (Isa. 53)

QUESTIONS OVER ISAIAH

1. How will Zion be redeemed? (1:27)
2. What name will the child to be born be called? (9:6)
3. How will the idols of Egypt react to the Lord's presence? (19:1)
4. What will God do with death? (25:8)
5. Who invaded Judah in the time of Hezekiah? (36:1)
6. What will be the character of God's chosen servant? (42:1-4)
7. Why was the individual of Isaiah 53 wounded, crushed, and scourged? (53:5)
8. What is God's throne and footstool? (66:1)

THE BURDEN OF ISAIAH
(Isaiah 1)

INTRODUCTION —

Here at the outset, a chapter which introduces and sets the theme for the book. The message is frighteningly appropriate to us.

I. THE DARK PICTURE OF JUDAH'S SIN.
   A. The point of view is that of the sorrowing father of wayward children. —never, "You're going to hell and I'm glad of it."
   B. Judah has rebelled against, and has not known God— this is the gist.
      1. They have gone off after idols.
      2. They have continued a formal worship without heart.
   C. The moral sins of Judah are described as the bruises of a drunkard.
      1. First, prosperous, cynical, forgetful.
      2. Materialistic, lustful, greedy.
      3. Dishonest, cynical, lacking in care for the needy.
      4. Punished by invasion, oppression, suffering.
      5. Still feverish for entertainment (22:12-14).
      6. The woes (5:18-23).
         a. Draw sin as with a rope; bound to it as beast of burden.
         b. Scornful of God—"Let's see You do some tricks."
         c. Call evil good and good evil:
            Vengeance made a virtue.
            (College teacher says skillful cheater will be successful.)
            Narcotics business justifies destruction of others for gain.
         d. Boastful and self-satisfied.
         e. Mighty in their cups.
         f. Takers and givers of bribes—influence in business.
   D. A frighteningly familiar picture of almost any mature civilization.

201

II. THE FORM OF RELIGION WILL NOT SUFFICE.

A. The activities here described are the things commanded in the law — Has God changed? — Israel has changed from obedience to form.

B. "Who hath required this at your hand, to trample my courts?"

　1. They came like unreasoning beasts — driven by others — coming by habit — fleeing through fear.

　2. No system of worship is without danger in this direction — The Roman pageantry. The Protestant testimony meeting.

C. The things commanded can be used wrongfully. "He that eateth and drinketh unworthily eateth and drinketh judgment unto himself, not discerning the Lord's body" (I Cor. 11:27).

III. GOD HAS AN ANSWER — THERE IS HOPE BECAUSE THERE IS GOD.

A. Come now and let us reason together — God deals as with children.

B. Chastening in order to salvation.

　1. Some are driven away and lost.

　2. The remnant are corrected, and become the center of future glories.

C. Cease to do evil; learn to do well; but moral reform is not enough.

D. *I* will thoroughly purge away thy dross. *I* will restore thy judges. Zion shall be redeemed.

CONCLUSION —

God provides the redeemer — This is the Gospel in Isaiah.

WHO WILL GO?

(Isaiah 6)

INTRODUCTION — The chapter preaches its own sermon.

A. One of those living and growing passages—let it live and grow and bear fruit in us.

B. For fifty years Uzziah had reigned—one of the greater, stronger, better kings (by tradition cousin of Isaiah).

  1. Yet the nation wandered ever farther from the way of God.

  2. Perhaps Isaiah asked, "Why doesn't somebody do something?"

I. THE LIFE-FILLING GLORY OF GOD.

A. "In the year that King Uzziah died, I saw the Lord." When the things in which we trust fail, we come to trust in Him (Dittemore).

B. The picture of glory.

  1. High—temple-filling train (no attempt at physical description of God). Circumstances most glorious.

  2. About Him the Seraphim—winged creatures. Their attitude and words of reverence. "And the four living creatures, having each one of them six wings, are full of eyes round about and within: and they have no rest day and night, saying, "Holy, holy, holy, is the Lord God, the Almighty, who was and who is and who is to come" (Rev. 4:8).

C. Smoke filled the house—symbol of the presence of God. Smoke and thunder at Sinai; pillar of cloud; smoke of the altar.

II. THE CONFESSION AND CLEANSING OF ISAIAH.

A. Here the mark of the kind of a man God can use: humble, aware of sin.

B. Hears how the seraphim praise God purely—has he done so? "If any stumbleth not in word, the same is a perfect man, able to bridle the whole body also" (James 3:2). "For out of the abundance of the heart the mouth speaketh" (Matt. 12:34).

C. Confession of imperfection, which is sin. Cf. Peter: "Depart from me, for I am a sinful man, O Lord" (Luke 5:8).

D. "I dwell among a people of unclean lips." — Not in the way of excusing himself, but of sharing their guilt.

E. The act of cleansing.

1. It was not an act of passing over; it was an act of taking away — pain?

2. Fire the symbolic agent of cleansing — cauterizing.

III. THE COMMISSION OF ISAIAH.

A. The Lord has need — "Whom shall I send, and who will go?"

1. The thoughtless in Israel; who will tell them?

2. Is there question that there is need in America today for God's servants? There are sinners, unsaved, unchurched, unloved, and lonely. There are those who should know better who do not know the word of God.

3. Why doesn't somebody do something?

B. The Lord invites and commands. — "If any man will be my disciple, let him deny . . ." (Matt. 16:24).

1. Early Christians obeyed the command — each one considered it his work to preach.

C. "Here am I, Lord, send me" — was this not presumption on Isaiah's part, to choose himself as God's ambassador?

1. God's question — *who will go?*

2. "Enthusiasm and willingness are 90% — they are 99%."

IV. THE RESULT — NOT IN APPARENT SUCCESS, BUT IN SERVICE TO HIM.

The remnant — you invite 100; one comes, thank God; teach a class; one hears and learns.

INVITATION —

The glorious Christ invites — who will hear?

THE PERFECT GOVERNMENT
(Isaiah 11:1-9)

INTRODUCTION — The world-wide interest in perfect government.

A. Speculation on what government ought to be has a noble heritage.
B. Plato—A wise man and his friend speculate on what the government should be like.
C. Sir Thomas More dreams of a perfect government on a far-away island, called Utopia, or nowhere.
D. They might well have saved their time, and studied instead the picture God gives us, of His perfect government.

I. THE RULER IS PERFECT.
   A. He is God through Christ. "All authority is given unto me . . ." (Matt. 28:18).
      1. Pilate testified to His moral perfection.
      2. The multitude said early in his ministry, "He doeth all things well" (Mark 7:37).
   B. The Spirit of Jehovah shall be upon Him.
      1. The spirit of wisdom and understanding.
         a. Compare Solomon's plea for wisdom.
         b. Gains understanding through a perfectly intimate knowledge of man—the man with wounds knows what war is.
      2. The spirit of counsel and might.
         a. He knew how to organize and to inspire His army.
         b. His might is testified by the results of His work.
      3. The spirit of knowledge and fear of Jehovah.
         a. *Knowledge* in the Old Testament sense — an experience of God. It was knowledge that Jesus had when He chose the Twelve.
         b. Fear of God—is Old Testament "religion"—which word is not found there. "I and the Father are one" (John 10:30). Every act of life has religious significance.

205

II. HIS RULE IS PERFECT.

   A. Does not judge by hearsay and appearances.

      1. The worthlessness of hearsay is evident.

      2. Appearances—Louise Moorman "saw" a friend smoking—but she believed his word above her own eyes when assured that it was not so.

   B. Brings justice to the poor with righteousness.

      1. God is no respecter of persons.

      2. Jesus healed and loved the dirty and downcast.

   C. Argues with equity (equalness for the meek).

      1. Pleads the cause for those too bashful to speak for themselves.

      2. The world accepts a man at his own valuation, but God knows.

   D. Smites the earth with the rod of his mouth, and with the breath of his lips shall he slay the wicked.

      1. "Whom the Lord loveth he chasteneth, and scourgeth every son whom he bringeth unto himself" (Heb. 6:12).

      2. Was Jesus wrong in being harsh?—It was the only way to save.

III. HE TRANSFORMS THE WORLD.

   A. Men would try to force others into a mold through pressure.

   B. Christ builds and transforms through an inward force. In the picture of Isaiah there is a *change in nature.*

   C. Hence the government is not a dictatorship, even with a perfect ruler.

      1. It is in the truest sense a democracy.

         a. The citizen chooses or rejects citizenship.

         b. He is free at any time to reject the rule once chosen.

         c. He is free at all times to obey or disobey.

      2. It is the willing allegiance of brothers to a Father.

CONCLUSION —

Will you join the Hallelujah Chorus to "King of Kings and Lord of Lords"?

PREPARE YE THE WAY OF THE LORD
(Isaiah 40:1-5; Luke 3:3-6)

INTRODUCTION — We all benefit from roadbuilding.

    A. We have come to our place on roads not built by ourselves.

    B. Roadbuilding as Isaiah knew it.

        1. The way prepared for a king to visit the provinces of his kingdom.

        2. The way prepared for an army, led by its king.

          a. An aggressive, winning army made roads.

          b. A besieging army built ramps for its siege engines, so a city could be conquered and occupied.

I. ISAIAH PROMISED A DIVINE DELIVERER-KING (vv. 1-3).

    A. His message directed to a people who had been punished for their sins.

        1. By prophetic insight Isaiah addressed the situation of the captives in Babylon two centuries after his time.

        2. Their God, "a great King above all the gods," was not limited to Palestine, but would come to Babylon as a rescuer to the outlands of His own realm.

        3. The herald-voice announces the coming and commands the preparation.

    B. Isaiah's message applies to a world, captive to sin and needing a Savior.

        1. Isaiah foreshadowed the situation of the Jewish nation seven centuries after his time.

        2. Their God so loved the world that He sent His Son to save it. — The Son came from Heaven to earth, as to a part of His created realm.

        3. The herald-voice, John the Baptist, announced the coming and prepared for it.

    C. Isaiah's message applies to our present-day world, sin-bound and needing salvation.

        1. The Son approaches the captives by way of the Word.

        2. The herald-voice and the preparer is the church, corporately and in person.

II. ISAIAH'S MESSAGE COMMANDS PREPARATION OF THE WAY (v. 3).

A. Why prepare the way?
   1. It is necessary in deference to the King.
   2. It is necessary to gain and assure His being received when He comes.
B. Who prepares the way?
   1. The soldiers and the subjects of the King.
   2. At Jesus' coming it was John the Baptist.
   3. In our time, it is the Christian who lives and speaks in such a way as to make Christ welcome.
C. How important is the preparation?
   1. The Romans took Masada after building a ramp reaching 200 feet above the plain.
   2. What is it worth, not to destroy a fortress, but to save a soul?

III. ISAIAH'S MESSAGE DESCRIBES THE PROCESS OF PREPARATION (vv. 3-5).

A. Build in the wilderness, where there is not a way available.
B. Valleys shall be lifted up. —Every man must be lifted to the consciousness that he is loved and can be saved.
C. Hills shall be brought low. —The proud and wealthy (Nicodemus?) must see their need as sinful humans.
D. The crooked must be straightened, the rough places smooth. Straighten things out for:
   1. The one perplexed by creeds.
   2. The one blinded by "hypocrites in the church."
   3. The one bewildered by inequities in this present world.

CONCLUSION —

The Great King approaches to rescue His captive people. In preparation He deserves not less, but infinitely more than the Cyruses and Caesars of old.

GOD'S SERVANT SERVES GOD!
(Isaiah 53)

INTRODUCTION — The Servant Songs of Isaiah speak of Christ.

   A. In poetry—imaginative, emotional, rather than precisely definitive, they describe:
   1. His gentle manner and world mission (Isa. 42:1-9).
   2. His mission and spiritual success (Isa. 49:1-13).
   3. His strength and perfection through suffering (Isa. 50:4-11).
   B. "Of whom speaketh the prophet this?" (Acts 8:34).
   1. Israel as a nation was to be God's servant.
   2. The prophet was to serve God and the nation.
   3. The Messiah was to serve and save the world. Here is the perfect Servant (See Acts 8:34, 35).

I. THE SERVANT DOES NOT SATISFY US (vv. 1-3).
   —He stands in stark contrast to all our ideas of supermen!
   A. His beginnings unimpressive by the world's standards.
   1. His virgin birth, an offense to many.
   2. Nazareth not highly regarded (John 1:46) and even Nazareth rejected Him.
   B. Physical appearance is not the basis of attraction.
   1. Jesus' appearance unknown; for any literal description would repel those to whom it contrasted.
   2. "Believe me for the very works' sake" (John 10:38).
   C. He was a man of sorrows ("Weep, and you weep alone.")
   1. He wept, literally, at the grave of Lazarus, and at the gates of Jerusalem.
   2. He knew the disappointment of betrayal and denial.
   3. Suffering is still wholly unacceptable to preachers of success and happiness.

II. THE SERVANT SAVES US (v. 4-6).
   A. We were wrong in rejection: all this was for us!
   B. He bore our griefs (sickness) and carried our sorrows (pain).
   1. It belonged to us, but we could not bear it.

    2. "Him who knew no sin [God] made to be sin on our behalf, that we might become the righteousness of God in him" (II Cor. 5:21, ASV).

    3. He bore the punishment that makes us whole.

  C. He suffered for our wanderings.

    1. We, like sheep, have gone astray.

    2. The Shepherd endured the search; laid down His life for the sheep.

III. THE SERVANT SUFFERS SILENTLY (vv. 7-9; compare I Peter 2:18-24).

  A. What shall He say?

    1. That He is innocent? It is known.

    2. That He is hurt? That is evident.

    3. Compare our self-justification, and explanations!

  B. He did finally say, "I have finished the work which thou gavest me to do" (John 17:4). — This explained it all, and introduces the final thought of the chapter.

IV. THE SERVANT SATISFIES GOD (vv. 10-12).

  A. He was God's provision from the first, the Lamb slain from the foundation of the world (John 1).

  B. He is God's hope for eternity. "He shall see his seed [posterity], he shall prolong his days, and the pleasure of the Lord shall prosper in his hand" (v. 9).

  C. For now, "He shall justify many." — God will attribute righteousness to multitudes who come through Christ.

  D. He is acknowledged as God's beloved Son.

    1. Authority and judgment are committed to Him.

    2. Peter said, "[Him] God raised up, because it was not possible that he should be holden of it [death]" (Acts 2:24).

    3. Paul: "God hath highly exalted him, and given him the name that is above every name . . ." (Phil. 2:9).

CONCLUSION —

God's Suffering Servant becomes the coming Judge, "Wherefore we make it our aim . . . to be well-pleasing unto him" (II Cor. 5:9, ASV).

PREACHING THROUGH JEREMIAH AND LAMENTATIONS

Jeremiah, the weeping prophet, member of a priestly family of Anathoth, a suburb of Jerusalem, received a call to be God's spokesman during the reign of Josiah, about 626 B.C. Under that king and the succeeding reigns of Jehoahaz, Jehoiakim, Jehoiachin, and Zedekiah, he saw the progressive decay, both moral and political, in Jerusalem, and he warned insistently that Judah's unrepentant sin would lead to destruction at the hands of the Babylonians. Jeremiah saw the reform that followed the finding of the Book of the Law by Josiah in 621, and the death of Josiah in 608. He saw the Babylonians sweep in successive conquests over Assyria (607), Judah (606), and Egypt (605). He saw the dread fulfillment of his prophecies with the final destruction of Jerusalem in 586 B.C.

The book of Jeremiah's prophecies was committed to writing by Baruch, his companion and scribe. It was destroyed by King Jehoiakim (see 36:23), and was later reproduced, the prophecies being in some instances arranged by content, rather than by the time of their utterances. A five-fold message persists throughout the Book: (1) Judah is to be destroyed by the Babylonians; (2) Genuine repentance will yet bring salvation by God's power; (3) The time of repentance past, submission to Babylon will save Judah from complete annihilation; (4) Judah, destroyed, shall be restored after seventy years' captivity; (5) Babylon shall at last be utterly and finally destroyed.

ANALYSIS OF THE BOOK

Chapters 1-36   Prophecies concerning Judah and Israel:
         During the reign of Josiah, with his outward reform. (1-12)
         During the reign of wicked Jehoiakim. (14-20)
         During the reign of Jehoiachin. (13)
         During the reign of Zedekiah. (21-24)
         Messages delivered at various times during these years. (25-36)

      37-43   Experiences of Jeremiah during the seige, fall and exile of Judah.

      44-52   Prophecies concerning the Gentile nations.

The Book of Lamentations is a group of five poems, supremely powerful in their pathos, written soon after the destruction of Jerusalem. They are believed to have been written by Jeremiah, and they complete the tragic story of his warnings unheeded by Judah.

Sermon Outlines Provided:

"Come Back Home!" (Jer. 3:11-17)
"The Former and the Final Will" (Jer. 31:27-34)
"Suicide With a Pen Knife" (Jer. 36:20-32)
"What Are You Complaining About?" (Lam. 3:21-39)

Other Suggested Sermon Topics:

"What Fault Do You Find With God?" (Jer. 2:4-8)
"The Old Paths" (Jer. 6:16-21)
"Citizens of the Kingdom" (Jer. 20)
"The Servant Teaches Gratitude" (Jer. 38:1-13)

QUESTIONS OVER JEREMIAH AND LAMENTATIONS

1. What was Jeremiah's excuse which he thought should disqualify him from prophet duty? (1:6)
2. Why was God going to bring destruction upon His people? (9:12-16)
3. What were some prophets prophesying in the name of the Lord? (14:13-15)
4. What did the example of the potter illustrate? (18:1-11)
5. What does God call Nebuchadnezzer King of Babylon? (25:9)
6. What prophet opposed Jeremiah? (28:10-11)
7. What is the new covenant which God will make with the house of Israel and Judah? (31:31-34)
8. What did King Jehoiakim do with Jeremiah's scroll? (36:23)
9. Who would conquer Egypt during Jeremiah's time? (46:26)
10. Why had Jerusalem become an unclean thing? (Lam. 1:8)
11. How great was the sinfulness of God's people? (4:6)
12. Why had the crown fallen from the head of the nation of God's people? (5:16)

COME BACK HOME!
(Jeremiah 3:11-17)

INTRODUCTION –

  A. The parent, punishing: "This hurts me worse than it does you."

  B. Jeremiah could say that truly of his beloved Jerusalem.
   1. The man: of priestly family, called to prophesy of coming exile. Patriotic, sensitive, reticent; still driven by "a fire in his bones."
   2. The audience: Jerusalem (Judah), beginning about 90 years after northern kingdom (Israel) destroyed by Assyria. Still he spoke as though to Israel, that Judah might get the message.
   3. The message, "repent or be destroyed."
   4. The result, the reforms achieved under Josiah, helped for a while.

 I. SIN DESCRIBED.

  A. It was essentially violation of the nation's marriage to God (vv. 8, 9, 14).
   1. Israel, openly idolatrous, had flouted the relationship through rebellion as a philanderer.
   2. Judah, more discreet, worshiped other gods on the side. Judah's judgment was more severe (v. 11) because Judah had received more warning.

  B. Moral and social sins grew out of this idolatry.
   1. Dishonesty and debauchery followed worship of lecherous gods.
   2. Cruelty followed worship of heartless gods.
   3. Breach of vows and contracts followed breach of covenant with God.

  C. Every aspect of this sin follows modern abandonment of God and His Word.

 II. SIN ACKNOWLEDGED.

  A. It is difficult, as Jeremiah learned in lifelong ministry.
   1. (Illus. Young men of family amuse selves by trying to press the noses of Grandpa's dairy goats to the

213

ground. It can't be done! The goat is a stiffnecked animal, and just won't "eat dirt." So is the sinner stiffnecked in refusal to say honestly, "I have sinned.")

    2. Jeremiah sought to avert the difficulty by reminding of Israel's fate.

B. It is necessary, as a prelude to any healing.

    1. Admit it honestly to yourself, in preparation for doing something about it.

    2. Admit it to others, in preparation for getting help.

    3. Admit it to the offended one (especially God), to gain forgiveness and restoration of relationship.

III. SIN ABANDONED IN REPENTANCE.

A. "Turn back, ye rebellious children" (v. 22).

    1. As the sin was like a faithless spouse's leaving home, repentance is essentially to renewed faithfulness.

    2. Compared is the wandering son's "I will arise and go to my father" (Luke 15).

B. Put away the false gods!

    1. Turning *to* God involves turning *from* sin.

    2. "The dearest idol I have known, whate'er that idol be, Help me to tear it from thy throne, and worship only Thee."

IV. SIN FORGIVEN.

A. This is according to God's nature and purpose: restoration, not destruction. Compare II Peter 3:9.

B. It is motivated by God's promise:

    1. "I will accept" each penitent individually (v. 14).

    2. "I will supply" instruction for godly living (v. 15).

    3. "I will be present" and available in limitless fellowship (vv. 16, 17) — God's presence no longer limited to Ark of Covenant, but all of Jerusalem will be blessed with His presence.

CONCLUSION —

So he who comes in the name of Christ, acknowledging his sin and committing himself to God, need not "wait for thee, sweet hour of prayer," but has the assurance of God's available presence for time and eternity.

THE FORMER AND THE FINAL WILL
(Jeremiah 31:27-34)

INTRODUCTION —

A man's inheritance depends on the will under which it is administered.

Many a person is under the delusion that God's inheritance is still under the Old Testament.

— Three words the same — *will, testament, covenant.*

I. THE BIBLE PRESENTS TWO COVENANTS.

    A. The New is promised in the Old — as in Jeremiah.

    B. The new is so recognized in its own writings.
"He taketh away the first, that he may establish the second" (Heb. 10:9). (See Rom. 7:6.)

    C. This is not a disparagement of the Old. The Old is a true representation of the will of God in the time for the people to whom it was given.
1. "Wherefore the law is holy, and the commandment holy, just and good" (Rom. 7:12).
2. It is often helpful to read an old will, for the better understanding of the new.

    D. Nevertheless the Old is completely set aside in the New. (See Galatains and Hebrews.)
1. Where a testament is, there must of necessity be the death of the testator.
2. Christ re-enacted most of the moral provisions of the law, but they are binding as from Him, and not as from the Old Testament.

II. DIFFERENCES BETWEEN THE COVENANTS.

    A. Old was for punishment of sin and sinner; New for salvation and forgiveness (27, 28).
"What the law could not do in that it was weak through the flesh, God sending His own Son in the likeness of sinful flesh and for sin condemned sin in the flesh" (Rom. 8:3).
Paul's recognition that "by the law is the knowledge of sin" (Rom. 7:2).

B. Old was for the nation; New is for the person.
   1. Old was given to the nation, and dealt with family unit—"as for me and my house . . ."
   2. New—He that loveth father or mother more than Me . . ."
    —"Repent and be baptized, every *one* of you" (Acts 2:38).

C. Old was made at Sinai; the new is to be unlike it (31, 32).
   1. Old Covenant the law as a whole, specifically ten commandments. (See Deut. 9:9.)
   2. New established at Jerusalem, at opening of Christ's will after His death.
   3. Old saw 3000 die at worship of calf; new saw 3000 saved.
   4. Old provided animals sacrificed to hold off God's wrath; new, salvation in Christ.
   5. Old, rituals and Sabbath; New, "Spirit on the Lord's Day."

D. Old was written on tables of stone; new to be written on the heart (33, 34).
   1. "Ye are an epistle of Christ . . . written not with ink, but with the Spirit of the living God; not in tables of stone, but in tables that are hearts of flesh" (II Cor. 3:3).
   2. There is voluntary, inward submission to Christ.
   3. In the New covenant we know God, not only by word, but through the Person of Christ (John 17:3).

III. and CONCLUSION—There are conditions to wills; the inheritance is still not wages.

A. Old Testament condition was obedience to the Commandments:
   "Ye shall walk in all the way which Jehovah your God hath commanded you, that you may live, and that it may be well with you, and that ye may prolong your days in the land which ye shall possess'" (Deut. 5:33).

B. New Testament conditions belief, repentance, confession, baptism, holy living—are all in Christ.

SUICIDE WITH A PEN KNIFE
(Jeremiah 36:20-32)

INTRODUCTION — The story of Jehoiakim.

A. Judah's heedless course halted in reign of Josiah by finding of the Law, and Josiah's reform.

B. Josiah opposes Pharaoh Necho, and is slain. The people make Jehoahaz king. Pharaoh deposes Jehoahaz, puts Eliakim on throne, changes name to Jehoiakim ("Jehovah raises up").

C. Josephus on Jehoiakim: "He was of a wicked disposition, and ready to do mischief; nor was he either religious toward God or good-natured toward men."

D. Egyptians defeated in battle at Carchemish; Jehoiakim then tributary to Babylon.

E. Rebelled against Babylon: this put him at odds with Jeremiah on two points.

 1. Jeremiah urged submission to Babylon.

 2. He rebuked sinfulness of Jehoiakim (Jer. 22:13-19).

F. The words of Jeremiah are gathered; read publicly; then before princes; then before Jehoiakim.

I. THE REASON FOR JEHOIAKIM'S ACT.

A. Given to selfishness, with little care for people, nation, or other.

B. Given to materialism, and dependence upon Egyptian support.

C. Basically opposed to Jeremiah — anything he had to say would be discounted.

D. Had committed his ways in opposition to God.

II. THE ACT OF UTTER DESTRUCTION (The cutting and burning of the roll).

A. A cold, calculating act of disdain for the messenger and the message.

 1. Counted that the Word could be destroyed by doing away with the parchment.

2. Accounted not the realities still behind the Word—Jeremiah—God.

B. Parallels in the act of destruction
1. Destruction of Bibles by Roman empire and by Communist rulers.
2. Editing of the Bible:
    a. Thomas Jefferson deleted accounts of miracles.
    b. Woman says, "That's not in my Bible."
    c. Liberal preacher: "You believe in everything that is in the Bible, and I don't."
    d. Church: "We don't have that kind of preaching in this pulpit."
3. Editing of the message in the hearing:
    a. Choose a church that agrees with the opinion. "Heap to themselves teachers, having itching ears" (II Tim. 4:3).
    b. Anger and absence when the message gets a little too close.

III. THE RESULTING SELF-DESTRUCTION
A. Jehoiakim's end: the record is not clear as the prophecy is; death in shame and defeat.
B. The destruction of the nation thus led is very clear.
C. His knife thrusts:
1. Cut himself off from the message of life— "Lord, to whom shall we go? thou hast the words of eternal life" (John 6:68).
2. Cut himself off from the possibility of repentance to salvation (cf. Acts 11:18).
3. Cut himself off from God. "He that rejecteth, rejecteth not man, but God" (I Thess. 4:8).
4. This becomes the unpardonable sin; the sin without desire for pardon; the disdain of the Spirit's testimony.

CONCLUSION —

"Men and brethren, what shall we do?"

218

WHAT ARE YOU COMPLAINING ABOUT?

(Lamentations 3:21-39)

INTRODUCTION —

A. As a breaking through of the sun in the midst of a stormy day, so is this passage in Lamentations.
   1. Book called the "funeral dirge over the desolation of Jerusalem."
   2. Tourists are shown "Jeremiah's Grotto" outside the north wall of Jerusalem, where Jeremiah is said to have composed this masterful elegy. (Six centuries later Jesus wept here over the *coming* destruction.)
   3. Composed within three months after city was destroyed, it is vivid in its references to the horrors.
   4. This passage speaks of hope, because it declares trust in God's goodness.
B. Even the hope is cloud-wreathed and turbulent.
   1. It was vigorously realistic for Jeremiah's time.
   2. It speaks to the troublous times in which we live.
C. Three notable themes are woven throughout the passage; climaxing in v. 39.

I. WHY COMPLAIN OF DESERVED AFFLICTION?

A. Recognition that *sin* caused the destruction.
   1. It was fulfillment of years-long warnings.
   2. The sin of Jerusalem is compared to the wantonness of a bad wife (Lam. 1:8, 18).
   3. The failures of prophets and priests (Lam. 2:14; 4:13). (Abandonment of sacred responsibility not limited to ancient Israel.)
   4. Jerusalem was worse than Sodom—it had received more of teachings and warnings, therefore had greater responsibility (Lam. 4:6).
B. The sin was not specifically Jeremiah's, but the suffering included him.
   1. Isaiah acknowledges participation in the sinful state of the people (Isa. 6:5).
   2. The prophet may suffer more than others, because of greater sensitivity.

219

C. There is the sin of unfulfilled obligation.
  1. Jerusalem had been expected to represent God in the world; it failed.
  2. So even the most faithful is still unprofitable, having only done his duty (Luke 17:10).

II. WHY COMPLAIN OF SURVIVED AFFLICTION?
  A. Survival itself is remarkable under the circumstances; "Doth a *living* man complain?"
    1. It is of the Lord's mercies that we are not consumed (v. 22).
    2. Said in nursing home: "I'm vertical, and warm; so what's to complain about?"
  B. Rigors of affliction enrich one's growth toward God (vv. 27-30).
    1. These verses seem autobiographical of Jeremiah.
    2. Willing, uncomplaining bearing of burden is mark of God's servant (Isa. 53).
    3. Acceptance of unfair attack is commended and exemplified by Christ (v. 30).
    4. Refinement in affliction's fire (I Pet. 1:6, 7).
  C. For Christians affliction for Christ brings closer to Him (I Pet. 2:21, 22).

III. WHY COMPLAIN OF GOD'S AFFLICTION?
  A. His total provision for us includes affliction (v. 38).
    1. "Shall we receive good at the hand of God, and shall we not receive evil?" (Job 2:10).
    2. Without affliction we are (spoiled, miserable).
  B. His affliction is for our good (vv. 31-36).
    1. Its purpose is to save, and not to destroy (v. 31).
    2. Even His causing of grief is that He might fulfill His compassion (vv. 32, 33).
    3. His purpose is to establish justice (vv. 33-36).
  C. His affliction is incidental to his changeless mercy.
    1. Punishment is limited in time (Jer. 3:5, 12).
    2. Punishment is only such as is necessary (Isa. 54:8).

CONCLUSION —
I have hope, because my hope is in God (See Hab. 3:17-19).

PREACHING THROUGH EZEKIEL

The man Ezekiel was a prophet-priest who was taken as a captive from Jerusalem to Babylon along with King Johoiachin and many Jewish nobles eleven years before Jerusalem was destroyed in 686 B.C. Daniel had been in Babylon nine years already, and had achieved fame as adviser to Nebuchadnezzar. Jeremiah was still in Jerusalem, warning against the coming downfall.

Ezekiel's prophetic ministry covered some twenty years in which he spoke to the Jewish people in captivity. For eleven years he prophesied the fall of Jerusalem as the necessary punishment to be meted out by a holy God for the sins of the people (chapters 1-24). During the sixteen months of the final seige of Jerusalem Ezekiel prophesied the later destruction of Israel's enemies on every side (chapters 25-32) as God's punishment for their sin, pride, and arrogance. These predictions came true during the next fifteen years, as Nebuchadnezzar continued his victorious march westward. After Jerusalem fell Ezekiel prophesied the return from captivity, the reestablishment of the Temple, and the coming kingdom of Messiah (chapters 33-48). The return took place in 536 B.C.; the Temple was rebuilt 515 B.C.; the Messianic prophecies were fulfilled in Christ. There remain a number of Ezekiel's predictions that have been fulfilled only in figure, not literally. Several of his expressions and figures have been repeated in the book of Revelation.

Figurative and dramatic expressions abound in Ezekiel. These appear in three forms: visions, parables or allegories, and symbolic actions. Among notable *visions* are those concerning the glory of God, all-seeing, all-knowing, ever-present, all-powerful, all-pervading, as in chapter 1. (Compare Isaiah 6, and similar visions in Revelation). A notable *allegory* is that of Israel as God's unfaithful bride, in chapter sixteen. Chapters 4-7 describe a series of *symbolic actions* by which Ezekiel illustrated the impending downfall of Jerusalem and its attendant suffering.

Great teaching in Ezekiel centers around his revelation of the glory, holiness and justice of God. "That they may know that I am Jehovah" is the refrain of the book. Based upon this revelation is the repeated insistence that God seeks not to destroy, but to convert His people; that each person is responsible before God

221

for his own life; that acceptance with God depends on the "new heart," or the inward, willing, loving obedience to God; and that the measure of righteousness includes obedience to God's ordinances and active practical goodness as well as the avoidance of the sins of lust and idolatry.

Sermon Outlines Provided:

"Blood on Our Hands" (Ezek. 3:15-21)
"What Noah, Job, and Daniel Could Not Do" (Ezek. 14:12-20)
"Forgetting Things That Are Past" (Ezek. 33:10-19; 18:31, 32)
"The Prophet and the People" (Ezek. 33:27-33)

Other Suggested Sermon Topics:

"God's Censorship" (Ezek. 3:22-27)
"The Sum of the Sins of Tyre" (Ezek. 28:15-19)
"They May Know That I Am Jehovah" (Ezek. 36:13-23)
"Healing Waters" (Ezek. 47:1-12)

QUESTIONS OVER EZEKIEL

1. How does God describe the sons of sons of Israel to Ezekiel? (2:3-5)
2. What kinds of wickedness and abominations was Israel committing? (8:9-18)
3. What is God's attitude toward death and dying? (18:32)
4. What had Israel despised and profaned? (22:8)
5. What was to happen to the city of Tyre? (26:1-14)
6. What will convince the scattered house that God is the Lord their God? (28:25-26)
7. Why was God going to cause the great nation of Egypt to fall? (31:10-11)
8. What will be required of the watchman who fails to sound the warning? (33:6, 8)
9. To what did God liken the ways of Israel? (36:17)
10. What did Ezekiel see come into the house of the Lord? (43:4-5)
11. What will grow on the banks of the river flowing out from the sanctuary? (47:12)

BLOOD ON OUR HANDS
(Ezekiel 3:15-21)

INTRODUCTION — The curse of blood on one's hands.

"Thy brother's blood crieth to me from the ground" (Gen. 4:10).
(Lady MacBeth trying to remove the spot of blood — "Out cursed spot!")
"His blood be upon us, and upon our children" (Matt. 27:25).

I. IS IT TRUE THAT THE BLOOD OF THE UNBELIEVER IS UPON *US*?

   A. Ezekiel, one who knew God, was placed *among the people,* and commissioned — the title he bears is "son of man."

   B. The New Testament commission is age-long, world-encircling, all-inclusive.

   1. Preach the gospel. Four words:
      Kerusso - Proclaim. "Go ye into all the world and preach . . . to every creature (Mark 16:15).
      Euangello - "Evangelize" - Usually in formal fashion, often informal; tell the good news.
      Katangello - Announce thoroughly; proclaim. "As often as ye eat this bread and drink this cup, ye do *proclaim* . . ." (I Cor. 11:26).
      Laleo - Talk "Now they that were scattered abroad upon the persecution that arose about Stephen travelled as far as Phenice and Cyprus and Antioch, *preaching* the word to none but unto the Jews only" (Acts 11:19).

   2. In this way every one becomes a bearer of the message — Andrew & Peter. The greatest preachers have done some of finest work this way — Jesus and the woman of Samaria.
      (Illus. — a child playing on the track and the train coming. Who says, "I am neither the child's parent nor a policeman; let them take care of it"?) Urgency often spoken but less often acted.

II. IT IS A LIFE-AND-DEATH PROPOSITION.

A. The past is not the issue — it is the present and future. Read Ezek. 33:11-19.
1. Leave bad past — "If any man be in Christ Jesus he is a new creature" (II Cor. 5:17).
2. Don't count on good past — "Let him that thinketh he standeth take heed . . ." (I Cor. 10:12).

B. "The soul that sinneth, it shall die" — warn the wicked. Question arises . . . "Can the untaught be saved?"
1. "And that servant, which knew his lord's will, and prepared not himself, neither did according to his will, shall be beaten with many stripes. But he that knew not, and did commit things worthy of stripes, shall be beaten with few stripes" (Luke 12:47).
2. More tolerable for the untaught than for the one who knew and failed to teach them.

C. Warn the righteous man.
1. We say we don't believe "once in grace, always in grace" — but what of our actions?
2. "The last state of that man is worse than the first" (II Pet. 2:20).
3. Time of warning is before he slips into sin — much harder after.
4. But "Brethren, if any *of you* do err from the truth, and one convert him, let him know that he which converteth a sinner from the error of his way, shall save a soul from death" (James 5:19, 20).

CONCLUSION —

The record of the great preacher:

"I am debtor both to the Greeks, and to the barbarians, both to the wise and to the unwise; so as much as in me is, I am ready to preach the gospel to you that are at Rome also" (Rom. 1:14, 15).

"Wherefore I take you to record this day, that I am pure from the blood of all men, for I have not shunned to declare unto you all the counsel of God" (Acts 20:27).

WHAT NOAH, JOB, AND DANIEL COULD NOT DO
(Ezekiel 14:12-20)

INTRODUCTION —

The situation in which Ezekiel spoke — prophesying destruction of Jerusalem.

  A. Noah - who alone was righteous, and made ark for saving of the few.
  Job - Who alone was patient and faithful, and was restored to prosperity.
  Daniel - who alone was even now bearing witness to true God in Babylon, at the capital.
  B. Mention of their names notable for —
  The stature of these heroes among the people, and
  The quality of their heroism.

I. COULD NOT SAVE THE LAND FROM FAMINE OR FROM WILD BEASTS.

  A. They could not even save themselves from suffering discomfort. — Flood came in spite of Noah; Job himself suffered; Daniel taken prisoner.
  B. Generalizings concerning natural tragedies as punishment are always dangerous. ("They must have been paying the preacher," oldtimers said when it rained.)
  C. In time of convenience the unrepentant enjoy the shelter of the saints.

II. COULD NOT SAVE THE LAND FROM WARFARE, INVASION, PESTILENCE.

  A. Daniel was one of the first to suffer from invasion — earliest captives.
  B. The presence of a few godly people is no guarantee; only a wise and godly policy on the part of the nation; as indicated by the prophecies of Jeremiah.
  C. When war comes, not even the godly are spared, or exempt from danger.

III. COULD NOT SAVE EVEN SON OR DAUGHTER—
No family safety by reason of one's faithfulness.
   A. Many even now depend greatly on family-unit religion.
      1. Some count the number of families in the parish—
         these are they who have the parents stand sponsor
         for the child in "baptism" of infants.
      2. Join husband's church.
         "The soul that sinneth, it shall die" (Ezek. 18:4, 5, 20).
   C. No such thing as family representation in religion.
      (One man "adequately represented" in church—and in
      Heaven.)
   D. There is a scriptural way to family solidarity.
      "The unfeigned faith that is in thee; which dwelt first
      in thy grandmother Lois, and thy mother Eunice; and,
      I am persuaded, in thee also" (II Tim. 1:5).
      Study of the word together.

IV. EACH COULD SAVE HIS OWN SOUL BY RIGHT-
EOUSNESS—NOT ARGUMENT AGAINST FAITH.
   A. There is no true faith without righteousness growing
      out of it. There is no Christian righteousness which
      does not grow out of faith.
   B. New Testament builds on personal responsibility.
      1. Noah could preach, but could not believe for others.
         "He that believeth and is baptized shall be saved."
      2. Job could repent for himself, but not for others; his
         prayer represented himself.
      3. Daniel could live righteously for none but himself.
         "But let each man prove his own work, and then
         shall he have his glorying in regard of himself alone,
         and not of his neighbor. For each man shall bear
         his own burden" (Gal. 6:4, 5).

CONCLUSION —

None, nor all, could face judgment for another.
"We must all be made manifest before the judgment-seat of
Christ; that each one may receive the things done in the body,
according to what he hath done" (II Cor. 5:10).

FORGETTING THE THINGS THAT ARE PAST
(Ezekiel 33:10-19; 18:31, 32)

INTRODUCTION —

A good driver on life's highway looks mostly through the windshield, not the rear view mirror.

A. There have been times and circumstances when God told men to remember; now He tells them they must not live in their memories.

B. The past can become a yoke hanging on one's neck — an opium cloud dulling the senses and destroying a life of service.

I. GOD IS NOT BOUND TO THE PAST.

A. His purpose is for growth in service, and for the salvation of His people.
1. The sinner is given a way of escape from his past.
2. The righteous is given a way of growth.
3. Both are given strong warning that there is death in self-trust.

B. God's concern is not in what you were, but in what you are; and much less in what you are than in what you are becoming.

II. THE NEED FOR A FORWARD LOOK IS ALIKE FOR SINNER AND SAINT.

A. The sinner must, and can turn from his sin.
— He cannot live it down, but he can give it up.
1. It takes the acceptance of responsibility; it will not be done by one who says he is shaped by circumstances and can't help it.
2. It takes faith in God. To erstwhile sinners in Corinth: "Such were some of you: but ye are washed, but ye are sanctified, but ye are justified in the name of the Lord Jesus Christ, and by the Spirit of our God" (I Cor. 6:11).
3. That faith must be part of the messenger's equipment as he addresses the sinner.

a. Shall Ezekiel say, "There is no use talking to them"?
b. (The farm boy, clearing ground, is told that big stumps come out the same way littles ones do, but with somewhat more digging.)

B. The saint must beware of overconfidence and lapse.
1. Observe the warnings:
Ezekiel 3:20, 21; 18:21-24; Hebrews 6:4-6.
(To believers and about believers) "My brethren, if any of you do err from the truth, and one convert him; let him know, that he which converteth the sinner from the error of his way shall save a soul from death, and shall hide a multitude of sins" (James 5:19). "Let him that thinketh he standeth take heed lest he fall" (I Cor. 10:12).
2. Observe difference in doctrine: one believes in "backsliding" and practices it; another does not believe in "backsliding," but practices it. — "Yousta bees" sting us! "Used to be" preachers, teachers, choir members, etc.
3. Time for the warning is before the lapse takes place: "Don't rest on past!"
4. Command to warn is serious: if the watchman fails, he is guilty with sinner.

III. CHRIST PROVIDES THE FOCUS FOR THE FORWARD LOOK.
A. Psychologist says that the way to forget is to switch attention to other and attractive subjects (reverse the process of fixing memory). "Turn eyes on Jesus!"
B. Christ is the sole hope for the sinner, and perfect goal for the saint. — Look ahead to Him, as example to follow, as friend to encourage, and as the King who is coming to receive us to His glory.

CONCLUSION —

"I count not myself to have apprehended: but this one thing I do, forgetting those things which are behind, and reaching forth unto those things which are before, I press toward the mark for the prize of the high calling of God in Christ Jesus" (Phil. 3:13, 14).

THE PROPHET AND THE PEOPLE
(Ezekiel 33:27-33)

INTRODUCTION –

Why do you go to church? To meet friends? To be entertained? God's messenger and God's people must never lose sight of God's purposes.

I. EZEKIEL

    A. The message - There is national punishment for national sin—repent!

    B. The response of the people

        1. Here is the first place that we learn of Ezekiel's popularity as an orator.

        2. They were entertained, but not converted.

    C. The faithfulness of the messenger.

        1. He was not turned aside by popularity—did not recognize it.

        2. He continued to mourn for the sin that destroyed, and preach the God who desired to save.

    D. Establishment of the message

        1. Fulfillment of Ezekiel's dire predictions proved that the message was far more than beautiful words.

        2. Took it out of the realm of theory into life-and-death reality.

II. THE GREATER THAN PROPHET—JESUS.

    A. Message - "I am come that they might have life, and have it more abundantly" (John 10:10).

    "To give eternal life to as many as thou hast given him" (John 17:3).

    "Let us go into the next town, that I may preach there also, for therefore came I forth" (Mark 1:38).

    B. The popular response —well shown in John 6, after feeding of 5000 they would take Him by force and make Him king. (Herod, at the time of trial, shows "entertainment" response in extreme form.)

229

C. Christ's faithfulness
1. Tested in the wilderness temptation, remained true throughout.
2. He had a way with compliments — Nicodemus, etc.
"Why call ye me Lord, Lord, and do not the things I say?"
"He that heareth these sayings of mine and doeth them not . . . (Matt. 7:26).
D. The message was established in the Resurrection. Will be established in the judgment.

III. THE CHURCH
A. First as hearer of the gospel
1. "These things are written for our admonition" (I Cor. 10:1-12).
2. Do not destroy the message by being merely entertained.
— Even the apostles were sometimes admired and worshiped, but not believed (Acts 14:8-18).
B. Then as messenger of the word
The church is a preaching institution. (No "great" preachers in 2nd century.)
1. Its message is the Gospel.
"Preach the gospel to every creature" (Mark 16:15).
"Repentance and remission of sins shall be preached in His name" (Luke 24:47).
— social betterment, peace of mind, etc. are proper *by-products*.
2. Drawing crowds must never obscure the purpose for which crowds may properly be drawn.

CONCLUSION —

There will come the sure fulfillment of God's word.
Where will it find us and our hearers? Entertained? Or saved?

PREACHING THROUGH DANIEL AND HOSEA

Is this true of you? God speaking through Hosea says, "I wrote for him the ten thousand things of my law; but they are counted as a strange thing" (Hos. 8:12). Is God's written Word a strange thing to you, or are you daily becoming more familiar with it?

Daniel was taken into captivity by Nebuchadnezzar, king of Babylon, twenty years before the general captivity of Judah. He was speedily recognized for his wisdom, his firmness of character, and his God-given ability to interpret mysteries. For seventy years he continued as officer and advisor to Babylonian kings and their conquering Persian successors.

The first six chapters of the book tell of various events in Daniel's life, widely separated in time:

Chap. 1 The capture and training of Daniel and his friends (607 B.C.).

2 He interprets Nebuchadnezzar's dream, foretelling events of six centuries of world history (603 B.C.).

3 The faithful Hebrews are preserved in the fiery furnace (580 B.C.).

4 He interprets a dream foretelling Nebuchadnezzar's madness (570 B.C.).

5 Belshazzar's feast, and the handwriting on the wall (538 B.C.).

6 Daniel is preserved in the den of lions (537 B.C.).

The last six chapters record four separate visions of Daniel, by which he foretold the successive rise of Persian, Greek, and Roman empires, the coming of Messiah's kingdom, and, by a figure, the resurrection and final judgment. Jesus made reference to Daniel's prophecy in speaking of the coming desolation of Jerusalem and of the final judgment. Many things in these visions appear again in John's visions on Patmos, as seen in the Book of Revelation.

For the prophetic ministry of Hosea we go back from Babylon to the kingdom of Israel, and back from the captivity to the time of Israel's corruption and decline, nearly two hundred years before Daniel. Under King Jereboam II, Israel was wealthy, powerful, and forgetful of God and goodness. Under his six successors, four of whom were assassinated after short reigns, it became progressively weaker as idolatry, immorality, and dishonesty increased. During this time and under these circumstances Hosea preached of Israel's terrible infidelity to God's justice and the restitution of the repentant by God's tender love.

The first three chapters of the book deal with Hosea's own tangled and tragic family life, as illustrative of God's patience toward His wayward bride, Israel. The final nine chapters are made up of short discourses in which the theme of sin, punishment, and restitution is developed.

Sermon Outlines Provided:

"When God Is With You" (Dan. 3)
"The Costly Habit of Prayer" (Dan. 6:4-16)
"I Called My Son Out of Egypt" (Hosea 11:1, 2)
"Return — With Words" (Hosea 13:15 — 14:9)

Other Suggested Sermon Topics:

"The Lasting Kingdom" (Dan. 2:31-45)
"A Writing of Judgment" (Dan. 5)
"Not Our Goodness, But God's Mercy" (Dan. 9:15-19)
"Who Wants to be Wise?" (Hosea 4:6-10)
"Flights of the Silly Dove" (Hosea 7:11-16)
"That Stormy East Wind" (Hosea 12:1, 2)

QUESTIONS OVER DANIEL AND HOSEA

1. What did God grant to Daniel? (Dan. 1:9)
2. What was the interpretation of the mysterious handwriting on the wall? (5:25-28)
3. What was Daniel's physical condition after seeing the visions? (8:27)
4. What was Daniel to do with the words he had received? (12:4)
5. What kind of a wife was Hosea to take to himself? (Hos. 1:2)
6. How long will God separate himself from His people? (5:15)
7. How should Israel have sown and reaped? (10:12)
8. What is the difference between the reaction of the righteous and the transgressors toward the ways of the Lord? (14:9)

WHEN GOD IS WITH YOU
(Daniel 3)

INTRODUCTION — The Story.

Nebuchadnezzar's vision - chap. 2 (esp. v. 47, his adulation of God.)

Later, perhaps near the time of Zedekiah's final revolt, he sets up image and demands worship of it.

Hananiah, Mishael, and Azariah refuse to worship the image, before or after personal threats.

Punishment inflicted, and they are saved from it.

Nebuchadnezzar convinced and again acknowledges God.

Two types of characters in the story.

I. THE VACILLATING KING: NEBUCHADNEZZAR.
   — History records prowess not only at arms, but in building roads, cities, palaces and gardens.
   A. Respectable, and of a certain nobility of character — this not enough. — So he becomes typical of respectable persons without real faith.
   B. Impressed by the spectacular — as Daniel's interpretation of the dream. (As "Christians" impressed by glory of special days, pageantry, revival, "faith healing.")
   C. Humble when bewildered, he worshiped when he was favored, but forgot when way was smooth. — So the way of half-hearted religion is downward.
   D. Became progressively forgetful of God, self-assertive, and finally blasphemous (see 3:15 end).
   E. Again "converted" by the spectacular, he became an outspoken advocate of Jehovah worship.

II. THE FAITHFUL HEBREWS.
   A. No former noteworthiness
      1. Had lost their own names and became Shadrach, Meshach, & Abedenego. (Daniel kept his Hebrew name against "Belteshazzar" — Dan. 1:7).
      2. Had been faithful companions and helpers of Daniel.

233

B. The test—threat of destruction
 1. Their faith grew out of what was past—there was no promise of security. —See vv. 16-18, for a remarkable confession.
 2. Complete faith in God's power—hard to see in the face of immediate force. —Faith did not depend on God's favor to themselves.
 3. Complete respect for God's will. Cf. Esther "If I perish, I perish" (Esther 4:16).

III. THE BLESSING IS FOR THE FAITHFUL.
 A. No indication of God's blessing on Nebuchadnezzar for his belated surrender. —He concluded his days, son reigned two years, was assassinated; end of dynasty.
 B. God's presence saved the Hebrews.
 In the furnace—the fourth, "like unto the Son of God," was present.
 "Lo, I am with you" is a promise dependent on obedient faith.

CONCLUSION —

Not all God's saints have been delivered from affliction and death, but all can know the glory that makes all suffering seem small (II Cor. 4:16-18).

THE COSTLY HABIT OF PRAYER
(Daniel 6:4-16)

INTRODUCTION —

    A. Jesus in Gethsemane
When Judas planned to betray Jesus, he knew where to find the Lord, at prayer in the Garden (John 18:2). Knowing all this, Jesus still went to pray!

    B. Daniel in Babylon, centuries before this.
When his enemies sought to destroy Daniel, they knew how to entrap him in his habitual times and manners of prayer. Knowing all this, Daniel still prayed!

I. THE EVENT RECOUNTED IN DANIEL 6.

    A. Darius' beureaucracy established (vv. 1-3).
        1. Contact with the people through 120 satraps.
        2. Executive branch, three "commissionsers" (NASB).
        3. Daniel the most distinguished of the three.

    B. Jealousy developed (vv. 4, 5).
        1. Daniel resented as a foreigner (v. 13).
        2. Daniel's goodness, Daniel's rebuke to evil.
        3. Daniel resented for efficiency, dependability, integrity.
        4. Daniel resented especially for Darius' favoritism.

    C. The trap laid (vv. 6-9).
        1. His religious devotion made him vulnerable. For it he would risk. In it he might seem to offend.
        2. Proposal made to exclude petition to any but Darius.
            a. Appealed to Darius' vanity. Seemed a way to unify the kingdom.
            b. Based on false claim to unanimity ("Everybody's doing it"; not so!).
            c. Proposal excluded God, from the consultation, and from trust.

    D. The response of Daniel (vv. 10, 11).
        1. He knew the plot, but was not deterred from life-long practice.
        2. He knelt, visibly; and prayed, audibly.
            a. Gave thanks to God for things Darius might have claimed credit for.

b. Made supplication to God, in violation of decree.
3. To change his custom in time, posture, voice, or subject or prayer would have constituted surrender to lesser authority, and dethronement of God.
E. The trap sprung (vv. 12-16)
1. Report to Darius.
2. His effort to avoid casting Daniel to the lions.
3. His yielding to the unchangeable decree.
F. The trap broken (vv. 17-28)
1. Did Darius pray to God during a sleepless night?
2. Inquiring at dawn, he rejoiced in Daniel's deliverance.
3. He punished the accusers, and decreed that "men tremble and fear before the God of Daniel."

II. THE COST AND THE WORTH OF PRAYER

A. Time consuming and inconvenient in a busy life.
— But Daniel accomplished more with the rest of his time than others did with all.
B. Subject of resentment among his peers.
1. It marked him as different, and it rebuked their carelessness.
2. Even so, it was part of the character that won him highest respect and favor.
C. Provided occasion for a plot against him.
— But it provided the foundation for failure of that plot.
D. Endangered his life; but it overcame that danger.
E. It was occasion of acute distress to Darius, his friend.
1. Parallel: Does a family man have a right to make his service to God the cause of distress and material sacrifice to his family?
2. It established in Darius a respect for God, which he shared with the kingdom.

CONCLUSION —

Victory from Daniel's praying came only after he accepted the cost, without seeing the victory.

236

I CALLED MY SON OUT OF EGYPT
(Hosea 11:1, 2)

INTRODUCTION –

The Exodus from Egypt a focal point in Israel's history. As well try to record American history without the American Revolution as to review Israel's history without the Exodus.

So Hosea (in time, halfway between Moses and Christ) spoke of God's dealing with His people in terms of the Exodus: "When Israel was a child, then I loved him, and called my son out of Egypt." This became prophetic of Christ (Matt. 2:15).

At several points in Biblical history Egypt became a place of refuge for God's people; though Egypt was an indifferent and sometimes reluctant host, and her land a place for coming out!

I. GOD CALLED YOUNG ISRAEL OUT OF EGYPT.
    A. Israel was a child.
        1. The sojourn in Israel occupied four hundred years, beginning with the man Israel and seventy of his clan; and ending with the departure of a million.
        2. Israel went into Egypt as a family, and emerged as a people, ready to become a nation.
        3. They had yet to develop the nationhood that comes with freedom and responsibility.
    B. "Then I loved him."
        1. God's love for Israel brought them into Egypt. Joseph said to his brothers, "God did send me before you to preserve life" (Gen. 45:5).
        2. God's love called them out of Egypt. He heard the cries of their affliction. He also saw the need to preserve their identity, and their faith in Him.
    C. "I called my son out of Egypt."
        1. Hosea uses the Father-son relationship between God and His people more than others do, but see also Deuteronomy 8:5 and Psalm 103:13.
        2. Moses was involved in that "calling out."
    D. "As they called them, so they went from them" (v. 2).
        1. Like a naughty child, Israel ran away from the pleading Parent.

2. At times they wanted to go back into Egypt: They missed the Egyptian onions in their diet (Num. 11: 4-6). They brought with them relics of Egyptian religion — the golden calf. They missed the security that went with their servitude.

3. At times they went into idolatrous relation with other peoples, denying the God who sustained them.

E. Most of us have "Egypts" from which God calls us.
   1. Slavery to sin.
   2. Bondage to the job, business, social relationship that offers security, but denies free responsibility.
   3. Ties to human tradition prevent freedom in Christ.

II. GOD CALLED HIS SON, JESUS, OUT OF EGYPT (Matt. 2:13-21).

   A. The experience in Egypt was an incident of early childhood; Jesus grew up in Israel.
   B. God's care sent Jesus to Egypt, and called Him away.
      1. The dream warned Joseph of Herod's murderous intent.
      2. Another dream instructed Joseph of Herod's death.
   C. Called out of Egypt — What if Joseph and Mary had decided to stay in the land of the Nile?
   D. Joseph and Mary obeyed more readily than the "naughty child" Israel. — They returned to Nazareth as directed.
   E. Application — Have you ever experienced a lapse in your relation to church, brethren, Christian development?
      1. Reasons may have been good, as false teaching in the home church.
      2. Don't linger in Egypt after Herod — whatever drove you away — is long dead!

CONCLUSION —

Lay hold now on God-given freedom, responsibility, and growing up in Christ!

238

RETURN — WITH WORDS
(Hosea 13:15—14:9)

INTRODUCTION —

What can I do for my nation? — the question of every sincere patriot when his native country is in danger.

Hosea's question, when he saw the decadence and danger of Israel, over a period of fifty years, beginning 2600 years ago.

A. Israel's gradual lapse into heathenism.
B. Strong reign of Jeroboam II followed by six brief weak reigns and then a fall to the Assyrians.

I. SIN, JUDGMENT, AND PUNISHMENT.

A. Hosea charges Israel with corruption of religion.
  1. It began with corruption on the part of priests.
     Apply - Christians are priests.
        How do we use God's day? His name?
  2. It ended in heathenism, idolatry, debauchery — as an unfaithful wife.
     Apply - Moral failure, with its eternal stain.
B. Hosea charges carousal in the king's house (ch. 7).
  1. Roger Babson interprets economic and political problems as being problems of *character, spirit, re-birth.*
  2. Truth takes a holiday — but will truth come back to school in diplomacy?
C. Commercial dishonesty is charged (Hosea chs. 11, 12).
  1. Sharp dealing in which weakness is exploited.
  2. How are *we* using the present world situation?
D. "*According to their pasture,* so were they filled; they were filled and their heart was exalted; therefore have they forgotten me" (13:6). — Prof. Walter M. Horton, Oberlin Seminary, "If a generation should skip the knowledge of the Bible, it would be calamitous. — It has been skipped."
E. "And they have not cried unto me with their heart; but they howl upon their beds; they assemble themselves for grain and new wine; they rebel against me."

239

"It is thy destruction, O Israel, that thou art against me, against my help" (13:9).
"They sow the wind and they shall reap the whirlwind."

II. RETURN.

A. Human effort inadequate — "Surely now shall we say, We have no King, for we fear no Jehovah; and the king, what can he do for us?" (10:3). — We will no longer say to the work of our hand, "Thou art our gods."

B. Return personally.
1. We can't heal the evils of all the world this morning, but we must let God heal our own evils.
2. We can confess our own sin, and accept Christ as our Forgiver of sin.

III. RETURN WITH WORDS.

A. We need a definite commitment to keep us from too-easy wavering.
1. "Your goodness is a morning cloud, and as the dew that goeth early away. Therefore have I hewed them with the prophets; I have slain them by the words of my mouth."

B. We need the spiritual cleansing of open confession. Before men we confess ourselves as sinners — to Him we confess the sin.

C. We need to glorify God with our confession.

IV. HEALING AND BLESSING — A RETURN TO GOD.

A. We have hopes for our nation.
1. That the work of men's hands shall be for building.
2. That homes may be united, and broken lives restored.

B. We have hopes for ourselves.
1. A calm courage in the face of all danger.
2. Unstained enjoyment of life, not dimmed by hate, jealousy, or guilt.
3. Assurance beyond — "I have all things, and am full."

CONCLUSION —

The price is a gift received; acknowledged with words.

PREACHING THROUGH JOEL, AMOS OBADIAH, JONAH, MICAH, NAHUM

JOEL (three chapters)

From evidence in the book itself it appears that Joel was one of the earliest of the prophets, writing about 800 B.C. The occasion of his message was a terrible plague of locusts, which he said came as God's judgment upon His sinful people. He also prophesied the coming of another Great Day of the Lord, when judgment would be pronounced. That was fulfilled in the Great Day of Pentecost, seven weeks after Christ's resurrection (See Acts 2:16-21).

AMOS (nine chapters)

Amos, a shepherd living not far from Jerusalem about 750 B.C., visited the center of idol worship at Bethel in Israel, and there proclaimed God's wrath upon the people for their moral and social corruption.

Chapters 1-2 He pronounces God's judgment on the nations, including Israel.

3-5 He describes Israel's sins of intemperance, injustice, and pride.

6-8 He gives a series of figurative predictions of destruction.

9 He tells of future glories to come through a faithful remnant.

OBADIAH (one chapter)

Writing soon after the destruction of Jerusalem, 586 B.C., Obadiah tells of the coming complete downfall of Edom. The Edomites were descendants of Esau, and had been persistent and cruel enemies of the descendants of Jacob.

JONAH (four chapters)

After an unsuccessful attempt to avoid the task, Jonah visited Nineveh, capital of the mighty Assyrian empire, sometime between 800 and 750 B.C., and brought the message of God's judgment. Modern archaeologists, led to a place called the "Munas (Jonah) Mound," discovered near the buried ruins of the ancient

241

city of Nineveh. Jesus referred to the incident of Jonah and the great fish as the "sign" of His own burial and resurrection (Matt. 12:39-41).

MICAH (seven chapters)

Brief records of prophetic messages delivered over a course of years, about 740 to 700 B.C., appear in this powerful little book. Micah preached in Jerusalem during the later days of Isaiah, found and condemned the same sins, and gave, especially in chapters 4 and 5, prophecies of the same Messiah.

NAHUM (three chapters)

Speaking in Palestine not long before the Chaldeans conquered and destroyed Nineveh, 607 B.C., Nahum prophesied that event in its completeness and finality. The repentance which had followed Jonah's preaching in Nineveh 150 years before had saved the city for some time, but cruel wickedness had returned so that judgment, complete and terrible, was the only answer.

Sermon Outlines Provided:

"The Day of the Lord" (Joel 2:28-32)
"Hunger for the Word" (Amos 8:11-14)
"God's Reluctant Messenger" (Jonah 3:1—4:3)
"From Bethlehem and Jerusalem" (Micah 5:2-5; 4:1-5)

Other Suggested Sermon Topics:

"Judgment Coming Near" (Amos 2)
"He That Reproveth" (Amos 5:10-15)
"God Like Mother" (Micah 7:18-20)
"The Great Stronghold" (Nahum 1:1-8)

QUESTIONS OVER JOEL THROUGH NAHUM

1. What will be poured out on all mankind? (Joel 2:28)
2. What did Israel not know how to do? (Amos 3:10)
3. What draws near on all nations? (Obadiah 15)
4. Where was Jonah to go? (Jonah 1:2)
5. What does the Lord require of man? (Micah 6:8)
6. What will people say about Nineveh? (Nahum 3:7)

THE DAY OF THE LORD
(Joel 2:27-32)

INTRODUCTION —
The Day of the Lord is theme of Joel's three chapters.

    A. Joel speaks with mixed emotions: "The Day of the Lord is great and terrible; and who can abide it?" (2:11).

    B. It is great with mercy to the penitent; it is terrible with judgment to the rebels against God.

I. JOEL'S MESSAGE COMBINES FIVE ASPECTS OF "THE DAY OF THE LORD"

    — The time of realizing God's presence with His people.

    A. It is the day when God pronounces judgment.

        1. He sits in judgment at "the Valley of Jehoshaphat" (the word means "Jehovah judges") where are gathered the nations of oppressors (3:2, 12).

        2. This is also called "the valley of decision" or "valley of determination" where the Divine Judge determines sentence on the sinners (3:14).

        3. Later tradition identified this valley with the Kidron Valley, or Hinnom.

        4. It is a terrible day for the sinner: "Alas for the day! for the day of the Lord is at hand, and as a destruction from the Almighty shall it come" (1:15).

    B. It is a day when God brings punishment.

        1. Chap. 1 describes a terrible plague of locusts which came as chastening for the sins of the nation.

        2. NASB speaks of "gnawing locust," "swarming locust," "creeping locust," "stripping locust" (1:4) and Chap. 2 speaks vividly of them as invading army.

        3. Joel 2:1, 2 speaks of a superlatively dark day.

        4. The beasts and the land suffer with the sinful people.

    C. It is a day for repentance and turning to God (2:12-17).

        1. Nation's leaders are to declare fasting, mourning, praying, and changing of ways.

        2. "Turn ye even to me with all your heart."

D. It becomes a day of God's relenting and bringing deliverance (2:18-27).
 1. Mercy, rather than destruction, accords with God's nature (v. 13).
 2. Deliverance and restoration may be promised confidently to the penitent.
 3. The beasts and the land shall share in prosperity.
E. It is a day when God's presence becomes evident in manifold wonders (2:28-31).
 1. God's Spirit made available to mankind.
 2. Visions and dreams, the means of divine revelation, experienced by young and old.
 3. Servants as well as masters will receive the divine presence.
 4. There is yet a final day of judgment, to be preceded by cataclysm.

II. THE GREAT DAY OF PENTECOST (ACTS 2) FULFILLS THE PROPHECY IN A SPECIAL WAY.
A. God's judgment was spoken in convicting the hearers of murdering His Son (22-36).
B. God's punishment had been borne by Christ, so "save yourselves from this . . ." (2:40).
C. God's offer of repentance became a focal point (2:37-39).
D. God's offer of salvation was confidently made and gladly received (2:38-41).
E. God's presence (visible in tongues of fire and audible in tongues of speech, for that occasion) was promised in less spectacular indwelling for all obedient believers.

CONCLUSION —

What does the Day of the Lord mean to you?
A. A generation tries to ignore God and shudders at the thought of His presence.
B. A people and a nation totter on the brink of destruction.
C. For repentance "Today is the day of salvation!"
D. Then the Day of the Lord is a time of supreme joy — "Even so come, Lord Jesus!"

HUNGER FOR THE WORD
(Amos 8:11-14)

INTRODUCTION —

Amos speaks of famine—it is a term not well known in America. It is not lack of television, autos, drinks. It is not *shortage* of the essentials—it is total lack of food.

Famine of the bread of life—see the story of Amos. (Man shall not live by bread alone.)

Israel had set up her calves to worship in Dan and Beersheba. She had neglected the moral law of God, guilty of sins of luxury and oppression. Amaziah had said of Amos, "The land is not able to bear all his words" (7:10). Amos says the unappreciated blessings shall be removed—famine. The people shall seek that which they have rejected, but not find it.

I. AMAZIAH COMPLAINS THAT THERE IS TOO MUCH OF GOD'S WORD IN ISRAEL.

Contrast: The word of Jehovah was precious in those days; there was no frequent vision (I Sam. 3:1).

A. Many things are little valued because they are with us all the time.

Air—how the trapped miners prayed for a breath!
Water—dust bowl picture shows a cow licking spigot of a dry pump.
Bread—Hungry men made soup of a mouldy loaf.
Home—last week a boy ran away for two days.
God and His Word—The godless lawyer seeks a place without a church; later sends back plea to preacher classmate to come and start one.

II. THE DESPISED BLESSING IS REMOVED—The time comes when the world is no longer heard.

A. Sometimes the action is deliberate—as a lawyer, or the one who "had too much church when he was a boy."
B. Sometimes it is hasty and rash, as one who breaks up a home in an angry quarrel.

C. More often it comes by long neglect.

Church—Ask your friends if they really want the doors closed.

Bible—How long would it take you to discover if someone substituted blank pages for the Word?

Prayer—How long since you availed yourself of the privilege?

Suppose that the things about which we complain were removed, one by one. . . .

III. THE LOSS IS FELT MOST KEENLY—a genuine famine.

A. A woman complains she can't pray—the minister forbids prayer—she comes back pleading to be released from the restriction.

B. "As the hart panteth after the water brooks, so panteth my soul after thee, O God.

My soul thirsteth for God, for the living God;

When shall I come and appear before God?"

(Psalm 42:1, 2).

IV. THERE IS SEEKING, BUT NOT FINDING, AND SUBSTITUTES WON'T SATISFY.

—One says after hearing a humanist sermon,

"They have taken away my Lord, and I know not where they have laid Him."

Carried to its limit, the picture of hell. The word is gone; God is gone; Christian friendship gone, beyond hope.

CONCLUSION —

At least twice God saw famine, and sent bread.

A. Manna in the wilderness.

B. "I am the living bread which came down out of heaven; if any man eat this bread, he shall live forever; yea, and the bread which I will give is my flesh, for the life of the world" (John 6:51).

What if the Christian gospel and the invitation were removed? They may be!

246

GOD'S RELUCTANT MESSENGER
(Jonah 3:1 — 4:3)

INTRODUCTION —

A. Whose preaching brought salvation?
   A popular professor made sport of Jonah as a "minus prophet," wholly wrong in his attitude and approach. But whose preaching brought salvation to Nineveh?

B. Jonah's reluctance understandable.
   1. What other prophet went to a foreign enemy capital, or vastly differing language, culture, and religion?
   2. Jonah was of Gath Hepher, north of Nazareth; hence acquainted with cruel raids of the Assyrians from the north.
   3. Nineveh described in Nahum 3:1: "Woe to the bloody city! It is all full of lies and robbery."
   4. Nineveh prepared? "Just before Jonah's time Assyria was torn by internal strife, weakened by revolt, and suffering from plague and famine." So God sent Jonah. . . .

I. JONAH RELUCTANT TO GO; BUT HE WENT (v. 1).

A. Difficulty evident in cultural differences.

B. Danger seen in announcing judgment on streets of the cruel enemy's capital city.

C. Distaste evident in Jonah's attitude (chap. 4).

D. Consider our own reluctance to "go where You want me to go."
   1. What is it that you don't want to do, so put off to another time?
   2. Do you say, or feel, with Jonah, "I'd rather die" (4:3)?
   3. Do you find some "necessary" other work to occupy your time and salve conscience?
   4. Do you say, "I have some things I need to straighten out first"? — Then find sympathy for, and instruction from, Jonah.

247

II. JONAH RELUCTANT TO PREACH GOD'S MESSAGE, BUT HE PREACHED IT (1:2; 3:2).
   A. God's prescribed message.
      1. Judgment: "Cry against it, for their wickedness is come up before me" (1:2).
         Nineveh shall be overthrown" (3:4).
      2. More? "Proclaim to it the proclamation which I am going to tell you" (3:2, NASB).
         a. The Ninevites learned somewhere that if they would repent, God might relent!
         b. Where did they learn about repentance and forgiveness? From Jonah?
   B. Ninevites' response indicates something of the message.
      1. They believed God ("Believed in God"—3:5, NASB).
      2. They fasted and wore sackcloth, expressing remorse.
      3. They heeded their king's proclamation "Let men call on God earnestly that each may turn from his wicked way" (3:8, NASB). "God saw their works" (v. 10). The message brought works of faith.

III. JONAH RELUCTANT TO ACCEPT GOD'S GENEROSITY (3:10; 4:1-3).
   A. Of what was Jonah afraid?
      1. Of failure, such as indicated in Isaiah 6:9-12?
      2. Or of success? That "those people" may become God's people and take over our church.
   B. Jonah's spirit still in rebellion.
      1. From the first he had known, and disagreed with God's grace, mercy, kindness.
      2. More concerned with pride than with salvation.
   C. Jonah faced the challenge of God's question.
      1. "Art thou greatly angry?" (4:4, 9, marginal reading).
      2. The Ninevites had only enjoyed the same divine grace that Jonah had known in rescue from the great fish: "Salvation is of the Lord" (2:7, 9).
   D. Did Jonah come to share God's care for people?

CONCLUSION —

God's obedient curmudgeon achieved divine purposes despite his reluctance. We, too.

FROM BETHLEHEM AND JERUSALEM
(Micah 5:2-5; 4:1-5)

INTRODUCTION —

    A. As Jonah was God's reluctant messenger, so was Israel.

    B. Micah chides them for their failure to make God known to the world. Predicts the punishment that follows their failure.

    C. There shall be the remnant and Messiah's kingdom, through whom God will accomplish His purpose.

I. BETHLEHEM, THE HOME OF THE SHEPHERD KING.

    A. Historically, Saul the first king had been a failure through disobedience. —David, the shepherd of Bethlehem, was chosen to lead in God's power. (One who would feed the flock rather than fleece it.)

    B. Prophetically, the kings have failed, since they depend on might, not on God. —The Great Shepherd shall be raised up, from Bethlehem.

        1. His goings forth are from of old
"In the beginning was the word" (John 1:1).
"Before Abraham was, I am" (John 8:58).

        2. (God) will give them up, until the great birth—400 silent years.

        3. He shall feed his flock
"I am the Good Shepherd" (John 10:14).

        4. He shall be great unto the ends of the earth—
"Go into all the world" (Mark 16:15).

        5. This man shall be our peace—"Prince of peace." (See Eph. 2:14-18.)

II. JERUSALEM, THE PLACE OF THE GOING FORTH OF THE GOSPEL.

    A. Following Messiah, the word shall go forth to all the world.
"Then opened he their mind, that they might understand the scriptures and he said unto them, Thus it is written, that the Christ should suffer and rise again

249

from the dead the third day; and that repentance and remission of sins should be preached in his name unto all the nations, beginning from Jerusalem" (Luke 24:45-47).
Compare events of the Day of Pentecost.
B. "They therefore that were scattered abroad went everywhere preaching the word" (Acts 8:4).
C. Thus, the "old Jerusalem Gospel" — That which went forth from Jerusalem. It is in this Gospel, and this alone, that God's plan lies. — The nations shall go to it for instruction. — Thus they come to the Bible as God's Word.

III. THE PROPHECY OF PEACE.
A. God is the judge — let men put aside vengeance. (See Rom. 12:17-21.)
B. The present situation causes many to be cynical.
— the proof lies in the accomplishment.
1. He has made peace between Jew and Gentile *in Him.*
2. He has made peace between nations. — Witness 3000 miles unarmed border Canada — U.S.
— "Christ in the Andes."
3. He has made peace and brought salvation to each individual who would receive.

CONCLUSION —

The gift is available; some have received it. It is not forced upon any; multitudes reject. What about you?

PREACHING THROUGH HABUKKUK, ZEPHANIAH, HAGGAI, ZECHARIAH, AND MALACHI

The reading of these books is like taking a trip, in which much of the scenery is ordinary, but where one occasionally comes suddenly on a view of breath-taking splendor. These views are abundant reward for the journey.

Habakkuk prophesied in the days of Jeremiah, about 625-605 B.C. He spoke of the coming Chaldean invasion of Judea, and of the later destruction to come upon the Chaldeans themselves. From him comes the thought which Paul later adopted as the theme for the Book of Romans: "The righteous by faith shall live!"

Zephaniah, a descendant of King Hezekiah and therefore distant cousin of King Josiah, prophesied in Josiah's time, about 610 B.C. telling of the coming day of God's judgment on Judah. His message seems to have had much to do with the reformation accomplished by Josiah, and recorded in II Kings 22 and 23.

Haggai and Zechariah prophesied in Jerusalem nearly a hundred years later, about 520 B.C. The Babylonian captivity had come and passed according to the prediction of God's early messengers, and now the people of Israel had returned to a ruined city to build again. These prophets spoke especially to urge the rebuilding of the Temple. Zechariah's series of sermonic visions include brilliant flashes of Messianic prophecy, including the fact of Christ's atoning death and amazing details related to it.

Malachi, speaking in Jerusalem in the days of Ezra and Nehemiah, not long before 400 B.C., gave God's final Old Testament message and warning to a disobedient nation. In it he shows how the people continue to show disrespect to God, even while following the forms of religion. He speaks of the coming day of the Lord, and of the messenger who shall be sent to prepare His way.

Commencement! This month's study brings to an end a four year course. Since then our Bible "Books of the Month," alternating between Old Testament and New, have covered the entire Bible, the New Testament being reviewed a second time during the latter half of the Old Testament study. This plan is completed,

251

but it has furnished only a sketchy introduction to the wonders and beauties of God's Word. Now is the time to commence studying the Bible with constantly greater enjoyment.

Sermon Outlines Provided:

"Yet I Will Rejoice" (Hab. 3:16-19)
"Time to Build" (Hag. 1:1-11)
"Thy King Cometh" (Zech. 9:9, 10)
"Who? Me? In Default to God?" (Mal. 3:7-12)

Other Suggested Sermon Topics:

"The Woes Men Work For" (Hab. 2:4-20)
"God's Pure Language" (Zeph. 3:9-20)

QUESTIONS OVER HABAKKUK THROUGH MALACHI

1. What nation does God tell Habakkuk he is going to raise up against Israel? (Hab. 1:6)
2. By what will the righteous live? (Hab. 2:4)
3. Under what conditions would Habakkuk still rejoice in the Lord? (Hab. 3:17-18)
4. What kind of a day would the great day of the Lord be? (Zeph. 1:14-18)
5. What will God do to all of the gods of the earth? (Zeph. 2:11)
6. What did Haggai tell the people God wanted them to do? (Hag. 1:7-8)
7. What did God say was abiding in the midst of His people? (Hag. 2:5)
8. Whom does God say He is going to bring in? (Zech. 3:8)
9. What are some of the things the Lord says He hates? (Zech. 8:16-17)
10. What wages did Zechariah receive and what did he do with them? (Zech. 11:12-13)
11. What is God's attitude toward divorce? (Mal. 2:16)
12. How did God's people rob Him? (Mal. 3:8-9)
13. Whom is God going to send before the coming of the day of the Lord? (Mal. 4:5)

YET WILL I REJOICE
(Habakkuk 3:16-19)

INTRODUCTION —

A funeral service opened with "Praise God from Whom . . ."
   A. This is the tone of Habakkuk's conclusion.
   B. The book, from the time, and in the spirit, of Jeremiah.
      1. God reveals that He raised up the Chaldeans to punish Judah.
      2. Habakkuk remonstrates, "How shall the godless prevail?"
      3. God replies that He will use, then destroy, Chaldea.
         —Woes against the cruel, idolatrous nation.
      4. Song of God's greatness and final justice. Now read 3:16-19.

I. FAILURES ON EARTH (vv. 16, 17).
   A. Failure in the affairs of men (v. 16, from ASV for clarity).
      —The prophet dreads, and is helpless before, the coming invasion.
      1. Fear makes him physically weak and ill.
      2. He can do nothing but await the calamity.
      3. We share his sense of dread when we see the collapse of authority around us, the decay of morals among us, and the pressures of advancing Sovietism.
      4. Yet we can at least pray!
   B. Failure in the world of nature—famine (v. 17).
      1. This is generally considered to be the province of God; has God himself failed?
      2. Described is agricultural plight as bad as farmers habitually say it is!
         a. Fruit failure (from blossom to harvest, from Washington apples to Florida citrus).
         b. Fields failure (no wheat, soybeans, or corn!).
         c. Flock failure (no beef or pork in the grocery cases this winter).
      3. Where shall we turn?

253

II. FAITH IN HEAVEN (vv. 18, 19).

   A. What will I do? Rejoice in the Lord! (v. 18).

      1. It is easier for Christians: "We glory in tribulation also. . . . For when we were yet without strength, in due time Christ died for the ungodly" (Rom. 5:2-6). "Rejoice in the Lord alway: and again I say, Rejoice" (Phil. 4:4, from Paul in prison to a church in poverty).

      2. (A city, New York, distraught at the news of President Lincoln's assassination, is brought to calm by James A. Garfield's shouted assurance, concluding, "God is in Heaven, and the government in Washington still stands.")

   B. What has God done to give me that assurance? (v. 19).

      1. He *is* my strength.

         a. The eternal *I AM* is untouched by the changes of earth.

         b. His creative power is available.

         (Arkansas country editor Jack Blanton printed in his weekly newspaper a prayer for rain, explaining to God that his readers knew the power of God, and how to avail themselves of it in prayer for themselves, but most would rather do without rain than go to the trouble.)

      2. He *makes* me to stand and to walk.

         —Again as Christians we have an advantage: "I can do all things through Christ which strengtheneth me" (Phil. 4:13).

CONCLUSION —

From Mark 14:26—The Lord's and apostles' hymn of praise between the betrayal-departure of Judas in the upper room and the agony and betrayal in Gethsemane:

"O give thanks unto the Lord, for he is good: because his mercy endureth for ever. . . . The Lord is on my side; I will not fear: what can man do unto me?"

                    (The Hallel hymn, Psalm 118:1-6).

TIME TO BUILD
(Haggai 1:1-11)

INTRODUCTION —

The common cry, "If things were just different." Last week we discussed the prophet's response to the despair before the captivity—"Yet I will rejoice in Jehovah." Now the circumstances of the return—still counsels of despair. Important thing is, "If *people* were different."

I. THE STORY OF HAGGAI.

A. There were reasons for trepidation.
1. Seventy years' captivity had sapped the nation's vitality.
2. First return, 538 B.C.—Temple started 535. Foundations laid—jealous Samaritans wrote letters to Artaxerxes, who ordered the building ceased.
3. Fifteen years brought general decline of spirits, health, and prosperity.
4. There was failure of crops.
5. Darius of Persia ascended the throne—Haggai's message timely.

B. There was trepidation beyond reason.
1. "It is not the time to build the Lord's house." When would the time come? No plan, just "not now."

C. Haggai makes a comparison and a rebuke.
1. Citizens had used the intervening years to foster their own interests. Some had houses planked with cedar.
2. Business, home building, agriculture went on.

D. Haggai makes an explanation of their sorry lot.
1. National prosperity is tied to national righteousness.
"I pray that thou mayest prosper and be in health, even as thy soul prospereth" (III John 3:2).
2. Human life is not satisfied with material things alone. "Is not the life more than meat and the body more than raiment?" (Matt. 6:25).

255

3. Big income is not necessarily prosperity. "He that earneth wages earneth wages to put into a bag with holes."

E. Haggai makes practical exhortation—"Seek ye first the kingdom of God" (Matt. 6:33).

1. There the Temple was the symbol of their love of God.

2. Go up to the mountain, get timber, build the house.

F. Results.

—Within 24 days building was recommenced. Finished in four years. Became center of national life.

II. FOR US.

A. Trepidation.

1. Change of ministry—"Just when we begin to get acquainted!" —"There never will be one to take his place." "It's going to cost so much more than we thought."

2. You can't do much in election year, anyway.

3. Building needs limiting growth.

B. Comparison.

1. Churches do grow with new or old leadership.

2. Business, work, and home building go on according to desire.

C. Explanation.

1. The right kind of zeal, enthusiasm, labor will make right circumstance.

2. Doing nothing will never bring it about.

3. So the individual with Christ, or the nation—conditions are never permanently better till in Christ.

CONCLUSION —

Exhortation—

1. Back up committees - pulpit - building planning, finance.

2. Enter boldly into that long-intended commitment to personal service in Christ.

256

THY KING COMETH
(Zechariah 9:9-10)

INTRODUCTION —

There was the sound of working again on Mt. Zion as Zerubbabel's temple arose.

In the city, the voice of Haggai, reminding of the glories of the former Temple, and urging that the glory of God be not forsaken.

Now the visions of Zechariah, speaking of those glories.
— There was the building of the Temple.
— More importantly there was the building of a Kingdom.

Flashes of the Messiah.

I. THE COMING OF KINGS IN GREAT PROCESSION
   A. Glorious to be among the victorious soldiers, but—
      The captives and victims, the seamy side of their triumph.
      The slaves brought back to wear out a dreary living death.
   B. So came the conquering human kings.
      Shalmanezer had returned in triumph to Damascus after Samaria's fall.
      Nebuchadnezzar, with the smoke of Jerusalem's ruin still about him, to Nineveh.
      Cyrus of Persia, with the tokens of his conquest over Assyria.
      Now Darius, who commanded that the obstructions to building be removed.
   C. God's kind of King goes beyond that. . . .

II. THY KING COMETH
   A. "The scepter shall not depart from Judah, nor the ruler's staff from between his feet,
      Until Shiloh come,
      And unto him shall the obedience of the peoples be.
      Binding his foal unto the vine

257

And his ass's colt unto the choice vine;
He hath washed his garments in wine,
And his vesture in the blood of grapes"
(Gen. 49:10, 11 — Jacob's blessing).

B. Just, and having salvation—How different from the wicked pride of many.

How shall one reconcile the two—*justice* and *salvation*?
"For the showing of his righteousness at the present season: that he might himself be just, and the justifier of him that hath faith in Jesus" (Rom. 3:26).

C. Lowly—How reconcile with the vain pomp and boastings of the kings?

"I am meek and lowly in heart, and ye shall find rest unto your souls" (Matt. 11:29).
"He that would be greatest among you, let him be your servant" (Matt. 20:26).
(Scene in the upper room, with the basin and towel).

D. Riding upon an ass.

1. The beast much respected—the useful servant of all. Contrast the horse, prize of the few, and worker of war. He shall come in peace.
2. Even upon a colt, the foal of an ass.
—His is the mark of purity—completely fulfilled in the Entry into Jerusalem.

III. THE FINAL COMING

A. The horse, chariot, and battle bow removed—coming in peace (Eph. 2:13-17).

B. His dominion from the River (Euphrates) to the ends of the earth.

"Make disciples of all nations" (Matt. 28:19).

CONCLUSION —

Thy King cometh!
Has your King come?

258

WHO? ME? IN DEFAULT TO GOD?
(Malachi 3:7-12)

INTRODUCTION —

    A. John Doe is stopped by a policeman and responds with injured innocence: "What did I do wrong?"

    B. When God, through His messenger Malachi, reminded His people of His patience and their manifold sins of selfishness and indifference, they responded again and again with injured innocence, "Wherein have we . . .?"

I. YOU ROBBED ME (GOD) IN WITHHOLDING TITHES AND OFFERINGS (vv. 7, 8).

    A. The paying of tithes was a national obligation.
        1. It had been accepted by Jacob (Gen. 28:20-22).
        2. It was made obligatory under Moses (Lev. 27:30).
        3. It was Israel's way of acknowledging material dependence upon God.

    B. Withholding, or defaulting upon an accepted contractual obligation becomes robbery, the appropriation to oneself of what belongs to another. (The Internal Revenue Service takes action against the tax defaulter.)

    C. So the people used God's money to finish off their own houses while His temple was neglected (Hag. 1:4, 9) and His ministry was unsupported (Neh. 13:10).

    D. What of our obligations to God as Christians?
        1. First is the giving of self to God in Christ (Rom. 12:1).
        2. It is as binding as taxes, (see Matt. 22:21).

II. YOU WERE CURSED (v. 9).

    A. Material robbery brought material affliction.
        1. Failure of field crops and vintage (v. 11).
        2. Haggai 1:6 and II Chronicles 7:13 describe this material curse: — Drought, locusts, pestilence, and lack of enjoyment in material things.

    B. What happens to Christians who renege on their commitments to God?
        1. Paul cites sickness and death of those who commune, "not discerning the Lord's body" (I Cor. 11:29, 30).

2. Even our hymns bewail the misery of those who "left their first love" (Rev. 2:4, 5). "Where is the blessedness I knew when first I saw the Lord?

III. MAKE GOOD ON YOUR OBLIGATION! (v. 10).
   A. God (through Malachi) commanded, "Bring all the tithes into the storehouse."
      1. It was needed for support of Temple and priesthood.
      2. It was needed as a symbol of God's relation to Israel.
      3. It was needed especially for renewal of relationship with God by His people.
   B. Even Christians are urged to bring money "as the Lord has prospered" (I Cor. 16:1, 2).
      1. This was for relief fund for poor in Jerusalem.
      2. Procedure is like "Faith-Promise," as God enables.
   C. The bringing of self is most important (II Cor. 8:5).
      1. "Now I belong to Jesus."
      2. This includes my time, pride, and ambition.

IV. YOU SHALL BE BLESSED (vv. 10-12).
   A. Malachi promised material blessings in abundance.
      1. This would prove that God was in it.
      2. It would become a testimony to the nations.
   B. Should Christians expect prosperity for faithfulness?
      1. Some cite the economic stability of tithers, and promise satisfaction in tithing.
      2. Kansas farmer, enthusiast for missions, says crops and markets have become more favorable. "If God sees fit to work things out for me, I'm grateful; but to take this as a way to financial success would be using God to improve your bank account; and that's all wrong. Love and serve Him for His sake, not for money!"
   C. The greater blessing: "Jesus' love is sweeter, Sweeter as the years go by."

CONCLUSION —

From Psalm 23: "I shall not want . . . My cup runneth over . . . Goodness and mercy shall follow me . . . and I shall dwell in God's house for ever!"

PREACHING THROUGH MATTHEW
THE GOSPEL

Read it!   Love it!   Live it!   Share it!

The most important part of the Bible is that which tells of Jesus Christ, who reveals God to man, saves by His sacrifice, and leads by His teachings and example. Without a thorough acquaintance with Him, as He is revealed in the Gospels of Matthew, Mark, Luke, and John, an intelligent Christian faith is impossible.

THE MESSAGE AND METHOD OF MATTHEW

The message of Matthew is that Jesus is the Messiah, sprung from the kingly line of David, and promised by the prophets. The Jews' Messiah becomes our Christ, as the words directed to the children of Israel come also to us.

Matthew builds around the confession of Christ as Messiah, as that confession was voiced by the apostle Peter (Matt. 16:13-20).

Leading up to this point, Matthew dwells much on the teachings and the miracles of Jesus, especially in Galilee.

After this point, the emphasis is on the opposition to Jesus (Matt. 16:21ff.), leading to His suffering, death, and resurrection. One-third of the book deals with the last week before the resurrection.

This plan prepares for the giving of the great commission (Matt. 28:18-20), which says that believers are to be brought first to a public acceptance of Christ, and then to be taught "all things whatsoever I have commanded."

PASSAGES TO MEMORIZE

Portions of the Sermon on the Mount   Matt. 5-7
The Great Invitation   Matt. 11:29
The Good Confession   Matt. 16:13-20
The Great Commandment   Matt. 22:37-40
The Great Commission   Matt. 28:18-20

Sermon Outlines Provided:

"Our Bread, Our Debts, Our Temptations" (Matt. 6:9-15)
"Where Your Treasure Is" (Matt. 6:19-21)
"The Power and Authority of Christ" (Matt. 8:1-22)

261

"Help Wanted" (Matt. 9:36—10:7)
"Time of Refreshment" (Matt. 11:25-30)
"Wise Men Listen" (Matt. 18:1-6)
"An Ordinance of Joy" (Matt. 26:17-29)
"Appointment in Galilee" (Matt. 28:7, 10, 16-20)
"The Life of a Christian—As a Disciple" (Matt. 28:18-20)

Other Suggested Sermon Topics:

"Fulfilling All Righteousness" (Matt. 3:13-17)
"Really Well Off" (Matt. 5:1-11)
"Walking on Troubled Water" (Matt. 14:22-33)
"Christ, the Unchanging Creed" (Matt. 16:13-21)
"When Forgiving Means Something" (Matt. 18:23-35)
"The Heat of the Day" (Matt. 20:1-16)
"He Shall Come to Judge" (Matt. 25:31-46)
"Thy Will Be Done" (Matt. 26:36-45)

QUESTIONS OVER MATTHEW

1. Who named Jesus? (1:20-25)
2. Why did Joseph and Mary take their child to Egypt? (2:13)
3. At Jesus' baptism what did God say from heaven? (3:17)
4. What is promised to the poor in spirit? (5:3)
5. How did Jesus describe a wise man? (7:24)
6. What was Matthew's occupation? (9:9)
7. Who requested John the Baptist's head? (14:8)
8. Quote Peter's great confession. (16:16)
9. Name the five people with Jesus on the Mount of Transfiguration? (17:1-3)
10. Whom did Jesus tell to "Go, sell that which thou hast and give to the poor"? (19:16-22)
11. What did Jesus say was "the first and great commandment?" (22:37, 38)
12. In whose house did the woman anoint Jesus with ointment? (26:6, 7)
13. What happened to the money Judas received for betraying Jesus? (27:6, 7)
14. What was done to prevent the soldiers from telling about the resurrection? (28:12-15)

OUR BREAD, OUR DEBTS, OUR TEMPTATIONS
(Matthew 6:9-15)

INTRODUCTION —

- A. Riches respond to request.
    1. Teaching of prayer came in answer to disciples' prayer to Jesus (Luke 11:1).
    2. It becomes a living well of truth from which to draw from now on.
- B. In Jesus' words we see (1) ourselves, (2) our God, and (3) our need.

I. "NONE LIVETH TO HIMSELF," AND HERE NONE PRAYS BY HIMSELF.

- A. The language is no merely polite editorial "we."
    1. "When thou [one] prayest, enter into thy closet."
    2. "When ye [a number together] pray, say, 'Our Father . . .'"
    3. Jesus himself prayed personal, rather than corporate, prayers.
        a. "I thank thee, Father . . ."
        b. "I have finished . . . Glorify thou me."
- B. The requested bread is *ours*.
    — Family concern, rather than self-interest, is expressed.
- C. The debts here acknowledged are shared debts.
    — See Isaiah's sense of corporate responsibility, "Unclean lips" (Isa. 6:5).
- D. Temptation and deliverance involve the whole church.
    1. Need for mutual encouragement in assembly of the saints (Heb. 10:23-25).
    2. He who helps a brother's deliverance today may be helped by him tomorrow.

II. WHETHER WE LIVE, WE LIVE *UNTO THE LORD*.

- A. Prayer is to Him, or it is not prayer.
- B. Bread comes from Him; and rich experience comes from discovering that.

C. Sins' debts are owed to Him, and forgiveness has to come from Him (Psalm 51:4).
D. Temptations yield ultimately to no other power.
   —God provides the way of escape (I Cor. 10:13).
E. Without the confessional quality of dependence, any prayer insults God.
   1. He is not willing that any should perish, but desires that all should come *to repentance.*
   2. He loves too much to give the unlimited indulgence by which men destroy themselves.

III. WE SEE *OUR NEED*, AND ARE NOT PROVIDED A TOOL FOR SELF-INDULGENCE.
   A. Here is no encouragement to expect material "security" or unlimited forgiveness for repeated and unresisted sins.
   B. A Laodicean church (Rev. 3:14-22) will not really pray for daily bread.
      1. "The world is too much with us" in emphasis on material security for the church.
      2. Dependence on denominational efficiency does not fit with this prayer.
   C. The prayer for forgiveness demands corporate humility and patience.
   D. The prayer for deliverance destroys the luxury of self-indulgent sin.

CONCLUSION —

In this prayer the church may have an experience like that of John and Andrew (John 1:35-40). Following Christ, we should learn where He dwells. Christ has invited, "Come and see!" This is where He lives!

264

WHERE YOUR TREASURE IS
(Matthew 6:19-21)

INTRODUCTION —

Two things are tied to "first day of the week": Lord's Supper and "Lay by in Store."

Jesus is talking about stewardship—the recognition of God's ownership of all. Most of what we hear about stewardship is complaint. We shall not complain about churches and missions neglected; they get on amazingly well. Jesus said almost nothing about the support of religious institutions, a little about giving to the poor; but much about generosity from the giver's standpoint.

I. LAY NOT UP FOR YOURSELVES TREASURES ON EARTH.
   A. Why? The results are unsatisfactory to the one who lays up.
   B. It is not a sound investment.
      1. See methods of hoarding in his day — fabrics, jewels, spices. — Adobe buildings offered poor protection ("dig through").
      2. "Labor not to be rich; cease from thine own wisdom. Wilt thou set thine eyes upon that which is not? For riches certainly make themselves wings; they fly away as an eagle toward heaven" (Prov. 23:4, 5).
      3. "Ye have sown much, but bring in little; ye eat, but ye have not enough; ye drink, but ye are not filled with drink; ye clothe you, but there is none warm; and he that earneth wages earneth wages to put into a bag with holes" (Haggai 1:6).
   C. Is it a better investment now?
      1. Inflation shows how fleeting is wealth.
      2. The government guarantees everything, but now the government bonds will buy less than the money put into them.
   D. Though the treasure remain and grow for all time, it is still temporary.

1. (Illus.) — Story of silk manufacturer who gave $25,000 for church organ; later failed and became custodian of the church. What he gave was all he had left!

E. The laying up of earthly treasure is soul-shrinking. "Covetousness, which is idolatry" (Col. 3:5).

II. LAY UP FOR YOURSELVES TREASURES IN HEAVEN . . . Why?

A. It is an experience satisfactory where the other is unsatisfactory in each point.

B. "He that giveth to the poor lendeth to God, and He shall recompense him."

C. It is an investment permanent for time and eternity. Fable of the rich and poor in heaven "We built with what you sent up."

B. It is an enriching experience of fellowship with Christ. "Though he was rich yet for your sakes he became poor" (II Cor. 8:9).

Paul — "For whom I suffered the loss of all things, and do count them but refuse, that I may gain Christ" (Phil. 3:6).

"Must I be giving again and again?
'O no,' said the angel, piercing me through.
'Just give till the Master stops giving to you.'"

III. WHERE YOUR TREASURE IS, THERE WILL YOUR HEART BE ALSO.

A. So true it needs only to be said. Perhaps you scan the market page for a certain line. It represents your investment.

B. There is the tragedy of a nation which has its heart in the liquor business eight times as much as in Heaven.

C. There is the need for every person to be included. Washerwoman in Richmond, "No one else can express my love to my Lord; so don't tell me not to give!"

D. "This is life eternal, that they may know Thee, the only true God" (John 17:3).

CONCLUSION —

"First they gave their own selves to the Lord" (II Cor. 8:1-5).

266

THE POWER AND AUTHORITY OF CHRIST
(Matthew 8:1-22)

INTRODUCTION —

See the conclusion of the Sermon on the Mount "He taught as one having authority." Chapter eight records a series of events which serve to illustrate—"All authority hath been given unto me—" Read Matthew 8:18-22.

I. CHRIST'S POWER OVER THINGS.
  A. Physical illness.
    1. The leper (vv. 2-4).
      a. Leprosy healed only by divine power.
      b. The leper recognized Jesus' power, but did not know His love. "If thou wilt, thou canst make me clean."
      c. Jesus touched him. Christ's power to heal was greater than the power of leprosy to defile.
    2. The centurion's servant (vv. 5-13).
      a. Here the power was exerted over a distance from where He was.
      b. The centurion knew what authority was. He commanded soldiers and servants, and they obeyed. He knew that Christ had the same power to command the disease and cause it to depart.
    3. Simon's wife's mother (vv. 14, 15).
      a. She was healed immediately with a touch.
      b. She who had been ministered to, now arose to minister.
  B. The natural world (vv. 23-27).
    1. Description of the sudden storm on Galilee.
    2. The apostles, with a lifetime on the lake, were afraid of *this* one.
    3. They knew His power and called on Him for help.
    4. The raging sea lay down quietly at the command of its Maker.
    5. The amazement of the apostles established the miraculous fact.

C. The spirit world—Healing of the Gadarenes (vv. 28-34).
  1. The demons recognized Him, knew His power.
  2. They knew that He would defeat them, but hoped it would be "later."
  3. They made their request before He spoke.
  4. His one word "Go" was enough. They obeyed instantly without question.

(Transition seen in the response of the citizens of Gadara, and the fact that Jesus acceded to their request to leave their borders. His power gives Him a right to command men, but his authority over people is a different sort.)

II. CHRIST'S AUTHORITY OVER MEN.
  A. It must be voluntarily accepted (vv. 18-20).
    1. His reply to the scribe indicated that He would have no blind, or forced, following.
    2. To force a man is to destroy his humanity.
    3. Thus the essential evil of infant "baptism," in which the unknowing infant is brought against his will, or without it.
    4. The Lord's army is made of volunteers, not draftees.
  B. Christ's authority is absolute (vv. 21-22).
    1. It is more important than the claims of one's own family.
    2. It must come above friends, business, property, or life itself.

CONCLUSION —

"The dearest idol I have known, whate'er that idol be,
Help me to tear it from Thy throne, and worship only Thee!"

268

HELP WANTED!
(Matthew 9:36—10:7)

INTRODUCTION —
Two items have called my attention to this Scripture:

I. *Christian Standard* survey of growing churches.
   A. Looked into churches that reported baptism (3 months) in large promotion to membership.
   B. Asked them, "To what do you attribute your growth?" 92 were asked; 49 answered—All over the country, all sizes, city/rural, old/new.
   C. "Visitation," "involvement," "commission centered," "people had a mind to work."
II. *Lookout* article on Sunday Schools, "not growing" and "growing."
   A. Inward-focused schools shrinking.
   B. "Outreaching" schools growing.

Read Matthew 9:37, 38.

I. THE HARVEST INDEED IS PLENTEOUS.
   (Cf. John 4:35: "Say not ye, there are yet four months, and then cometh harvest? behold, I say unto you, Lift up your eyes, and look on the fields; for they are white already to harvest.")
   A. What harvest? (Kansas spoke of "harvest" beginning mid-June. That was wheat. They never spoke of "wheat harvest." They grew corn, beans, etc., too. But "harvest" was wheat.)
      1. So Jesus, who came to seek and to save the lost—that was harvest! That was what He did. (See Matt. 9: concluding with 35, 36.)
      2. He invites us to share that enthusiasm; or what will we talk with Him about forever in glory?
   B. Need we document the millions needing the gospel now? (Some resistant fields.) But what about the lonely, purposeless neighbor? (Some shattering grain.)

II. THE LABORERS ARE FEW.
   A. Here is the *want*—the need/lack—in "help wanted."

269

B. Jesus' experience: multitudes followed to hear, see miracles, receive benefit.
— They were the harvest that needed to be brought in. But where were the ones who would bring them?

C. So today the large attendances in church, including those who wish to be religious without being involved in religion. The laborers are still few!

III. PRAY YE THE LORD OF HARVEST.

A. It's His enterprise; talk to Him about it!

B. What about the appeal letters that request prayer first? Religious gimmickery? But would you charge Jesus with religious gimmickry?
(Cf. Earl Hargrove's request for Lincoln Bible Institute: "If we get folk to give to the Lord, and if we serve the Lord, we'll get our share.")

C. So also the growing churches report, "God's power, God's Word, God's Spirit."

IV. PRAY THAT HE WILL SEND FORTH LABORERS INTO HIS HARVEST — HIS WORK, HIS APPOINTMENT.

A. "Whom shall I send, and who will go for us?" (Isa. 6:8).

B. This is not necessarily the time to hand out assignment cards.
(Do we pray that the committee will send forth laborers? The committee assigns, but few go. We need the motivation of God's sending!)

C. Some are afraid to join in the praying because they don't want to join in going. So help is still wanted, and wanting.

CONCLUSION —

Did the apostles pray as Jesus asked? At least, He followed up by saying "You go!" and they went. Those who went would be prepared to answer, "What will you talk with Jesus about forever in glory?" In life their praying has talked with Him about harvest. They'll pick up where they left off.

TIME OF REFRESHMENT
(For a Bible College Dinner)
(Matthew 11:25-30)

INTRODUCTION —

A. It is appropriate to speak of refreshment at a dinner. Observe, "restaurant" — a place for being restored.
B. For sheer restorative quality nothing more dramatic than cold water for the sweating worker in the hayfield. He was ready to go back to work!
C. So Jesus called men — all men — to refreshment, in Him.
  1. "Rest" here is *anapausis:* "cessation, refreshment, rest."
  2. Not a rest from work, but *in* work.
  3. So Isaiah promised refreshment from the unfainting God to weary Israel (40:28-31).
    1. See Isaiah's fulfillment in Jesus: Soul refreshment is a learning experience.
    2. Come; take; learn? No! — "Come unto Me!" "Take My yoke!" "Learn of Me!"

I. COME UNTO ME — It wasn't a correspondence course.

A. Invitation inclusive, to those needing refreshment.
  1. Any selectivity was self-applied by prospects.
  2. Burdens and weariness well known:
    (Lyndon B. Johnson said of the day he left the White House that he felt as though a 100-pound sack of cement had been lifted off each shoulder.)
  3. Jesus may have referred to burdens of the law, increased by the weight of traditional obligations laid on by scribes and Pharisees (Matt. 23:4).
  4. Young people served by your college: burdened with personal past; perplexed present; problematical future.
B. Invitation personal and definite — "Unto Me."
  1. "Come and see" where and how I live (John 1:39).
  2. "Come and follow me," to rich young ruler.
  3. "Come ye after me, and I will make you . . ." to disciples (Mark 1:17).
  4. "Him that cometh to me I will in no wise cast out" (John 6:37).

II. TAKE MY YOKE UPON YOU — Not mere academic theory; Christ required commitment.

A. Christian college offers what no state university can: affirmative faith.

1. Teaching without religion is offering a world hollow at the core.

2. Teaching about religion is negative; detached objectivity is impossible.

3. (A judge, asked what was constitutionally acceptable in public schools, said, "If the ABC's are taught as devotion, it's unconstitutional."

The Christian college says, "If the ABC's are taught without devotion, it's unChristian!")

B. Christ's college offers partnership.

1. Contrast the Pharisees who refused the yoke; Christ came to earth to bear our burden.

2. "My yoke is easy" — well fitted to the shoulder.

3. "My burden is light" — bearable, according to bearer's developing strength.

III. LEARN OF ME — Otherwise you just don't know!

A. See preceding verses: "hid these things from the wise and prudent . . ."

— "Neither knoweth any man the Father, save the Son, and he to whomsoever the Son will reveal him."

B. Full curriculum:

1. Learn about Me: demonstration of life, "meek and lowly" — accessible.

2. Learn from Me: explanation of what has been seen: Christ preached what he practiced!

3. Learn with Me: realization from the yoke-fellow experience on the job.

CONCLUSION —

In Him is the boundless refreshement of life eternal and unwearied! "In him a well of water springing up into everlasting life" (John 4:14).

WISE MEN LISTEN
(Children's Day Sermon)

(Matthew 18:1-6; 11:25-30)

INTRODUCTION —

This nation has never needed its children more than now.
— Not with the idea of making soldiers or workers in future.
— We need them to teach us the qualities that make life worth while.

I. TURN, AND BECOME AS LITTLE CHILDREN.
   A. Childlike qualities needed for entrance to kingdom.
      1. Humility and innocent trust.
         — One would never be suspicious if he were never lied to.
         — He learns attitudes of superiority from his elders.
      2. Teachableness.
      3. Quickness to forgive.
      4. Enthusiasm — closely akin to consecration.
      5. Honesty.
   B. Warning against occasion of stumbling. — It is the adult who robs the child of these attributes.
      1. False example of parents and friends.
         "One hour in Sunday School can't compete with thirty godless hours at home."
      2. False teaching of "knowledge falsely so-called."
   C. Well-meaning parents rob children of heritage by hurrying them to grow up.
      1. "When I was a child I spake — understood as a child."
      2. Smoke — dress — hours — company — responsibility; all "rushed."
      3. (Illus.) — Alexander Campbell relatively slow growing up; he matured.

II. "THOU HAST HIDDEN THESE THINGS FROM THE WISE AND PRUDENT."
   A. Intelligent people need not be left out.
      1. Sir James Jeans, astronomer, a noted Christian.
      2. Borden P. Bowne, philosopher, also.

3. Roger Babson, business man, wrote of Christ and the Bible.
4. Prime Minister Churchill said he found the Bible far more accurate than many of the records of battles that happened today.

B. The Word must be approached as a revelation — to deny it raises more questions than it settles.
1. It must be approached for its message, and not for superstition.
2. The message is plain to those who read plainly.
   a. A decipherer of codes is stumped by message in plain language.
   b. "The purloined letter" is found in plain sight (Poe).
3. Peter and John before the council puzzle the doctors (Acts 4). — Farmer preachers in Restoration were the despair of the learned.

III. COME UNTO ME — and I will give you rest.

— Comfort possible to those who *humbly receive* the revelation.

A. Many would not listen to Old Testament prophets. "Thus saith the Lord, stand ye in the ways, and see, and ask for the old paths, where is the good way, and walk therein, and ye shall find rest for your souls. But they said, We will not walk therein. Also I set watchmen over you, saying, Hearken to the sound of the trumpet. But they said, We will not hearken" (Jer. 6:16, 17).

B. "We preach Christ crucified, unto the Jews a stumbling block and unto the Greeks foolishness; but unto them which are called . . . Christ the power of God . . ." (I Cor. 1:23, 24).

CONCLUSION —

The American woman who was proud of her skepticism lives in Berlin; at last finds life unbearable; goes to American church — small, unimpressive; ministered to by young man without outstanding talent — (the symbol of the weak power in the midst of puny might) and says, "We received it as a starving man takes food."

274

AN ORDINANCE OF JOY
(Matthew 26:17-29)

INTRODUCTION —

Matthew presents with great emphasis the death and resurrection of Jesus, as the fulfillment of prophecy; the trial and the glory of the Heavenly King.

The Lord's Supper presents, in form that all can understand, these great facts. It is a memorial ordinance, but not a memorial of sorrow to one who has gone on; a memorial of joy to One who lives.

I. IT IS AN ORDINANCE OF FELLOWSHIP WITH GOD IN CHRIST—"EMMANUEL."
   A. Its elements are of the humble common sort available to all men. So is Christ.
   B. We rejoice in the present fellowship of the great.
      (Illus.) In Revolutionary War, soldiers building a protective breastwork of logs against expected British attack. Corporal commanded "Heave ho," but a great log would not rise. A stranger on horseback came and helped to lift. In parting he identified himself as George Washington. Men cheered.
   C. Christ at the well—look at Him from the woman's point of view. He asked for water, and they fell into conversation—common language; common need. "If thou hadst known who it was that asked thee . . ." (John 4:10). The woman was changed from that day when He came asking for a drink.

II. IT IS AN ORDINANCE OF GENEROUS LOVE.
   A. "This is my body, which is given for you" (I Cor. 11:24).
   B. Nothing so cheers as love—nothing so depresses as hate or disregard.
   C. (Illus.) —The departing pastor in *How Green Was My Valley* gives his watch of the young boy he had befriended. The hours of every day took on more meaning as they were counted by the hands of that watch.

D. "The Good Shepherd giveth His life for the sheep" (John 10:11).
Which hour of His life could you say He claimed for Himself. The very hours of prayer were used that He might gain strength for service. "No man taketh it from me, but I lay it down of myself" (John 10:18).

III. IT IS AN ORDINANCE OF SPIRITUAL NOURISHMEN. "TAKE, EAT."

A. "My flesh is meat indeed, and my blood is drink indeed."
B. "Come unto me, all ye that labor and are heavy laden and I will give you rest. Take my yoke upon you and learn of me; for I am meek and lowly in heart; and ye shall find rest unto your souls" (Matt. 11:28, 29).
C. (Illus.) — The laborer in the field welcomes the waterboy, and the relief of a parched throat, aching muscles, dull weariness of spirit.
D. We — "Six days exposure to the full weight of the world's temptation; thorns and thistles springing in the hearts; the scattered wheat has been snatched from the heart by this bird and the other . . ." Sinking in the weight of world, we cry "Save, Lord, or I perish."

IV. IT IS AN ORDINANCE OF HOPE AND PROMISE: "I DRINK IT NEW WITH YOU IN THE KINGDOM."

A. "As oft as ye eat this bread and drink this cup ye do show the Lord's death, until he come" (I Cor. 11:26).
B. I think when I read that sweet story of old, when Jesus was here among men, How he called little children as lambs to His fold; I should like to have been with them then. I wish that His hands had been placed on my head; and His arms had been thrown around me, And that I might have seen His kind look when He said, "Let the little ones come unto me."

CONCLUSION —

He, the Host, at the final feast — "That they may be with me where I am."

APPOINTMENT IN GALILEE
(Matthew 28:7, 10, 16-20)

INTRODUCTION —

A. The visitor to Israel is shown the sacred scenes related to the passion of Christ — all in and around Jerusalem. Temple, *Via Dolorosa,* Holy sepulchre, (or Gordon's Calvary and the Garden Tomb), Gethsemane and Mount of Olives.

B. What, then, is the meaning of insistence on an appointment in *Galilee?* (The area bounding most of the Sea of Galilee — a hill country sixty to one hundred miles from Jerusalem. Hours by bus, or days walking.)

The appointment made in connection with prediction of death (Matt. 26:32). Reiterated by the angel at the tomb (28:7); repeated by Jesus (28:10). Some suggestions:

I. IT WAS HOME — THEIRS AND HIS.

A. Galileans not too highly regarded by sophisticated Judeans.

1. Mixed races, not highly cultured in speech, excitable emotionally, but a stout hearted, freedom loving people.

2. Those apostles could have been called "briar hoppers."

B. "When you go home, I'll be there ahead of you!" (Bethsaida, Capernaum, etc.) (cf. the scene at Emmaus).

II. IT WAS WHERE THEIR PEOPLE WERE — THEIRS AND HIS.

A. Andrew set the pattern, finding his brother Simon.

B. The healed demoniac was commanded to remain among his own people and tell what great things God had done for him.

C. So, apparently in Galilee, the five hundred brethren saw him at once, and some of them still doubted His resurrection.

D. "When you go among your own people, I'll be there ahead of you!"

277

III. IT WAS WHERE THEIR WORK WAS—THEIRS AND HIS.
  A. Levi (Matthew) the tax collector of Galilee (perhaps Capernaum). —A new work, keeping the accounts of the Savior. He it was who wrote of this appointment in Galilee.
  B. The four fishermen—Peter, Andrew, James and John "I will make you fishers of men" (Matt. 4:19). "Feed my lambs!" (John 21:15).
  C. In Galilee they shared His ministry of healing, teaching, serving. —Here is where you get down to work!
  D. "When you go to work, I'll be there ahead of you!"

IV. SO HE MADE AN APPOINTMENT TO MEET THEM ON A FAMILIAR MOUNTAIN—WHICH ONE?
  They knew and they met the appointment. That is enough.
  A. Mount of Transfiguration? "This is my beloved Son, hear ye Him" (Matt. 17:5). —"All authority hath been given unto me. . . ."
  B. Mount Hermon, near the scene of the Confession? —"On this rock I will build my Church"—"Go and make disciples of all nations, baptizing them in the name. . . ."
  C. Mount of Beatitudes (the Sermon)? —"Teaching them to observe all things, whatsoever I have commanded you."

CONCLUSION —

The closing scenes are in Judea, with ascension from the Mount of Olives, but they were not allowed to forget.

"When you go home, the risen Lord will be there ahead of you, and He has work for you to do, and He'll be right with you as you do it."

THE LIFE OF A CHRISTIAN—AS A DISCIPLE
(Matthew 28:18-20)

INTRODUCTION — How did we get that way?

   A. This is a key question to understanding any relationship or institution. — Nation, church, friendship, vocation, or business.

   B. So to understand our experience as Christians we refer to Christ's descriptive command through which we became Christians.

   C. *Disciple*—one who follows in order to learn, and learns in order to follow.

 I. THE BEGINNING OF DISCIPLESHIP—Recruitment.

   A. "Make learners"; but much of the initiative in learning is with the learner.

      1. "We are . . . present . . . to hear." (Cornelius and friends) (Acts 10:33).

      2. "They received the word with all readiness of mind, and searched the scriptures daily, whether those things were so" (Acts 16:11).

      3. (World War II instructor in aerial navigation attributed success to that first lecture: "There are two kinds of aerial navigators; good ones and dead ones." The students were motivated to learn!)

   B. The learning centers in Christ.

      1. "Take my yoke upon you, and learn of me" (Matt. 11:29).

      2. A believing person is the teacher, and the believed-in Person is the lesson.

   C. The learning focuses in commitment.

      1. Taking the yoke is the "following" in discipleship.

      2. Thus the command to baptize; but note the example at Pentecost that baptism was not for reluctant ones being pressured into it: "They that gladly received his word were baptized" (Acts 2:41).

 II. THE GROWTH OF DISCIPLESHIP—Received instruction.

   A. "Teaching them to observe all things . . . commanded."

1. Having learned about Jesus and confessed Him, we must learn from Jesus and follow Him.
2. They "continued steadfastly in the apostles' (teaching) and fellowship" (Acts 2:42).
3. When one ceases to be a learner he ceases to be a disciple.
4. Here is the message of the Sermon on the Mount, *to the disciples.*

B. This teaching also centered in the person of Christ.
   1. Rebuke to the Ephesians: "Ye have not so learned Christ" (4:20).
   2. The goal, "That I may know him, and the power of his resurrection, and the fellowship of his sufferings" (Phil. 3:10).

C. This learning also demands commitment.
   1. The learning is in order to "observe" (to do) what Christ commands.
   2. The sermon is not a good one until it is lived.
   3. See Hebrews 5 and I Corinthians 3 — the rebuke to those who must still be fed with spiritual milk.

III. THE FRUITION OF DISCIPLESHIP — The presence of the Lord, "with you always."
   1. Even beyond this life there is something to learn: "Then shall I know even as also I am known" (I Cor. 13:12).
   2. The beloved Person is the center of the promise, to "receive you unto myself; that where I am, there ye may be also" (John 14:3).
   3. They who have enjoyed a serving discipleship here will be prepared to glory in Heaven, where they "serve him day and night in his temple" (Rev. 7:15).

CONCLUSION —

The Commission promise is extended: "I am with you . . ." becomes "You shall be with me after the world has ended."

PREACHING THROUGH MARK

Of the four Gospels Mark gives the most concise account of the life and ministry of Jesus. For a re-reading of priceless records, and for new acquaintance with more of divine truth, we invite you to share in this reading.

This book was written, probably about 50 A.D. by John Mark, a friend and perhaps a convert of the Apostle Peter (I Pet. 5:13). He was a kinsman of Barnabas (Col. 4:10), and accompanied him on certain of his missionary tours (Acts 13:5; 15:37-39). Mark's mother owned a house in Jerusalem which was used as a meeting place for the church (Acts 12:12). A very early tradition outside the New Testament tells that Mark traveled much with Peter, and that, at the request of the people of the church, he wrote the things which Peter told concerning Jesus. Thus his record of the Gospel begins with the events which Peter witnessed (see Mark 1:29-31) and does not tell of the birth and early life of Jesus.

Mark wrote, apparently with the Roman people in mind, to tell of the power and divinity of Christ. Thus his Gospel—

1. Stresses the miracles which Jesus performed.
2. Explains Jewish words and customs, as to a people who did not know them.
3. Gives many intimate and interesting details, as they came from one who was there when these things happened.
4. Says little about the prophecies of the Messiah.
5. Includes only a few of the discourses of Jesus.

ANALYSIS OF THE BOOK

Chapter		
	1:1-13	Jesus' preparation for His ministry
	1:14 — 2:12	Early works and miracles
	2:13 — 6:5	Actions and attitudes which set Him apart from the religious leaders of His day.
	6:6 — 13:37	The main period of His ministry.
	14:1 — 15:47	Opposition, leading to the Crucifixion.
	16:1-20	The Resurrection, appearances, and Commission.

Sermon Outlines Provided:

"The Beginning of the Gospel" (Mark 1:1-15)
"He Knew Success" (Mark 1:35-39)
"The Harvest Depends on the Soil" (Mark 4:1-20, 26-33)
"You Give Them Something to Eat" (Mark 6:30-44)
"Command and Traditions" (Mark 7:1-13)
"He Does All Things Well" (Mark 7:31-37)
"Two Commands to the Christian" (Mark 12:28-34)
"They All Drank of It" (Mark 14:17-26)
"The Lonely Shepherd" (Mark 14:32-42)

Other Suggested Sermon Topics:

"Have You Never Read?" (Mark 2:25)
"Of Such Is the Kingdom" (Mark 10:13-16)
"God of the Living" (Mark 12:13-34)

QUESTIONS OVER MARK

1. For whom did Jesus say the Sabbath was made? (2:27)
2. In the parable of the sower Jesus said that when the word is sown in some hearts who takes it away? (4:15)
3. Name the brothers of Jesus listed in Mark 6:3.
4. Which disciple rebuked Jesus for saying He would be killed? (8:32)
5. What would be the measure of punishment for a person who caused a little one to stumble? (9:42)
6. Jesus said He came not to be ministered unto but to do what? (10:45)
7. What did Jesus reply to those who asked if it were lawful to pay tribute to Caesar? (12:17)
8. Who knows the time of the second coming of Christ? (13:32)
9. How did the disciples locate the room where they were to eat the Passover with Jesus? (14:13)
10. Pilate released what murderer to please the crowd? (15:15)
11. After His resurrection Jesus appeared to what woman from whom He had cast out seven demons? (16:9)

THE BEGINNING OF THE GOSPEL
(Mark 1:1-15)

INTRODUCTION — No wasted time in Mark's Gospel.

   A. Mark's is a bold, brief presentation of the Gospel, without unnecessary introduction.

   B. It stands as inspired rebuke to our tendency to believe what is not taught in the Word, and thus to crowd out the truth that is taught.

   C. Mark gets down to business in telling us how Christ got down to business.

I. THE LORD IS INTRODUCED (v. 1).

   A. Don't neglect the beginnings!

      1. If you would understand a person or an institution — or a gospel — find out how it all began.

      2. Genesis 1:1 and John 1:1 speak of the beginnings of the world and human life; Mark 1:1 speaks of the beginnings of salvation in Christ.

   B. The good news (gospel) begins with Christ; all else is prologue.

   C. The whole glory of Christ is declared at the beginning.

      1. Jesus, the prophet of Nazareth in Galilee is He of whom we speak.

      2. This Jesus is Christ, the promised Messiah, divinely anointed.

      3. This Jesus Christ is the only begotten Son of the living God.

         a. Matthew and Luke tell how God's Son came into the world.

         b. His Sonship is more than family resemblance; it is identity and partnership.

   D. Without this identity between God and man, there is no revelation of God's character or His love.

II. PROPHECY IS FULFILLED (vv. 2-8).

   A. Isaiah 40:3 announced the voice of preparation, and Malachi 4:5 (compare Luke 1:17) identified that voice with a later prophet coming in the spirit and power of Elijah.

B. The fulfillment of prophecy was so significant that Mark, who wrote for Romans (not specially interested in prophecy) still made an issue of it.

C. John the Baptist is boldly declared to have fulfilled the prophecies.

1. In his rough and vigorous way (v. 6) he was like Elijah.

•2. In preaching repentance he sounded the theme of the prophets.

3. In baptizing he added new force to the hearers' commitment. Repentance was more than a mere word, promise, or gesture; it was total involvement.

4. In declaring the supremacy of Christ, John fulfilled the promise of preparing the way (vv. 7, 8).

III. PREPARATION IS SEEN IN JESUS' EARLIEST ACTS (vv. 9-13).

A. He was baptized in the fulfillment of righteousness (vv. 9-11).

1. His was not a minimum ministry, but a maximum one.

2. He asks nothing that He has not led in doing.

3. He received the seal of divine approval for what He was and what He did.

4. Having obeyed (beyond necessity?), He was ready to command in God's name.

B. He was tempted, sharing the experience of those He came to save (vv. 12, 13).

1. "We have not an high priest which cannot be touched with the feeling of our infirmities, but was in all points tempted like as we are, yet without sin" (Heb. 4:15).

2. Temptation experience reaches all levels: Satan tempted; beasts (spiritually neutral) were there to observe; angels strengthened. So also our temptation

includes potential relationships all the way from Hell to Heaven.

IV. PREACHING THE PROMISE—THE GOSPEL IN MOTION (vv. 14, 15).

    A. This was the beginning; all else was preliminary.

    B. The King had come in His kingdom—Good news!

    C. Repentance was available—Good news! You don't have to stay lost!

CONCLUSION — The time is fulfilled!

    A. The gospel (good news) began in Judea when Christ preached and was heard.

    B. Good news begins for you and me when Christ enters our lives.

    —Now is the accepted time; . . . Now is the day of salvation (II Cor. 6:2).

HE KNEW SUCCESS
(Mark 1:35-39)

INTRODUCTION — Do we know what we want?

Some years ago a Bible college student spent time in a city bus station interviewing the waiting passengers with this question: "What do you want more than anything else in life?" The dominant replies centered around "success" and "happiness." "Success" was usually thought of in terms of wealth, popularity, and power.

Success, then, is the achievement of a goal. If you don't know the goal, you'll never know whether you are successful; and if you lose sight of the goal, you'll probably not reach it.

Our text finds Peter exulting in Jesus' popularity (success), and Jesus saying, "That's not my goal."

I. PETER ADMITS A WRONG VIEW OF SUCCESS.
   A. Mark's gospel reflects Peter's preaching.
      1. Papias (about 130 A.D.) quoted the testimony of an elder, saying, "Mark, having become Peter's interpreter, wrote all that he remembered (or all that Peter related) . . ."
      2. Peter thus did not spare himself, as his preaching included accounts of Jesus' repeated rebukes to his own faulty understanding.
   B. Mark's Gospel recounts confrontations between Peter and Jesus.
      1. Peter rebuked Jesus for talking about the cross; Jesus rebuked Peter as the tempter (Mark 8:31-39). (Success is not escaping trouble.)
      2. Peter would build tabernacles and stay on the mountain; God said listen to Jesus (Mark 9:2-8). (Success is not basking in the company of saints.)
      3. Peter boasted of unfaltering devotion; Jesus warned that Peter would deny (Mark 14:27-37). (Success is not self-assurance, nor wielding a sword against the enemy.)

286

C. Our text from Mark 1:35-39 indicates the first of such confrontations.
  1. Peter (and his friends) seem excited (elated) at Jesus' popularity. —Jesus' beginning ministry seems to have met with "instant success."
  2. Shortly afterward they saw that multitudes actually hampered Jesus' work (Mark 1:43-45).
  3. But didn't Jesus owe His public some attention? Why was He out here alone?
  4. Jesus said, "Let's leave the multitudes here and preach the kingdom in other towns; that's what I came for!"

II. JESUS DEMONSTRATED A RIGHT VIEW OF SUCCESS.
  A. He never forgot the purposes for which He came to earth (v. 38).
    1. "I must be about my Father's business" (Luke 2:49).
    2. "I came down from heaven, not to do mine own will, but the will of him that sent me" (John 6:38).
    3. "I am come that they might have life, and that they might have it more abundantly" (John 10:10).
    4. "The Son of man is come to seek and to save that which was lost" (Luke 19:10). (His purpose to seek men, rather than to have them seeking Him?)
    5. Jesus' wisdom is badly needed by:
      a. Students too busy with extracurricular activities to study!
      b. Teachers too busy promoting attendance, and so not having time to teach!
      c. Christians so busy making contacts for the Lord they never get around to using those contacts for persuading men of Christ.
  B. He never forgot the source of His power (v. 35).
    1. Prayer time and privacy were hard to come by. (Josephus' descriptions of Galilee indicate a fertile, intensively cultivated, and densely populated area, including 240 towns and villages and perhaps two

million population in the space of two or three small Ohio counties.)

2. Jesus "lost sleep" in the prayer support for His ministry. — Spiritual conditioning was more important than physical conditioning.

3. Notable servants of God such as John Wesley and Alexander Campbell have followed Jesus' example in the early morning prayer times, and youth in Christian camps will remember the "morning watch."

4. Whatever the time and place, the fact of prayer must not be neglected. The doer of God's will must have that constant relationship of self to God.

5. What seemed to Peter and the others a waste of time and a neglect of the people was actually the most valuable time towards serving the people!

C. Jesus worked at His task (v. 39).

1. Did He preach in 240 village and town synagogues? At least He covered the territory.

2. He laid down His life, day by day, for His people.

3. He felt strength go out of Him as He healed others (Mark 5:30).

4. How did He keep it up? Moved with compassion, He considered the needs of others rather than His own comforts and concerns (Matt. 9:36).

5. At last He could report ultimate success to the Father: "I have finished the work which thou gavest me to do" (John 17:4).

CONCLUSION — What, then, of our success?

A. The goal: "We make it our aim, whether at home or absent, to be well-pleasing unto him" (II Cor. 5:9, ASV).

B. The evidence of having reached the goal: "Well done, thou good and faithful servant."

THE HARVEST DEPENDS ON THE SOIL
(Mark 4:1-20; 26-33)

INTRODUCTION — Jesus' contact with the things of the soil

    A. Business affairs may change, but the matters of seed time and harvest, never.

    B. So the religion of Christ is more popular and better understood in the rural districts than in the cities.

I. THE LITTLE SEED AND LARGE HARVEST.

    A. The foolishness of preaching.

        1. Its disrepute in the modern world. The question remains, how shall they believe without hearing?

        2. "It pleased God by the foolishness of preaching to save them that believe" (I Cor. 1:21).

        3. "We preach Christ crucified, unto the Jews a stumbling block and unto the Greeks foolishness; but unto them which are called, both Jews and Greeks, Christ the power of God and the wisdom of God" (I Cor. 1:23, 24).

    B. The wise do not regard the littleness of the beginning in a forecast of the ending.

        1. Christ was not great as the world sees greatness.

        2. "Behold how great a matter a little fire kindleth!" (James 3:5).

    C. The little beginning of Paul's preaching at Lystra.

        1. Driven from Antioch and Iconium by the Jews.

        2. He heals the man lame from birth.

        3. The inhabitants would worship Paul and Barnabas as Apollo and Jupiter.

        4. Paul turns their attention to the true God.

        5. The Jews come, and Paul is stoned.

        6. Healed, he departs.

    D. The great shrub at Lystra

        1. When Paul next came to Lystra, there was a certain disciple named Timothy.

        2. Paul's lieutenant in all his missions.

        3. Trusted as an ambassador to Jerusalem.

    4. Left as director of affairs at Ephesus.

    5. Meanwhile sent to Philippi: (See Phil. 2:19-22).

E. But there were many at Lystra who saw the same things and heard the same preaching that Timothy did, and were left haters and hateful, blasphemers, and despisers.

II. THE HARVEST DEPENDS ON THE SOIL

We have spoken of the letter to the Philippians, a church in a town. As all churches, it had in it various people.

A. The seed that fell by the wayside

    1. Paul heals the girl with the spirit of divination, and her owners prosecute.

    2. They had heard the preaching, but their greed had so hardened their hearts that it was like sun baked clay, where no seed could find lodging.

B. Stony ground

    1. "And they came and besought them, and brought them out, and desired then to depart out of the city" (Acts 16:39).

    2. Those who are like a poorly insulated house, hot in summer and cold in winter.

    3. The thin soil on which the plow rides to the surface.

C. Some among thorns

    1. "For many walk, of whom I have told you often, and now tell you even weeping, that they are enemies of the cross of Christ; whose end is destruction, whose God is their belly, and whose glory is in their shame, who mind earthly things" (Phil. 3:18, 19).

    2. "Demas hath forsaken me, having loved this present world" (II Tim. 4:10).

    3. Cares of the world . . . . duties of the daily task. Deceitfulness of riches . . . . owned and kept or desired and coveted.

        Lusts of other things . . . . . the approval of the crowd and of pleasure.

D. Good ground

"He which hath begun a good work in you will perform it until the day of Jesus Christ" (Phil. 1:8).

YOU GIVE THEM SOMETHING TO EAT
(Mark 6:30-44)

INTRODUCTION — Review the well-known story

The busy days when the apostles went forth healing and casting out demons. The popular turmoil that forbade privacy even to eat and sleep. The notoriety that attracted Herod's attention — John the Baptist returned from dead? The day of teaching and healing. Then the apostles' impatience and Jesus' compassion: "You give them something to eat!"

I. *YOU* — A disturbingly indefinite reference "to whom it may concern."
   A. The apostles
      1. Busy, beleaguered, and beset. "And they cast out many demons, and anointed with oil many that were sick, and healed them" (Mark 6:13).
      2. Had not privacy to eat and sleep (vv. 31, 32).
      3. Limited in resources: "What are these among so many?" Where do you start? (cleaning attic, feeding the hungry, converting the world).
      4. But they were His apostles — had limitless resource!
   B. Ourselves ("who shall believe on me through their word" — John 17:20).
      1. Very busy with our own affairs?
      2. Hopelessly limited in resources?
      3. But we, too, are His!

II. *THEM* — Again a disturbingly pointed indefinite reference. "Who is my neighbor?"
   A. As the apostles saw them —
      1. The thrill-seeking throng — "Because they beheld the signs which He did on them that were sick" (John 6:2). (Always a crowd at a dog-fight.)
      2. Thoughtless, thankless, undeserving.
         Consider the home town at Nazareth; they sought to kill Him. Always the carping critics, the layers of snares.
   B. As Jesus saw them —

"He had compassion upon them, because they were as sheep not having a shepherd."
1. How much different were they from ourselves?
2. But Jesus loved and died for the people who rejected Him and cost Him His life!

III. *SOMETHING TO EAT* — Again Jesus did not say what, and so gave no excuse or way out.
   A. "What do you have?" A very little and that very common — but give it!
   B. Food for the hungry. "Not what we give, but what we share; For the gift without the giver is bare . . ."
   C. Gracious gestures of providing a meal . . . on moving day . . . in sickness . . . at death.
   D. The nourishing grace of gratitude — the kind word and the smile. Cf. the waitress, on being told, "You served us well." "You don't know how much that means to me; I had a horrible day yesterday; now today is better."
   E. Most important is the Bread of life. Shall we not share that, too? But what is my ability in so great need? What *do* you have?

IV. *GIVE THEM* . . .
   A. "Inasmuch as ye did it unto one of these, ye did it unto me" (Matt. 25:34-46). — All of Jesus' commands included care for people.
   B. We have become tragically fearful to become involved. It's dangerous! It was dangerous then, too. That road down to Jericho was no safe place, and the Samaritan could have found himself in a trap (Luke 10:30-37).
   C. How much of our "giving to the Lord" is giving, and how much is serving ourselves? The church building; the teaching, preaching program; camps, colleges, etc.

CONCLUSION —

The apostles gave — no, they let Him give through them — thank God! What did Jesus say in giving thanks? "And they all ate, and were filled." "All things are ready; Come to the feast!" Peter and John at Temple: "Such as I have, I give . . ." (Acts 3:6).

COMMAND AND TRADITIONS
(Mark 7:1-13)

INTRODUCTION —

Question arises, what is the church's rule on this point?

A. If we can give answer in the very words of the New Testament, knowing that the apparent meaning of the passage is in harmony with all else on same point, we can reply most gladly.

B. If we cannot do this we cannot give a positive answer. We can give a personal opinion, as such.
   We may tell what one or many congregations have found wise to do in regard to an untaught subject. We cannot make rules and doctrines for the church of Christ.

C. The experience of the Jews in the 1500 years between Moses and Christ is very much in point.

I. THE GROWTH OF THE TRADITIONS OF MEN.

A. Law given through Moses on Mt. Sinai, recognized as divine law.

1. Prophets spoke for God, but gave no new commandment; applied old.

2. Mishna, "laws" or "teachings" grew up; oral then; written later. These were the "traditions of the elders" so revered by Pharisees.

B. Grew as sincere attempt to clarify and apply the law.

1. Washings — Law prescribed washing of person, garments, etc. when defiled as from leprosy, running sores, dead body, etc. "That they die not be reason of their uncleanness when they defile my Temple" (Lev. 12:15; esp. 15:31).
   Application — extended from Tabernacle to eating; idea that soul became defiled by ceremonially unclean thing coming into body. — Fear lest one might unconsciously touch unclean thing. — at home, *nipto* (wash); after market *baptizo* (bathe; plunge).

3. Jesus said, "Ye leave the commandment, and hold fast the tradition."

293

C. Explanation or defense of custom which came from other source.

Corban and the law, "Honor thy father and thy mother." Things of God are more important than things of men. Therefore dedicate property now and change the arrangement later, at your will.

D. Pharisees claimed that traditions originated with Moses, and were oral, parallel to written, and of equal authority.

II. CHRIST DENIED THE AUTHORITY OF TRADITION, POINTED TO FAULTS IT INTRODUCED.

A. He respected the Law, but refuted traditions.
1. Twofold purpose: to sweep away traditions and get to source. To bring higher law through authority as Son.
2. We must not allow traditions to bury, hide, and nullify His Word.

B. Fault of tradition:
1. Give too much importance. "Ye leave the commandment." Where do commands end and traditions begin (some necessary)? Frailty of human mind, prone to do more for men than for God. Won't attend Lord's Table at His request; will at Easter Sunrise. Won't be baptized; will do without sweets in Lent.
2. Traditions nullify and contradict the commandment. "I know the Bible says, but . . ." Regarding the spiritual significance of infant baptism, a pastor says, "I'm uneasy myself about the way the practice works out, but that's the way our denomination does it."

CONCLUSION — The better way.

Dr. J. L. Gaur, Hindu Brahmin physician, read and studied the Bible, wished to accept Christ in scriptural manner; found himself at odds with preachers and missionaries who insisted that baptism, especially immersion, was not necessary; and that their systems were. Found church of Christ, now hangs sign, "Charitable dispensary - church of Christ" - gives money to mission and self to helping fellow men. He never met Thomas or Alexander Campbell, but same book led to same conclusions.

HE DOETH ALL THINGS WELL
(Mark 7:31-37)

INTRODUCTION — We love Jesus more each time we read this story, because it tells in another and interesting way how much He loves us.

I. HE GRASPED THE OPPORTUNITY TO DO GOOD AS THE OPPORTUNITY CAME.
  A. We discover only one appointment Jesus had—that was with the cross, and He kept it.
  B. Otherwise the conversations, sermons, healings, were the products of the moment.
    1. Cf. Nicodemus, woman at well, Widow's son.
    2. The greatness of His ministry is the sum of many little opportunities accepted.
  C. Different from men.
    1. Missionaries not concerned for their neighbors.
    2. Preachers who refuse to talk to one, on the way to addressing many.
  D. Stewardship - "It's not what you'd do with a million
        If a million should e'er be your lot;
        It's what you're doing right now
        With the dollar and a quarter you've got."
  "Say not unto thy neighbor, Go and come again, and tomorrow I will give, when thou hast it by thee" (Prov. 3:28).

II. HE UNDERSTOOD.
  A. The sensitiveness of the man who could not speak plainly.
  B. The difficulties of youth in being understood.
    1. Nobody understands you—not even yourself!
    2. There is One who does understand.

III. HE WAS CONSIDERATE AND RESPECTFUL.
  A. Manner of healing—took the man aside so as not to make embarrassing spectacle. Showed intention through gestures. —Spoke words that could be lip-read.
  B. He dealt with people as people, not as things—gave them a part in their own healing—so, too, in salvation.

295

C. God is often more considerate and respectful of us than we of Him.

IV. HE DEALT EFFECTIVELY WITH THE SITUATION.
    A. That had come to be expected routine, but not when it is *you* being healed.
        1. What were the dumb man's first plain words? "Hallelujah"? (A tongue-tied person can't say it.)
        2. What was the effect upon the audience?
    B. Have faith in His power for you:
        1. To forgive sin.
        2. To conquer temptation.
        3. To bring contentment—"I can do all things through Christ . . ." (Phil. 4:13).

V. "HE DOETH ALL THINGS WELL."
    A. Vastly different from the invented supermen.
        1. Nietzche's philosophy.
        2. The heroes of our own entertainment world—always "successful."
        3. He saved others—Himself He could not save.
    B. Yet where is the fault that can be found?

VI. MAN'S RESPONSE LIMITS HIM.
    A. He commanded silence—they disobeyed. Whatever he tells you, do it!
        "But he went out and began to publish it much, and to blaze abroad the matter, insomuch that Jesus could no more openly enter into the city, but was without in desert places" (Mark 1:45).
    B. They no doubt thought they did Him a favor by the publicity. "Behold to obey is better than sacrifice" (II Sam. 15:22).
    C. They made it impossible for Him to bless them as He would like.

CONCLUSION —

How about you? He said, "Don't tell anyone." They told everyone! To us, He says, "Tell everyone." Do we?

TWO COMMANDS TO THE CHRISTIAN
(Mark 12:28-34)

INTRODUCTION —

A new covenant brings a new relationship to the commandments. Deuteronomy 4:13 identifies the ten commandments as the center of a covenant between God and Israel.

I. THERE IS A NEW COVENANT.
   A. It is predicted in Jeremiah 31:31-34 and declared in Hebrews 8:6-13.
   B. The writing on stone gives way to the inscription in human hearts (II Cor. 3:2, 3).
   C. The old covenant is of the law, the new is of grace.
   D. The old tends to prohibit; the new directs to fullness.
   E. The law, *as such,* is not binding on the Christian.
      1. "Except your righteousness shall exceed the righteousness of the scribes and Pharisees, ye shall in no case enter into the kingdom of heaven" (Matt. 5:20).
      2. (Analogy) An athlete will never challenge the new records until he has surpassed the old.

II. THE CHRISTIAN HAS A NEW RELATIONSHIP TO THE TEN COMMANDMENTS.
   A. He is taught to build a life of love; not merely to tear down a life of sin. —Still, he will avoid the sins that destroy (I Cor. 6:9, 10; Gal. 5:19, 20).
   B. The command to love God covers the obligations of the first four Commandments.
      1. No other gods—the principle reaffirmed by Christ.
         a. "Ye cannot serve God and mammon" (Matt. 6:24).
         b. "Idolatry, witchcraft" condemned (Gal. 5:20).
      2. Graven images are forbidden in the New Testament. —"We ought not to think that the Godhead is like unto gold or silver or stone, graven by art and man's device" (Acts 17:29).
      3. Blasphemous use of God's name is not Christian.
         a. He is to "swear not at all" (Matt. 5:34) with or without the divine name.

297

    b. He is not to accept the identity of "Christian" lightly or vainly, "having a form of godliness, but denying the power thereof" (II Tim. 3:5).

  4. The Sabbath as such is not binding on the Christian.

    a. There is no New Testament command for keeping it (Compare John 5:18).

    b. The first day of the week is observed among Christians (Acts 20:7; I Cor. 16:2).

    c. Justin Martyr (died 165 A.D.) — "The Lord's Day is understood to be the first day of the week."

C. The command to love one's fellowmen covers the other commandments (Rom. 13:8-10).

  1. Honor to father and mother (Eph. 6:2).

  2. Command to refrain from murder is superceded by positive command to love.

    a. "Whosoever hateth his brother is a murderer: and ye know that no murderer hath eternal life abiding in him" (I John 3:15).

    b. "Bless them that curse you, do good to them that hate you . . ." (Matt. 5:44).

  3. Adultery is condemned in the wish as well as in the act (Matt. 5:28).

  4. Stealing is to give way to earning and to generosity (Eph. 4:28).

  5. False witness is only one form of the lying that Christ condemns — He is Truth! (Rev. 21:8; 22:15). False witness is also the denial that Jesus is the Christ (I John 2:22).

  6. Covetousness rebuked by Christ and apostles.

    a. Jesus warned against the greed which loves too strongly what is one's own (Luke 12:13-21).

    b. Covetousness identified with idolatry (Col. 3:5).

CONCLUSION —

Emphasis on the commandments is a humbling, even hopeless, experience. But the grace of God and the cleansing, empowering sacrifice of Christ offer the way out. See I Corinthians 6:9-11!

THEY ALL DRANK OF IT
(Mark 14:17-26)

INTRODUCTION —

Why should this Passover be so important to Jesus? "With desire I have desired to eat this Passover with you before I suffer."

I. THE STORY
- A. First Day of Unleavened Bread — setting in the Passover.
  1. Preparations for Jesus' eating with His disciples as a family.
  2. Peter and John make arrangements for the upper room.
  3. Ambition and humility, the washing of feet (John 13).
- B. "One of you shall betray me."
  1. Each asking, "Is it I?"
  2. "The Son of Man goes, as it is written, but woe to that man. . . ."
- C. "This is My body."
  1. Already He had used the flesh of the lamb, with the customary words, "This is the body of the lamb which our father's ate in Egypt."
  2. In neither case — the Egyptian lamb or the Lamb of God — could the reference be literal.
- D. "They all drank of it."
  1. See what variety of men were here together. Fishermen, tax collector; Jews, Galileans, Canaanite, Zealot; "Sons of Thunder," quiet men.
  2. Their behavior afterward would show as great variety.
     a. John who was near and Peter who followed afar.
     b. But the presence of Christ made of these two a great team in evangelism.
  3. "Are ye able to drink of the cup that I drink of?" James, beheaded at order of Herod — John exiled to Patmos. Traditions concerning others. They were marked men from this time forth.
- E. "When they had sung a hymn" — Hallel (Psalms 115-118).

"The Lord is my strength and song, and is become my salvation.

The voice of rejoicing and salvation is in the tabernacle of the righteous;

the right hand of the Lord doeth valiantly.

The right hand of the Lord is exalted: the right hand of the Lord doeth valiantly.

I shall not die, but live, and declare the works of the Lord.

The Lord hath chastened me sore: but he hath not given me over unto death" (Psalm 118:14-18).

II. APPLICATION

A. The church, as the Twelve, is made up of many varied persons.
  1. Today's fellowship at the Lord's Table reminds of it.
  2. Each congregation may have, and should have, a varied fellowship, that the unifying center may be faith in Christ.

B. The hand of the betrayer at the Table.
  1. "Let a man examine himself," and he will know.
  2. The betrayer was not the weak one; he was the deliberately hypocritical.

C. "They all drank of it."
  1. Monday to Friday — and Saturday — must feel the spiritual impact of the Table.
  2. There will be failures — pray that there be no betrayals or denials. "Watch and pray that ye enter not into temptation."

D. There are other cups to share with Him.
  1. Service rendered in His name.
  2. Difficulties suffered in that service.

CONCLUSION —

The hymn of faith triumphant over any circumstance. "The Lord Christ is my strength and song, and is become my salvation."

300

THE LONELY SHEPHERD
(Mark 14:32-42)

INTRODUCTION —

The records of the later days of Jesus' ministry emphasize the pathos of his loneliness.

I. THE SHEPHERD BEARS THE STROKE ALONE.
   A. I will smite the shepherd, and the sheep will be scattered abroad.
   B. In much of Jesus' ministry it was impossible for others to share.
   C. From His habitually going off to pray we gain the sense that He was least lonely when He was alone with God. (The experience of almost any person will furnish instances in which the greatest sense of loneliness came when one was in a crowd who did not know or care for the things which most concerned him.)

II. HE WAS ALONE IN UNDERSTANDING THE ISSUES INVOLVED IN HIS SACRIFICE.
   A. He knew the need for His death, and the fact of His resurrection. Peter, told of it, said, "Be it far from thee, Lord."
   B. He urged, "Watch and pray, that ye enter not into temptation." They did not know the need, and did not watch.

III. HE WAS ALONE IN THE AGONY OF HIS SUFFERING.
   A. Gethsemane, place of the oil press.
   B. Matthew tells that He fell on His face in the intensity of anguish.
   C. "Watch with me." They slept. "Could ye not watch with me one hour?"

IV. HE WAS MOST ALONE ON THE CROSS.
   A. Friends forsook Him and scattered.
   B. God turned His back—"Why hast thou forsaken me?"

C. As the high priest entered the holy of holies in the Temple alone with the sacrifice on the Day of Atonement, so Christ entered the place of sacrifice alone.

(Here read the words of the hymn, "Alone"
— "It Was Alone . . .")

V. HE IS ALONE IN HIS RULE.

A. Men left Him alone in His suffering; they seek to share His rule. (Note fable of the Little Red Hen: The cat, the dog, and the pig, were willing to let her labor alone in planting, weeding, reaping, and grinding the wheat, but all wanted to help her eat the bread.)

B. James and John sought places at His side in glory.

C. In later times, men have sought, and have been given places of authority.
1. In the rule of His church.
2. In the names of glory borne by it.

D. God set Jesus alone: "This is my son; hear ye Him!" (Matt. 17:5).

CONCLUSION —

He was alone in His suffering; He must be alone in His authority; but He does not wish to be alone in His heavenly glory:

"I go to prepare a place for you, that where I am, there ye may be also" (John 14:3). "If we die with him we shall also live with Him; If we suffer with him, we shall also reign with him" (II Tim. 2:11, 12).

PREACHING THROUGH LUKE

Doctor Luke, the author of the Gospel and of the book of Acts, was not one of the twelve apostles, but he made careful inquiry among them, and among other eye witnesses of Christ (Luke 1:1-4) in preparing his record of the Lord's life. He seems to have received from Mary, the mother of Jesus, the story of His birth. With the Holy Spirit's guidance he recorded faithfully, in order that the believer in Christ might be established more firmly in his faith. Luke was the "beloved physician" and helper of Paul during much of his missionary work and especially during his final imprisonments. (See Col. 4:14; Philemon 24: II Tim. 4:11.)

Observe these things as you read the gospel:

Luke ties the events of the gospel in with the records of the kings of Rome. He emphasizes the ministry of Jesus to the outcast and the stranger. He tells more than others do concerning the prayer life of Christ. He gives large place to godly women and to the home. He gives much place to praise. The Gospel begins and ends with praise in the temple. There is an unusual beauty of literary style in Luke. This, with its subject matter, has caused this to be called "the most beautiful book in the world."

ANALYSIS OF LUKE

Chapter 1	Introduction to the gospel
2	Birth and early years of Jesus
3:1—4:13	Opening events of Christ's ministry
4:14—9:50	The ministry of Jesus in Galilee
9:51—19:28	His teaching ministry in Perea
10:29—23:56	The last week and the crucifixion
24	The resurrection and later appearances

The center of the gospel with Luke, as with others, is Christ. We would introduce you to the book, only that the book might introduce you to Jesus.

Sermon Outlines Provided:

"Prayer and the Editor" (Luke 1:1-4)
"Together, With God" (Luke 1:5-17)
"Growing Up" (Luke 2:52)
"The Kind of Workman God Can Use" (Luke 5:1-11)

"Laughter and Tears" (Luke 6:25)
"Christ, the Life of the Party" (Luke 10:38-42; John 12:1-9)
"Bread, Please!" (Luke 11:1-13)
"The Greater Triumph" (Luke 19:28-44)
"Known in the Breaking of Bread" (Luke 24:13-35)

Other Suggested Sermon Topics:

"Promise to a Father" (Luke 1:5-25)
"Tempted" (Luke 4:1-13)
"Why Did Jesus Go to Church?" (Luke 4:16-25)
"The Whole Garment" (Luke 5:33-39)
"What Did You Go to See?" (Luke 7:24-30)
"More Favored than Kings" (Luke 10:17-24)
"On Being Afraid" (Luke 12:1-12)
"Strengthen Thy Brethren" (Luke 22:31-34)

QUESTIONS OVER LUKE

1. Name the angel who announced the birth of John the Baptist and of Jesus. (1:19, 26)
2. What does Luke say Jesus did when He was baptized? (3:21)
3. Why did Jesus say He healed the paralyzed man? (5:24)
4. What did Jesus do for the widow of Nain? (7:11-15)
5. For whom did Peter want to build tabernacles on the Mount of Transfiguration? (9:33)
6. In Luke 12 what does Jesus say about the man who lays up treasure for himself? (12:21)
7. Jesus said one must renounce all that he has before he can do what? (14:33)
8. How did Abraham explain his refusal to send Lazarus to testify to the five brothers of the rich man in torment? (16:29-31)
9. What did Jesus say about the publican who said, "God be merciful to me a sinner" (18:13, 14).
10. Who was Malchus and what did Jesus do for him? (22:50)
11. Name one of the disciples to whom Jesus appeared on the road to Emmaus. (24:18)

PRAYER AND THE EDITOR
(Luke 1:1-4)

INTRODUCTION — Consider Dr. Luke, the evangelist:

A. No record of any spoken sermon by Luke, but because of him we know: Jesus' messages of the lost sheep, lost coin, lost son, etc. Peter's sermon and Pentecost; Paul's sermon at Athens, etc.

B. Luke evangelized the believer—"That thou mightest know the certainty."

C. No record of Luke's praying, but because of him we know Jesus' prayers at His baptism; at the teaching of prayer; at Caesarea Philippi; before choosing the apostles—besides other prayers told by other writers. Because of Luke we know of the disciples' praying before, at, and after Pentecost, at Paul's conversion, at Peter's imprisonment, at the sending of Barnabas and Paul, etc. Didn't Luke pray? Of course he did! He just didn't talk of himself.

D. Many Christians don't think to pray for writers and editors. They pray for: Teachers—but teachers use what writers and editors produce. Preachers—but preachers get sermons from writers' research. Missionaries—but missionaries rely on news contact with homeland. —Pray, then, for the writer, that, like Luke, he may be faithful, capable, effective.

I. RECRUITMENT (v. 1). "Pray the Lord . . . that He will send forth laborers" (Matt. 9:38).

"Many have taken in hand." These are colleagues, not competitors; Holy Spirit may use one more.

A. Editors of church publications ("Christian churches don't have bishops; they have editors").

B. Preacher-editors of church papers.

C. Writers of articles, etc. *Christian Standard* uses 279 articles per year (average five years 1971-1975).

D. Editors of lesson literature. One such editor has this on her desk: "Are you working for them or for Me?"

II. RESEARCH (v. 2).
—Luke's evident securing of information from Mary, apostles in Jerusalem.
   A. The writer-editor needs roots: In facts, in language.
   B. Pray for thoroughness and honesty.
      Not as the politician, using whatever will serve his party. Check the sources. Beware the temptation to pick up and repeat whatever says what you want to hear!

III. RECORDING (v. 3). Orderly presentation.
   A. Luke's order differs from Matthew (teaching) and Mark (miracles).
   B. Advantage of writing over speech—it can be done orderly. —Arrange and rearrange, word and reword.
   C. Writing *must* be orderly—for the unforgiving permanence of print.
   D. Pray that we may exercise discipline to be worthy, skill to be effective.

IV. REINFORCEMENT (v. 4).
   A. Luke's "Theophilus" becomes all-inclusive (write for one reader at a time).
   B. Purpose to convince (cf. Campbell-Rice debate; Rice was clever when heard; Campbell was convincing when read).
   C. Purpose to establish.
      1. "To write the same things unto you, to me indeed is not grievous, but for you it is safe" (Phil. 3:1).
      2. So pray that the writing and publication of timeless truth be fresh, so as to be read, foundational, so as to be worth reading.

CONCLUSION —
   A. A lonely ministry? No, although contacts are less immediate or personal. Seldom does one say, "You helped me when I needed it."
   B. Ephesians 6:18-20—A writer requests prayer on his behalf!

TOGETHER, WITH GOD

(Luke 1:5-17)

INTRODUCTION —

Here is the story of a godly family, Zacharias and Elizabeth. It isn't a family if it is only one; and it isn't what a family ought to be, without God.

I. THEIR RIGHTEOUSNESS WAS TOGETHER, WITH GOD.

Both righteous

Age is honorable; they approach it so modestly you hardly know they are doing it.

A. It was in God's sight.
1. Their growing up in priestly families gave them a congeniality that was important for all their life together. "Ye also, as lively stones, are built up a spiritual house, an holy priesthood, to offer up spiritual sacrifices, acceptable to God by Jesus Christ" (I Pet. 2:5).
2. Zacharias known for doing, more than for saying— He spoke one grand hymn!
3. Their awareness of God precluded hypocrisy—God knew.

B. It was in God's way.
1. Familiarity with the Law removed any confusion in right and wrong.
2. In the days of Herod the king—the court and the kingdom were ruled by standards far different from the law of God. —"Everybody's doing it"—not everybody! Zacharias and Elizabeth weren't!

C. It was in God's approval.
1. If God be for us, who can be against us? This really mattered!
2. As a bonus they had the good will of their neighbors. The neighbors wanted to name the baby "Junior" for Zacharias. The whole story reflects the love of the people for their priest.

Here was real achievement in righteousness!

307

II. THEIR FAMILY WAS TOGETHER, WITH GOD.
  A. *The fact* of the coming birth was not mere human partnership; it was divine intervention. So, Isaac, of Abraham and Sarah. But Jesus, divine intervention alone.
    1. Our gynecologist had no trouble at all with the virgin birth; since every life and birth is an act of God.
    2. This is what families are all about, under the command, "Be fruitful . . ."
  B. Their *fame* was in their son, because of God. (Better to be father of a great man than the son of one.)
    1. Thou shalt have joy . . . many shall rejoice.
    2. "He will be a great man in the Lord's sight" (1:15, TEV).
    3. Except for John they would be unknown—to men.
  C. Their *influence* was in their son, with God.
    1. He will go as God's messenger. —Did they live to see the crowds at Jordan?
    2. He will bring fathers and children back together. —Nothing new about generation gaps, nor about God's bridges for them. The family, and God— "Nurture and admonition of the Lord."
    3. He will turn the disobedient back to the way of righteousness. —It is the healing of the earth's brokenness.
       Read Luke 1:68, 69, 76-79. "To guide our feet in the way of peace." (One wonders when he considers the tragic death of John; but go to Damascus and see the shrine of John the Baptist in a Mohammedan mosque—he is salve to the family feud that began with Isaac and Ishmael and burns in the hearts of Jews and Arabs.)
    4. He will get the Lord's people ready for Him.
       The glory of the family, Zacharias and Elizabeth. The glory of John the Baptist. The glory of the Christian family.

CONCLUSION —

The basis of invitation — Has someone prepared you to receive Christ?

GROWING UP

(Luke 2:52)

INTRODUCTION — The universal desire to "grow up."

    A. Picture of a small boy in a college town.

    B. Jesus was once our age—that is where we have it over the old folks.

    C. Where growth ceases, death begins. Even the adult body is continually growing to renew itself. The mind does not become completely mature until age fifty.

    D. The aim of all teaching is to help you grow up.

I. ADVANCED IN STATURE.

    A. Such advance is natural and cannot be helped. All we can do is to make the conditions so nature can work properly.

    B. Food—the simple fare of the country Palestinian.

    C. Play—the hills and villages about Nazareth furnished ample opportunity. That He played hard and was used to His share of winning is shown by His set-to's with the Pharisees later.

    D. Work—the oldest son in a poor family of six has to work.

        1. He was known as a carpenter's son, and as a carpenter.

        2. His parables are about people at work.

    E. Danger in growth only in stature—

        1. Absolom, perfect physically, met a dismal end.

        2. Samson, the childish giant, was a failure.

        3. Saul of Tarsus did well with a limited physique.

II. ADVANCED IN WISDOM

    A. (Illus.) with Paul—able to be "all things to all men."

        1. With the Jews he proved Christ by their Scriptures.

        2. With the Greeks he talked philosophy.

        3. Felix said his education had driven him insane.

        4. To the heathen he could talke in their learning.

    B. Jesus

        1. "Knew all the answers" with the wisest of the Pharisees.

        2. His wisdom was largely in the knowledge of the will and the Book of God.

3. "Behold, to fear God is wisdom, and to depart from evil is understanding" (Job 28:28).

III. ADVANCED IN FAVOR WITH MAN.

A. Dale Carnegie's *How to Win Friends and Influence People*
1. Don't criticize, learn first names, smile, be appreciative, etc.
2. All this is included in one verse: Matthew 7:12.

B. Illustration with Joseph
1. He failed in favor of his brothers when he spoke of his own dreams and boasted himself.
2. He succeeded when he interpreted dreams for others and became so deeply concerned with the affairs of others that he forgot himself.

C. So was Jesus.
1. That even in death, concerned himself with others.
2. Even after 1900 years is the world's best loved man even among those who deny His divinity.

IV. ADVANCED IN FAVOR WITH GOD.

A. Without this all else is transient.

B. Illustration with David.
1. Saw the stars of God.
2. Saw the shepherd-sheep relation as of God and His.
3. Sang of God.
4. Attributed success to God.
5. Became a king after God's own heart.

C. Christ's approved status was often declared by the Father himself.
1. At baptism (Matt. 3:17).
2. At transfiguration (Matt. 17:5).
3. By the resurrection (Acts 17:31).

CONCLUSION —

The proof of our own maturity is to be found, finally, not with size nor wisdom, nor favor with man, but in the final declaration, "Well done, thou good and faithful servant."

THE KIND OF A WORKMAN GOD CAN USE
(Luke 5:1-11)

INTRODUCTION —

    A. The Lord needs many kinds of workers for many purposes, but there is a core of character that will be found in the more useful ones.

    B. In spite of his weaknesses, the apostle Peter had qualities that made him useful.

    C. What did Jesus see in Peter that morning on the Sea of Galilee that persuaded Him to "sign on" the fisherman as a fisher of men?

    D. Recount the story. It spells out W-O-R-K-M-A-N.

WORKING WORKMAN (vv. 2, 5).

    A. Endured the night-long drudgery in spite of failure.

    B. If a man cannot see work to be done in the world, he will not be able to see work to be done in the kingdom.

    C. There is a discouraging tendency for folk to feel that if one is religious, he should not be expected to toil.

    D. West Virginian Myron Taylor insists that a preacher needs to work at his ministry — especially his sermons, "like a miner under a landslide."

ODERLY WORKMAN (v. 2) — One who knows how to use and care for his tools.

    A. "A workman that needeth not to be ashamed, handling aright the word of truth" (II Tim. 2:15, ASV).

    B. See James' warning about the teacher's tricky tool — the tongue (James 3:1-12).

    C. Illustration — A preacher borrows and uses a paint brush, cleans it, and returns it. The lender's wife examines the brush and says, "You'll pass. My husband said we'd know a lot more about our preacher when the brush came back."

RESPECTFUL WORKMAN (v. 3) — Not too busy to do a favor for another.

    A. The weary and discouraged fisherman still lent his boat to the Lord's use.

B. Not how much of Jesus' ministry took place informally "as He passed by." He needed workers who could catch the opportunity of the moment to render ministry.

C. The follower of Christ will give the "cup of cold water" to another because of Jesus.

KNOWING-THE-LORD WORKMAN (vv. 4, 5)—Accepting the Lord's authority.

A. The fisherman, Peter, followed a preposterous directive, from a carpenter, about fishing!

    1. He knew this was no ordinary carpenter.

    2. As a confession that Jesus Christ is Lord, this is almost more significant than the confession recorded in Matthew 16:16.

B. The fisherman would accept responsibility and do more than his share in obeying. —"At thy word, *I* will let down the net."

C. Show me a businessman who will take Jesus' directives in the conduct of his business, and I'll show you a workman who can be trusted to accept the Lord's authority in the church.

MEEK WORKMAN (v. 8)—Definitely not weak, but aware of his relationship to God.

A. Peter acknowledged the power and the purity of Christ.

B. He showed appreciation for the miracle of provision.

C. Confronted with what he saw in Jesus, Peter did not need anyone to accuse him of weakness and sin, but said, "I am a sinful man."

ABLE-TO-CHOOSE WORKMAN (vv. 10, 11) — He selected the best in preference to the good.

A. He left an honorable and profitable calling when the Lord invited to something better.

B. It is an ability sorely needed by all of us amid the multitude of opportunities.

    1. Don't ask "what's wrong" with what you are considering!

2. Ask "what's right" with it; is this the best investment of time and energy to the glory of God?

NOW-CONSCIOUS WORKMAN (v. 11).

A. The fishermen's immediate, radical change in life-style and occupation probably seemed hasty to their friends, but consider:
   1. Sufficient evidence was at hand; the validity of the Lord's claim was established.
   2. Nothing was to be gained by delaying decisive action.
B. The same decisiveness would be required in their work.
   — Consider the answers to those who would forbid them to preach (Acts 4:18-21).
C. "Now is the accepted time; behold, now is the day of salvation" (II Cor. 6:2).

CONCLUSION —

Am I the kind of workman God can use? The answer may depend on my answer, *now,* to the question Peter and his partners answered that day: "Is Jesus the kind of Lord I want to follow?" Well, is He? Now!

313

LAUGHTER AND TEARS
(Luke 6:25; I Peter 4:1-11)

INTRODUCTION —

Modern emphasis on smiles and cheerfulness is not always right.
> We are told that Jesus wept, but never that He laughed — we assume that He did.
> The least desirable are often very cheerful, and vice versa.
> So in poetry —
>> Milton's Il Penseroso:
>>> "Hence, all you vain deluding joys —" — His poem praises the solemn enjoyments.
>> John Fletcher:
>>> "Hence all you vain delights, as short as are the nights
>>> Wherein you spend your folly.
>>> There's naught in this life sweet, if men were wise to see 't,
>>> But only Melancholy, O sweetest Melancholy."

"Woe unto you that laugh now, for you shall weep and mourn."

I. YOU SHALL WEEP FOR POWER AND OPPORTUNITY LOST.
> A. The fable of the futile fiddling grasshopper and the industrious ant has many counterparts. (The ant ate well in winter while the grasshopper froze.)
>> Illustration — Madame Tolstoi.
>>> Reared a family of ten children.
>>> Took, in longhand, the dictation for all her husband's many books.
>>> Some of them went through seven longhand copies before they reached the printer.
>>> One alone went into 1600 closely printed pages.
>>> (There was no time for seeking entertainment.)
>> Illustration — Alexander Campbell.
>>> Recognized in England as a fit representative of the earth to Mars.
>>> Had a standing order for all theological books from a great publisher.

Arose at 4:00 a.m. to read Hebrew and Greek; then went into the day's work.

(He didn't see any movies or TV.)

B. So the church has an urgent message to the world, and cannot waste its time in light pleasantries and entertainment.

1. It is not a club.

2. Its music should be thoughtful, not frivolous.

C. Classes in their meetings may well put in the time for the Lord, rather than in mere entertainment.

— The class that laughs now may weep for its members lost and dead.

II. YOU SHALL WEEP FOR THE LOSS OF YOUR HOLD ON LIFE.

1. There is an innate pessimism among those who seek only light entertainment.

2. Much of "swing out" is fear to face the facts of life.

3. The aquaplane that skims the surface, sinks when the speed is gone.

4. The bitterest mourners at funerals are the thoughtless and gay otherwise.

III. YOU SHALL WEEP FOR A LOST HOLD ON ETERNITY.

1. One who can laugh with the world cannot laugh with God.

2. The things in which the world finds pleasure will be gone in ruin.

3. "What doth it profit a man if he gain the whole world and lose his own soul?" (Matt. 16:26).

CONCLUSION —

"Blessed are ye that weep now, for you shall laugh."

CHRIST, THE LIFE OF THE PARTY
(Luke 10:38-42; John 12:1-9)

INTRODUCTION —

From two incidents, some very untheological observations (but nothing that affects God's children is really untheological), dealing with questions that plague young people from age ten onward: How can I say and do the right thing in company?

The two incidents—same place, same principal characters; one before, the other after, raising Lazarus; house guest on journey; honored guest at banquet.

Similar observations could be made on basis of many other incidents: Wedding feast at Cana; Matthew's banquet; the supper at Emmaus on resurrection evening.

I. JESUS ACCEPTED AN INVITATION.

   He was not the pale Galilean recluse.

   A. Why did He accept?
   1. He loved these people (enjoyed their company).
   2. He "was moved with compassion"; He "came not to call the righteous, but sinners."
   3. He was found where the currents of life ran strongest; marketplaces, synagogues; and the currents of life ran strong about Him.

   B. Why was He invited? Same reasons; they loved Him.
   1. He was not social climbing: "When you make a feast, invite the lame and blind . . ."
   2. They could count on His genuine respect to host and guests.
   3. The gathering would be infinitely more meaningful with Him present.

II. MATERIAL EXPRESSIONS OF HOSPITALITY WERE PROVIDED, AND RECEIVED (*Martha served*).

   A. When people get together, it is usually "over" something: a meal, or a cup of tea, a game, a play, a stack of records, a campfire.

1. It overcomes awkwardness in getting acquainted; provides for a meeting of minds.
2. It is a buffer for people who haven't yet learned to regard each other highly.
3. It can become a social crutch, never outgrown.
4. It can be vicious, thwarting every good purpose (drink, gambling, etc.). (Physical attraction can prevent meeting of minds.)

B. Jesus accepted the service.
1. Generosity is as much in honoring a gift as in giving one.
2. There is sharp rejection in "Please! I'd rather do it myself!"
3. The fine art of grateful acceptance, never blandly taking for granted.

III. MARY LISTENED AS JESUS TAUGHT; SHE HONORED HIM WITH HER TREASURE.

A. The meeting of minds; the sharing of treasure; is the real reason for gathering, and nothing should be permitted to thwart it.
B. Here is the complete integrity of Christ; He was not "getting away from it all," but relaxed with the word of God on His lips.
C. (What do you talk about when you have pushed back the plates or the checker board?)
D. Mary's enthusiasm responded to His teaching and His gift of life.

IV. SOMEONE RAISED PRACTICAL OBJECTIONS TO THE "WASTE" OF TIME AND TREASURE.

A. Martha objected sincerely; Judas hypocritically.
B. How obtrusive are the practical limitations of time and material program!
C. How fine is the balance between orderliness and obtrusiveness in worship!

V. JESUS, THE GUEST, BECAME HOST AND TEACHER — giving the party eternal life.
   A. In this, we can hardly do as He did; we have not the right; but —
   B. We can make Him the Host and Teacher at our get-togethers.
      1. This is better than acknowledging Him as "unseen guest, silent listener."
      2. Let Him be Lord of the gathering over punch and cookies as well as over the loaf and the cup of the Communion.
      3. His the constructive goodness that forbids moral compromise, and makes every social contact leave each participant better for it.
      4. His the love of God that forbids spiritual compromise, and draws friends to become brothers in Christ.

CONCLUSION —
He is the secret of successful get-togethers: He knows their value, so He provided for a get-together, every week, to talk about Him over His table, and "Father, I will that they also, whom thou hast given me, be with me where I am; that they may behold my glory, which thou hast given me" (John 17:24).

BREAD, PLEASE!
(Luke 11:1-13)

INTRODUCTION —

    A. Before us are three paragraphs on prayer. They all talk about bread.

        1. "Give us day by day our daily bread."

        2. The friend supplies bread when asked, at midnight!

        3. The father gives bread to his family.

    B. Bread is basic food, coming in many sizes, and kinds.

        1. From Eden, "In the sweat of thy face shalt thou eat bread" (Gen. 3:19).

        2. Even in fancy finger sandwiches, you still eat bread.

    C. Yet, "Man shall not live by bread alone" (Matt. 4:4).

        1. Physical nourishment is not enough. There is a hunger it does not fill.

        2. Jesus said, "I am the bread of life" (John 6:35).

    D. God provides bread both material and spiritual.

        1. We sometimes have to become hungry to appeciate it, and to express our dependence on God for it.

        2. Material bread is provided daily and generously.

        3. Spiritual bread is available for our souls' malnutrition.

    E. We examine the paragraphs of our text in reverse order.

I. THE SON SAYS, "BREAD, PLEASE!" (vv. 11-13).

    A. The situation is totally normal in any family.

    B. The wise father knows what is good for his child.

      —God is wiser, especially at the points where we disagree with Him!

    C. The kind Father gives what is good.

      —God is kinder, especially as we are undeserving.

    D. The plea is normal also in the family of the church.

        1. Provide the word, the bread of life, faithfully.

        2. Provide leaders and teachers willing to feed the flock (family).

        3. Pray the Lord to send forth laborers.

II. THE NEIGHBOR SAYS, "BREAD, PLEASE!" (vv. 5-10).
   A. The situation is special—unexpected company.
   B. The friend understands the need.
      —God understands better, our need to meet the opportunities around us.
   C. The friend is generous; the petitioner has no legal claim to assistance. —God is more generous; He didn't get us into trouble.
   D. The friend is responsive, though the response may be punctuated with sleepy grumbling.
      1. God is more reponsive, and without grumbling—the point of the parable.
      2. The problem is with the requester, who would often rather complain of God's "injustice" than ask for God's mercy.
      3. The request is still a request, not a demand. Say "Please!"

III. THE CHRISTIAN SAYS, "BREAD, PLEASE!" (vv. 1-4).
   A. His is a daily expression of daily dependence.
      1. There are no standing orders with God. Needs change, so must requests.
      2. Tragedy of lifelong repetitions of "Now I lay me...," never adjusting the request to growing circumstances.
   B. Christ himself expressed this daily dependence.
      —He was praying, and the disciples said, "Teach us Your skill at prayer."
   C. Bread of life must be renewed daily.
      1. This is like the daily provision of manna (Exod. 16).
      2. How will you stock and preserve a month's supply of love; inspiration; goodness; generosity; purity?
   D. The prayer Jesus taught deals with living perishables, made eternal by daily renewal. —Reverence; submission; dependence; forgiveness.

CONCLUSION —

There is never vain repetition in the trusting child's grateful petition, "Bread, please!" and "Thank you, Father!"

THE GREATER TRIUMPH
(Luke 19:28-44)

INTRODUCTION —

    A. The world loves a parade of pomp and glory. There-
fore it makes much of the "Triumphal Entry."

    B. There is that about the story which indicates that Jesus
did not consider this type of glory so important.

    C. "He that is slow to anger is better than the mighty; and
he that ruleth his spirit than he that taketh a city" (Prov.
16:32).

I. THE GREATER TRIUMPH OF SELF-FORGET-
FULNESS IN SERVICE.

Matthew 20:20-29 (across the page) is the story of the ambitious sons of Zebedee.

    A. The request - "When thou comest in Thy kingdom,"
brought by mother. — Christ seemed to brush aside the
reference to the kingdom. (Freely rendered.)

    B. "Can you drink of the cup that I drink, can you be
baptized with the baptism wherewith I am baptized?"

    C. The ten by their indignation are scarcely less guilty, so
all are taught—

    D. Princes of the Gentiles exercise dominion over them
and their great ones exercise authority; it shall not be
so among you.

    E. The greatest among you shall be your servant.
For the "Son of man came not to be ministered unto,
but to minister, and to give His life a ransom for
many" (Mark 10:45).

    F. "And as they departed from Jericho a great multitude
followed him."

    Apply - The servant is greatest.
In *The Robe* Demetrius is made to say, "He is some-
thing more important than a king."
There have been other kings; never another like
Jesus; hence to call Him king is no honor.

321

II. THE GREATER TRIUMPH OVER HUMAN SUFFERING.

Blind Bartimaeus (Mark 10:46-52).

A. The story—Begging—"Jesus, Son of David, have mercy on me"—rebuked—calls the more—Jesus stops, asks that he be called—"Be of good comfort; rise; He calleth thee." Casts away garment—"What wilt thou that I should do to thee?"—"Lord, that I might receive my sight." "Go thy way, thy faith hath made thee whole" —He follows; "Thy way" becomes Christ's way.

B. Others have had processions—none for this reason.

C. Why are we in the Easter parade? Rise; He calleth thee.

III. THE GREATER TRIUMPH OVER NATURE, SIN AND GREED.

Zacheaus (Luke 19:1-10).

A. The story—another parable, but that is not important. —Zachaeus up a tree—"Make haste and come down, for today I must abide at thy house." Murmuring of the Pharisees—Zacheus stood, "The half I give; if I have taken anything wrongfully, I restore fourfold." —"This day is salvation come to this house for the Son of man is come to seek and to save that which was lost."

B. Napoleon's tribute to Christ —"He conquered through love; he is the greater conqueror."

C. There was real honor in the Entry if Zachaeus was there.

IV. THE GREATER TRIUMPH OF HUMBLE KINDNESS (John 13:1-17).

The washing of the disciples' feet. (Told in intimate detail—e.g. of Peter.)

Many heroes receive a royal welcome, but which of them has with complete naturalness so served his friends?

CONCLUSION —

John takes us for the final evening as a guest. We return with tear-wet eyes and say, "How cheap and futile the shouts of yesterday!"

KNOWN IN THE BREAKING OF BREAD
(Luke 24:13-35)

INTRODUCTION —

It is the afternoon of the resurrection day; the excitement of the resurrection evidences has ebbed a bit, and now Jesus himself appears to some not-very-prominent friends.

I. THE RISEN LORD IS KNOWN IN THE BREAKING OF BREAD.
   A. He is revealed in a familiar gesture at a family table.
      1. He appeared to two as they walked, conversing about Him.
         a. Why not to a multitude in Jerusalem? That would lack personal touch.
         b. Why not to one alone? That might be dismissed as subjective imagination.
      2. He taught them the Scripture in private conversation. —That was impressive, but He was not revealed in that teaching.
      3. He came into their home as invited Guest; then remarkably He became the Host, breaking bread and giving it to them!
         a. The mealtime fellowship is intimate and meaningful.
         b. In anyone else, His presumption would have been bad manners; in the Lord, His place as Host is natural and necessary.
      4. In the breaking of bread, He became known to them. Consider:
         a. At feeding the five thousand, He "blessed and brake the loaves."
         b. At feeding the four thousand, "having given thanks, he brake the loaves."
         c. At institution of the Supper, "when he had given thanks, he brake it." —No one knows how many other times.

323

d. After this, "They see a fire of coals there, and fish laid thereon, and bread" (John 21:9). "Jesus cometh and taketh the bread and giveth them" (Luke 24:13).

e. Peter's statement to Cornelius: Jesus showed himself "unto witnesses that were chosen before of God, even to us, who ate and drank with him after he arose from the dead" (Acts 10:41).

B. He chose to be known by the church in the breaking of bread.

1. "This do ye, as oft as ye do it, in remembrance of me."

2. "The breaking of bread" was a regular reference to the Communion: Acts 2:42; 2:46; 20:7; I Cor. 10:16.

3. "He that eateth and drinketh, eateth and drinketh judgment unto himself, if he discern not the body" (ASV) (I Cor. 11:29).

4. If Christ is not known in the breaking of this bread, the act is mockery!

Transition: The table of acquaintance at Emmaus has two sides. Cleopas and his friend also became known in that breaking of bread with the risen Lord.

II. THE FOLLOWER OF CHRIST IS KNOWN IN THE BREAKING OF BREAD.

A. The Christian is known in his familiar gestures at the family table.

1. Shall we say, "Christ is the Head of this house; the unseen Guest at every meal; the silent Listener to every conversation"? If He is Head of the house, He is Host at every meal and the dominant Personality in every conversation!

2. At meals, do you thank God for the food and then complain to Mother about it?

3. Ought not "grace at meals" include graciousness to those around the table?

324

4. There is reason for the emphasis on meals and meal-times in books of etiquette; here most significantly we show respect or disregard for others.

B. The Christian is known at the church in the breaking of bread.

1. John 6:35, 52-58 may not refer to the Communion, but it does refer to Christ.

2. How great is your love of Christ? How much does it take to keep you away from His table?

3. How much do you appreciate His sacrifice? How reverently do you "proclaim the Lord's death till he come"? (ASV) (I Cor. 11:26).

4. How do you regard your partnership with Him? In what other matters do you participate after you have participated in the body and blood of Christ? (I Cor. 10:16-22).

CONCLUSION —

Hear again the excited report from Emmaus: "The risen Lord was with us at the table!" Let's enjoy His presence, at His table and ours!

QUESTIONS OVER JOHN

1. Who identified Jesus with these words, "Behold, the lamb of God who takes away the sin of the world"? (1:29)
2. What was Jesus' first miracle? (2:1-11)
3. Jesus told Nicodemus that "Except a man be born again" he cannot do what? (3:3)
4. Jesus told the Samaritan woman that true worshipers will worship the Father how? (4:23, 24)
5. In His sermon in John 5 what are the four witnesses He cites? (5:32-39)
6. Which apostle brought the lad with five loaves and two fishes to Jesus? (6:8, 9)
7. When Jesus said, "Out of his heart shall flow rivers of living water" he referred to what, according to John 7:39?
8. How did the Jews respond to Jesus' statement, "Before Abraham was, I am"? (8:58, 59)
9. Who said, "We know that God heareth not sinners"? (9:31)
10. The good shepherd will show his love by doing what for his sheep? (10:11)
11. What man had been dead four days before Jesus raised him from death? (11:39)
12. What does Jesus say will be our ultimate judge? (12:48)
13. What act of humble service did Jesus perform for the disciples at the last supper? (13:1-15)
14. Who is the comforter Jesus promised to send to the apostles? (14:26)
15. Believers are the branches. God the father is the husbandman. Who is the vine? (15:1)
16. Jesus prayed that believers would be one in order to have what influence on the world? (17:21)
17. Why did the soldiers not break Jesus' bones? (19:33)
18. What did Thomas say when Jesus showed His hands and feet? (20:28)

PREACHING THROUGH JOHN

"Everybody ought to know who Jesus is!" This book tells it! John sums up the purpose of his writing to show that "Jesus is the Christ, the Son of God" (John 20:30, 31). It is the central message of the Christian faith. It is needed by all—by the mature Christian, to keep him in touch with his Lord, as with an old friend; by the new Christian, to become better acquainted with his new-found Savior; and by the non-Christian, that he may make the soul-saving acquaintance with Christ.

GREAT PASSAGES

Great passages stand out like tall peaks in a mountain range, as one reads John. These you will cherish:

John 3:1-21 Jesus' conversation with Nicodemus; verse 16 is the "Golden Text."
John 10:1-8 The Good Shepherd.
John 15:1-7 The Vine and the Branches.
John 14:1-6 The Many Mansions.
John 17:1-26 Christ's Prayer for Us.

THE WRITER AND THE WRITING

John, the "Beloved Disciple," brother of James and son of Zebedee, was one of the four fishermen first called to follow Jesus. He was the companion of Peter, both before and after the resurrection of Christ. In his old age he preached in Asia Minor, about the city of Ephesus, and there he wrote the Gospel, the three epistles of John, and the book of Revelation.

JOHN, AND THE OTHER GOSPELS

Matthew, Mark, and Luke had written their records of Jesus' life nearly thirty years before John committed his message to writing. He knew of these other Gospels, and in his record he repeated only the most important things which they had written, especially the accounts of the crucifixion and resurrection. John wrote mostly about the teaching Jesus did in and around Jerusalem, whereas the others recorded principally the miracles and ministry of Jesus in Galilee. The book of John is called the "Universal Gospel," being addressed to all men everywhere, while the others had particular nations in mind when they wrote.

ANALYSIS OF THE BOOK

Its theme - Belief in Jesus as the Son of God.

1:1-18	Introduction.
1:19 — 4:54	Early Manifestations of Jesus.
5:1 — 12:50	Fuller revelation: Growth of unbelief among the Jews.
13:1 — 17:26	Fuller revelation: Growth of faith among the disciples.
18:1 — 19:42	Climax of unbelief: His surrender and crucifixion.
20:1 — 21:25	Climax of faith: resurrection and proofs.

Sermon Outlines Provided:
"In the Beginning" (John 1:1-14; Gen. 1:1)
"He Dwelt Among Us" (John 2:1-11)
"Just Between the Two of Us" (John 3, 4)
"When Messiah Comes" (John 4:25; 7:25-36)
"The Judgment of Jesus" (John 8:1-11)
"A Man Came Seeing" (John 9:1-12)
"The World Is Gone After Him" (John 12:12-19)
"Peace — What a Bequest" (John 14:27)
"That Other Disciple" (John 20:1-10)

Other Sermon Topics Suggested:
"What Do You Say of Yourself?" (John 1:19-28)
"The Sign of Christ" (John 2:18-25)
"That Nothing Be Lost" (John 6:1-14)
"One Flock and One Shepherd" (John 10:1-21)
"Shepherd or Hireling" (John 10:12-14)
"One of You" (John 13:13-21)
"The Finished Task" (John 17:1-10)
"Keep Them From the Evil" (John 17:9-19)
"On Seeing and Believing" (John 20:24-30)

IN THE BEGINNING
(John 1:1-14; Genesis 1:1)

INTRODUCTION —

    A. There are beginnings for all of us. For many this is a time of special beginnings.
        1. A new experience or a new year at college in new surroundings.
        2. A new business or a new home.
        3. For all, a new week, and a new day.
    B. Beginnings are important for the prospects that are before them and the possibilities that are in them.
    (Maple sprouts in the lawn are only potentially the beginning of tall trees.)
    C. Learn from the beginning of all things.

I. GOD WAS IN THE BEGINNING.

    A. The writer gives by revelation what otherwise we guess at and grope for.
        1. We are not left to speculate about "whatever gods may be."
        2. Even from everlasting to everlasting Thou art God.
    B. The simple term, God, excludes the possibility of there being others.
        1. It is exclusively singular.
        2. It declares ultimate supremacy.
    C. He is personal, active, willing, evaluating.
    D. He is known by what He does.
    So are you and I known by what we do.
    E. *Apply* — unless God is in our beginnings, and kept there, we are empty. — Do we need the warning? Yes, especially if we think we don't.
    "I can get along by myself."
    "I have already all the help I need."

II. THE ACTIVITY OF GOD BROUGHT ABOUT THE BEGINNING.

    A. "Except the Lord build the house they labor in vain that build it."

B. He has the right to be heard concerning the things He has made:
   1. His Body the Temple.
   2. His Church, the bride.
   3. In business, honesty, dependability, service.
   4. In the home, unselfish devotion.
   5. In our studies: Reverence for God is the beginning of wisdom.

III. THERE IS OPPOSITION FROM THE BEGINNING.
   A. We surmise from Bible that Satan was early with God, but rebelled.
      —He was active in man's earliest experience.
   B. Adam turned to disobedience.
   C. "Jesus came unto His own, and His own received Him not."

IV. THERE IS GOD'S WAY OF CORRECTION THROUGH CHRIST.
   A. "To as many as received Him, gave He the power to become sons of God."
   B. "The word was made flesh and dwelt among us."
   C. Hebrews 1:1.

CONCLUSION —

The beginnings of the world, the church, and our lives are established. Let us follow faithfully the God who authored them!

The beginning of a new life and a new day in Christ is available. Let us accept it!

HE DWELT AMONG US
(John 2:1-11)

INTRODUCTION —

    A. At the occasion of Missionary Roger Clark's death in the Belgian Congo (now Zaire) the natives spoke of their love for him. "He spoke our language," they said. He was one of the very few white men who had learned the language of the drums.

    B. Likewise John writes of Jesus, that He "dwelt among us" (John 1:14).

        "We have not a high priest who is not touched with a feeling of our infirmities" (Heb. 4:15).

I. JESUS WAS INVITED.

    A. He was naturally included where life's current ran strongest. —With Him were the disciples whom He had recently called.

    B. The feast—

        1. Center of the whole community life for a week.

        2. Groom, garlanded with flowers. Bride veiled, and be-jeweled.

        3. Bridegroom goes to the home of the bride, when the feast starts—no set time.

        4. The gathering procession to the home of the bridegroom, where the feast goes on.

    C. Jesus' presence sanctifies the simplest and most natural incidents of life.

        1. His every contact with people left them better for receiving it—or worse for their rejection of it.

        2. He moves about the feast, enjoyed and enjoying, taking a guest's place.

II. THE WINE FAILED.

        1. It was always the center of the feast—to have it fail was a disgrace.

        2. "Grape-growing countries know its use as northern countries cannot."

   3. Mary approaches Him, and makes known the fact—
      "Lady, why approach me? I am not in charge."
      (He is never in charge until He is invited to be so.)

III. THE PROBLEM WAS REFERRED TO HIM.
   A. "Whatever He tells you to do, do it," said Mary.
      —He is now in charge.
   B. This the invitation of those who would preach Him—
      not our way but His.
   C. Mary had learned that, whatever was done, obedience
      to Him was a part of it.
   D. His command was to fill the six water jars, of nine gal-
      lons each.
      1. It was done without question, apparently on Mary's
         authority.
      2. Perhaps even you first turned to Jesus because a re-
         spected friend urged it. —Later you followed for His
         own sake.

IV. THE WINE DIPPED OUT WAS BEST.
   A. The comment of the governor of the feast to the bride-
      groom.
   B. God always provides the best—
      1. Manna, meal, oil, etc., in Old Testament.
      2. The Son Himself in the New Testament.

V. HE BECOMES THE SANCTIFIER OF ALL OF LIFE.
   A. Each nation claims Him, believing, as its own.
      —So in art and literature, He is represented as a native
      of the artist's land.
   B. Each party finds in Him the reflection of its own char-
      acteristics.
      —One says, "Don't you know that Jesus Christ was a
      Dumb Dutchman?"

CONCLUSION — contrast between John Baptist, the recluse,
and Christ.

John forever the preacher, condemning our sins. Christ forever the Teacher, leading us into His way, and saving us.

   —He dwelt for a lifetime among us, that we might dwell forever with Him.

JUST BETWEEN THE TWO OF US
(John 3, 4)

INTRODUCTION — The marvelous, fragile gift of human speech.

A. To none of His creatures but man, has God given the powers of spoken language.
  — How then shall it be used?

B. The occasions of formal, public speeches are commonly approached carefully.

C. Most of our talking, though, is informal and at least semi-private.
  1. Do we escape responsibility for what is said "between the two of us"?
  2. Much time is wasted on trivia, or worse than wasted on gossip.

D. Look to Jesus for example in conversations "between the two of us."
  — John tells of His talks with Nicodemus and a Samaritan woman.

I. THE OCCASIONS WERE VERY DIFFERENT.

A. One at night in Jerusalem, the other in daytime outside a Samaritan village.
  — Yet Jesus' occupation, His Father's business, was the same.

B. One evidently a formal interview, the other a chance meeting. — Yet the same basic truths dominated both conversations.

C. One a man who was a ruler of the Jews; the other a woman of questionable repute even among the Samaritans. — Yet Jesus maintained the same attitude toward both.

D. Nicodemus initiated the interview with a question; the woman responded with surprise to Jesus' introductory request.

E. The principles that cover these occasions can cover almost anything.

333

II. THE LORD MET BOTH IN MUCH THE SAME WAY.

A. He respected each as a person.
    1. He was neither awed nor resentful in the presence of the ruler.
    2. He was neither disdainful nor condescending in the presence of the woman.
    — She was amazed that He even spoke to her.

B. He addressed each one at the level of that one's interest, understanding the need.
    1. To do so He perceived more than was evident on the surface. — In this we are limited in our following of His example.
    2. His awareness centered in the other person; He offered Himself to help. — In this we can follow Him more completely than we usually do.
    3. To each He gave His full attention and His best self.

C. To each He taught things eternal, based on that one's own experience.
    1. Nicodemus had trouble with the idea of birth from above, but he would never forget the teaching.
    2. The woman had difficulty understanding "living water," but would not forget the teaching of the Teacher.

D. To each He showed boldly and kindly that one's fault, error, and need.
    1. The ruler may have doubted that he needed much of anything.
    2. The woman may have doubted that her great needs could ever be met.
    — In our following of His example we can present Jesus and His word; we cannot imitate His authority in judgment.

E. To each He declared His Messiahship and Sonship to God.
    1. The Nicodemus conversation produced the "Golden Text of the Bible" (John 3:16).

334

2. To the woman He said, "I that speak unto thee am he [Messiah]" (John 4:26).

F. Both conversations brought important results.

1. The less likely prospect brought more immediate returns, in persuading the people of Sychar (John 4:39-42).

2. Nicodemus identified himself at last as a follower of Jesus and assisted in His burial (John 19:38-42).

CONCLUSION —

"Every idle word that men shall speak, they shall give account thereof in the day of judgment" (Matt. 12:36).

A. Doesn't that put one under an awful strain, never able to cut loose and say what you want to?

1. To the nominal "Christian," seeking the appearance of religion while loving the world, yes!

2. But not to the one of whom we can say, "His delight is in the law of the Lord."

B. "Out of the abundance of the heart the mouth speaketh" (Matt. 12:34)—

even when it is just between the two of us.

WHEN MESSIAH COMES
(John 4:25; 7:25-31)

INTRODUCTION —

    A. What grand things almost any of us will do, when . . .

        1. "When my ship comes in."

        2. "When I get things squared away."

        3. "When the right time comes."

    B. The Jews had great anticipation and some sense of obligation for — "When Messiah comes." Illustrated in two episodes in our text.

        1. John 7 tells of Jesus in Jerusalem at the Feast of Tabernacles, facing opposition.

        2. John 4 tells of Jesus' conversation with a Samaritan woman beside Jacob's well.

        3. In both instances the Messiah was at hand; would they confess Him?

    C. The hearer of the Gospel probably has some expectation of Christ's (Messiah's) coming into his or her life. When? — The words of the text become a common expression.

I. EXPRESSION OF DISBELIEF (7:27-29)

    A. Faith is balked by preconceived ideas.

        1. The Jews assumed, without Scriptural warrant, that the Messiah would appear suddenly, mysteriously, as though falling from Heaven.

            a. This lent force to Satan's temptation for Jesus to float down from the pinnacle of the temple.

            b. Scripture identified Bethlehem as birthplace and Nazareth as dwelling (Matthew 2:5, 6, 23).

            c. They refused to acknowledge potential grandeur in the known commonplace.

        2. Many hearers of the Gospel assume, without Scriptural warrant, that Christ's coming to them must be mysterious and spectacular.

            a. Some insist on emotional seizures, visions, and "feelings."

  b. Some insist that their lives must be cleaned up first.
  c. They refuse to acknowledge Christ's presence according to the Word.
 B. The Lord's reply fixed responsibility squarely on the hearer.
  1. The Jews knew the town He came from, but not the Father from whom He came.
  2. The present-day hearer needs to see the power of God, not in latter-day miracles, but in the supreme miracle of Christ.

II. EXPRESSION OF PROCRASTINATION (4:25)
 A. The Samaritan woman tried to dodge responsibility for thinking and doing.
  1. To her, worship centered in a place; Jesus said it centered in a Person.
  2. She was willing to postpone such topics to the conveniently indefinite future, "When Messiah comes."
 B. Hearers of the Gospel may also dodge and procrastinate.
  1. Many avoid the basic question, "What think ye of the Christ?"
  2. Many would delay commitment to a "more convenient season" (Acts 24:25).
  3. Many would wait for a great occasion, such as Easter, Christmas, "revival," or when Grandma is here. — You are asked, not to confess a great occasion, but a great Lord.
 C. The Lord's reply nailed the woman's responsibility to the here and now!
  1. "I that speak unto thee am He!"
  2. For us, "Now is the accepted time" (II Cor. 6:2).
  3. We do make a decision for this day, one way or the other.

III. EXPRESSION OF COMMITMENT (7:31)
 A. The believers accepted the convincing evidence.
  1. Their prejudices and questions were not all answered.

337

2. Yet they saw enough of Jesus' power to convince them He was Messiah.
3. They acknowledged that no essential proof was still lacking.
4. They passed over the circumstances of His coming, to the worth of His person.

B. We are asked to confess Christ, rather than times or circumstances.
   1. It is Christ in the life that is important, not the vision or feeling.
   2. As to occasions, the acceptance of Christ, not the calendar date, is what makes the occasion meaningful and memorable.
      a. The coming of Christ made—and makes—Christmas!
      b. The resurrection of Christ makes Easter.
      c. The coming of Christ into my life makes the supreme occasion.

C. The grandeur of Christ overrides all questions and uncertainties.
   1. Compare Job 42:1-6. Job's questions were not answered, but he saw God, and that was enough.
   2. Our queries and curiosities about many things may remain, but we have seen Christ in the Gospel, dying for our sins and raised for our life eternal. That should be enough.

CONCLUSION —

When Christ comes to you—what essential element can that hour possess that is not available here and now?

THE JUDGMENT OF JESUS
(John 8:1-11)

INTRODUCTION —

Someone says that God denied to man the virtue of justice, and man chose another emotion, labeling it justice. He chose revenge for the masquerade.

They stand before us, the characters in this incident.

I. THE GUILTY SINNER.

A. No doubt of her guilt — guilty both of sin and of getting caught.

B. What about those who are not caught?

"Thou hast set our iniquities before thee, our secret sins in the light of thy countenance" (Psalm 90:8).

C. There is the story of the preacher ministering to a condemned prisoner, who was the companion of his own early escapade, but could not run quite so fast as the one who escaped and became a minister.

II. THE GUILTY JUDGES.

A. They had backing of the law of Moses; the law has no better thing to offer.

B. "He that is without [the] sin among you, let him first cast stone at her."

"I say unto you, that whosoever looketh on a woman to lust after her hath committed adultery with her already in his heart" (Matt. 5:28).

They seem to have had a morbid interest in this sin, and the apprehension.

Thou art inexcusable, O man,

whosoever thou art that judgest: for wherein thou judgest another, thou condemnest thyself; for thou that judgest doest the same things" (Rom. 2:1).

C. "Who art thou that judgest another man's servant. To his own master he standeth or falleth" (Rom. 14:4).

D. They departed, from the oldest to the youngest — The oldest had the greater sense of sin.

III. THE GUILTLESS JUDGE.
   A. Able to pass sentence without condemning Himself.
      —But He refused to pass sentence.
   B. Able to read accurately the temptations of the sinner.
      "Not an high priest which cannot be touched with
      the feeling of our infirmities" (Heb. 4:15).
   C. Purpose of judgment is not destruction but reforma-
      tion: God is not willing that any should perish, but
      that all should come to repentance.
   D. "God was in Christ, reconciling the world unto him-
      self" (II Cor. 5:19).
      His act does not lightly regard sin—"lest a worse thing
      come unto thee" (John 5:14).
   E. This does not remove finality of last judgment, which
      is condemnation to the unrepentant.
      (The jurist sentences the man he had rescued from an
      earlier accident. "Your savior then; your judge now."

IV. THE SINNER REMADE.
   "No man, Lord [condemns me]."
   A. If any man be in Christ Jesus he is a new creature.
      (A man cannot be tried twice for the same crime.)
      "Such were some of you, but ye are washed, but ye are
      sanctified . . ." (I Cor. 6:11).
      The crushing load of the past slips away.
   B. As we have stood in judgment as sinners, we may stand
      in God's presence whole.
   C. "The publicans and harlots go into the kingdom of God
      before you" (Matt. 21:31).
      Where were those who condemned her?

CONCLUSION —

   "Joy shall be in heaven over one sinner that repenteth more
than over ninety and nine just persons which need no repenting"
(Luke 15:7). Hence, "Joy to the world, the Lord is come" in
judgment!

A MAN CAME SEEING
(John 9:1-12)

INTRODUCTION —

Two parts of one sermon "A Man Came Seeing"; "The Seer Came, a Man."

    A. The event took place rather late in Jesus' ministry.
        1. He was well known, so that His name meant something to the blind beggar.
        2. Pharisaic opposition to Him had crystalized.
    B. He walked with His disciples in the Temple area on the Sabbath of the feast.

I. A MAN.
    A. Member of a minority group—a beggar, because blind, had never seen.
        1. Knew only that others could do what he couldn't. (We all are members of various minority groups.)
        2. But in one thing he shared a universal status; he had a need that only God could meet!
    B. What was he to himself?
        1. We know little of his self-esteem.
        2. He faced a hopeless existence.
    C. What was he?
        1. The object of scorn; or pity, or academic interest.
        2. Apostles saw in him an interesting question: "Who sinned, . . . that he should be born blind?"
            a. The question thoroughly in Jewish tradition; suffering considered a punishment; judgment inherited; sin in earlier life or prenatally.
            b. We are not so foolish; or are we?
               One sin, committed before birth, is regularly met with death penalty: the sin of being conceived by a mother who doesn't want you! Abortion. This blind beggar at least was born!
    D. What was he to Jesus? — *"He saw."*
        1. The man was an object of God's love, to be applied.
        2. Others analyze the problem; He corrects it.
        3. Others might diagnose; He would heal!

II. CAME.
   A. The coming involved work, even on the Sabbath: An idea rejected and opposed.
   B. He came to Jesus' attention, and under His care.
      — This is the only way of salvation, and often the work of others.
   C. Jesus worked!
      1. The symbolic anointing of the blind eyes was outlawed as a sabbath activity by Jewish tradition.
      2. "I must work the work of Him that sent me."
         What did this take out of Jesus? "Virtue is gone out" (Luke 8:46).
         (Ministers feel drained after a day of counseling.)
   D. The man worked.
      1. The pool of Siloam, the meaning is "sent" — "The sent One sends you."
      2. A half mile or more, from the Temple area, down along the Kidron Valley, through the old city of David, to the rock-hewn pool to which Hezekiah had brought water from Gihon.
      3. Here was participation in the act of God, but it wasn't easy for the man.

III. SEEING.
   A. A totally new experience, opening up areas of life not known or imagined!
      "Eye hath not seen, nor ear heard . . ." (I Cor. 2:9).
   B. A new man, different enough in appearance that neighbors weren't sure of his identity.
   C. He didn't see it all yet, and it didn't bother him.
      "How did the healing take place?" He *did* and said; "I did"; "I see"! "Where is He?" "I don't know!"
   D. There are unexplained mysteries in such as baptism and Lord's Supper.
      How is Jesus present at the table, here and in Japan, Manila, Adelaide?

CONCLUSION —

Even the unseeing have the right to life! — In Christ!

THE WORLD IS GONE AFTER HIM
(John 12:12-19)

INTRODUCTION — The setting, as might be viewed by a stranger.

A. Spring Sunday on Mt. Olivet.
B. The strange procession shouting its way to Jerusalem.
C. Contrast with the processions of conquering monarchs.

I. ENEMIES.

A group by the way, and one says, "See how ye prevail nothing." Ask him questions:

A. Are you His friend that you say, "*Ye* prevail nothing"? No, just human.
B. Why are you opposed to Him?
  1. We were leaders, and He made us a laughingstock:
    a. Respected for piety; He calls us hypocrites, and prefers sinners.
    b. Admired for wisdom; He makes fools of us.
    c. Ruled the people; and He neither submits nor lets others submit.
C. What is the meaning of this display?
  1. The thing most provoking—
    a. A public acceptance of glory.
    b. A proclamation of Messiahship.
    "Thy king cometh unto thee; he is just and having salvation; lowly, and riding upon an ass, and upon a colt the foal of an ass" (Zech. 9:9).
    c. We even urged Him to silence them, but He said that truth came from the mouth of babes.
  2. The thing which gives occasion for His destruction —His presumption becomes a weapon with Caesar.
D. What will you do about it?
  1. Use His proclamation for His destruction.
  2. Use the same mob to secure His downfall.

Apply — Are His enemies our friends?

343

II. THE MULTITUDE.

—Visitors, many from Galilee, to the feast.

A. Why do you shout His praises?
1. He is the Prophet of Nazareth, in our own Galilee (so answered to citizens).
2. He did many wonderful works in Galilee.
3. He recently raised Lazarus from the dead.
4. It is the feast time, and occasion to honor great men.

B. What is the meaning of this particular occasion?
1. Some say He is the Messiah.
2. It is a possibility to exult over.

C. What will you do about it?
1. We will shout with the people, and be glad.
2. We will rejoice in His popularity.
3. (This group, loudest to acclaim, were first to desert.)

Apply 1. The world goes after Him at Easter—what does it mean? Where will they be next week?
2. His weaker disciples join the multitude, and for like reasons.

III. DISCIPLES.

A. Why are you in this crowd?
We are always with Him, wherever He is.

B. What means this occasion?
1. We are not sure; it is different from any other.
2. We rejoice to do Him honor at any time.

C. What will you do about it?
1. We will continue to follow and to learn.
2. We will remember this occasion for future understanding.

IV. AND CONCLUSION —

Christ alone the complete master of the occasion, and knows its meaning.

A. Proclamation of Messiahship, for all time to come.
B. Teaches the nature of Messiah's Kingdom; humility; voluntary character.
C. Dedication of the Passover Lamb.

PEACE — WHAT A BEQUEST!
(John 14:27)

INTRODUCTION —

See the stark contrast between Christ's conversation in the Upper Room and the labored pronouncement of a cease-fire in any modern warfare. It is only because we have faith in the one that we can see any hope in the other.

Peace — what is it?

Shalom (Hebrew) — "completeness, peace, wholeness." The peaceful person is all there! He has it all together.

Eirene (Greek) — Peace, unity, concord — "Of the two, one person, so making peace."

I. CHRIST'S PEACE IS PERSONAL.
   A. It is as personal as Dad's leaving you his watch.
   B. The whole conversation is "I" and "you."
   C. It is the conveyance of a gift from Him who has it to the person who needs it.

II. IT IS A BEQUEST, "Peace I leave with you."
   A. Compare the sending of the Holy Spirit — If I do not go He cannot come.
   B. It is purchased by the same conditions — Christ's departure in death.
      — We can't have peace without His sacrifice!
   C. "A testament is of none effect without the death of the testator" (Heb. 9:17).

III. NO ONE CAN GIVE WHAT HE DOESN'T HAVE. "My peace I give unto you."
   A. So Jesus at the conclusion of a tense week, filled with controversy, was at peace.
   B. The apostles had been wrangling about who'd be captain of the team — He quietly washed the feet of them all.
   C. He announced that one of His own would betray Him, and told Judas so in such a way that none of the others caught on.

345

D. Later that night — "Pilate before Christ."
 1. Pilate thought He didn't know what was going on.
 2. Had He been smoking pot? Was His mind "way off in some ethereal meditation"?
 3. No! The Lord's reply showed Him keenly alert to all that was going on: "You would have no power at all if it hadn't been given you by someone else" (cf. John 19:10, 11).
E. Jesus refused the pain-killing drug on the cross. His peace was His own!

IV. "NOT AS THE WORLD GIVETH."
 A. The world can provide an uneasy cessation of hostility, and perhaps make it stick.
  (Compare Sheriff Andy Taylor's effort to quiet a wrangling pair by making them say sweet things to each other. They became unbearable to everybody.)
 B. Personally, the world can give the temporary peace of satiated appetite —
  "Soul, take thine ease — thou hast much goods laid up for many days" (Luke 12:19). (He would have been hungry again tomorrow.)
 C. The world offers the killing of desire through drugs, or meditation, etc.
  These are now popular in a world hungry for peace — but not with Jesus.

V. LET NOT YOUR HEART BE TROUBLED — Believe!
 Believe in God — His Word and His reign beyond the world.
 Believe also in Me — "I have overcome the world."
  Overcame time, space, sin, temptation — "I go to pre-prepare a place for you."
  "I will receive you unto myself, that where I am, there ye may be also" (John 14:1-3).

CONCLUSION —

We receive His peace now; we share His triumph forever. Arise — let us go hence — to Gethsemane — trials — crucifixion — resurrection — glory!

THAT OTHER DISCIPLE
(John 20:1-10)

INTRODUCTION –

There is much in the story to encourage one to identify with that unnamed "other disciple." He is not the headliner in the story, but the one through whose eyes we behold the scene, and through whose words we hear of it.

    A. It is elsewhere established to be John, the apostle—someone special.

        (In the eyes of self and of God, each of us is someone special.) John, the inner circle—closest to Jesus at the Supper, Gethsemane, Calvary.

    B. Willing to claim special prerogatives (Matt. 20:20); asks for place at the right hand of Christ in the kingdom. *"Boanerges"*—Willing to bring down fire on a Samaritan village (Luke 9:51ff.). Forbade one to cast out demons in the name of Christ—"followed not with us" (Luke 9:49).

    C. But here he steps back into the common place—He was not first to see the risen Lord. He comes near to taking his place with us.

    D. Fulfilled the admonition, "Whatsoever thy hand findeth to do, do it with thy might" (Eccl. 9:10).

I. *HEARS* THE WORD OF THE RESURRECTION FROM ANOTHER.

    A. Apparently at his own lodging in Jerusalem.

    B. The words of the women.

        "They have taken away the Lord out of the sepulchre, and we know not where thy have laid him." (Apparently the definite word of the resurrection came later.)

        But see Luke 24:11: "And their words seemed to them [Peter and John] as idle tales, and they believed them not."

347

C. But much concerning Jesus seemed at first incredible. (Experience is in slow motion; and events of years pass in review.)

See: The event of Luke 5:1-11, and the call to be a fisher of men.

The transfiguration, and "Hear ye him."

The manifold miracles—"I suppose the world itself could not contain the books that should be written" (John 21:25).

D. What are you prepared to hear? Only what is already familiar? Then you'll not "Learn of me"—for He is full of surprises.

II. *COMES* TO THE EMPTY TOMB.

A. Response a little like that of Thomas later: "Except I see . . ."

B. He came to learn, to observe, and to share.

C. He was willing to be involved.
   1. It could be dangerous—safer places were far away.
   2. Let someone else stick his neck out first.

D. But John outran Peter (he couldn't outtalk him), and came first to the tomb.

III. *OBSERVES* AND SHARES THE OBSERVATION IN VIVID DETAIL.

A. The open tomb, with stone removed; the soldier guards perhaps by now gone.

B. Leans down and looks inside, seeing the grave wrappings lying empty.

C. Then after Peter enters the tomb, John goes in too.
   —sees the head kerchief, folded by itself.

D. Not the blase attitude of the lad who had "seen a circus already," nor the unimpressed attitude of the one who said, "I was there, but I don't remember anything."

IV. *BELIEVES.*

A. It had to be resurrection; that tomb was not robbed!

B. Then He had to be Messiah—"My Lord and my God!"

C. He believed now what he had been told before: "From that time forth began Jesus to show unto his disciples, how that he must go unto Jerusalem, and suffer many things of the elders and chief priests and scribes, and be killed, and be raised again the third day (Matt. 16:21).

D. But John is the one who recorded Jesus' words to Thomas: "Blessed are they that have not seen, and yet have believed" (John 20:29).

V. *DECLARES*.

(Read John 20:30, 31; 21:24.)

A. To the other disciples who were not present (Thomas later).

B. To Jerusalem: "But Peter and John answered and said unto them, Whether it be right in the sight of God to hearken unto you more than unto God, judge ye. For we cannot but speak the things which we have seen and heard" (Acts 4:19, 20).

"With great power gave the apostles witness of the resurrection of the Lord Jesus" (Acts 4:33).

C. To Ephesus, and to the world.

Rev. 1 — Receives message from the risen Lord.

"I was in the Spirit on the Lord's Day, and heard behind me a great voice, as of a trumpet" (1:10).

CONCLUSION —

There is place in this program of faith and declaration for still another disciple — you!

"The Lord himself shall descend from heaven with a shout, with the voice of the archangel, and with the trump of God . . ." (I Thess. 4:16).

"Even so come, Lord Jesus."

QUESTIONS OVER ACTS

1. Who was chosen to replace Judas as an apostle? (1:26)
2. The early church continued steadfastly in what four things according to Acts 2:42?
3. What Old Testament person predicted God would raise up a prophet like unto himself? (3:22)
4. Who said, "We cannot but speak the things we have seen and heard"? (4:19, 20)
5. What did Peter say was the sin of Ananias and Sapphira? (5:3)
6. The disciples were to choose seven men to serve tables so the apostles could devote themselves to what two things? (6:4)
7. What were Stephen's last words when he was stoned to death? (7:60)
8. What did Philip preach to the Ethiopian treasurer? (8:35)
9. After Saul's conversion what did he preach in the synagogues in Damascus? (9:20)
10. Who was Cornelius? (10:1, 2)
11. Where were the disciples first called Christians? (11:26)
12. In whose house did the disciples meet in prayer for Peter when he was in prison? (12:12)
13. Why did Paul and Barnabas turn to the Gentiles? (13:46)
14. Why did Paul not want to take Mark on his second journey? (15:38)
15. What co-worker did Paul enlist at Lystra? (16:1)
16. What was Paul's trade? (18:3)
17. On what day did Paul preach and break bread with the church at Troas? (20:7)
18. When Paul started following Jesus what did Ananias tell him to do? (22:16)
19. Paul preached to Felix about what three things? (24:25)
20. What strange thing happened to Paul when he was shipwrecked on the island of Malta? (28:3)

PREACHING THROUGH
ACTS OF THE APOSTLES

Rightly called by many the "most important book in the Bible," the Acts of the Apostles will make enjoyable and profitable reading for you this month. Join with us as we study this book together.

IMPORTANCE OF THE BOOK

This book alone carries the whole load of inspired history, telling how Christ's Church was established and grew under the leadership of the apostles. There are four records of Jesus' life. There are twenty-one letters to the churches. There is only one record telling how the life and commission of Christ took form in the churches to which the letters were written. That record is in the book of Acts.

IT TELLS

How the church was established.
How the Gospel was preached by inspired men.
How men in every age are to be saved through Christ.
How missionary work was done when men followed Christ most closely.
How the heroes of the faith lived and suffered joyously for their Lord.

THE WRITING OF ACTS

The book was written about A.D. 63 by Luke, the "beloved physician" and companion of Paul. Even the most critical scholars marvel at its historical accuracy.

OUTLINE OF THE BOOK

Chapters 1-12: The Church in Jerusalem and Judea (Peter is the main character).
1   Preparation for Pentecost.
2   Establishment of the Church.
3-5   The church in Jerusalem.

351

Chapters 6-8   Choosing of the seven, and the preaching of two of them.

9   The conversion of Saul.

10,11   Extension of the gospel to the Gentiles.

12   Persecution of the Christians.

13-28   The Church "Unto the Uttermost Parts of the Earth" (Paul is the main character).

13,14   Paul's first missionary journey.

15   The council at Jerusalem, concerning the Law and the Gospel.

16-18   Paul's second missionary journey.

19,20   Paul's third missionary journey.

21-26   Paul's arrest and imprisonment.

27,28   Paul's voyage to Rome.

Sermon Outlines Provided:

"Ye Shall Be My Witnesses" (Acts 1:1-11)

"The Christian College and the Churches" (Acts 2:41-47)

"Conversion of a Thoughtful Man" (Acts 8:25-40)

"Conversion of a Just Man" (Acts 10)

"Why Call for a Preacher?" (Acts 10:24-33)

"Marks of a Good Man" (Acts 11:19-26)

"Contending in the Faith" (Acts 15:36-41)

"Timothy Comes to Corinth" (Acts 16:1-5; 18:5)

"The Conversion of an Active Man" (Acts 16:19-34)

Other Sermon Topics Suggested:

"Preachers of Pentecost" (Acts 2:1-4, 22-31)

"Prayer for the Preacher" (Acts 4:23-31)

"The Things that He Possessed" (Acts 4:32-37)

"The Conversion of a Religious Man" (Acts 9:1-19)

"Marks of Nobility" (Acts 17:10, 11)

"Partners" (Acts 18:1-5, 24-28)

YE SHALL BE MY WITNESSES
(Acts 1:1-11)

INTRODUCTION —

When one is given a job to do, he wants to know the nature of the work. We have a job in the life of the church, immediately and continuing. We must obey our Great Employer.

I. "YE SHALL BE MY WITNESSES"
  — the Apostles were addressed.
  A. The qualification of a witness.
    "Him God raised up the third day, and showed him openly; not to all the people, but unto witnesses chosen before of God, even to us who did eat and drink with him after he rose from the dead" (Acts 10:40, 41).

    "Wherefore of these men which have companied with us all the time that the Lord Jesus went in and out among us, unto . . . that same day when he was taken up from us, must one be ordained to be a witness with us of his resurrection" (Acts 1:21, 22).
  B. Witnesses were appointed by Christ:
    1. Such as would bear testimony without conscious interpretation.
    2. They were capable, plain men, without sophistication or subterfuge.
  C. Witnesses were given ample evidence of His Lordship, especially in resurrection.
    — They were prepared by close living acquaintance.
  D. Witnesses promised special power of recollection.
    1. "But the comforter, which is the Holy Ghost, whom the Father will send in my name, he shall teach you all things, and bring all things to your remembrance, whatsoever I have said unto you" (John 14:26).
    2. It was recollection, not discovery or invention.
  E. Witnesses given the promised power.
    "But ye shall receive power, after that the Holy Spirit is come upon you."

353

II. WITNESSES TO JERUSALEM, JUDEA, SAMARIA, AND UNTO THE UTTERMOST. . . .

    A. Beginning at Jerusalem, the apostles preached and led in establishing the Church.

    —They covered Judea, through the persecution and scattering.

    B. Samaria is specified in the ministry of Philip.

    C. To the uttermost part of the earth, theirs is the testimony through Scripture.

        "Forasmuch as many have taken in hand to set forth in order a declaration of those things which are most surely believed among us, even as they delivered them unto us, which from the beginning were eyewitnesses and ministers of the word; it seemed good to me also, . . . to write unto thee in order, . . . that thou mightest know the certainty of those things, wherein thou hast been instructed" (Luke 1:1-4).

        (Illustration)— When a court case is appealed, but the recorded testimony of the original witnesses, perhaps now dead, is reviewed by the higher court, as it is presented and argued by counsel. the original witnesses are the only witnesses.

III. AND CONCLUSION —

What then is our position?

    A. *First,* to accept and build on apostolic testimony.

    B. We can be *witnesses* only of those things which we have seen and heard.

    C. But far more importantly, we are *messengers* of the apostolic testimony to the uttermost part of the earth.

    D. This is the purpose of Christ, that the good news of His death for our sins reach all men. (Illustration—the warning of a flood must reach all in the valley. There are newspapers, radio, telephone—but some don't have them.)

    E. So, too, we have the Bible, church, etc., but some do not hear them—each person must be a messenger.

THE CHRISTIAN COLLEGE AND THE CHURCHES
(Acts 2:41-47)

INTRODUCTION —

Meet Lucius, the teacher at Antioch (Acts 13:1).

    A. Came to Antioch from Cyprus (Acts 11:19-21).

    B. Scattered from Jersualem (Acts 8:1-4).

    C. Why in Jerusalem? (Acts 2:42).

    D. When did he come? (Acts 2:10).

I. THE EARLY CHAPTERS OF ACTS DESCRIBE A BIBLE COLLEGE ALMOST AS MUCH AS A CHURCH.

    A. The apostles were teachers (Acts 2:42; 4:2, 18).

    B. The Christians were disciples, learners — (See Acts 5:12, 13; Matt. 28:20).

    C. The place of the daily teaching is named; Solomon's porch of Temple (5:12).

    D. Curriculum — "Whatsoever I [Jesus] have commanded."

    E. Graduation and activity (Acts 6, 7, 8).

II. WHAT EDUCATION DID THESE MEN (LUCIUS AND OTHERS) RECEIVE?

    A. It was not accredited — They were "unlearned and ignorant men" (4:13).

    B. Something is more important than accreditation.

    C. What is necessary to do the job? Any other standard may be misleading.

        1. One needs to know and respect the Word of God.

        2. He needs to express himself clearly, accurately, simply.

        3. He needs to have vital touch with life, past and present.

        4. He needs to think for himself.

        5. He needs to be perpetually a student — otherwise comes mental deterioration. ("He isn't a student any more; he got his degree last June" — a horrid calumny!)

III. THE CURRICULUM WAS ESSENTIALLY CHRIST.
Matthew 11:28, 29 — Student does the learning.
   A. Come unto Me, and *I will give you rest* — refreshment.
      1. The unburdening of hindering guilt, fears, loneliness, jealousy, selfishness.
      2. The renewing of zest and strength for labor.
   B. *Come unto Me* — Learn of Me.
      1. Personal acceptance of a life.
      2. We may we can not avoid personalities in learning principles.
      3. Love, light, and life is in the flesh.
         Thus also Christian teaching — Be imitators of me as I am of Christ. ("I want to be the kind of a man Mark Hopkins is.")
   C. Take My yoke upon you — Learning involves commitment.
      1. Commitment to the task of learning — how efficient are we?
      2. Commitment to the doing of the thing learned.
   D. Acts 2:42 introduces one to classroom, campus, cafeteria, and chapel.
      — Small Christian college is best equipped to meet these needs — relationship, attitude, personalities, commitment, atmosphere. *Has something money can't buy. That doesn't mean it doesn't need money.*

IV. EDUCATION REQUIRES FINANCIAL STEWARDSHIP IN HEROIC PROPORTIONS (vv. 44, 45).
   A. Here is explained the "communism" in Jerusalem. Not a mistake that was given up; not a pattern for all; but the meeting of a special need in a special way.
   B. Acts 2:41-47 tells of Christians far from home without support; "students on full scholarship."
      1. The need was seen and it was met.
      2. Couldn't call on neighboring churches; there were none; this was beginning.
   C. Others were asked to help later (Rom. 15:26).

CONCLUSION —
The results — the best possible investment (see I Thess. 3:8).

CONVERSION OF A THOUGHTFUL MAN
(Acts 8:25-40)

INTRODUCTION — the time is spring or early summer in the year about A.D. 35.

The place is a lonely ravine in the south of Judea.

A chariot, marked with the official emblems of dignity of the Ethipoian monarchy, moved along the stone paved Roman road.

I. THE MAN IN THE CHARIOT.

In all probability a black man.

A. A slave, physically mutilated so that he must always be a slave.

B. By sheer ability and dependability he has reached an eminence known to few freemen . . . now a person of grandeur.

C. Still humble, and devout. (The horses are not running —perhaps because of road conditions.)

    1. A proselyte to Judaism, he came 1500 miles to worship (at the feast).

    2. He knew that he would be allowed only in the court of the Gentiles, and must send his offering into the Temple by other hands.

D. Now on return, he is reading the Prophet Isaiah.

    1. A thoughtful man, he is using the time—but not for business.

    2. The Temple worship has lifted him spiritually, and he continues to seek the will of God in His word.

    3. He reads aloud, perhaps to fix his attention, perhaps to instruct his driver.

    4. Unwilling simply to read and to pass by, he seeks the meaning—probably knows that this passage has given great concern to the scribes.

II. THE PREACHER MEETS HIM IN THE WAY.

Here some things the eunuch doesn't know.

A. That this preacher was selected of God because of his kindly approach to strangers. He is the one who has gone to the despised Samaritans.

B. That an angel of God made this appointment with Philip while the Ethiopian was still worshiping in the temple at Jerusalem, and that Philip has been traveling a full day more to this place than he himself has traveled.

C. That the Spirit has just commanded him, "Join thyself to the chariot."

(The preacher, not the prospect, is subject of angelic visitation.) "The Scriptures were opened to him by the ministration of angels and of the Holy Spirit, but all became effective to him through the words of the preacher" — *McGarvey*.

D. "Understandest thou what thou readest?" — the preacher's wise question.

The understanding of that particular passage is a key to the man's faith and attitude. If a Christian, he will; if not, he won't.

III. THE TEXT.

God apparently knew he would be reading it.

IV. THE SERMON.

Beginning at the same scripture he preached to him Jesus. — by comparison with sermons of others, we know something of its content.

A. It spoke of the prophecies concerning the Messiah, perhaps facing difficulties.

B. It spoke of the life and person of Jesus, fulfilling these prophecies.

C. It emphasized His atoning death, and His resurrection.

D. Probably in this case it mentioned what Christ offers — "There is neither Jew nor Greek, bond nor free, male nor female, but one man in Christ" (Gal. 3:28).

E. It told what Christ commands — how else did the Ethipian know of baptism?

358

V. THE DECISION.
   A. It was his own decision, not forced upon him by another.
   B. It seems hasty for a thoughtful man—but mark what kind of a man he was.
   C. The facts were all in, established by the Word of God —what more to come?
   D. On those facts he made a decision, and on the decision he based immediate action. —To delay action unnecessarily is to break down the force to act.
   E. The necessity of faith (v. 37); its fact evident, whether or not in text.

VI. THE BAPTISM.
   A. They came to a certain water—perhaps in Valley of Elah, where David crossed to meet Goliath.
      1. Farther, in the Philistine plain, the Wady el Hasy, a year round stream.
      2. Many artificial pools, built to hold water for stock and crops through seven dry months, as Kentucky ponds.
   B. The action clearly described.

VII. THE RESULT.
   He went on his way rejoicing.
   A. The Abyssinian church has traditions of his ministry in Africa.
   B. The inspired record closes with this . . . No more perplexing problems—He is the answer. No more weary pilgrimmages—"Ye are the Temple." No more sacrifices carried in by other hands—"You are a living sacrifice, acceptable" (Rom. 12:1, 2).

CONCLUSION —

O happy day that fixed my choice
On thee my Savior and my God
Well may this glowing heart rejoice,
And tell its raptures all abroad.

Happy day, happy day,
When Jesus washed my sins away.

THE CONVERSION OF A JUST MAN
(Acts 10)

INTRODUCTION —

"There is a way which seemeth right unto a man, but the end thereof are the ways of death" (Proverbs 14:12).

God and men see differently in many things.

There is no better illustration of the way of salvation through Christ, than in the case of Cornelius.

I. THE CHARACTER OF THE MAN WOULD HAVE LED MEN TO THINK HE WAS SAFE.
   A. A devout man—personally pious.
   B. Feared God with all his house—traditionally religious as a Jew.
   C. Giving much alms—Charitable with his fellowman.
   D. Praying continually—an expression of religion and piety.

II. SEE THE EFFECT OF HIS CHARACTER.
   A. His prayers were heard.
      —It is not said that they were answered nor that they saved him.
   B. He was remembered for his alms.
      —There is no indication of salvation in either or both of these statements.
   C. It is quite evident, however, that God thought such a man very much worth saving, and went far out of His way to make it possible that he should hear the Gospel.

III. THE CLEAR EVIDENCE IS THAT HE WAS NOT YET SAVED.
   A. "He shall tell thee what thou oughtest to do."
   B. "Who, when he is come, shall speak to you."
   C. "Send to Joppa and bring hither Simon, whose surname is Peter, who shall speak words to you, by which you and all your family shall be saved."
   D. Man would ask why God didn't save both Himself and Peter a great deal of trouble by giving an immediate saving revelation.

— the truth is that we have no scriptural evidence that any man ever was saved in that way, and consequently no assurance whatever than one can be thus saved. Turn to God (Acts 20:1).

IV. PETER PREACHED TO THEM CHRIST.
  A. Here is one reason the salvation could not come by immediate means.
      It must come through an acceptance of the good news about Jesus, and so it was referred to one who knew it.
  B. The preaching of the Gospel was the basis for the action and acceptance on the part of the hearts.
  C. "There is none other name under heaven, that is given among men, whereby we must be saved" (Acts 4:12).

V. PETER COMMANDED THEM TO BE BAPTIZED.
   This was the promised directive (see v. 6).
  A. They had already received the baptism of the Holy Spirit.
      1. This was a sign of the fact that they were fit candidates for the kingdom, but it was not enough for salvation.
      2. Here again God's way and man's diverge sharply.
  B. "Who can forbid water?"
      There was enough water involved so that it was an item to be considered.

CONCLUSION —

How was this a conversion? A change?
  A. Cornelius surely did not change from being devout, prayerful, generous, and a spiritual leader in his home.
  B. Consider an analogy. We know a Pennsylvania woolen mill that produced excellent shirts and blankets. During World War II it was converted to war production. What did it produce? Shirts and blankets! But for the armed forces, rather than for the civilian market.
  C. Cornelius was not less new than the veriest sinner is new. Each is a new man in Christ Jesus, living in Him and for Him. To Him be the glory!

WHY CALL FOR A PREACHER?
(Acts 10:19-33)

INTRODUCTION —

The Apostle Peter still asked the little boy's question: "Why?" It was a good question, and it brought a remarkable answer.

 A. The story.
   1. Peter raised Dorcas from the dead in Joppa, and stayed there for a time.
   2. Cornelius, at Caesarea, was instructed to send for Peter, who would bring him the words of life.
   3. By a threefold vision, God prepared Peter to receive and communicate with Gentiles.
   4. Peter received Cornelius' messengers and returned with them to Caesarea, some thirty miles along the Mediterranean coast.
 B. Twice Peter asked "Why did you send for me?"
   1. He asked the messengers when they arrived at Joppa (v. 21).
   2. He asked Cornelius after Peter and his companions arrived at Caesarea (v. 29).

I. PETER'S QUESTION: A WISE APPROACH.

 A. He wanted to know the assignment before he addressed himself to it.
   1. God had already directed Peter to go, but where? and for what?
   2. The present-day preacher, not thus directed, must also decide whether to go.
   3. In any case, the ministry must be fitted to the need.
 B. He wanted his hearers to see clearly their own motivation.
   1. Folk often do good things for bad reasons; they need to clear up the reasons before they fail and the good things are no longer done.
   2. Why does your church want a preacher? To fit the usual pattern? To lead in a program? To call on the sick? To pat hands and console the lonely?

3. Cornelius' motivation was clear: he wanted to hear the God-given gospel (vv. 22, 33).

C. Peter wanted to establish a relationship with his hearers.
   1. Their first welcome, "worshiping," was cause for concern (v. 25).
      a. Too many Christians "worship" their ministers, then turn bitterly against them when they discover some human weakness, or cease coming to church when the minister moves on.
      b. God, in Christ, must be the sole center and focus of worship.
   2. Peter's reply was and is needed: "I also am a man."
      a. Not more than a man to be "reverenced," nor less than a man to be disregarded.
      b. The saving power and divine quality was in the message, not the messenger.

II. CORNELIUS' REPLY: A WORTHY AUDIENCE (v. 33).
   A. We are all here present.
      1. Many "kinsmen and near friends" were gathered (vv. 24, 27; 11:14).
      2. Cornelius was not one to see others starve while he feasted, physically or spiritually (compare v. 2).
      3. The preacher did not have to round up his audience; the hearers did that!
      4. Anyone's attitude toward the preached message will be much improved if he has brought a friend to hear it.
   B. We are present before God.
      1. God had instructed the gathering; He was present and they knew it.
      2. There was no problem with reverent behavior.
      3. When you enter God's house, it is well to greet your friends, but speak first to the Host, before whom you all are guests.
   C. We are present to hear.
      1. They were purposeful and responsible: they would gain much more from the gathering.

363

2. They *attended* (gave attention in) that gathering. Attend to what is said!

3. Peter had no need for a long, amusing "introduction" to his sermon.

4. If speakers need training and preparation, so do listeners; just as your radio receiver needs to be operative before the broadcast does you any good.

D. All things that are commanded thee of God.

1. It was an inclusive demand, and willingness ("all things").

   a. They were godly folk, but they were still to hear new and unfamiliar facts of the Gospel, plus new and unfulfilled obligations (v. 48).

   b. Nothing must be left out of the words by which they were to be saved.

2. It was an exclusive demand ("commanded thee of God").

   a. No place for a travelogue of Peter's trip through the Sharon Plain.

   b. Did they know that God had needed to overcome Peter's personal inclinations? (He had admitted it! v. 28).

   c. Another great audience, hearing Paul, "searched the scriptures daily, whether these things were so" (Acts 17:11).

CONCLUSION —

A responsible preacher rose to the occasion with a remarkable audience and made history. So the household of Cornelius heard the words of life; they believed; they received the seal of the Holy Spirit (God's approval); they were baptized into Christ; and the door of the Church was opened to the Gentiles.

Great things will still happen when folk assemble themselves in large, expectant gatherings, before God, to hear all things that God has given His messenger to speak.

MARKS OF A GOOD MAN
(Acts 11:19-26)

INTRODUCTION — Who is great?

Paul was great; but he had a partner who was "good."

That designation available to us, even if the other is not.

I. RECORD OF A GOOD MAN.
   A. Acts 4:36, 37 — Introduction: Joseph - given an honor name, "son of encouragement."
      1. Levite — but different from the one who walked the Jericho road, and chose "the other side."
      2. "Native of Cyprus" — Mediterranean island.
      3. "Having property, evidently in Judea.
      4. Sold (all of it?); brought the price and "laid it at the feet of the apostles."
      5. Related to Mary, mother of Mark, whose home became a meeting place.
   B. Acts 9:27 — Gained Saul's acceptance among disciples in Jerusalem.
      1. Took Saul to the apostles — accepted here, Saul would be accepted by others.
      2. Told of Saul's experience on Damascus road.
      3. Told of Saul's bold and hazardous preaching in Damascus. — How did he know?
   C. Acts 11:19-30 — Ministry in Antioch.
      1. Sent by the Apostles to investigate.
      2. Observed, rejoiced, encouraged.
      3. Went to Tarsus and brought Saul.
      4. Taught and built the church first called Christian.
      5. Sent by brethren, with Saul, to Jerusalem with famine relief.
   D. Acts 12:25 — 13:13.
      1. Returned from Jerusalem with Saul and Mark.
      2. Listed first (Saul last) among prominent teachers in Antioch.
      3. Commissioned by the Holy Spirit and set apart by the church "Barnabas and Saul."
      4. Went to his own native *Cyprus,* and there the lead changed hands!

365

   a. Confrontation with Elymas the sorcerer—"Paul and his company."
   b. Conversion of Sergius Paulus. (Mark leaves soon after.)
E. Acts 14—In Galatia—Lystra: He was called Jupiter, Paul called Mercury.
F. Acts 15—In Jerusalem reporting, insisting that Christ was enough—
   1. Gentiles did not need to follow the rituals of Judaism.
   2. References are again to "Barnabas and Paul." Did the elders see in Barnabas the steadier influence?
G. Acts 15:36-41—The controversy over John Mark.
   —Barnabas and Mark go back to Cyprus; Paul and Silas on Paul's second missionary journey.
H. I Corinthians 9:6 "Are Barnabas and I the only ones who need to work for a living?" Paul asks.

II. REFERENCES OF A GOOD MAN.
A. Attributes.
   1. Full of the Holy Spirit—"Paracletes"—comforter.
      —No record of any miracles—not associated with "tongues."
   2. Full of faith—not in material things.
      a. Faith in God.
      b. Faith in God's people.
   B. Attitudes.
      1. Generosity, material and spiritual—Sharing with all.
      2. Optimism, hopefulness.
      3. Interest in the home folks—back in Cyprus.
   C. Actions.
      1. Saw—as he had seen in Saul, etc.
      2. Rejoiced—in others' accomplishments.
      3. Exhorted—from him the exhortation was accepted.

CONCLUSION — Much people added to the Lord.

"None greater than John the Baptist; but he that is least in the kingdom is greater than he" (Matt. 11:11).

"Well done, good and faithful servant; enter thou into the joy of thy Lord."

CONTENDING IN THE FAITH
(Acts 15:36-41; I Corinthians 3:1-6)

INTRODUCTION —

Even the Apostles had a touch of human weakness.

    A. Rough spots in the early Church become warnings.

    B. This does not take away from the inspiration of the gospel or the administration of the church.

    C. "Enmities, strife, jealousies, wraths, factions, divisions" —are listed as works of the flesh (Gal. 5:20).

    D. Paul urges peaceableness (Phil. 2:1-4).

    E. When we come to know and do God's will perfectly, contention will cease.

    F. The growing family quarrels; the grown family should not.

I. THE PROGRAM OF THE APOSTLES

    —to visit and encourage the churches.

    A. Both men were firmly committed to the Gospel.

        1. Paul, the apostle, with his vision of Christ.

        2. Barnabas, the generous—surety for Paul; partner in former journey.

    B. But their very zeal made possible the contention.

        1. There is no contention among those who don't care.

        2. There is no contention among slaves and puppets.

II. THE ISSUE—the choice of a partner for the journey.

    A. Personal issues entered only slightly—but too much.

        1. Barnabas never contended for himself, but here for a relative.

        —His very generosity was behind it.

        2. Paul considered that the work would be hindered by Mark's presence.

        Lingering resentment over former defection.

    B. It was a question to which there could be no sure answer.

        1. A "thus-saith-the-Lord" would have cleared the matter.

        2. "In essentials, unity; in non-essentials, liberty, in all things, love." —Now just what is essential?

3. We sometimes fight most savagely to prove to ourselves that we are right, where we can't be sure.

III. THE CONTENTION—"SHARP."

 A. Of Peter's defection, "I withstood him *to the face.*"
—There was no talking behind the other's back—nothing *anonymous.*

 B. Probably each thought it was principle with him, personal with the other.

 C. They retained respect and kindness for each other.

 D. They kept it in the family; it wasn't spread abroad.

 E. They proved their sincerity by godly life and work.

IV. THE RESULT.

 A. They did not allow personal slight to interfere with usefulness in Gospel.
—(President Lincoln, ignored at a ball by McClellan, refuses to relieve him of his command.)

 B. Another team went forth to preach.
"Some indeed preach Christ even of envy and strife" (Phil. 1:15-18).

V. POSTSCRIPT-RECONCILIATION.

 A. "Be angry and sin not. Let not the sun go down upon your wrath" (Eph. 4:26).

 B. How was reconciliation accomplished? Perhaps not directly at all, but see:
"Or I only and Barnabas, have we not a right to forbear working?" (I Cor. 9:6).
"If he (Mark) come unto you, receive him" (Col. 4:10).
"Send Mark, for his is useful to me for ministering" (II Tim. 4:11).

CONCLUSION —

We have growing to do. The Church is to edify "the body of Christ; till we all come in the unity of the faith, and of the knowledge of the Son of God, unto a perfect man, unto the measure of the stature of the fullness of Christ" (Eph. 4:13).

TIMOTHY COMES TO CORINTH
(Acts 16:1-5; 18:5; II Tim. 1)

INTRODUCTION —

Churches speak of their Timothys, serving in many places. But where is the church that produced the Biblical Timothy?

A. Much more is said of the people with whom he served, and the places to which he came.

B. Acts 16 tells of a team ministry: Paul, Silas, Timothy, Luke. It calls to mind others: Paul and Barnabas and Mark; Peter and John.

C. Acts 18:1-5 reflects the results of a team ministry. The work is done, as each member contributes his own special skill to the total effort. Job descriptions are good, and necessary; but the essential element is personal, and not organizational or mechanical.

D. II Timothy 1 reflects the personal qualities of the Paul-Timothy team.

I. CHARACTER THAT GROWS FROM FAITH.

A. See II Timothy 1:3, 12, 5.

B. II Tim. 3:10, 11 "Thou hast fully known my doctrine, manner of life, purpose, faith, longsuffering, charity, patience, persecutions, afflictions, which came unto me at Antioch, at Iconium, at Lystra" (where Timothy met him). — So the relationship provides an unsparing revelation of character.

C. One becomes aware of "good faults," good-bad aspects of the same quality.

1. (As "a squeal goes with disc brakes." And beauty takes a long time in the bathroom.)

2. Some unyielding insistencies came with Paul's zeal.

3. And some lack of aggressiveness came with Timothy's tender affection.

II. CARE AND PRAYER, BOTH WAYS.

A. "Timothy my son" ("As a son with a father, so he has served with me in the gospel" — Phil. 2:19-23).

369

"Remembering thy tears, that I might be filled with joy."

B. The relationship makes demands: Paul becomes responsible for things he doesn't do; Timothy "plays second fiddle."

C. The relationship brings privileges, blessings, benefits.
1. Paul enjoys accomplishments he could not make alone (Who remembers Timothy at Corinth?)
2. Timothy's errands became responsibilities and finally notable leadership.

III. CHOICE IN ESTABLISHING THE RELATIONSHIP.

A. Paul knew Timothy's family, heard recommendations concerning him; invited him to go along.

B. Timothy seems to have concurred in the agreement.

C. Dual purpose: Doing the work and building the worker. Strangely, the two purposes are served together.

IV. CONFIDENCE (vv. 1, 13).

A. Each must have confidence in himself.
1. Otherwise the leader becomes like King Saul with David: jealous, destructive.
2. Otherwise Timothy becomes restive and ambitious.

B. Each must have confidence in the other.
—You can't watch him all the time; that would stall the work.

C. This confidence becomes loyalty and protectiveness toward the partner.
"I am a part of this ministry; my part cannot prosper without his."

V. COMMUNICATION.

A. Appreciation and prayer—includes memories and hope.

B. Exhortation—Stir up the gift (v. 6); Guard the treasure (v. 14).

CONCLUSION —

Rewards are shared: "Not to me only" (II Tim. 4:8).

370

THE CONVERSION OF AN ACTIVE MAN
(Acts 16:19-34)

INTRODUCTION —

We usually identify ourselves with the hero of a story. For variety, identify yourself with the jailer.

I. THE MAN YOU ARE.

A veteran of the Roman army—(garrison at Philippi; a Roman colony).

A. Given to obedience without question.

B. Given to action without delay whatever the occasion—
1. Your life has sometimes depended on it.
2. The occasions have sometimes been brutal.

C. Rome has shown you:
1. Might without mercy—the Empire demands it.
2. Ethics without morals. There are standards, but they concern what will serve the Empire.
3. Punishment without qualms for criminals and enemies.
4. Vengeance without limit.

Strange men come into your life.

II. INTRODUCTION TO PAUL AND SILAS.

A. Babblers teaching a strange doctrine that doesn't concern you.

B. "Salvation" is involved.

C. They are handed over for keeping.
1. In bad shape when they come.
2. Don't fit picture of common criminals—not cursing or reviling.

D. You obey, putting them in maximum security without asking why.

—Nothing here to keep you from sleeping.

III. THE EARTHQUAKE AND ITS RESULT.

A. At the awakening, things begin to concern *you*.

B. Security of prisoners is first care.
1. Inner and outer doors of prison found open; surely they escaped.

371

    2. Code of honor demands death before dishonor.

    3. The choice is prompt and automatic.

C. Then the cry—"Do yourself no harm; we are all here!"

    1. The reaction of a narrow escape—fear and trembling.

    2. Why did he do it?

    3. "What must I do to be saved?" (I'll do it promptly.)

IV. THE COMMAND THAT REQUIRED TEACHING.

A. Believe on the Lord Jesus Christ—(you can't salute and do that pronto.)

    1. Paul's purpose to prevent thoughtless outward action.

    2. Your friends are given the same promise you are.

B. "Spake [unto him] the word of the Lord."

    1. The *power* of Christ is all mercy—made men out of "cases."

    2. The *ethics* of Christ are all purity—in this He led.

    3. *Punishment* is borne by Him, for us.

    4. Vengeance gives way to "Father, forgive them."
    —That is why the apostles cried out to save you!

C. Spake the word of the Lord to all in the house.

    1. Same Christ, on same terms for all.

    2. Infants obviously not included here.

V. THE ACTS THAT FOLLOWED—washed their stripes!

A. Were baptized immediately.

    1. Teaching of it was a part of "the word of the Lord."

    2. There was cause for delay here if anywhere—"untaught"—illegality—danger—*but there was no delay*!

B. Brought them into the house and set meat before them—hospitality, a normal expression of membership in Christ's body.

C. Believing and rejoicing.

CONCLUSION —

    Buried with Christ and raised with Him, too.

    What is there left for me to do?

    Simply to cease from struggling and strife.

    Simply to walk in newness of life.

PREACHING THROUGH ROMANS

According to our custom in encouraging every Christian to be a regular reader and student of God's Word, we invite you to read with us during this month the sixteen chapters of Paul's letter to the Romans. If there are questions which arise in your reading, your preacher will be more than glad to help you find their solution. Questions of public interest will be handled publicly.

Samuel Taylor Coleridge called Romans "The most profound work in existence."

THE WRITING OF ROMANS

While at Corinth during his Third Missionary Journey Paul wrote this epistle to the Christians at Rome. He had never been to Rome, but had many friends there. He desired to go to Rome, and wrote the letter partly to introduce himself ahead of his arrival to the Roman Christians. This book gives a very thorough answer to the question, "How may a man be acceptable to God?"

DIFFICULTY OF THE BOOK

Two things make this book harder than some others to understand. First is its literary style. Some sentences are very long and complicated. Second is the fact that it treats prominently a question which is less important to us than it was to the Roman Christians of Paul's day—"Can one be a Christian without first being a Jew?" In spite of these difficulties, this is one of the grandest books in the entire Bible. It contains much that is as new as today.

GREAT PASSAGES IN ROMANS

The Preaching of the Gospel	1:13-17 and 10:8-15
"Judge Not"	2:1-23
Justification by Faith	3:19-26
The Meaning of Christian Baptism	6:1-14
The Christian's Comfort	8:33-39
The Practical, Consecrated Christian Life	12:1-21

OUTLINE OF THE BOOK

Chapters 1-11 The Doctrinal Part of the Book.

1:1 — 3:21 Man's failure to save himself by deeds of the law.

3:22 — 6:23 Salvation is through faith in Jesus Christ.

7, 8 The law is weak; the Spirit is strong.

9-11 The unbelief of the Jews does not change God's plan.

Chapters 12-16 The Practical Part of the Book.

12 God's goodness must be reflected in a good life.

13 The Christian has duties to the government and to others.

14, 15 The Christian must respect those who differ with him.

16 Paul sends concluding greetings.

Sermon Outlines Provided:

"Not Ashamed" (Romans 1:13-25)

"The Need of the Gospel" (Romans 3)

"Justification by Faith" (Romans 3:19-31)

"A Matter of Death and Life" (Romans 6:1-14)

"Law and Conscience" (Romans 7:1 — 8:3)

"What We'd Rather Not Say" (Romans 10:9-15)

"Citizenship" (Romans 13:1-8)

"Responsibility to Brethren" (Romans 14:1 — 15:13)

Other Sermon Topics Suggested:

"In Debt to Strangers" (Romans 1:10-16)

"Accessories After the Fact" (Romans 1:18-33)

"Peace — Past, Present, and Promised" (Romans 8:1-11)

"Children and Heirs" (Romans 8:9-17)

"Your Gift to the Great Giver" (Romans 11:33 — 12:8)

QUESTIONS OVER ROMANS

1. In Romans 1:16 Paul says he is not ashamed of what?
2. Paul says that pagans had worshiped what instead of the Creator? (1:25)

3. How does Paul describe a true Jew? (2:29)
4. What advantage did the Jews have over the Gentiles? (3:1, 2)
5. Paul concludes that how many have sinned? (3:23)
6. Was Abraham justified by faith before the law was given? (4:1-3)
7. Who has shed abroad the love of God in our hearts? (5:5)
8. How have Christians been buried with Christ? (6:4)
9. Did Paul say the law was sin? (7:7)
10. Paul says there is no condemnation for whom? (8:1)
11. How does Paul say we can be "more than conquerors"? (8:37)
12. What is Paul's prayer for Israel? (10:1)
13. Faith comes by hearing what? (10:17)
14. Paul calls himself an apostle of what group of people? (11:13)
15. Instead of conforming to the world, Paul asks that Christians be transformed by what? (12:2)
16. We are to owe no man anything except what? (13:8)
17. Who all must stand before the judgment seat of Christ? (14:10)
18. How does Paul say we are to receive one another? (15:7)
19. Paul hopes to see the Romans on a trip he wanted to take to what country? (15:24)
20. What name of the church is given in Romans 16:16?

NOT ASHAMED
(Romans 1:13-25)

INTRODUCTION —

One of the world's brilliant personalities writes to the Christians at Rome, the center of the affairs of the world, "I am not ashamed of the gospel." Startling suggestion that he, and they, might have been ashamed of it. There were many who had already become ashamed of it.

I. I AM NOT ASHAMED OF THE GOSPEL.
   A. That Jesus of Nazareth is the Messiah.
      1. "He was despised and rejected of men" (Isa. 53:3).
      2. Celsus scoffs that so humble a man should be Messiah.
      3. "Nevertheless even of the rulers many believed on him; but because of the Pharisees they did not confess it, lest they should be put out of the synagogue: for they loved the glory that is of men more than the glory that is of God" (John 12:42).
      4. Circles today in which acceptance of the deity of Christ marks one as less than well-informed, and bordering on superstition.
   B. That Christ died to save sinners.
      1. "We preach Christ crucified, unto Jews a stumblingblock, and unto Gentiles foolishness; but unto them that are called, both Jews and Greeks, Christ the power of God and the wisdom of God" (I Cor. 1:23, 24).
         a. Jews ashamed of a Messiah who would die thus (Celsus).
         b. Gentiles thought it meaningless.
      2. Peter at first ashamed at the death of Christ — "All ye shall be offended."
      3. Modern trend shying away from unpleasant subject of sin and death.
   C. That Christ rose from the dead the third day. Not ashamed to believe it.
      1. "When they heard of the resurrection of the dead, some mocked; and others said, We will hear thee again of this matter" (Acts 17:32).

2. Intellectuals try to find a way around it.
3. Hardened paganism.
    When Elmer Kile preached in 1945, from trailer on street corner in New York City, the boys say, "Don't give us that stuff; when you're dead, you're dead!"

II. IT IS THE POWER OF GOD.
A. Not the power of men.
    1. Strange that men would insist on God's using *their* brand of "dynamite."
    2. Paul doesn't say that this is the way he would have chosen to preach.
    3. "My ways are not your ways, nor my thoughts your thoughts" (Isa. 55:8).
B. Difference
    — Man blasts a rock with explosivess; God plants a seed in a crevice, drops water into the earth and freezes it.
C. The gospel is the power of God.
    1. It changed head-hunters into missionaries in the Pacific islands.
    2. It made a Kagawa out of a "Jap," which is more than all the armed might of America could do.

III. IT IS UNTO SALVATION.
A theme of which the pagan world is ashamed.

A. Romans are reminded of the results of their civilization
    — producing all manner of unutterable sin.
B. Civilization, without God, is more destructive than uncivilization.
C. See the refinements of destruction in German prison camps; mass production methods; scientific control of crematories; use of heat to warm dwellings; use of human ashes for fertilizer. This is the natural result of man's worship of himself and his own power. The gospel is God's power unto salvation from world suicide.
D. Individual and eternal salvation.

1. No other plan offers anything in this direction; here we have a promise—and here alone. . . . "I am the resurrection and the life."
2. A brilliant student once said, "There are many beautiful things about the Christian religion, but when any system attempts to tell a man whence he came and where he is going, that is attempting too much."
   a. But that young man was studying in a college made possible by that faith.
   b. He was protected by laws that were made under that faith.
   c. The freedom out of which he spoke, came from the teaching of Christ that the single man is eternally worthwhile.
3. I am not ashamed to believe, "I go to prepare a place for you."

IV. TO THEM THAT BELIEVE.

1. No universalism here. "He that believeth not shall be condemned" (Mark 16:16).
2. "Without faith it is impossible to please Him."
3. There is no teaching of faith-alone.
   a. Paul assumes that those who believe will act as though they believe.
   b. "All we who were baptized into Christ Jesus were baptized into his death" (Rom. 6:3).

CONCLUSION — II Timothy 1:7-13.

Written at *Rome* near the end, when Paul himself was an offense to some. Demas hath forsaken me—ashamed of the Gospel, but "be not ashamed!"

THE NEED OF THE GOSPEL
(Romans 3)

INTRODUCTION —

The test of a physician is in his practice.

    A. So, one test of the Bible lies in the fact that it does with unerring accuracy diagnose the ills of mankind and prescribe for them.

    B. The opening chapters of the book of Romans are diagnosis. — What has happened that man needs the gospel?

I. GOD HAS REVEALED HIMSELF TO ALL MEN.

    A. To the Gentiles through the things that He has made: "The invisible things of God are seen in those things which appear" (Rom. 1:20).
Power — the greater is not made by the less.
Godhead — "The hand that made us is divine."

    B. To the Jews through the law and the prophets. These spoke concerning His nature and His will, as far as they were able.

    C. To us is added the revelation in His Son (Heb. 1:1, 2).

II. MEN HAVE REJECTED OR NEGLECTED THE REVELATION.

(Here lies the key to the need of the Gospel — the terrible lag between knowing and doing.)

    A. The Gentiles worshiped the creature rather than the Creator.

        1. Made God in the likeness of man — Greek and Roman.
Birds and beasts — Egyptian, Canaanite.
Creeping things — India.
"When the universe began,
 God, they say, created man.
 Later, with a mocking nod,
 Man annihilated God."

        2. In none of it is there power or cleansing.

    B. The Jews rested in being the "chosen people" — heard

only half the law. Judged others, but were unwilling to judge themselves.

C. What have we done? That is a very personal and individual question.
  1. Many, like the Gentiles, neglected entirely or denied.
  2. Many like the Jews, have formally accepted and neglected.
  3. Some have accepted and live their acceptance.

III. THE REJECTION IS SEEN IN MAN'S MORAL FAILURE.

—Here is the climax of lag between knowing and doing.

A. "God gave them up" (1:26, 28). What an epitaph! They first gave Him up.
  1. The description is a shock—historically accurate—an understatement.
  2. What must be the thought of God?

B. The Jew—the teacher who lived no differently from his pupil (Rom. 2).

C. Our own day:
  "I fear God, and next to God I chiefly fear him who fears Him not." —*Saadi*
  1. A statesman more recently diagnosed the problem: "Our intelligence, sir, has outrun our goodness."
  2. Our generation knows how to save life, but destroys it instead.
    a. Private morals — "It is absolutely true that God has in large measure been set aside, and we are reaping the rewards of doing it."
    b. Not statistics, but people, show it.

CONCLUSION —

Yet we have hope, as all Christians have. And we have power —What can change a life can change a nation! Prayer can change things.

JUSTIFICATION BY FAITH
(Romans 3:19-31)

INTRODUCTION —

What is important this week? The most important thing is not in the headlines. The far bigger thing is our relationship to God.

I. THE LAW'S USE AND LIMITATIONS.

Here speaking of the Torah—moral and ceremonial law.

A. It gives the knowledge of sin.

B. It points to something better.

C. It cannot remove the guilt or stain of sin; it has only a limited power to keep one from sinning.

D. It cannot bring a person into right relationship with God—square him up with God; it can only compel an outer conformity, or punish guilt.

II. FAITH BRINGS ONE INTO RIGHT RELATION.

A. Illustration with the modern world.

1. One has not faith in modes of transportation, currency, postal system, food prepared by others, etc.—hence a recluse scratching a meager existence. How different when he gains faith.

2. Faith puts one in a position to benefit by all things. Soil and weather, insurance office and bank, car, bus or plane.

B. It must be a living faith, not just a willingness to flatter. "What think ye of the Christ?"

1. Thomas—"My Lord and my God."

2. Peter—"Our Lord and Savior Jesus Christ."

C. The Gospel must be "preached until we are all aflame with it, rather than being flattered and fawned on until we are bored with it."

III. "GOD IS JUST AND THE JUSTIFIER OF THEM THAT BELIEVE."

—Faith in Christ is:

A. Faith in God's goodness and justice. We have no respect for indulgence.

381

    1. God's holiness demands holiness.

    2. Sin cannot be condoned in His sight; it must be forsaken.

    3. "We do not destroy the law; we establish it" — perfect sacrifice, "Sacrifice of reconciliation."

B. Faith in God's mercy.

    "God so loved the world . . ." (John 3:16).

    "God commended his love toward us . . ." (Rom. 5:8).

C. Faith in God's plan.

    "The Gospel is the power of God unto salvation" (Rom. 1:16).

(The boaster hasn't faith, and the faithful doesn't boast.)

IV. BOASTING IS EXCLUDED.

Self is forgotten — it isn't self that has done it.

A. Here is a reality that changes things — e.g. attitude toward gambling.

    "My pleasure" vs. God's will, and my brother's good.

    "Get mine" vs. "It is more blessed to give" (Acts 20:32).

    "Easy money" vs. "Work with his hands the thing that is good" (Eph. 4:28).

    "Everybody does it" vs. "Strait is the gate . . . and few there be that find it." "Love not the world, neither the things that are in the world."

    "Can't see any harm in it" vs. "Provide things honest in the sight of all men."

B. We don't boast of our baptism — it is life's most unboastful act.

    1. It is not of our choosing, but of His.

    2. It is a humble (humiliating) act.

    3. It is a submergence of self.

    4. We are saved not by baptism, but by Christ, into whom we are baptized.

CONCLUSION —

Have we faith?

Story of performer on tight rope, who would wheel man over Niagara abyss in wheelbarrow. Did any one believe him? "Get in the wheelbarrow."

A MATTER OF DEATH AND LIFE
(Romans 6:1-14)

INTRODUCTION —

A. Matters of life and death.
   1. You are being rushed to the hospital, with police escort, sirens screaming.
   2. Appointments are forgotten, traffic rules are set aside.
   3. There is desperation and dread, as life is clutched with slipping fingers, and death is the final word.
B. The matter of death and life.
   1. You are involved in loving and serving the Lord.
   2. Obligations, appointments, and rules are adjusted to "living in Christ," as the urgent first priority.
   3. There is delight in the anticipation of life even more complete in the resurrection. Life is the final word.
C. If you are unsure of this, then remember the gospel (as Paul reminded the Romans).
   1. Christians, as well as sinners, need to be evangelized — told and reminded of the evangel — the good news concerning Christ Jesus.
   2. So in Romans 6, Paul reminded of Gospel facts and their relation to them.

I. THE GOSPEL FACTS IN CHRIST ARE A MATTER OF DEATH AND LIFE (Cf. I Cor. 15:1-4).
   A. In His crucifixion, Jesus laid down His life.
      1. He declared it beforehand (John 10:17, 18).
      2. The Gospel records detail the fact.
      3. The epistles recount it as the key to God's grace (Rom. 5:6-8; Phil. 2:5-11).
   B. In His resurrection, Jesus broke the bonds of death.
      1. The gates of Hades (death and the grave) did not prevail over the Rock on which Christ has built His church (Matt. 16:18).
      2. "Death hath no more dominion over him" (v. 9).
   C. In His eternal glory, Christ lives, sustaining His own.
      1. He "lives unto God" (v. 10).

2. His coming in glory will be the end of this age (I Thess.
4) but only an incident in His ongoing reign.

II. FAITH'S RESPONSE IN YOU IS A MATTER OF
DEATH AND LIFE.
 A. You are dead to sin (v. 2).
  1. Once dead *in* sin, you accepted the Lord's invitation
  and died *to* sin.
  2. The old man is crucified with Christ (v. 6).
  3. Death frees from every obligation to the old life.
  4. "Ye are dead, and your life is hid with Christ in God"
  (Col. 3:3).
 B. You are "alive unto God through Christ Jesus" (v. 11).
  1. Death to the world becomes life in Christ.
  2. Risen with Christ, we walk in "newness of life."
  3. It is a positive, affirmative, active experience of
  service to God and man.
 C. The total experience is impossible without Christ.
 "If we be dead with Christ, we believe we shall also live
 with him" (II Tim. 2:11-13).

III. YOUR BAPTISM LINKED YOU WITH JESUS IN
THE MATTER OF DEATH AND LIFE.
 A. You don't make enough of it (Paul told the Romans).
  1. If you live in sin, you deny the experience.
  2. A lifeless religion, negates the resurrection aspect.
  3. Learn from your baptism, live by it, show what it
  means!
 B. Be what you are (as the M.D. who spends his life being
 a doctor)!
  1. You were baptized into Christ; accept the identity.
  2. You were buried with Him; accept His death for
  you and your death for Him.
  3. You were raised to "be in the likeness of His resurrection."

CONCLUSION — The triumph of death and life is available.
 A. The Christian's possession, to be claimed.
 B. The sinner's hope, to be accepted.

LAW AND CONSCIENCE
(Romans 7:1—8:3)

INTRODUCTION — the place of law and conscience.

    A. Reference to Rom. 1 and 2: Law for the Jew and conscience for the Gentile serve the same purpose.

    B. Presentation of the claims of each to provide salvation.

    C. Note the reference of Paul in Acts 26 as to his relation to both.

    D. What shall be said of law fits the conscience as well.

I. LEGAL BIOGRAPHY OF PAUL.

    A. Relation to the Law.
Pharisaic rigors—and he was of the "straitest sect," and blameless.

    B. Confidence in the Law.

    C. Discovery of failure of the Law.

        1. The tenth commandment—the Law could not kill desire, and in condemning what it could not kill, it made life impossible.

        2. Life without the Law was blissful ingnorance, only an ignorance that leads to death.

        3. The hopeless death in the Law.

II. THE PURPOSE OF THE LAW.

    A. By law is the knowledge of sin—it is a measure of the character.
—Illustration with traffic laws that point out violations and warn against them, but cannot prevent the violation or redeem the violator.

    B. It points out the seriousness of sin.
—"That sin might be exceeding sinful."

        a. There is no little sin. It is separation from God, and the distance makes little difference.

        b. Welshimer—"When you hit sin, use a sledgehammer." (It is not a way to be popular.)

    C. It points out the sins of desire.

        1. The tenth commandment.

2. Christian interpretation of the law includes mental attitudes. "But I say unto you . . ." (See Matthew 5:20-28).

III. LIMITS OF THE LAW.
    A. Its only deterrent value is the fear of punishment. It cannot change desire.
    B. It does not heal the hurt of the sinner, but leaves him as sore and as far from God as he was before.
       1. Note the effect of preaching of sin that does not include the preaching of healing in Christ Jesus.
    C. Note similar limits of conscience. (Illustration—The murderer found in the north woods, moaning alone in a cabin. He could escape the police, but was tortured by his conscience.)

IV. RELIEF THROUGH CHRIST.
    A. Paul's hymn of praise.
    B. "What the law could not do, in that it was weak in the flesh" Christ did!
    C. We are no more tied to law or conscience than we are to a dead partner.
    D. Christ not only points out sin as set against His perfection, but keeps from sin with His love and His example, and heals the sinner with forgiveness.

CONCLUSION —

The story of Jean Val Jean, (Dumas' *Les Miserables*), who stole a loaf of bread to feed his sister's hungry family, and suffered the limit under the law. Then was at last saved to a useful life through the expression of the love of Christ.

386

THE SAVING CONFESSION
(Romans 10:9-15)

INTRODUCTION — You can't go beyond the end of the line! All that God has done for you heretofore has been leading to Christ: "For Christ is the end of the law for righteousness to every one that believeth" (Rom. 10:4).

Therefore confess (acknowledge) Christ!

- A. Confession, not profession, is required.
  1. Profession is a claim or assertion that is often self-advertising.
  2. Confession is acknowledgment of that which pride would rather deny.
  3. To confess Christ is to say, "He must increase and I must decrease" (John 3:30).
- B. Confession of Christ, rather than confession of sins, or of faith, is needed.
  1. Christians do confess sins, but that is in different context (I John 1:9).
  2. Scripture does not use the phrase, "Confess faith," but Jesus said, "Confess Me," and the apostles required the confession of Christ as Lord.
- C. Our text indicates the acknowledgment of Christ on three levels: to oneself (in the heart); to one's fellows (with the mouth); and to God (calling on His name).

I. BELIEVE: ACKNOWLEDGE IN THE HEART THAT JESUS IS GOD'S SON.
- A. "Believe in thine heart."
  1. Scripture presents the heart as the center of thinking, believing, originating action (When emotion rather than thought is indicated, Scripture speaks of "bowels").
  2. Christian belief involves the center and the whole being.
- B. Believe that God raised Jesus from the dead.
  1. In this God acknowledged Jesus as one above all others (Acts 17:31).

    2. His place as Son of God is thus established, and must be confessed (I John 4:15; compare I John 4:2; II John 7).

    3. Human pride balks at confessing this, but would rather profess the "universal Fatherhood of God and universal brotherhood of man."

C. Believe unto righteousness (v. 10).

    1. The moral life follows the faith: "As he thinketh in his heart, so is he" (Prov. 23:7).

    2. This belief brings one into right relationship (justification) with God.

D. Believe and avoid shame (v. 11).

    1. Accept the world's ridicule for Christ's sake, and avoid the ultimate frustration of all you have built upon.

    2. Be not ashamed of the gospel (Rom. 1:16), and rejoice in God's final acceptance.

II. CONFESS: ACKNOWLEDGE WITH THE MOUTH THAT CHRIST IS LORD.

A. Confession is the outward action growing out of the inward faith.

    2. Words of the mouth, communicating with others, are necessary.

B. Confession declares the Lordship (ultimate authority) of Christ (Phil. 2:11).

1. It acknowledges, "I am not my own"; "I belong to Jesus."

    2. It renounces the boast of "doing it my way."

    3. It requires obedience to Christ in all things: "Why call ye me Lord, Lord, and do not the things which I say?" (Luke 6:46).

C. Confession is unto salvation (v. 10).

    1. It assures that Christ will confess the confessor (Matt. 10:32; Luke 12:8).

    2. A one-time confession of Christ, never repeated, would be as empty as a momentary salvation without life, growth, and eternity following.

3. Confession is a way of speech and life for as long as salvation lasts.

III. CALL UPON CHRIST: ACKNOWLEDGE WITH PRAYER THAT HE IS SAVIOR.
   A. "Call upon the name" is equivalent to "pray to, or in the name of."
      1. It acknowledges the deity of Jesus.
      2. It offends the humanism that boasts divinity for all mankind.
      3. It was directed at least three times in Jesus' last conversation with His disciples before His death (See John 16:23).
   B. Calling upon the Lord acknowledges our need of salvation.
      1. It admits that we are guilty of sin that would destroy us.
      2. It acknowledges that we cannot save ourselves.
      3. It identifies us with the stricken multitude at Pentecost, crying out, "Men and brethren, what shall we do?" (Acts 2:37).
   C. It brings us into contact with Him who is able and available to save.
      1. He is "rich unto all that call upon him" (vv. 12, 13), without distinction as to status or nationality.
      2. As our great High Priest He is "able to save them to the uttermost that come unto God by him" (Heb. 7:25).

CONCLUSION —

Acknowledging Christ by (1) belief in Him as God's Son, (2) confession of Him as Lord, and (3) calling upon Him as Savior, we can hear most gladly the inspired directive of Pentecost: "Repent, and be baptized every one of you in the name of Jesus Christ for the remission of sins, and ye shall receive the gift of the Holy Ghost. For the promise is unto you, and to your children, and to all that are afar off, even as many as the Lord our God shall call" (Acts 2:38, 39).

CITIZENSHIP
(Romans 13:1-8)

INTRODUCTION —

Most of us have a partial view of Christianity—other world or this. Some desire doctrinal preaching exclusively—some exclusively practical. Probably some such in Rome—but Paul gave both—practice based on doctrine.

Chapter 12 deals with personal spiritual living; 13 with politics.

I. THE POWERS THAT BE ARE ORDAINED OF GOD.
   A. God is the ultimate ruler of all, and would be the Father of all.
      1. Some will not accept His rule—they, too, must be ruled—so we have government.
      2. Certain services rendered by government to all.
   B. The basic needs of civil government.
      1. Protective.
         a. Police, local and military ("a minister of God, an avenger of wrath to him that doeth evil").
         b. Protection against fire, flood, etc.
      2. Co-operative commercial.
         a. Highways.
         b. Legal provisions for exchange of property, etc.
      3. One phase of protection our government has *not* faced adequately—alcohol.
         a. Of deep concern is the slaughter on the highways.
         b. Here is a murderer guilty of two an hour, and left free.
         c. Here is a robber who enters every home, and takes—
               cash to pay for wares,
               more cash to pay for crimes caused,
               part of cost of every article purchased.
         d. Here is a contributor to every crime.
   C. Even bad governments exist by divine sanction, and have their needs.

II. BE SUBJECT.

   A. Godly folk are ever the best citizens, even under difficult circumstances.

   B. "And seek the peace of the city whither I have caused you to be carried away captives, and pray unto the Lord for it; for in the peace thereof shall ye have peace" (Jer. 29:7).

   "And pray for the life of the king, and of his sons" (Ezra 6:10). See I Peter 2:13-17.

   C. Christianity has never been the source of rebellion by force.

      If there are bad laws and bad men in office (especially in a republic) there is a proper way to change them.

   D. Thus the refusal of Jehovah's Witnesses to salute the flag is refusal of a proper part of the ordinance of God.
      —Be subject for conscience' sake.

III. RENDER TO ALL THEIR DUES.

   A. Ye pay tribute also—Jesus paid His tax: "Render unto Caesar."

     1. Government services cost money, and must be paid for.

       Taxes (debt means later taxes, and shortens life). Inflation—Much of the savings of all Americans already confiscated.

     2. Honest recognition would save many ills.

   B. Honor to whom honor.

     1. Curse of American politics is mud slinging, before and after election.

     2. Prayer (I Tim. 2:1-8). (Include "I'm praying for you" in letter to legislator.)

   C. The great responsibility upon the citizens of a republic; we are in control.

      If good men will not control politics, they have no reason for complaint if bad men do.

CONCLUSION —

We are citizens of another kingdom, and better citizens of this, as Christians. Where is your citizenship?

391

RESPONSIBILITY TO BRETHREN
(Romans 14:1—15:13)

INTRODUCTION —

    A. Perhaps first responsibility is to see brothers as brothers:

        1. Not fathers, to obey instead of Christ.

        2. Not children, subservient to our authority.

        3. Not nieces and nephews to be loaded down with advice.

    B. Our text is helpful. In the ASV it appears in three convenient paragraphs.

        1. It says little about discovering who is and who is not a brother.

        2. It speaks of the weaker brother, perhaps recognizing that each of us tends to think of himself as being strong.

        3. Implications of "weakness" (scrupulous concern for particulars) reverses popular ideas of strength.

I. RECEIVE—DON'T DESPISE THE BROTHER (14:1-12).

    A. He doesn't have to agree with you, or you with him.

        1. "If a man is weak in his faith you must accept him without attempting to settle doubtful points" (NEB).

        2. How different from the young preacher who thinks that all you have to do in order to agreement is to explain and come to an understanding.

        3. Compare the woman who "never lost an argument; just failed to make herself clear."

    B. Christians have differences over what seem to be vital matters.

        1. Paul's readers in Rome differed over—

           a. Eating flesh (sacrificed to idols?).

           b. Observing times and seasons (prescribed in the Old Testament).

        2. These seem unimportant to us because we do not face them.

        3. We have our own areas of disagreement:

a. I take the scrupulous (weak?) position on tobacco, alcohol, card games, dancing, and some organizations. My conscience could not condone these.

b. Others object to dominoes, television, new versions of the Bible, instrumental music, racial equality (or inequality), missionary organization.

C. Each is free to choose. (Thomas Campbell, in *Declaration and Address,* insisted that the brother is bound by the *implications* of Scripture only insofar as he is able to perceive the connection.)

D. Each must answer to God!

II. RESPECT—DON'T DESTROY THE BROTHER (14:13-23).

A. Turn judgment around.

1. Judge yourself, your motives, your actions in relation to brothers.

—One may find himself championing good causes for very bad reasons.

2. What are you trying to prove, in your application of judgment?

—Paul knew his strength; he didn't have to prove or justify it.

B. Don't tear down what Christ died to build up.

1. Let not your example lead another to do what he is convinced is contrary to God's will.

2. Let not your words mortify, discourage, or confuse a brother.

3. In works and in words, affirm Christ always!

III. REENFORCE—DON'T DISCOURAGE THE BROTHER (15:1-13).

A. Bear the infirmities of the weak; bear one another's burdens.

B. Please God, and others, rather than selves.

1. Follow the example of Christ.

2. Seek genuinely to please, rather than to expect others to be pleased with us (II Cor. 5:9).

3. Consider—not merely tolerate or endure—the other's conscience.

B. Sustain one another in glorifying God.

1. (In battle, one protects the comrade beside him, is protected by that comrade, and together they win.)

2. Agreements in Christ, overriding disagreements in controversy, strengthen all.

—If such diverse peoples can give themselves to Christ, He must be worthy!

3. With one spirit render one praise.

—In hymns, Scripture teaching, in Communion.

CONCLUSION —

A. Herein is the recognition, that we are *God's* children, through the mind, the words, and the works that bind us to Him, and hence to each other.

B. Observe the focus of each section with which we have dealt:

1. Brothers do different things, but each to the glory of God; and each must give account to God.

—Our judgmentalism usurps God's right!

2. The kingdom of God is righteousness, peace, and joy in the Holy Spirit. Overthrow not the work of God.

—Our selfishness thwarts God's purpose!

3. With one mouth glorify the God and Father of our Lord Jesus Christ.

—Our separatism denies God's glory!

C. "By this shall all men know that ye are my disciples, if ye have love one to another" (John 13:35).

—Thus only are we brotherly, and thus only can we meet our responsibilities to our brethren.

PREACHING THROUGH
I AND II CORINTHIANS
REQUIRED READING

To the present-day Christian, confused by many conflicting claims and urges, within the church and without, the letters to the Corinthians bring needed strength from the Lord's inspired apostle Paul. Growing out of Paul's experience and relationship with the church at Corinth, the letters meet directly the problems of the Church in a worldly setting. No person who is not familiar with them can be well-informed concerning the Lord's will for His Church.

GREAT PASSAGES

The great passages in Corinthians are not single verses easily memorized. They are grand treatments of great themes. Memorizing should be done in blocks of half a dozen verses to a chapter. Here are some of them:

Christ's Church is one—I Cor. 1:10-15
God's building—I Cor. 3:5-15
The Communion—I Cor. 10:14-22; 11:23-32
The body of Christ—I Cor. 12:12-27
The best gift is love—I Cor. 13
The resurrection—I Cor. 15
The future life—II Cor. 5:1-10
The ministry of Christ—II Cor. 5:17-21
Christian generosity—II Cor. 8:1-5

BACKGROUND

Read the eighteenth and nineteenth chapters of Acts. They tell that Paul established the church at Corinth while on his second missionary journey, and that he went to Ephesus, from which city he wrote the first epistle to the Corinthians. The first letter deals with practical problems in the Corinthian church, as those problems had come to Paul's attention—factions in the church; the presence of evil-doers; marriage problems; the relationship of Christians to the pagan feasts and customs about them; the conduct of public worship; death and the resurrection.

395

The second epistle, written from Macedonia several months later, deals largely with Paul's ministry as an apostle, and with the gathering of gifts for the poor in Jerusalem. This epistle answers the question, "How can one know the true servant of Christ from the false teacher?"

Sermon Outlines Provided:

"Building the Temple" (I Cor. 3:10-17)
"All Things Are Yours" (I Cor. 3:18-23)
"Get in the Game" (I Cor. 9:24-27)
"As Oft as Ye Eat" (I Cor. 11:26)
"Where Is Thy Victory?" (I Cor. 15:54-58)
"Heaven" (II Cor. 5:1-10)
"The Unequal Yoke" (II Cor. 6:14-21)
"Loans and a Gift" (II Cor. 9:8-15)
"Reaching With the Gospel" (II Cor. 10:13-18)

Other Sermon Topics Suggested:

"Is Christ Divided?" (I Cor. 1:10-17)
"I Know Nothing Against Myself" (I Cor. 4:1-6)
"Communion With Whom?" (I Cor. 10:14-22)
"The More Excellent Way" (I Cor. 12:31 — 13:13)
"The Uses of Adversity" (II Cor. 1:3-11)

QUESTIONS OVER I AND II CORINTHIANS

1. What was a stumbling block to the Jews and foolishness to the Greeks? (I Cor. 1:23)
2. Paul said he was determined not to know anything among the Corinthians except what? (2:2)
3. Whom does Paul say he sent to the Corinthians to remind them of Paul's work and teaching? (4:17)
4. Instead of brother going to court against a brother Paul recommends what? (6:7)
5. In I Corinthians 6:19 we read that what is the temple of the Holy Spirit?
6. If a wife's husband dies she is free to remarry, but with what restriction? (7:39)

7. If eating meat causes our brother to stumble, what is our duty? (8:13)
8. Paul said he became all things to all men for what purpose? (9:22)
9. As often as we partake of the Lord's Supper we show forth what? (11:26)
10. In I Corinthians Paul compares the church to what? (12:13-27)
11. Which chapter in I Corinthians describes and tells the importance of love? (13)
12. Paul closes chapter 14, "Let all things be done decently" and in what? (14:40)
13. More than how many people saw the risen Lord at one time? (15:6)
14. Paul says, "Let him be anathema," for the person who does not do what? (16:22)
15. Paul said when Moses was read by the Jews what was on their hearts? (II Cor. 3:15)
16. Paul said he was willing to be absent from the body and to be what? (5:8)
17. "Be not unequally yoked with" whom? (6:14)
18. God loves what kind of a giver? (9:7)
19. Paul says some people say his letters are what? (10:10)
20. With what benediction does II Corinthians conclude? (13:14)

BUILDING THE TEMPLE

(For the dedication of a church building.)

(I Corinthians 3:10-17)

INTRODUCTION — Congratulations on securing a good tool for your building program!

A. The church is in a constant building program, building temples for the indwelling of God's Spirit.

B. The material structure about us is an instrument to be used in that program.

C. Paul wrote to the Corinthians about their own building program.

I. GOD'S TEMPLE IS YOU (vv. 16, 17).

A. God's dwelling is in persons, not in material buildings. (See Acts 7:48; 17:24; I Cor. 6:19; II Cor. 6:16.)

B. It is made for His occupancy and in His likeness.

C. The temple is holy.

1. Christ came to make holy people, not holy places.

2. He cannot condone the occupancy of His temple by other gods.

3. He cannot condone the defilement of His temple by willful sin.

4. He recognizes our holiness, even if we don't; He respects us more than we often respect ourselves.

II. GOD'S TEMPLE HAS A PLAN AND A PLANNER (v. 9).

A. The architect sees the total design.

1. He knows the stresses the structure must bear.

2. He provides for all the components: plumbing, wiring, heating.

—The workman does well to follow the plan, though he may not understand.

B. The architect knows how to make the plan work.

(A visitor to a nursing home once found telephone workmen pondering a complex layout for an intercommunication system. In a few quiet sentences the visitor showed them how to hook up the system, and

398

then went on. "Who is that?" a workman demanded. "Oh, just the man who dreamed up this little jewel when he was doing research and development for Bell Telephone," the owner replied. Wire up as the visitor directed, the system worked! So God in His revealed Word shows us how to order our lives. "Who is He to give orders to us?" we demand. "Oh, just the One who made the system." If we follow His directions, it will work!)

III. GOD'S TEMPLE HAS A BUILDER AND BUILDERS (v. 10).
   A. Christ himself is the ultimate builder (Matt. 16:18).
   B. Paul as an apostle served as masterbuilder of Christian lives and churches.
      — Wise workmen must respect the directives conveyed by such a one.
   C. Others must help and complete the structure.
      1. They must receive instruction and bear responsibility.
      2. They must sometimes accept correction. (The architect-overseer spots faulty workmanship and demands that it be done over.)
   D. Each of us bears responsibility in building his own life.

IV. GOD'S TEMPLE HAS A FOUNDATION THAT MUST BE LAID (vv. 10-12).
   A. Christ is the only possible foundation for a Christian life (Acts 4:11, 12).
      — A life centered and built on anything else is doomed.
   B. This is the one standard item in all Christian building.
      — A rich and amazing variety is possible as each builds on this foundation.
   C. Foundations are laid, and that requires time (v. 10; Luke 6:48).
      1. Church steeples have been lowered into place by helicopter; not foundations!
      2. Laying the Christ-foundation involves a steadily growing acquaintance with Him.

399

V. GOD'S TEMPLE REQUIRES QUALITY MATERIALS (vv. 12-15).
   A. The materials will be tested by fire.
      1. Old Corinth had been destroyed by fire, and Paul's Corinth displayed all the varieties of remaining structures, new structures, and structures built from fragments of fire-blackened materials.
      2. So the Christian life will be tested and will survive, or be damaged or destroyed, as by fire at life's (or the world's) end (II Pet. 3:7-11).
      3. There is no fire-proof life, no fire-proof building.
         —The contents, if not the structure, include flammable material.
   B. Some materials last, as gold, silver, precious stones.
      1. Faith, hope, and love are lasting (I Cor. 13:13).
      2. The Word of God: "My word shall not pass away."
      3. Christian influence preserved in faithful lives (I Thess. 3:8).
      4. "One life to live; 'twill soon be past.
         What's done for Christ alone will last."
   C. Some valuable materials will be lost in the fire, as wood.
      1. Material substance, necessary for life and Christian service (Cf. Eph. 4:28).
      2. Use it wisely as an investment in things eternal.
   D. Some is worthless from the beginning and will be utterly destroyed, as hay, stubble.
      1. Light pastimes are gone with the moment, and may be destructive.
      2. The praise of men claims no standing with God, and may lead to destruction.

CONCLUSION — The material building around us is by nature temporal if not temporary.
   A. Use it wisely and carefully, but use it; perhaps use it up!
   B. Use it as an investment in building God's eternal temples—human souls. "We know that if our earthly house of this tabernacle were dissolved, we have a building of God, an house not made with hands, eternal in the heavens" (II Cor. 5:1).

ALL THINGS ARE YOURS
(I Corinthians 3:18-23)

INTRODUCTION — At the end of a war a sudden change makes prison camp guards into prisoners and prisoners into guards.

    A. Paul points out the danger of such trading of places between the people of God and the things which are designed to serve them. The servant becomes too soon the master, etc.

    B. Cause of division in Corinthian church was that the people had come to *belong* to their leaders.
"Ye are Christ's." This was written to those who had made Him Lord.

I. PAUL, APOLLOS, CEPHAS, ARE *YOURS.*

    A. The Corinthians were calling themselves by those leaders' names, as though they belonged to them — "I am of Paul," etc.

    B. Foolishly the church has bowed to great leaders.
Illustration — In N. Carolina certain Christian churches named their congregations for the saints. In one year we counted 8 St. James, 8 St. Pauls, 4 St. Lukes, 3 each St. John, St. Mark, St. Peter, St. Stephen; also St. Thomas, St. Matthew, St. Joseph, St. Jude, St. Mary (2), St. Rose, St. Percy and St. Galilee!

        1. Put your tag on the great leaders, and not theirs on you!
Claim Paul's faith, Apollos' personality, Peter's power.

        2. The reformation and restoration leaders belong to us.
Martin Luther's crusading courage; Calvin's vision of God; Knox' zeal; John Wesley's warm, prayer-filled life; Jacob Albright's simple devotion; Alexander Campbell's intelligent understanding of the Gospel; Walter Scott's plain view of the truth; Barton Stone's lovable Christian character.

    C. *All* are yours.
You cheat yourself if you follow only one, to learn from him.

401

II. THE WORLD IS *YOURS*.

A. On what shall we lay our hands — *not* on that which takes possession of us!

— That which one can't let go quickly is too dangerous.

B. "Possessing our possessions lest they come to own us."

1. "I have a property that I must fix up."
2. "I'm too busy to spend time with my family."
3. "I can't leave my store."
4. "If I leave, someone will rob my hen roosts."
5. There are almost more men whom money owns than there are who own money.

   (They will spend, and risk, life to gain money, and then again to save it.)

III. LIFE, DEATH, THINGS PRESENT, THINGS TO COME.

A. Young people; life belongs to you, in Christ; and not you to it.

1. The fashion is yours to examine and perhaps enjoy; don't be a slave to it!
2. The club is yours; don't let it own you.
3. The crowd is yours — you don't belong to it!

   a. With some you may keep company profitably.

   b. Others are for your warning and instruction.

B. Beware of slavery to one's own body; it belongs to you, and not you to it.

   "I buffet my body and keep it in subjection" (I Cor. 9:27).

   See warning to those "whose God is their belly" (Phil. 3:19).

C. Death is yours

   "For me to live is Christ, and to die is gain" — death is the instrument of freedom and God's presence.

IV. AND CONCLUSION —

Ye are Christ's; and Christ is God's.

A. This is the key to the whole passage.

B. You will belong to something "His servants ye are to whom ye lend yourself."

C. "Ye are not your own." We are bought with a price.

GET IN THE GAME
(I Corinthians 9:24-27)
(For men's class meeting.)

INTRODUCTION –

    A. College alumnus at track meet says, "I'd give every cent I own if I were young again and could run a race like that."

        – But the runners themselves will soon outgrow that physical prowess.

    B. There must be a game that will include more than the few for a short time. (See I Tim. 4:7, 8.)

I. GET IN THE GAME EARLY.

    A. Tom Brown breaks into football his first day at Rugby.

    B. Paul starts preaching before he leaves Damascus after his conversion.

    C. The personal evangelist says, "Now you go and get somebody else."

    D. Every notable servant of God from Moses through Paul started early.

II. EVERYBODY IS IN IT (v. 24).

    A. We are not represented by champions, as David and Goliath –

        In modern warfare, the entire nation is enlisted.

    B. In the church, all are needed.

        1. The organization – to usher, sing, pray, pay.

        2. To call – not everyone will come to church until he first knows Christ.

           a. Learn to introduce Christ gracefully.

           b. Train callers and organize calling.

        3. To serve; from taking groceries to furnishing a car to shut-ins.

        4. To be responsible for teaching.

           a. To learn – Be ready always to given an account.

           b. To teach – either formally in class or informally in private.

    c. To back the preacher—Never the cop-out "That is our preacher's belief."

    d. To check the preacher, as Aquila and Priscilla (Acts 18:26).

III. "NOT BEATING THE AIR."

    A. (I recall that in my Scout football games I made every play a personal contact, and got bruised, while the opponent used his head and made plays count.)

    B. For Christ, too, the meaningful service is better than the frantic activity.

IV. RUN WITH PATIENCE.

    A. Honor "the cloud of witnesses" (Heb. 12:1ff.).

    B. "Ye were running well" (Gal. 5:7).

    C. The cross-country runner is sustained by knowing— "The other fellow is as bad off as you are."

V. STAY IN THE GAME.

    A. Prof. Arthur Holmes says you are not grown up until you are fifty.

    B. The coach doesn't put the scrubs into a tough game, so don't "step out to give the young folks a chance."

VI. AND CONCLUSION — Finish the course.

    A. Not as Demas.
        Thrice mentioned as a companion of Paul—then "hath forsaken."

    B. As Paul (II Tim. 4:7, 8).

    C. Rewards are for those who cross the finish line.

AS OFT AS YE EAT

(I Corinthians 11:26)

INTRODUCTION —

This rite is typical of the whole church of Christ.
Where the church is, it is, and vice versa.
The true apostolic succession will be found in the ordinances.

I. "AS OFTEN AS YE EAT."
   A. Here is an invitation to willing service.
      It is not a categorical command, but a request.
      John 6 presents conditions of the request.
   B. The Christian is not a slave, lashed into unwilling service, but a friend, giving his all to One he loves.
   C. Christ gave Himself willingly.
      1. "No man taketh it from me, but I lay it down of myself" (John 10:18).
      2. The other view of Gethsemane — He prayed that He might be spared to die.
      3. "If love had not bound the Savior to the cross, the nails would never have held Him there."

II. "YE DO SHOW FORTH" — "Declare," "proclaim," "preach."
   A. Every Christian becomes a preacher when the Supper is spread.
   B. Why does one partake?
      1. Because others do? Because it is commanded? Simply to remember a thing of the past?
      2. Also to proclaim, "This happened for me."
         With the acted sermon of the Supper being preached by every Christian every Lord's Day, we need to write no creeds to hold the church together.
   C. How does one partake?
      1. Commander Booth said of Joseph Parker "If he comes from his study and addresses his audience with light cheerfulness, you won't hear much, but if he comes thoughtfully and quietly and addresses

the Book as though his were the vast responsibility of proclaiming its truth, then listen."

2. He who preaches thoughtlessly does not say much. — How much does the fact you proclaim mean to you?

III. "THE LORD'S DEATH"

A. Here is the center of the Supper and of the Christian religion. It is made the substance of the Gospel (I Cor. 15:3, 4).

B. Forget theology — let each theorize for himself, but not attempt to lay his thought on others.

1. In this, the meaning of the word *communion* has sometimes been reversed, so as to be a term of division, referring to only a certain small group.

2. Transubstantiation — not taught, but don't divide on it. Consubstantiation — the two elements at once in the matter. Calvin's theory of the real presence — The presence seems to be taught. Zwinglian theory of simple memorial of past event.

3. Religious conferences meet in discussion, but split up to take "communion" in separate groups — How false to the purpose!

C. Where theology divides, the fact unites.

1. The Supper is centered in fact, and the fact is unchangeable.

2. The Supper is a confession of the fact.

3. As such it can be partaken by all, and be a uniting force on a united Christ.

IV. AND CONCLUSION — "TILL HE COME"

A. There is prediction as well as declaration in the Supper.

B. Again the fact is unitive and the theories divisive. Declare the fact.

C. He who established the Supper will at that time be Host and Participant (Matt. 26:29).

WHERE IS THY VICTORY?

(I Corinthians 15:54-58)

INTRODUCTION —

The way of the Cross a way of victory, although it seems not so.
- A. Christ's enemies were all converted or routed.
- B. It was the way looked for from the foundation.
  1. Death is swallowed in victory (Isa. 25:8).
     God's day of jubilee fulfilled in Christ.
  2. Death, where is thy sting? (Hos. 13:14).
     Promised salvation is accomplished.

I. DEATH IS SWALLOWED IN VICTORY.

- A. The last enemy—unconquered until Christ arose.
  1. Pictured as the venomous creature, inflicting poisoned and fatal wounds.
  2. Christ entered death once and for all.
  3. Promised that He should conquer death, and fulfilled promise.
- B. The last enemy for us.
  1. Disease is conquered by science.
  2. Ignorance conquered by means of communication.
  3. But men still helpless in the face of death.
- C. Paul realized the value of resurrection as he beheld death finally conquered.

II. GOD GIVES THE VICTORY THROUGH CHRIST.

- A. Christ's resurrection predicts our own.
  1. The firstfruits of them that slept.
  2. The farmer pulls the first ripened heads of grain.
- B. So we follow Christ to victory.
  1. Over sin—"I can do all things through him who strengtheneth me" (Phil. 4:13).
  2. Over death—He returned as evidence of that victory.
     (As the aged woman who would—but could not—go to see beyond the mountains, and so asked another to get the view for her.)
     So Christ has gone and come back to tell us of what is fair.

   C. The victory is through Christ, and not of our own
      selves.
      1. "As in Adam all die, so in Christ shall all be made
         alive" (I Cor. 15:22).
      2. He has opened the way for us, where we could not
         have gone.
      3. "Because I live, ye shall live also" (John 14:19).

III. YOUR LABOR IS NOT IN VAIN IN THE LORD.
   A. The seeming futility of human effort.
      1. To amass wealth—came a depression.
      2. To amass property—come storm and flood.
      3. To gain a place in the world—no opening—What's
         the use?
   B. Then view the risen Christ.
      1. The picture of victory—survival and more.
      2. The picture of a victorious Christ. Death did not
         end His ministry.
      3. The picture of a victorious Christian—engaged in a
         winning cause.
   C. The ultimate triumph—someone has said it:
      "To see this victory accomplished and to have no
      part in it will be the sorest humiliation and the most
      painful reflection to every generous mind."

CONCLUSION —

   "Where is thy victory?"
   With the world which conquers Christ for a time? or
   with the suffering Christ who rises from death for eterntiy?

HEAVEN

(II Corinthians 5:1-10)

INTRODUCTION — The need for emphasis on that which is God's purpose for creation.

I. PURPOSE OF GOD (v. 5).
   A. Reasons for creation cannot be known fully except by revelation. —God made us to be with Him!
   B. "God is not willing that any should perish" (II Pet. 3:9). Heaven is the kingdom "prepared for you from the foundation of the world" (Matt. 25:3, 4).
   B. This purpose motivated Paul in the ministry.
      1. It overcame discouragement (II Cor. 4:16, 17).
      2. It directed his service to others (II Cor. 4:15).

II. PROVISION OF GOD (vv. 1, 2).
   A. Beyond the imagination (I Cor. 2:9).
      (Illustration—Vernon Newland tells of trying to tell native Tibetans about America. They had neither the language nor the imagination to understand things so completely beyond their experience.
   B. The resurrection body—"We shall be like Him" (I John 3:2).
      1. Not disembodied spirits, but recognizable persons.
      2. Neither dependent upon material bodies.
         "Mortal shall have put on immortality" (I Cor. 15:52-54).
   C. The place prepared.
      1. Beggars description; but in Revelation.
         "John bankrupts human language to provide a glimpse."
      2. Riches of gold and precious stone.
         —The values of Heaven are immeasurably greater.
      3. Beauty of the bride.
         —Where in human experience is anything more fitting?
      4. Comfort of the tears wiped away.
         —How shall it be known to those who have not wept?

III. PRESENCE OF GOD—this is central in every description (vv. 6-8).
   1. "So shall we ever be with the Lord" (I Thess. 4:17, 18).
   2. "Having a desire to depart and to be with the Lord" (Phil. 1:20-23).
   3. "That where I am there ye may be also" (John 14:2, 3). (Illustration—The boys disliked the rich schoolmate, but liked his well stocked play room. If they could have been turned loose there without him, they would have liked it fine. So are many in respect to God.)
   4. The presence of God is actually a threat to those who love Him not.

IV. PLEASING GOD—Here the purpose of man comes into harmony with God (v. 9).
   1. A means of getting acquainted with Him. (As we come to know a friend or spouse by learning and doing what pleases.)
   2. "Your labor is not in vain in the Lord" (I Cor. 15:58). (Illustration—Father decided to turn his attention from matters of health to those things that will not meet with defeat. "Physical health will come to an end." Twenty years later he found his victory of the spirit in defeat of the flesh.)

CONCLUSION —

"I know whom I have believed" (II Tim. 1:12). With that for a beginning all else that is heaven follows naturally.

THE UNEQUAL YOKE
(II Corinthians 6:14-18)

INTRODUCTION —

Picture the camel and the donkey yoked to the plow. In Corinth, the wide divergence between Christian and heathen.

I. BE NOT UNEQUALLY YOKED.
A. Friendship.
  1. Sammy gets Bobby into trouble and runs. He plays according to different rules.
  2. "He that walketh with wise men shall be wise: but a companion of fools shall be destroyed" (Prov. 13:20).
  3. See Proverbs 1:10-19.
B. Schoolmates and roommates.
  — Everyone knows some horrible example of pains in "room-mate-ism."
C. Business.
  1. Abe Lincoln's partnership left him with bankruptcy and bills to pay.
  2. A wise man refused partnership with one who said, "I have the experience; you have the money." "No!" he said, "Soon I'd have the experience and you'd have the money."
D. Marriage.
  1. The woman carries the load, while the man does as he pleases, unkindly, or
  2. The man left with a family of children.
     In each case, the believer is imposed upon by one who operates under other rules.
     But there is an even more serious side of the matter:

II. COME OUT AND BE SEPARATE.
A. The theme of all God's dealings with His people.
  1. Noah; Abraham; the children of Israel;
     "Ye shall not be like the nations round about"; serve their gods; do as they.

411

"Strait is the gate and narrow is the way which leadeth unto life, and few there be that find it" (Matt. 7:14).

B. Real danger is that the Christian partner will lose hold on Christ.

"It was just a fight every time I went to church, so I gave it up."

C. How much separate?

I Cor. 5:9-11 directs refusal of communion with the flagrant sinner.

Let it be known that this is no part of Christianity.

III. WHAT FELLOWSHIP HAVE RIGHTEOUSNESS AND INIQUITY?

(*Belial*, "worthlessness.")

A. Amos "How can two walk together except they be agreed?"

—As far as men go together, they must be going the same way; when one changes direction, they must part.

B. Ordinary business and social contact can be carried on with most people.

—the more intimate and constant the contact, the more agreement is required—and developed.

C. With unbelievers Christians can not have, must not have, the agreement necessary for partnership.

CONCLUSION — "I will be to you a father."

A preacher's teen-age boy comes home in bitterness—the gang doesn't want the preacher's kids around. Then he considers, and says at last, "But it's worth it to come home to a Dad and Mother like you!"

What separation is it worth now to come home to God as our Father?

412

LOANS AND A GIFT
(II Corinthians 9:8-15)

INTRODUCTION — Thanksgiving.

It is particularly an American institution, with its thanks expressed for: material blessings, a good crop, a great land in which to build a great nation, the nation itself, and life and health. But all these are mere loans.

I. ALL OF THIS THANKSGIVING IS FOR LOANS.
   A. Material blessings—a good crop (vv. 9, 10).
      1. Story of the man whose fields brought forth plentifully.
         "Then whose shall these things be?" They are no longer his (Luke 12:16-21).
      2. "We brought nothing into this world, and it is certain we can carry nothing out" (I Tim. 6:7).
      3. "Naked came I out of my mother's womb, and naked shall I return thither. The Lord gave and the Lord hath taken away; blessed be the name of the Lord" (Job 1:21).
   B. The great land is also a loan.
      1. Its life span is longer than that of the individual only by comparison.
         "But the day of the Lord will come as a thief in the night; in the which the heavens shall pass away with a great noise, and the elements shall melt with fervent heat, the earth also and the works that are therein shall be burned up" (II Pet. 3:10).
      2. If the earth is to come and go without anything further, what is the purpose to creation?
   C. The nation is a loan.
      1. The tenure of the enjoyment of the loan depends on how it is used.
      2. Many nations have thought themselves imperishable.

         I met a traveller from an antique land
         Who said: Two vast and trunkless legs of stone

Stand in the desert. Near them, on the sand,
Half sunk, a shattered visage lies, whose frown,
And wrinkled lip, and sneer of cold command,
Tell that its sculptor well those passions read
Which yet survive, stamped on those lifeless things,
The hand that mocked them, and the heart that fed:
And on the pedestal these words appear:
My name is Ozymandias, king of kings:
Look on my works, ye mighty, and despair!
Nothing beside remains. Round the decay
Of that colossal wreck, boundless and bare
The lone and level sands stretch far away!

3. Now we would warn that the seeds of decay which honeycombed the Roman Empire and caused it to crumble—liquor, luxury, immorality,—are sown in the U.S. some 400 years earlier in its national life, and whereas Rome lasted some 1250 years, we are not well started.

D. Life and health are loans.
1. It is only a blind and foolish optimism which makes us say that all will be well, and that we shall recover perfectly from every ill.
2. As national life, this may be lengthened and made more enjoyable by care.
3. But the loan will be recalled soon or late, in complete physical defeat.

II. CHRIST WITH THE THINGS WHICH HE GIVES, IS THE ONLY GIFT.

A. Given from above, He gave himself completely in life.
B. His body and the cross, He made the giving complete with a prayer.
C. Resurrected, he made it plain that that, too, was for us.
D. Ascended, He is still ours, at the right hand of God making intercession for us.
E. The life, love, joy, peace, temperance, patience, meekness, all abide.

CONCLUSION — the non-Christian has no gift from God. Let us accept the Gift with the loans.

REACHING WITH THE GOSPEL
(II Corinthians 10:13-18)

INTRODUCTION —

    A. Present world contacts are bringing Christianity into collision with other religions. It is charged that the Christian overreaches himself in his claims for Christ.

       1. Collision with atheism—itself an aggressive religion.

       2. Collision with agnosticism—a part of human pride.

       3. Collision with world religions, drive into contact for mutual protection against communism.

       4. Collision with denominationalism, with teachings so near the truth.

    B. Bold claims are inherent to Christianity.

       Half measures will not accomplish what it proposes to do.

    C. Paul, in his ministry to Corinth, collided with the ego of some there.

       They charged him with overreaching his rightful authority.

I. WE MAKE NO CLAIMS LARGER THAN OUR ASSIGNMENT (v. 13).

    A. Paul had assignment as apostle to the Gentiles. That took in Corinth.

       1. Assignment given at the time of his conversion (Acts 26:16-18).

       2. Re-affirmed in vision at Jerusalem (Acts 22:17-21). Positive witness indicated.

       3. Recognized by the other apostles (Gal. 2:7-9). Demands and direction given.

    B. Christians have an assignment to the world.

       1. Inclusive of the whole world; not to be limited by agreement.

       2. Inclusive of all people, economically, socially, intellectually, morally.

       3. Includes the whole of every man; total commitment totally accepted—unconditional surrender.

II. WE MAKE NO CLAIMS LARGER THAN DEMON-
STRATED ACCOMPLISHMENTS (v. 14).
  A. Paul had reached to the Corinthians.
    1. Geographically, the journey took longer than to any
       place on earth now—the westward limit of Chris-
       tian invasion to the time.
    2. Morally—if Corinth could be reached, any could be.
    3. Religiously—The revealed faith separated from the
       religions. —Accomplished at a cost: (11:23-28).
  B. The church has accomplished much.
    1. Probably no place is harder to reach than Tibet and
       upper Burma have been.
       —Yet there are places unreached.
    2. No convert more improbable than Augustine.
       —Yet such conversions are all too few.
    3. The town drunk becomes mayor, beginning with
       conversion to Christ.
       —Yet the demonstration is incomplete.

III. WE MAKE NO CLAIMS LARGER THAN THE
POSSIBILITIES FOR THE FUTURE (v. 16).
  A. Paul's self-prediction: "We shall be enlarged by you."
    1. No cause for satisfaction or basis of development
       in the easy way.
       Paul no seagull following a pelican for a free meal.
    2. The reaching developed the reach.
       "Reaching forth unto those things that are before,
       I press toward the mark . . ." (Phil. 3:13, 14).
  B. Possibilities in them.
    1. "When your faith is increased" "Grow in grace . . ."
       (II Pet. 3:18).
    2. " . . . May grow up into him in all things, which is
       the head, even Christ" (Eph. 4:15).
  C. Possibilities beyond them—"To preach the gospel in
     the regions beyond you."

IV. AND CONCLUSION — WE MAKE NO CLAIMS
LARGER THAN OUR LORD (v. 17).
  Here arises the balance between humility (not ourselves) and
courageous boldness (II Cor. 4:5).

PREACHING THROUGH GALATIANS, EPHESIANS, PHILIPPIANS, COLOSSIANS

These are letters written by the Apostle Paul under various circumstances to Christian friends in Asia Minor and Greece. Galatians is a teaching epistle, written to the churches in the province of Galatia (See Acts 13:1—16:5), where certain Jewish Christians were troubling the church by teaching that one could not be a Christian without keeping the Old Testament ritual laws.

Ephesians, Colossians, (and Philemon) are companion letters, written at the same time and sent together, from Paul in Rome to Christians in the province of Asia. Ephesians (See Acts 19 and 20:17-38 for Paul's labors at Ephesus) speaks of the divine character and unity of the Lord's church. Colossians (to the church at Colosse) warns against false teaching. Philemon is a personal letter sent to a Christian at Colosse.

Philippians is written to the church at Philippi (See Acts 16:6-40 and I Corinthians 8:1-5), to thank them for a gift sent to Paul in prison by Epaphroditus, one of their number.

ANALYSIS OF THE EPISTLES

Galatians 1:1—2:21   The Gospel as preached by Paul came by revelation.

3:1—5:12   Christian faith and grace are enough; the Law is done away.

5:13—6:18   The Gospel lays upon the Christian some practical duties.

Ephesians 1:1—2:10   Greeting, thanksgiving, and prayer for the readers.

2:11—3:21   The conversion of the Gentiles is the Apostle's great aim.

4:1-16   God's plan for His one Church.

4:17—6:9   Practical obligations of believers to one another and to God.

6:10-23   Concerning the Christian warfare — concluding greetings.

417

Philippians	1:1-26	Paul reports on his own condition.
	1:27—2:30	He encourages and exhorts the Philippians; plans for them.
	3:1-21	Contrasts true and false teachers.
	4:1-23	The basis of Christian optimism.
Colossians	1:1—3:4	Christ is sufficient, without other objects of worship.
	3:5—4:6	Christian faith demands a consistent life.
	4:7-18	Personal matters.

Sermon Outlines Provided:

"No Hasty Arrival" (Gal. 4:4-11, 19, 20)
"Freedom, a Gift of God" (Gal. 5:13-24)
"A Killer Killed" (Eph. 2:13-19)
"The Church Christ Founded" (Eph. 4:1-16)
"The Christian Warfare" (Eph. 6:12)
"Thanks for You" (Phil. 1:1-11)
"God Exalted Him" (Phil. 2:1-11)
"The Missions Program of First Church" (Phil. 4:10-19)
"Epaphras' Prayers" (Col. 4:10-17)

QUESTIONS OVER GALATIANS, EPHESIANS, PHILIPPIANS, COLOSSIANS

1. Paul says "It is no longer I that live, but" who lives in him? (Gal. 2:20)
2. How does Paul say we put on Christ? (3:27)
3. List the fruit of the Spirit. (5:22, 23)
4. What is the body of Christ? (Eph. 1:22, 23)
5. Husbands are told to love their wives in what way? (5:25-28)
6. What is the sword of the Spirit? (6:17)
7. Paul says that to live is Christ but to die is what? (Phil. 1:21)
8. What statement in Philippians 3 shows that Paul was still growing as a Christian? (3:12-14)
9. Paul had learned to have what attitude whether in plenty of poverty? (4:11, 12)
10. Name the faithful minister from Colosse who was with Paul in Rome. (Col. 1:7)
11. Covetousness is said to be what? (3:5)

NO HASTY ARRIVAL
(Galatians 4:4-11, 19, 20)

INTRODUCTION — Christmas, so long anticipated, is soon over. What will we be saying at the day's end? When the last grandchild has departed, and the lights have been turned off on the tree? "That's over again?"

But the coming of God among men is not over; it is just begun.

I. CHRIST CAME IN THE *FULNESS OF TIME.*
  A. Paul wrote of Israel's national childhood, while God was preparing.
     — The nation's history, all prophecy, all Scripture is involved.
  B. But consider the leisurely course of events immediately involved with "Christmas." (They can't be compressed into one "nativity scene" anywhere!)
     1. An angel appeared to Zacharias promising the fore-runner — more than a year — nearer to two years before the birth of Christ.
     2. The angel appeared in promise to Mary almost a year ahead of the event.
     3. The tax-related journey to Bethlehem, a matter of probably a week, and taking place some time in the last three months.
     4. *While they were there,* "the days were fulfilled." Several days at least.
     5. No "place" (*topos*) or opportunity (for the birth) in the inn. The inns semi-public shelters. Cf. The accused ones "*opportunity* (*topos*) to make his defense" (Acts 25:16).
        "Avenge not self, give *place* (*topos*) unto wrath" (Rom. 12:19).
        "Neither give *place* (*topos*) to the devil" (Eph. 4:27). So, while they had been in Bethlehem for some days, there was no maternity ward in the public guest chamber!
     6. Circumcision of Jesus at eight days (Luke 2:21).
     7. Presentation and purification in temple at Jerusalem, forty days (Luke 2:22ff.).

419

8. Some time after that the Wise-men came, finding Mary and Jesus in house.
   a. They had made a considerable journey since seeing His star, which indicated the time of His birth (Matt. 2:1-12).
   b. Herod's destruction of infants up to the age of two is significant.
9. Departure immediately thereafter to Egypt.

II. CHRIST COMES (FORMED IN YOU) IN THE FULNESS OF TIME.
   A. Don't be too hasty in singing.
      "O holy child of Bethlehem, Descend to us, we pray.
      Cast out our sin and enter in; Be born in us today."
   B. Not every believer was baptized after hearing the first sermon (Cf. Saul of Tarsus).
   C. After one's birth *into* Christ (the figure is used both ways), there is infancy.
      1. Paul charged the Galatians with immaturity.
         (or with premature birth, almost like an abortion.)
         a. Part of the immaturity was overemphasis on "days, and months, and times, and years"—these were integral parts of the legal system.
         b. For comparison, I found that the "sunrise service" faithful were not always present at other times.
   D. Until Christ be formed in you—"Yet not I, but Christ liveth in me" (Gal. 2:20).
      (Mary is unknown but for Him. She is Mother of Jesus.)
      Take time to be holy; the world rushes on;
         Spend much time in secret with Jesus alone.
      By looking to Jesus, like Him thou shalt be.
         Thy friends in thy conduct His likeness shall see.
      Take time to be holy, be calm in thy soul
         Each thought and each motive beneath His control.
      Thus led by His Spirit to fountains of love,
         Thou *soon* shalt be fitted for service above.

CONCLUSION — Celestial service? Perhaps not, but it is eminently worth whatever time it takes! Service soon?

A GIFT OF GOD: FREEDOM
(Galatians 5:13-24)

INTRODUCTION — The month of February is an important one in the memories of American liberties. Washington — who led in the establishment of independence. Lincoln — so much nearer to most of us — who preserved and extended freedom. The honoring of their memories will do the nation good.

I. YE HAVE BEEN CALLED FOR FREEDOM.

A. Paul spoke of freedom from the Law of Moses, yet he laid down a principle that applies in every field.
— The tendency of the Gospel is toward freedom, personally, economically, politically, morally, religiously.
— American institutions have religious beginnings.

B. Freedom is not a ten-cent-store plaything, but is hard-won and hard kept.
Edwin Markham's "Man Test."

When in the dim beginning of the years,
God mixed in man the rapture and the tears
And scattered through his brain the starry stuff,
He said, "Behold! Yet this is not enough,
For I must test his spirit to make sure
That he can dare the Vision and endure.

I will leave man to make the fateful guess,
Will leave him torn between the No and Yes;
Leave him unresting till he rests in Me,
Drawn upward by the choice that makes him free;
Leave him in tragic loneliness to choose,
With all in life to win or all to lose.

C. Freedom given when God breathed into the man the breath of life and made him a living soul.
1. All about is choice-less nature moving in its ordered ways.
2. Man blunders like a drunkard through history because he must choose.
3. In Christ is the divine beacon Light that can end the blundering, but He must be freely followed.
4. We must hold and cherish the freedom we have in Him. It is a gift.

II. USE NOT YOUR FREEDOM FOR AN OCCASION TO THE FLESH.
   A. Is this handing you a thing with one hand and taking it back with the other?
   B. The better things you buy (autos, glassware, silver) have instructions with them.
   C. The lust of the flesh destroys freedom — you can't have your cake and eat it.
      1. Fornication, uncleanness, lasciviousness.
         — A girl who once attended Sunday School with us decided to be "free." Dark stories circulated; no longer free to chose companions. The circle in which she was welcome narrowed and worsened.
      2. Enmities, strife, jealousies, wraths, factions, divisions, parties.
         — A man in the church is hurt, by action of the congregation, and leaves. The wound becomes deeper and more lasting. Now he "can't come back."
      3. Drunkenness, revellings, and such like.
         — A brilliant young imbiber, shut out of athletics, makes debating team; then is shut out there, because he would be "free," and can't be dependable.

III. THROUGH LOVE BE SERVANTS ONE TO ANOTHER. — A surprising way to freedom.
   A. Love — "Looking out for the other fellow's interests, and enjoying doing it."
   B. Remember Joseph, who was free in, and from, an Egyptian prison, because of service to fellow prisoners.
   C. Abraham Lincoln the symbol of American freedom — *for others.*
      "If I ever get a chance to hit that, I'll hit it hard."
      "This nation cannot longer exist half slave and half free."

CONCLUSION — A greater than Lincoln is here.

Was Christ ever driven to any deed against His will?
— Yet, I "came not to be served, but to serve" (Matt. 20:28).
"For freedom hath Christ set us free" (Gal. 5:1).

A KILLER KILLED
(Ephesians 2:13-19)

INTRODUCTION — "Having slain the enmity thereby."
Man's great enemy is enmity—the conflict that tears the world
apart and destroys peace, which is wholeness—oneness.

    A. The conflict of man's will against God.
    B. The conflict of selfish interests, man versus man.
    C. The conflict of conscience and lust. The difference
       between "ought to," and "do."

This is what Jesus killed by dying on the cross.

I. HE BROKE DOWN THE MIDDLE WALL OF
PARTITION.

    A. The barrier between Jew and Gentile—
      —It was most evident in traditional animosities.
    B. Illustrated in the wall between the court of the Gentiles
      and the inner court of the Temple. The wall bore an
      inscription warning of death for intrusion.
    C. The wall of the Law, which stood between Jew and
      Gentile—
        1. Between God and man—that sin might be exceeding sinful.
        2. Between man and self—to condemn the wrong shamefully done.
    D. Jesus fulfilled and went beyond the Law.
        1. He replaced form with reality.
        2. He offered the last sacrifice under the Law.

II. HE RECONCILED MEN, BOTH JEW AND
GENTILE, TO GOD (II Cor. 5:18, 19).

    A. "And this is the judgment, that the light is come into
      the world, and men loved the darkness rather than the
      light; for their works were evil. For every one that
      doeth evil hateth the light, and cometh not to the light,
      lest his works should be reproved (John 3:19, 20).
    B. Illustration—Adam hid; Jacob fled; the injurer holds
      the grudge.

Peter said, "Lord, depart from me, for I am a sinful man" (Luke 5:8).

C. We come together as we are reconciled to Him.

D. Reconciliation is "through His body on the tree."

    1. There is that which humbles the observer of Christ and the cross. "Why should He love me so?"

    2. "I, if I be lifted up from the earth, will draw all men unto me" (John 12:32).

III. PREACHED PEACE TO THEM THAT ARE AFAR OFF, AND PEACE TO THEM THAT ARE NIGH.

A. Afar off—the Gentiles.

    1. Neither knowing nor caring about God.

    2. Far from both the spiritual and moral qualities of faith.

    But see the Samaritan woman and the thief on the cross.

B. Them that are nigh—the Jews—they are often hardest to reach.

    1. So near and yet so far.

    2. These include Nicodemus, the believing priest, and the apostles.

IV. PROVIDED ACCESS TO THE FATHER.

(Illustration—Tad Lincoln and his friend see Tad's father, the President, while "important" people wait.)

A. The broken relationship of Eden restored at Calvary.

B. "Whatsoever ye shall ask in my name" will be done.

CONCLUSION — "Reaching up to God, Reaching out to man,
Reaching down to the depths of shame.
The Cross of Christ, it reaches me,
O glory to His name."

THE CHURCH CHRIST FOUNDED
(Ephesians 4:1-16)

INTRODUCTION —

Here as elsewhere, Paul answered practical problems with doctrinal teaching. "At Ephesus" (1:1) could be "at your town."

Thesis: The church is the continuing body of Christ, doing the continuing work of Christ.

I. THE WORK IS CENTRAL.

Fulfillment of purpose; "Walk worthily of the calling."

A. Christ's purpose — To do the will of Him that sent.
That they may have eternal life. That they might have life, and have it more abundantly.
Christ's program — Matthew 4:23; 9:35.

B. The church's purpose the same; described in Commission — Not self-saving nor self-serving.
1. To make disciples, baptizing, and teaching the way of Christ.
2. Immediate purposes and side issues must not confuse (Examine every item of "church work.")

C. The tools of accomplishment are at every point divinely provided — God has given.
Hence to be respected, not leaving out what is given, nor demanding more.

Keep the unity of the Spirit in the bond of peace. (Remember Demetrius and Alexander?) "Till we *attain* unto the unity of the faith" (4:13).

II. THE GIVEN UNITIES MAKE DISUNITY IMPOSSIBLE (Repeated emphasis on the *one*.) Cf. T. Campbell, *Declaration and Address*, Proposition 1.

A. One body.
Its birth predicted, divinely provided, proclaimed — Luke 2; Matt. 2; Acts 2.
I Corinthians 12:12, 23, identifies the Church with Christ.
Ephesians 1:22, 23; Colossians 1:18 declares headship.

425

B. One Spirit, one hope.
C. One Lord, the head of the church—brooks no competition.
   Observe the care to make human agencies *plural* and subservient.
D. One faith, *the* faith, delivered—this is the creed (Not "I believe" but "Christ is.")
   1. Answers the question whether the church produced the Word.
   2. The revealed faith is Christo-centric, factual.
   3. The gospel is the message, for unbeliever and believer.
   4. None other to be brooked (Galatians 1; II John 8, 9).
E. One baptism
   1. The ordinances, Christo-centric, dramatic of the Gospel.
   2. Initiating, teaching (Rom. 6).
   3. Relating to gospel (cf. I Pet. 3:21).
F. One God and Father of *all*.
   1. He permeates the whole.
   2. He permeates every one who makes up the whole. (Then what of those whom He permeates?)

III. THE GIVEN VARIETIES MAKE UNITY POSSIBLE
   This is New Testament polity.—The necessary flexibility.
   A. He gave some officers—Some temporary, gifted tasks. Some permanent, trained workers. See the task and the worker.
   B. He gave a responsibility, the edifying of saints to do the work. Christ directs, each member *supplies*.
   C. He gave the means of growth—teaching love, and knowledge of Christ (II Pet. 3:17, 18).

CONCLUSION — John writes thirty years later to the same church (Rev. 2:1-6).
   A. You have left your first *love*.
   B. Repent and do the first works. —Restoration was needed!

426

THE CHRISTIAN WARFARE
(Ephesians 6:10-13)

INTRODUCTION — There is a certain attractiveness in a struggle.

A. Let a fight start on a school ground or anyplace else, and the crowd gathers.
   1. In the strain of proving one's worth against that of another, is a challenge which is interesting to all.
   2. Often it takes real combat to bring it out.
B. So in Christ.
   1. We are challenged to bring our best into the service.
   2. There is no lack for competition, if we will but see it, and the competition is such as to challenge our best.

I. OUR WARFARE IS NOT AGAINST FLESH AND BLOOD.

A. After one experience in Eden, Satan found that the physical embodiment was too easily combatted physically, and the snakes have been suffering ever since.
B. Often we wish it were simple as flesh and blood warfare, even as the soldiers in recent wars wished they could see and get their hands on the enemy that was shelling and bombing them from some place out of sight.
C. Yet there is little or nothing to be gained spiritually from physical conflict. Jesus used it twice, but in neither case was there any spiritual good to the sufferer; only immediate relief of material evils.

II. OUR WARFARE IS "AGAINST."

It is an agressive warfare.

A. It was thus that Paul saw it.
   1. He never waited for another to bring the battle to him, but went and kept going to carry the Gospel into new fields.
   2. His very defenses were aggressive gospel sermons.
B. Illustration—The small man in the football line wins if he can "crack the other fellow before he cracks you."

C. Illustration—The desert tribes in World War I were impossible to capture because they wouldn't dig in; they were always attacking.

D. So the church is seen storming the very stronghold of hell in aggressive warfare (II Cor. 10:4).

III. THE FOE.

A. Principalities—first things.
1. "The stone that was set at nought of the builders has been made the head of the corner."
2. Christ has an uncompromising warfare against anything that would come first in the life of man. In Ephesus it was idols, the State, lustful pleasure.

B. Powers.
Influences, appetites, habits, desires, or anything that exerts a power over the life of the individual.

C. The rulers of the darkness of this world.
1. Here we have the forces embodied.
2. We may speak of gambling, liquor, and vice.

D. Spiritual wickedness—high places—evil spirits on high.
A man may war alone against material things, but where the warfare is, as it is here, against powers on which he cannot lay his hands, he needs a spiritual ally on his own side. Holy Spirit to combat evil spirit; Christ to conquer Satan.

CONCLUSION — The victory—
See it in the book of Revelation.

A. Theme of desperate conflict.
B. Ultimate victory to the Lamb and those that are His.
C. Song of triumph
—"Worthy Is the Lamb!" (Rev. 5:12, 13).

THANKS FOR YOU
(Philippians 1:1-11)

INTRODUCTION — Take a Thanksgiving trip via Trans-History Dreamliner (cost only attentive imagination, no congestion, no pollution) to Philippi, on a day in A.D. 64.

The church is gathered. Expectancy. Epaphroditus is back from Rome, wan from his recent illness. He has a letter from Paul.

Look around and you see some friends. Lydia, nearing retirement now. The girl who once told fortunes now has her own treasure, a family. The jailer who can tell you about the two big cleanups after the earthquake — his baptism and the cleanup of the buildings.

Hear the letter.

I. "I THANK MY GOD UPON EVERY REMEMBRANCE OF *YOU.*"

   Note the object of thanks.

   A. We sent Paul money, but he doesn't say, "I thank God for your money."

   B. We heard that Paul was in danger of his life and it was spared, but he doesn't say, "I thank God for the preservation of my life."

   C. We hear that his ministry in Rome is meeting with success, but he says, *you.*

   D. After all, mankind is the climax of God's creation; why stop with lesser things?

      The magic word *you* is a word of tender or turbulent meaning, depending on context and tone.

II. FOR YOUR FELLOWSHIP IN THE GOSPEL FROM THE FIRST DAY.

   A. Remember that first day: Lydia by the river, the demoniac girl, the jailer. See Acts 16.

   B. Fellowship — what strange fellowship that was!

      1. It had little of "Blest be the tie . . . fellowship of kindred minds."

429

They weren't kindred minds at first. They *lacked* what he *had*.

2. "Ye all are *partakers* of my grace."

Paul had spread a feast and they, hungry, had partaken.

3. Later "When I departed from Macedonia, no church *communicated* with me as concerning giving and receiving, but ye only" (4:15).

He lacked what they *had* — money. They weren't alike, and the matching up of their strengths and weaknesses was fellowship.

4. The basis was the Christ, who supplies to all alike.
— In the gospel.

III. "HE WHO HAS BEGUN A GOOD WORK IN YOU WILL PERFORM IT" — *Growing*.

A. "With the bishops and deacons . . ." Was the jailer now a bishop?

B. "Now we live, if you stand fast in the Lord" (I Thess 3:8).

C. Love may abound more and more — approve the excellent (Phil. 1:9-11).

1. Paul was hard to please!

2. But compare 3:13-15 — "I count not myself to have apprehended." He had not yet pleased himself.

IV. UNTIL THE DAY OF JESUS CHRIST.

A. Philippi provided a good testimonial to Paul's ministry. He had reason to be thankful for them; but the accounts were not complete.

B. "What is our hope, our joy, our crown of rejoicing? Are not even ye at the presence of our Lord Jesus Christ at his coming?" (I Thess. 2:19).

— Then the measure of his labors will be evident.

CONCLUSION — Other thankworthy items have faded.

Money is spent; life and health are finally surrendered. *You* remain. Thank God for you!

GOD EXALTED HIM
(Philippians 2:1-11)

INTRODUCTION — Read Psalm 2.

Here is the conflict between God's way and man's way. "My thoughts are not your thoughts; neither are your ways my ways, saith the Lord" (Isaiah 55:8).

I. THE STORY OF THE CRUCIFIXION AND RESURRECTION—ON GOD VERSUS MAN.
  - A. "He came unto his own and his own received Him not" (John 1:11).
  - B. "Show us the Father" (John 14:7)—Jesus did and they killed Him.
  - C. Christ crucified because He crossed their ideas on:
    1. The nature of righteousness.
    2. The nature of greatness.
    3. The center—God—and not self.
  - D. Even the church is permeated with man's rebellion.

II. MAN WINS A TEMPORARY VICTORY IN THE CRUCIFIXION.
  - A. He taught love, and hate triumphed.
  - B. He taught service, and the law of the jungle proved more strong.
  - C. He taught the importance of God's will, and man's will dominated.
  - D. He claimed to be the Son of God with power, and He lay in the grave.
      - —In the present world, all this seems to be true.

III. GOD HIGHLY EXALTED HIM—God wins a permanent victory in the resurrection.
  - A. The very deeds of Christ's enemies assured their defeat.
    1. Killing Him, they made possible the glory of resurrection.
    2. Desiring to destroy His influence, they made possible world evangelism.
    3. Attempting to make removal of His body from the grave impossible, they proved resurrection.

B. No joy in the resurrection for His enemies.
  1. Judas had already gone to his own place.
  2. The soldiers fled in terror, and then jeopardized their lives with a lie.
  3. The priests invented an excuse, confused and confounded by resurrection.
    —They continue to fight against Him, but it is like trying to keep the grass from growing.
    (Annas and Caiaphas are mentioned in Acts 4.)
  4. The Jewish nation finds no comfort in it.
    a. Those who refuse His Lordship try to deny the resurrection.
    b. The Jews, with promises and threats of Deuteronomy 28, have reaped the threats—why?
C. Christ will not be bound—
  1. By the grave—"it was not possible that He should be holden of it" (Acts 2:24).
  2. By the church—(a picture shows Jesus chained to steps of a church building).
    He will escape, even if it destroys that church.
  3. By special times and seasons.
    Significant that many celebrate the death and ignore the weekly observance of the resurrection.

IV. EVERY KNEE SHALL BOW, AND EVERY TONGUE SHALL CONFESS.
  "Sit thou on my right hand until I make thy foes thy footstool" (Acts 2:35).
  A. The resurrection becomes a threat and a danger to those who oppose.
  B. His will shall be done; He shall be glorified as Lord.
    1. It promises complete frustration to opposers.
    2. It promises complete victory for those who follow Him.
  Read Philippines 3:18-21.

CONCLUSION — Christ our King lives, with unlimited power either to save or to judge.

432

THE MISSIONS PROGRAM OF FIRST CHURCH
(Philippians 4:10-19)

INTRODUCTION — Speak on Missions Sunday as representative of missions committee.

    A. Purpose—To educate, promote, disburse.
       Make materials and speakers available to whole church.
    B. The "first church" is at Philippi, the first in Europe.
       —It was not called missions, but fellowship, or communication.

I. PHILIPPI HAD RECEIVED THE GOSPEL FROM OTHERS.

    A. Second missionary journey—"Come over into Macedonia" (Acts 16:9).
       Conversion of Lydia, the jailer, and others.
       —a Gentile church.
    B. Circumstances put them under obligation to those who sent gospel.
       1. The Jewish Christian (Rom. 15:26).
       2. Paul himself (II Cor. 8:5).
       3. To the Lord.
    C. Circumstances also put them under obligation to those who had not heard (Rom. 1:14, 15). (The package doesn't belong to the messenger, but to the addressee.)
    D. They established a direct connection for a substantial expression of faith. (How many letters of this kind could Paul have written without crippling his work in Rome? Don't expect major reply for a minor gift).

II. PHILIPPI SENT A BENEVOLENT GIFT OF GRATITUDE IN RELIEF TO JERUSALEM (II Cor. 8, 9).

    A. It did not pass over the material needs of the Jewish Christians.
    B. We have opportunity to help the needy in age, as orphans, etc.

III. PHILIPPI GAVE EARLY AND SUBSTANTIALLY TO EVANGELISM NEAR AT HAND (4:15, 16).
   A. They didn't have much gospel to give; it was new to them.
   B. They didn't have much money to give; they were poor and persecuted.
   C. Compare our own labors through local fellowship.

IV. THEY GAVE MONEY AND MANPOWER EPAPHRODITUS) TO EVANGELISM FARTHER AWAY.
   A. The rent had to be paid on Paul's dwelling in Rome; contacts had to be maintained with Christians in the community.
   B. Lockland church sends its own members to overseas mission fields.

V. PHILIPPI GAVE HELP AND COMFORT TO AN AGED PREACHER IN NEED—PERSONAL ANGLE.
   (Pensions and ministerial relief.)
   A. "Fellowship with my affliction"—an expression of gratitude and affection.
   B. Removes a handicap concerning future evangelism; younger preachers are encouraged.

VI. PHILIPPI WAS MOST BLESSED IN THEIR GIVING.
   A. Like Christ, they emptied themselves and God filled them.
   "Whosoever will save his life shall lose it, and whosoever will lose his life for my sake shall find it" (Matt. 16:25).
   B. "For your fellowship in the gospel from the first day until now . . ." (Phil. 1:5).
   It was a fellowship that included Paul, the saints in Judea, and Christ himself.

CONCLUSION — Most blessed is the giver of the Gospel.

But you can't give what you don't have.

EPAPHRAS' PRAYERS
(Colossians 4:12, 13)

INTRODUCTION —

A. "I pray daily for you," said a mother to her troubled neighbor. "I didn't know that, Mamma," said her little daughter afterward. "What time each day do you pray for her?" "O, I don't really say prayers," said Mama. "It's just to make her feel better, thinking I care."

B. Our text reports a man's praying for his friends; but it is a report by someone other than himself.

C. Epaphras is known to us only by three references in two letters of Paul, written from prison in Rome to friends in Colosse: Philemon 23 expresses greetings from "Epaphras, my fellow-prisoner in Christ." Colossians 1:7 speaks of "Epaphras our dear fellowservant, who is for you a faithful minister of Christ." Was Epaphras helping Paul on behalf of the church in Colosse?

Colossians 4:12, 13 — our text. Paul testified that Epaphras prayed for the home folk!

I. FOR WHOM DID EPAPHRAS PRAY?

A. He prayed for others.
   1. Surely he prayed for himself also, but he was not consumed with self-pity or self-interest for his station as a prisoner along with Paul.
   2. Like Jesus (Matt. 9:36), he was moved with compassion for the needy.

B. He prayed for the home congregation.
   1. As one of them, he was naturally concerned about them.
   2. Their doctrinal troubles (noted in Colossians) stirred, rather than stilled his interest.

C. He prayed for neighboring congregations (v. 13).
   1. Laodicea, twenty miles from Colosse, had the "lukewarm" church (Rev. 3:14-22).
   2. Hierapolis ("priest town") is otherwise not known to us.

II. HOW DID EPAPHRAS PRAY? (v. 12).

    A. He prayed in a manner clearly observed by Paul.
- 1. Probably they engaged in sessions of praying together, and with others.
- 2. Times of personal prayer observed by his friend.
- 3. How much do our friends know of our prayer habits, and how do they know?

    B. He prayed "always."
- 1. He did not give up on prayer (I Thess. 5:17).
- 2. The habit of prayer was established.

    C. He prayed "laboring fervently for you."
- 1. This was no mere habitual recitation of words.
- 2. It speaks the urgency of genuine concern.
- 3. It reflects something approaching the fervency of Jesus in Gethsemane.
- 4. Our own prayers would accomplish more if we worked harder at praying.

III. FOR WHAT DID EPAPHRAS PRAY? (v. 12).

    A. He prayed concerning their relationship to God.
- 1. A natural concern for their health and material well-being is not ruled out, (Compare III John 2).
- 2. In talking to God about them, he was most concerned with the things of God.
- 3. On their behalf he sought first "the kindgom of God and his righteousness" (Matt. 6:33).

    B. He prayed with awareness of their problems.
- 1. The doctrinal confusions at Colosse were known to him as well as to Paul.
- 2. His prayers were not limited to their correction; it was not simply, "Lord straighten them up."
- 3. His plea for their growth and maturity: "Lord, build them up!"
- 4. It is an excellent example of Christian prayer for the church, here and elsewhere.

CONCLUSION — We don't know much about Epaphras; but the little we do know centers in his praying for his friends. Would that we might be thus known!

PREACHING THROUGH
I AND II THESSALONIANS, I AND II TIMOTHY, TITUS AND PHILEMON

THESSALONIANS

Paul established the church at Thessalonica, in Macedonia, while on his second missionary journey (Acts 17:1-9). When he was at Corinth, later on the same journey (Acts 18:1-17), he learned that some of the Thessalonian Christians had already laid down their lives for the faith, and their friends were much concerned over them. He wrote these letters to establish them in the faith and to comfort them concerning their departed faithful friends. The letters were among the earliest New Testament books to be written — about A.D. 52.

TIMOTHY

For the character and work of Timothy, see Acts 16:1-4; I Thessalonians 3:1-8; Philippians 2:19-22; Acts 18:5; 19:22; Hebrews 13:23; II Corinthians 1:19. Paul had completed his major missionary labors when he wrote these epistles to Timothy at Ephesus, giving instruction and exhortation concerning the conduct of the work. Some time elapsed between the writing of the two letters. The second is Paul's last preserved writing, from prison in Rome about A.D. 66.

TITUS

For the character and work of Titus, see Galatians 2:1-3; II Corinthians 2:13; 7:6-14; 8:6-23; II Timothy 4:10. He was given charge of the work of the church in the Island of Crete, as Timothy was in Ephesus, but his problems were different. The chief trouble at Ephesus arose from false teachers; in Crete it came from the immorality of the heathen world.

PHILEMON

Philemon was a wealthy Christian in Colosse, a city near Ephesus. His slave Onesimus escaped to Rome, and was there converted by Paul, who sent him back to Philemon with this beautiful letter, written about A.D. 64.

You are cordially invited to share in this fellowship of reading God's Word, and to share in the worship as these messages are presented.

Sermon Outlines Provided:

"Your Election of God" (I Thess. 1:2-10)
"On Wholesome Diet" (I Tim. 1:1-7)
"Add Godliness" (I Tim. 6:3-16)
"Workers Together for God" (II Tim. 1:1-8, 13, 14)
"He Abideth Faithful" (II Tim. 2:13)
"The Workman and His Tools" (II Tim. 2:7-15)
"Completely Furnished" (II Tim. 3:10-17)
"Ready to Every Good Work" (Titus 3:1-9)

Other Sermon Topics Suggested:

"The Word of God" (I Thess. 2:13-16)
"On Playing Fair With the Family" (I Thess. 4:1-8)
"Concerning Them That Sleep" (I Thess. 4:13 — 5:11)
"His Own Bread" (II Thess. 3:6-12)
"Of Shepherds and Servants" (I Tim. 3:3-13)
"Train the Young Women" (Tit. 2:1-8)
"Our Brother" (Philemon)

QUESTIONS OVER I AND II THESSALONIANS, I AND II TIMOTHY, TITUS AND PHILEMON

1. Paul says he is constantly remembering what three things about the Thessalonians? (I Thess. 1:3)
2. After the return of Christ vengeance will be given to what two groups? (II Thess. 1:8)
3. What does Paul say is the goal of his instruction or charge? (I Timothy 1:5)
4. What did the false teachers Paul warns against in I Timothy 4 say about marriage? (4:1-3)
5. Name Timothy's mother and grandmother. (II Tim. 1:5)
6. Though Paul was imprisoned he said what was not imprisoned or bound? (2:9)
7. What does Paul call Titus? (Tit. 1:4)
8. Who was the runaway slave Paul asks Philemon to receive back? (Philemon 10-12)

YOUR ELECTION OF GOD
(I Thessalonians 1:2-10)

INTRODUCTION — In addressing this subject one has to be comforted by the exhortation to "tackle the great texts, even if they throw you." What is election, and how can one know it?

I. WHAT IS ELECTION?

Ekloge, choice, selection. (Of Paul, Acts 9:11.)

A. This in accord with eternal purpose of God. What?
  1. See Ephesians 1:9-12. Introduces fore-ordination (predestination). See Romans 8:28-30.
  2. "The Lord is . . . longsuffering to usward, not willing that any should perish, but that all should come to repentance" (II Pet. 3:9).
  3. "This is good and acceptable in the sight of God our Savior; who will have all men to be saved, and to come unto the knowledge of the truth" (I Tim. 2:3, 4).

B. Thus He has ordained — set in order — before hand.
  1. It is not a matter of force, but of plan.
  2. As the ordination of church officers, it is a plan, sometimes broken by the free choice and action of the one ordained.

C. The selection — the act of choosing — is the act of God. As with Jesus' choice of the twelve:
  "Ye did not choose me, but I chose you, and appointed you, that ye should go and bear fruit . . ." (John 15:16, ASV).
  "Many are called, but few are chosen" (Matt. 22:14).

D. The will to accede or not to accede to the choice is still with man. Compare the rich young ruler — the man also who would go and bury his father. "Come unto me, all ye that labor and are heavy laden" (Matt. 11:28).

E. The old definition of election is still good: (You announce yourself a candidate; God votes for you, Satan votes against you; you vote, and the way you vote you are elected.) Many are not elected because they decline the nomination!

439

II. HOW CAN ONE KNOW THAT HE, OR ANY OTHER, IS ELECTED?

   — By their fruits ye shall know them.

   A. Our gospel came unto you not in word only, but in power . . .

      "When ye received from us the word of the message, even the word of God, ye accepted it not as the word of men, but, as it is in truth, the word of God, which also worketh in you that believe" (I Thess. 2:13, ASV).

   B. You became imitators of us, and of the Lord — so that you became examples to all that belive.

      Be ye imitators (not followers) of me, even as I also am of Christ (I Cor. 11:1).

      The fruit of the Spirit is manifest (Gal. 5:22, 23).

   C. You turned from idols, to serve a living and true God.

      "The dearest idol I have known, whate'er that idol be,
      Help me to tear it from thy throne,
         and worship only Thee."

   D. From you hath sounded forth the word of the Lord — Macedonia and Achaia and beyond.

CONCLUSION —

   "Give diligence to make your calling and election sure" (II Pet. 1:10).

ON WHOLESOME DIET
(I Timothy 1:1-7)

INTRODUCTION —

A. The unpopular position of doctrinal preaching.
  1. The worst slur one could make on a preacher, that he preached nothing but doctrine.
  2. I am announcing the subject boldly.
     Like taking castor oil without orange juice.
B. Doctrine is teaching, and soundness is wholesomeness.
  1. Some have denied the Pauline authorship of the Pastorals because they and no others of his letters refer to "sound doctrine."
     a. But Paul was at this time in prison, attended by Luke, his physician.
     b. The medical term under the circumstances is natural—wholesome spiritual diet (Heb. 6:1; I Pet. 2:1, 2).

I. ON GETTING ENOUGH.

A. It is unfortunate that our spiritual appetite dies with starvation and does not demand food as our stomachs do when they are denied.
B. But this is not the center of our thought.

II. WARNING AGAINST POISONED FOODS.

A. Parallel.
  1. We have pure food laws to protect us against getting poisoned or inferior foods for our bodies.
  2. The labels must tell the exact truth about what is inside.
  3. Perhaps some would not know the difference if teachings were so labeled.
B. Genealogies—socially significant, but spiritually unprofitable.
  1. To Paul they were the carry-overs from Judaism.
     a. Introducing to religion the things that were of no importance.
     b. Disturbing the mind of the people with guesses.

441

2. So occupied are they who base much teaching on the uncertain prophecies.
   a. If it is even true, for instance, that Revelation refers largely to the last things, still it is subject to many and varied interpretations, none of which can be authoritative.
   b. Such things are those on which division is based. Beware the young preachers of Ezekiel and Revelation.
   c. Beware the Russellites with their queer mixture of dogged literalism and wild allegorizing, all according to their own fancy. Entertain them if you must, but expect only fruitless questionings to arise from them.
C. Myths—Fascinating, but misleading.
   1. These came in the pagan element of the church at Ephesus.
      a. The knowledge falsely so called.
      b. The vagaries and dogmatics of the pagan mind.
   2. Of such is the "science" that makes the present day superstitions.
      a. "A true scientist keeps his mouth shut until he knows what he is talking about."
         i. Yet one hears the dogmatic assertion that the Peking man is our ancestor of a million years ago.
         ii. The basis of all science is hypothesis.
      b. Science, dogmatic as it is, is ever changing, yet would claim in its more brazen state, allegiance away from the stable Gospel. Illustration—The young sailor, who, off the course, wanted another star to follow: "We have passed this one up."
      c. Beware of the scientific teachers, who want to be teachers of the law, yet do not know what they are talking about.
         i. If they knew science, they would know and admit its limits, as do really eminent scientists such as Jeans, Millikan, etc.
         ii. They know only enough to cast doubts.

442

III. THE REAL FOOD.

A. "If any man teacheth otherwise, and consenteth not to wholesome words, *even the words of our Lord Jesus Christ,* and to the doctrine which is according to godliness; he is proud, knowing nothing, but doting about questions and strifes of words" (I Tim. 6:3).

B. Milk—I Peter 2:2.

1. Faith in Christ, repentance toward Christ, confession of Christ, baptism into Christ, and living in Christ.

2. Milk is foundation food—it is completely essential doctrine.

3. When one lingers too long on this it becomes (Heb. 6:1) not doctrine but dogmatics and systematics.

C. Meat—II Pet. 1:5-7.

Virtue — manliness, beauty, worth.

Knowledge — there is no limit to the knowledge which is in God.

Temperance (self-control) in all things — it may mean abstinence.

Patience — that which is learned through enduring and staying kind.

"Let patience have her perfect work" (James 1:4).

Godliness — God-likeness, and to that there is no limit.

Brotherly kindness — It is without limits inside the world.

Love — "for God is love" (I John 4:8).

When we have achieved that in perfection, we have achieved God.

CONCLUSION — Where do you find wholesome diet?

"All scripture is given by inspiration of God, and is profitable for doctrine, for reproof, for correction, for instruction in righteousness: that the man of God may be perfect, throughly furnished unto all good works (II Tim. 3:16, 17).

ADD GODLINESS
(I Timothy 6:3-16)

INTRODUCTION — The ugly phrase, "pious hypocrite," has but piety or godliness under a shadow, even among its friends.

    A. There are two bases for it:

        1. One without knowledge becomes a pious fanatic.

        2. One without temperance becomes a pious fraud.

    B. In II Peter 1:6 this attribute is put late in the list, for a purpose, but it is given great significance.

I. PIETY ESTABLISHED ON SOUND DOCTRINE.

    A. Sound doctrine is "the words of our Lord Jesus Christ, and the teaching which is according to godliness."

    B. "One cannot have the Holy Spirit without knowing and following the word of God."

    C. If it is not founded in Christ it becomes a display of oneself—"puffed up, knowing nothing."

    D. If it is based on fragmentary knowledge it becomes "a striving about words to no profit."

II. PIETY ESTABLISHED ON SOUND PRACTICE.

    A. Basic is a proper attitude toward the Creator and the created.

        Godliness is fundamentally an attitude toward God, impossible to the materialist. *Read again verses 6-11.*

        (Illustration—Two families following a flood; one "lost everything"; the other "saved everything"; though their experience identical, in destruction of property, survival of people.)

    B. True piety impossible with any willful sin.

III. EMPHASIS ON PRACTICAL MORALITY HAS GONE TOO FAR.

    A. The fashion of John Hay, the poet (which see).

    B. In discussion of "week-day religious education," Dr. P. feared that the teaching would "degenerate to doctrine"—that it be kept strictly ethical.

C. In Church:

(Original hymn)　　　　　　　　　*Lines 2 & 3 as edited:*

From all that dwell below
　the skies,
Let the Creator's praise arise;　Let faith and hope and love
Let the Redeemer's name be　　arise
　sung　　　　　　　　　　　　Let beauty, truth, and good
Through every land, by every　sung
　tongue.

D. Thus to be ashamed of the deep piety that is at the base of all true good is like a child ashamed of his parents.

IV. NOTE THE ENTHUSIASTIC PIETY OF THE APOSTLE.

A. On God's honor roll are those soldiers of the Cross who have dared to march with His banner flung out for all to see, not caring about the ugly taunt of "hypocrite."

B. It is God-consciousness in practice—awareness of God; frank and honest humility before Him; willingness to praise Him before men.

C. Deep and daring piety characterizes great men.
1. Lincoln frankly admits his dependence on God.
2. The Campbells' conversation and letters steeped in expressed faith.

D. Surprising evidences of piety.
1. "God bless you," says our physician, genuinely.
2. Editor Jack Blanton, Monroe Co., Mo., in *Appeal*—headlines "Rain, Rain, Praise God from Whom All Blessings Flow!" "Lord, We Confess Our Sin, We Ask Forgiveness, We Pray for Rain."

CONCLUSION −

Let our lives be rooted and grounded in faith; let them grow the strong trunk of manly virtue; let their branches be bolstered with knowledge; let them grow through winter storm and summer sun with steadfast patience; but let them never forget to lift high their boughs in prayerful honest piety, drinking the warmth of God's love and the sweet rain of His mercy.

445

WORKERS TOGETHER FOR GOD (Teamwork)
(II Timothy 1:1-8, 13, 14)

INTRODUCTION — Our restoration of New Testament Christianity needs to recognize its rural beginnings.

A. The elements of God's kingdom are not identical pieces stamped out in a factory; they are living growths, springing from good seed and producing good fruit.

B. Recognition, then, is not like identifying the make of an auto off an assembly line; it is like finding a walnut tree in a winter woods, by walnuts on ground.

C. Consider our stereotyped reference to "Timothies" (with the impersonal *ies* plural), as products of a Timothy factory, home church and ministry. The New Testament Timothy was not sent into ministry, but *brought*, apprenticed, companioned with, interned, trained, loved, and directed by Paul. Thus, if I am a "Timothy," it is not so much of the Salem church, where I grew up, as it is of P. H. Welshimer at First Church, Canton, where I served as assistant, and learned *teamwork*. —Christian friends and partners, working together.

Let's restore teamwork, a la Paul and Timothy (more Biblical *Timothys*) as seen here, and in Acts.

I. THIS TEAMWORK WAS FIRST A RELATIONSHIP BETWEEN PERSONS.

A. They knew each other from long and close association.
1. Some twelve years of "father-son" service between first joining and the writing of the letter (Phil. 2:19-22).
2. Acquaintance with the family for two generations back.
3. (By comparison, P. H. Welshimer wanted dinner-table acquaintance with me and Mrs. Hayden.)

B. They maintained affectionate regard for each other.
1. Timothy was Paul's "beloved son."
2. Paul was subject of Timothy's tears (perhaps at stoning—Acts 14:19, 20).

446

3. Each was the object of the other's fervent prayers.
4. This relationship cannot be forced; it can be deserved and encouraged.
   (One member of the team does not entertain fault-finding against the other.)
C. Their personal relationship was centered in Christ, in whom they were brothers before they were partners.

II. THIS TEAMWORK WAS THE OPERATION OF PERSONS, NOT MACHINES, IN MINISTRY.
A. It centered in tasks and functions, rather than positions. There was work to be done, and each did the part for which he was then fitted and able.
B. It defies any mechanical and absolute job descriptions.
   1. The fitting of pegs and holes, square and round, has limited value.
   2. The Christian ministry is a vast area, growing and changing.
   3. The Christian minister is his own person, not like any other.
   4. Teamwork is the operation of two or more individual, growing persons, in a field that is itself growing and changing.
C. It demands the recognition of "good faults" — qualities good in one situation, but less desirable in another.
   1. Paul perhaps like P. H. Welshimer, a "steam engine in breeches" — watch the safety valve!
      — Comes out in relation to Barnabas. Paul took over; conflicted over Mark.
   2. Timothy's self-forgetful tenderness (perhaps delicate health — I Tim. 5:23) became a lack of needed energetic aggressiveness when he was in charge.
   3. So the perfectionist worker may be a very poor trainer of others.

III. THIS TEAMWORK WAS GEARED TO ONE ESSENTIAL TASK TOGETHER.
A. Doctrinal — "Retain the standard of sound words" (v. 13).

447

"Guard the treasure entrusted" (v. 14).

"Endure hardship as a soldier of Christ."

B. Moral — as seen in the admonitions related to Ephesus' needs.

C. Mutual — each supplying the other's need.

1. Paul (and the presbyters) had supplied some special gift for Timothy's use in the ministry.

— Consider what you have from teachers, mentors, parents.

2. Timothy supplied an element of encouragement without which Paul was less than wholly effective (Acts 15:5).

"Every man is my superior at some point."

CONCLUSION — Teamwork is still found.

"He is not only a good worker himself. His influence (presence) makes everyone around him a better worker because he is there."

The coaches', score sheet includes not only goals, but *assists*.

HE ABIDETH FAITHFUL
(II Timothy 2:13, ASV)

INTRODUCTION — From present situation.

    A. Some lose faith in time of difficulty.
        1. Rebellious at personal affliction.
        2. Swamped in national calamity.
        3. Blame everything and everybody but themselves.
    B. Contrast Paul:
        1. Charitably forgetful of others' failures.
        2. Everlastingly sure of God.
        3. Concerned lest he himself prove faithless.

Probably no one ever suffered more from faithlessness of others than Paul.

I. HIS OWN PEOPLE THE JEWS, PERSECUTED HIM.

    A. Hounded from city to city.
        1. Stoned at Lystra.
        2. Jailed and beaten at Philippi.
        3. Driven from Thessalonica.
        4. Opposed at Corinth.
        5. His work destroyed in Galatia.
    B. Betrayed in the Temple while doing the Jews a favor.
    C. Still he prayed for them—(Rom. 9:1-3; 10:1).

II. THE CHURCHES FAILED HIM.

    A. Corinth quarreled and divided.
    B. Galatians proved untrue.
    C. Caesarea sent no visitor in two years of imprisonment there.
    D. "Some even preach Christ of envy and strife" (Phil. 1:15).

III. CIVIL AND GOVERNMENTS FAILED HIM.

    A. Beaten contrary to law in Philippi.
    B. Held without charges for two years in Caesarea.
    C. Felix waits for a bribe.
    D. Falsely condemned by Caesar in Rome.

IV. FRIENDS TURNED THEIR BACKS ON HIM.
   A. "All that are in Asia are turned away" (II Tim. 1:15).
   B. "Demas hath forsaken me, having loved this present world" (II Tim. 4:10).
   C. "At my first answer no man stood with me, but all men forsook me" (II Tim. 4:16).

V. HE FELT HE COULD TRUST TIMOTHY.
   1. "I have no other one likeminded, who cares for your souls, for you know the proof of him, how that as a son with a father he has labored with me in the gospel" (Phil. 2:20-22).
   2. "Yet, Timothy, though you yourself and I myself prove faithless . . ."

VI. GOD ABIDETH FAITHFUL.
   "Faith, beaten back to its last stand, rallies there and turns the tide, then ventures forth upon those who bear the image of God."
   A. "God is not a man, that He should lie; neither the son of man that he should repent; hath he said, and shall He not do it: or hath he spoken, and shall he not make it good" (Num. 23:19).
      1. Promises to Israel had all been fulfilled, even after much time.
      2. We see but for a day and are impatient with delay.
   B. Paul's faith had been tested.
      1. "I besought the Lord three times . . . My grace is sufficient for thee" (II Cor. 12:8, 9).
      2. "I know whom I have believed" (II Tim. 1:12).
      3. "The Lord stood by me" (II Tim. 4:17).

CONCLUSION —
   A. "If we die with him, we shall also live with him,
         [remembering Stephen]
      If we endure, we shall also reign with him:
         ["Be thou faithful unto death, and I will give unto thee the crown of life" Rev. 2:10.]
      If we shall deny Him, He also will deny us.
   B. He is faithful that promised.

WHERE HAVE ALL THE CRAFTSMEN GONE?

(II Timothy 2:15 — chapter as basis)

INTRODUCTION — Is workmanship a lost quality?

A. Is it true as often reported that job-holders in our time are: — Lazy, incompetent, unconcerned, unskilled, and unwilling to learn?

B. Consider Paul's exhortation to Timothy.
   1. Philippians 2:19-22 describes Timothy as selflessly dedicated and experienced in Christian service.
   2. Yet Paul's second epistle to Timothy is full of vigorous admonitions to more aggressive and fruitful workmanship (II Tim. 1:6-8 and chapter 2).

C. No harsh criticism need be found, then, in our application of Paul's words: "Give diligence to present thyself approved unto God, a workman that needeth not to be ashamed, handling aright the word of truth" (2:15, ASV).

I. DILIGENT WORKMEN NEEDED.

A. This seems to be the key to Timothy's problem.
   1. His gentle disposition and perhaps delicate health (I Tim. 5:23) rendered him less persistent and aggressive than Paul wished.
   2. The same quality that rendered him easy to work with, seems to have rendered him also easily discouraged and dissuaded.
   3. The epistle urged stirring up and using his talents to the full.

B. This is the key to the workman-examples in 2:3-6; all speak of single-minded application to the task at hand:
   1. The soldier endures the rigors of service and avoids competing involvements.
   2. The contestant submits to the discipline of the rules. (Remember the racer who came in first but was disqualified for infraction?)
   3. The fruit grower invests enormous labor in bringing his crop to harvest.

451

C. Beware the temptation to consider that hard work is not to be expected in the field of religion!
— It is the laborer, not simply the position occupier, who is worthy of his hire.

II. GOD-CONSCIOUS WORKMEN NEEDED.

A. If one would succeed in any enterprise, he must keep his purposes clear.

B. The Christian's purpose is like that of his Lord: "I seek not mine own will, but the will of the Father which hath sent me" (John 5:30).

C. If God approves, we can bear the disapproval of all else; if God disapproves, other approvals mean nothing.

D. "Wherefore we labor, that, whether present or absent, we may be accepted of him" (II Cor. 5:9).

E. Our aim must be to adjust our ways so as to please God; we cannot expect Him to adjust His judgment so as to be pleased with what we have chosen to do.

III. WORK-PROUD WORKMEN NEEDED.

A. One should find gratification in worthy accomplishment.
  1. Do you like to be around when the inspector looks your job over?
  2. Then take pride in what is designed to please God, for He is the final judge.

B. Did Timothy have a problem with timidity?
"Be not thou therefore ashamed of the testimony of our Lord, nor of me his prisoner" (II Tim. 1:8).

C. Confidence before God may rightly grow into a "holy boldness" before men.

IV. SKILLED WORKMEN NEEDED.

A. "Handling aright" or "rightly dividing" (AV) was literally "cutting straight," and by usage "dealing correctly" with the matter at hand.
  1. It suggests the plowman or the user of a saw cutting straight and square.
  2. It agrees with Proverbs 4:27: "Turn not to the right hand nor to the left."

B. The straight course in Scripture teaching is urged: Don't wander off.
   1. "Strive not about words to no profit, but to the subverting of the hearers" (v. 14).
   2. "Shun profane and vain babblings, for they will increase unto more ungodliness" (v. 16).
C. ("Happy is he born and taught Who serveth not another's will; Whose armor is his honest thought, And simple truth his utmost skill.")
D. The basic task is to convey accurately to others the Word that has been received (v. 2).

V. TRUTH-TAUGHT WORKMEN NEEDED.
   A. One cannot be God's workman without a commitment to God's Word.
   B. That is the Bible, to be known, loved, lived, and taught.
   . "Handling aright" demands awareness of the way in which any book or passage relates to the whole.
   D. It is not enough to assert, "The Bible says." Each passage must be weighed by:
      1. Who said it?
      2. To whom was it said?
      3. When and under what circumstances was it said?
   E. The Word of truth demands that Bible words be used with Bible meanings. Examples:
      1. Scripturally the *heart* is the center of thinking, rather than of emotion.
      2. *Conversation* (AV) is the manner of life; not just talk.

CONCLUSION — Where have the craftsmen gone? Ask rather, "Who is a craftsman?" and "Who is to judge my workmanship?"

(The Boy Scouts built bird houses and brought them to the troop meeting place. Tommy's wren box, solid and brown, looked dull and awkward among the brightly painted models around it. Some boys were embarrassed to have it in the display. But Tommy took it home and mounted it firmly on a tall pole, where it sheltered families of happily approving wrens for many years. Tommy's work was approved by the ultimate authority!)

By whom is your workmanship approved?

THE BOOK WE NEED
(II Timothy 3:14-17, ASV)

INTRODUCTION — What can we do about the mess we're in?

A. The third chapter of II Timothy reads somewhat like today's paper or TV news.
   1. Increasing wickedness in the "last days."
   2. Sufferings endured by the faithful.
   3. Warnings of persecutions to come.
B. What shall Timothy do under the circumstances?
   1. He shall not waste time wailing and hand-wringing.
   2. "Abide thou in the things which thou hast learned."
   3. The Bible is what you need; make use of it!

I. SCRIPTURE IS TO BE KNOWN (v. 15)

A. Timothy knew the Old Testament Scriptures.
   1. It involved rote learning of much material.
   2. His learning began very early, with Grandmother Lois and Mother Eunice (II Tim. 1:5).
      a. The Psalms were probably their lullaby songs.
      b. Scripture was taught and discussed at mealtimes, etc. (Deut. 6:4-9).
B. We have many advantages toward knowing Scripture.
   1. The New Testament material is briefer and more interesting.
   2. Copies are readily available and convenient.
C. Reverence for the Book is of little worth if the Book itself is not known.
   1. Some are like the housekeeper who will not allow anything to be placed on top of a Bible, but admits that she knows very little of its content.
   2. The content, not the container, is valuable.
D. We could bewail the modern lack of knowledge of Scripture; but what shall we do about it?
   1. If you have not known the Bible from childhood, you can start learning it now!
   2. You can act so that another generation will not be so cheated. Teach now!

II. SCRIPTURE IS TO LEAD TO SALVATION IN CHRIST (v. 15).

A. It is able to make wise.
   1. It provides *information* about God and His will; it also directs to the *useful employment* of that information.
   2. It separates between the wise and the fool (Prov. 1:7).
B. This wisdom directs toward Christ and salvation.
   1. Old Testament Scriptures foreshadowed the Messiah.
   2. Jesus and the apostles used the Old Testament in setting forth the Gospel.
   3. Hearers examined the Old Testament to check on their preaching (Acts 17:11).
C. Salvation was not through the law, but through faith in its Messiah.
   1. The way of salvation is much easier for us to trace in the New Testament.
   2. John 20:30, 31 identifies this salvation as the purpose of the writing.

III. SCRIPTURE IS TO DISCIPLINE ONE FOR GROWTH IN CHRIST (v. 16).

A. The "profitable" writings are those inspired of God.
   1. Some writing is inspired of the devil and is most destructive.
   2. Unbridled "freedom of the press" can work harm.
B. The useful discipline appears in four elements.
   1. Teaching or doctrine, the subject matter for study.
      — In the Old Testament it was the Law; for us it is basically the Gospel.
   2. Reproof, showing the error of one's way.
      a. Through the law is the knowledge of sin.
      b. Seeing perfection in Christ, Simon Peter said, "I am a sinful man."
   3. Correction, showing the right way to the erring.
      a. Timothy saw the right way according to the prophets: "What doth the Lord require of thee, but to do justly, and to love mercy, and to walk humbly with thy God?" (Micah 6:8).

b. To us, Christ provides correction by His teaching and example, in New Testament.
4. Instruction in righteousness—the drill that makes the right way a habit.
   a. Parents were to give daily instruction (Deut. 6:4-9).
   b. The New Testament reiterates the Gospel facts and commands (to love, etc.) "To write the same things to you, to me indeed is not grievous, but for you it is safe" (Phil. 3:1).

IV. SCRIPTURE IS TO EQUIP ONE FOR GOOD WORKS (v. 17).
   A. The man of God is to grow to maturity in Christ (Eph. 4:13-16).
      ("The vigor of our spiritual life will be in exact proportion to the place held by the Bible in our life and thoughts." —George Müller)
   B. For that maturity, Scripture offers the needed and balanced diet.
      (A noted educator once said that a knowledge of the Bible, without college training, was a better education for life than college training without a knowledge of the Bible.)
   C. The purpose of Christian maturity is active service to God and man—"good works."
      1. Matthew 25:31-46 relates Jesus' demand for acts of love to the needy.
      2. Romans 12 spells out Paul's exhortation to good works built on sound doctrine.
      3. Book of James warns against a dead, inactive, faith.

CONCLUSION — The Bible is designed for these things: (1) to be known, (2) to lead to salvation in Christ, (3) to provide discipline for growth, and (4) to equip one for good works.

The Bible is God's provided instrument for our blessing. It accomplishes His purpose only if we use it!

READY TO EVERY GOOD WORK
(Titus 3:1-9)

INTRODUCTION — "Good works" to Titus.

1. We are impressed by repeated emphasis on "good works." Read Titus 1:16; 2:7, 14; 3:18, 8, 14.

2. Strange from the same pen that wrote, "By grace are ye saved through faith; and that not of yourselves: it is the gift of God: not of works, lest any man should boast" (Eph. 2:8, 9).

3. Sound living and sound teaching are all part of the same pattern, here given.

4. Special need to write of good works to Crete: see Titus 1:12.

     We shall see that the advice given for Crete in Nero's time is good for us.

I. "THE THINGS WHICH BECOME SOUND DOCTRINE."

 A. The pattern for aged men. Of one such it was said "His presence a benediction."

 B. Aged women—Not china figures for a picture, but "teachers of good things."

 C. The younger women taught by the older.
    —Centering at home, and loving it.

 D. Younger men—the insistence on soberness is significant for every age. —Where that is necessary there is danger.

 E. Servants—a special need.
    Perhaps we need also here: "Ye masters, do the same things unto them, forbearing threatening; knowing that your master also is in heaven; neither is there respect of persons with him" (Ephe. 6:9).

 F. Citizens.
    Obedience to authority.
    Peaceableness, without groveling.

This quality of life doesn't come by wishing for it, nor talking about it; then or now.

II. *WE* OURSELVES ARE A CHANGED PEOPLE.

   (Here a before-and-after picture).

   A. Reasons for wickedness.
      1. Foolish—"Thou fool, this night shall thy soul be required of thee" (Luke 12:20).
         Absorption with things seen; no appreciation of eternal values.
      2. Disobedient—Either not knowing, or deliberately rejecting, God's will.
      3. Deceived—"Be not deceived, God is not mocked; whatsoever a man soweth, that shall he also reap" (Gal. 6:8).
         "Be ye doers of the word, and not hearers only, deceiving your own selves" (James 1:22).

   B. Nature of wickedness.
      1. Serving divers lusts and pleasures.
         Note "serving"; pleasure seekers become slaves.
      2. Living in envy, hateful, and hating one another.
         The self-seeker, confronting other self-seekers, is in position of the terrier that ruled the block till an airedale came.

III. "BUT *AFTER* THE KINDNESS OF GOD'S LOVE APPEARED." (What worked the change?)

   A. God's love in Christ.
      1. Reaches the heart that won't bend to the bludgeon.
      2. If He can love us, we can love one another.

   B. According to His mercy He saved us.
      Not that we are saved unwilling, any more than a drowning man is saved against his will.

   C. By the washing of regeneration, and renewing of the Holy Ghost.
      "Except a man be born of the water and of the Spirit" (John 3:5).

CONCLUSION — A great vessel at the shipyard has been years in the building. Now it is ready—fitted, commissioned, manned. Let it sail! That's what it was built for! Christian, what were you made ready for? Good works!

458

PREACHING THROUGH HEBREWS AND JAMES

Written to Jewish Christians in the first century, these two books containing a total of eighteen chapters are addressed to two different problems, both of which have modern parallels and applications.

The book of Hebrews is addressed to those who were tempted to let their Christian faith and commitment slip away in favor of the more convenient forms of their traditional Judaism. They are told that such a course would be spiritual suicide. The message of Hebrews is needed by every Christian today as he is faced with the overwhelming busy-ness of the present world which tempts him to "get out of the habit" of the practices of Christian faith.

The book of James is a brief and practical preachment addressed to the problems of a living faith—temptation, lust and sin; patience, wisdom and prayer; poverty, riches and respect of persons; faith and good works; sins of the tongue, quarrelsomeness, worldlymindness, and self-sufficiency. These problems are modern as well as ancient. So is the Christian answer to them.

The writer of Hebrews is not named in the book. His thinking is like that of Paul; the fine literary polish of his writing is different from the informal character of Paul's other letters. The time of the writing is near the end of Paul's life. The theme of the book is "Christ, God's Perfect and Final Revelation."

Chapters 1-4   Christ Supreme
5—7:10   Christ the Universal High Priest
7:11—8:13 Christ the Mediator of the New Covenant
9-10   Christ the Perfect Sacrifice
11-13   The Achievements of Faith; the past inspiring the future.

The writer of James is not James the Apostle who was the brother of John, but rather "James the Just," the half brother of Jesus (Matt. 13:55; Gal. 1:9) who became a believer after the resurrection of Christ (I Cor. 15:7) and achieved a place of influence in the church at Jerusalem (Acts 15). He was known for his piety and wisdom, and although he was himself a strict observer of the Jewish Law, he insisted upon the freedom of Gentile Christians from the Law. His letter to the Christian Jews everywhere speaks of the daily temptations by which their faith will be tried, and advises them to meet the temptations with steadfast faith, prayer, and active good deeds.

Sermon Outlines Provided:

"A Revealed Word" (Heb. 1:1-4)
"The Starting Point" (Heb. 6:1-12)
"The Old and the New" (Heb. 8)
"Let Us . . ." (Heb. 10:19-25)
"The Joy of Thy Lord" (Heb. 12:1-6)
"Swift to Hear" (James 1:19-27)
"Show Me Your Faith" (James 2:14-24)
"Occupational Hazards in the Ministry" (James 3)

Other Sermon Topics Suggested:

"If We Neglect" (Heb. 2:1-9)
"Pilgrims" (Heb. 11:13-16)
"Whence Come Wars?" (James 3:13—4:4, 10)
"Add Patience" (James 5:7-11)

QUESTIONS OVER HEBREWS AND JAMES

1. God has spoken in the last days through whom? (Heb. 1:2)
2. Who is called apostle in Hebrews 3:1?
3. Jesus learned obedience in what way according to the Hebrew writer? (5:8)
4. When the priesthood is changed, what else necessarily changes? (7:12)
5. It is appointed unto men to do what? (9:27)
6. Hebrews 10:31 says what is a fearful or terrifying thing?
7. Moses chose to suffer ill-treatment with the people of God rather than to enjoy what? (11:25)
8. What is the descriptive title of Jesus used in the benediction to the Hebrew letter? (13:20)
9. How does James define pure religion? (James 1:27)
10. We should say what when we declare our plans? (4:15)
11. Who is given as an example for our prayer life? (5:17, 18)

A REVEALED WORD
(Hebrews 1:1-4)

INTRODUCTION — From his ignorance and sin, man is rescued, as it were, by helicopter!

    A. Men do get themselves into predicaments where they can be reached only from above.

    B. The knowledge of God cannot be attained by seeking, striving, searching.

        1. Discovery is limited to knowing God's power and divinity (Rom. 1:19-20).

        2. For His nature, His will, and His purpose for men, we must depend on revelation.

    C. Genesis 1:1 and Hebrews 1:1 overleap all human discovery by declaring a revealed truth: God created, and God has spoken to His creatures.

I. GOD SPEAKS.

    A. The very name of God, found in the Old Testament, is revealed and revealing.

        1. God identified himself to Moses at the burning bush (Exod. 3:13-15).

        2. It speaks of one absolute; there can be no other god or gods.

        3. It speaks of one eternal, without beginning and without end, dwelling in an unchanging present tense: I AM.

        4. Most importantly, it speaks of one who makes himself known to His people.

    B. God is personal: He thinks, feels, wills, judges, and makes known His thoughts, feelings, and will.

    C. God is interested in His creation, and so communicates with it.

II. GOD SPOKE TO THE FATHERS THROUGH THE PROPHETS.

    A. In this sentence, as in the rest of Hebrews, the writer includes the whole sweep of sacred history.

461

1. It is summed up in what God did, and what He said (Compare Acts 1:1, of Jesus).
2. God did nothing more important than to speak.
3. Revelation is thus a matter of history, rather than of philosophy.
    a. Solomon used experience as a source and learned only that experience is vain. (theme of Ecclesiastes). Experience teaches the limitations of experience.
    b. Job spoke of man's search (mining) for wisdom, and concluded, "Behold, the fear of the Lord, that is wisdom; and to depart from evil is understanding" (Job 28:28).
    c. The prophets, to whom and through whom God spoke, became witnesses to the fact of God's speaking (Heb. 3:5 declares this of Moses).
B. God's word came to various prophets in various ways.
    1. To Elijah the word of the Lord came at least once in the still small voice.
    2. Isaiah could testify to an introduction, "I saw the Lord" (6:1).
    3. Amos was taken from following the sheep (7:15).
    4. Joseph and Daniel recounted dreams and interpretations.
C. For all the prophets Peter summarized, "Holy men of God spake as they were moved by the Holy Ghost" (II Pet. 1:19-21).

III. GOD HAS SPOKEN TO US THROUGH HIS SON.
This is the central declaration and emphasis in the book of Hebrews.
    A. It is the same God speaking in various times and manners.
        1. Jesus identified with the prophets, quoting, "It is written."
        2. The Gospel writers (Matthew especially) declared Jesus' fulfillment of prophecy.

462

B. God gave many assurances that He did indeed speak and act through Jesus as His Son.
1. The assurance was verbal at Jesus' baptism and His transfiguration (Matt. 3:17; 17:5).
2. The assurance reached its climax in God's raising Jesus from the dead (Acts 17:31).
C. God-given glories became the basis of Jesus' miracles.
1. As "heir of all things," He became host in feeding the multitudes (Matt. 14:19).
2. As Maker of the worlds, He controlled the storms on Galilee (Matt. 8:23-27).
3. The "brightness of [God's] glory" was seen in the transfiguration (Mark 9:2-8).
4. The "image of His person" was declared: "He that hath seen me hath seen the Father" (John 14:9).
5. The "word of His power" is also declared: "As the Father hath life in himself; so he hath given to the Son to have life in himself" (John 5:26).
6. Of Him who "purged our sins" it is declared, "God was in Christ, reconciling the world unto himself, not imputing their trespasses unto them" (II Cor. 5:19).
D. Eyewitnesses testified to the acts and the words by which God spoke through Christ.
— Their testimony is in the Gospels (Luke 1:1-4).

CONCLUSION — One declaration is not yet supported by eyewitnesses. "He sat down at the right hand of the majesty on high." Your own coming experience will establish that!

THE STARTING POINT
(Hebrews 6:1-12)

INTRODUCTION — The point where preachers become impatient with their people.

The point where they discover that they can't deal with them as men and spiritual equals, but must deal with them as babes.

W. E. Sweeney says a preacher gets tired of pushing 25-year old Christians in baby carriages.

The writer of the Hebrew letter (5:11) knows he is talking over their heads and bemoans the fact.

"By reason of time ye ought to be
teachers, ye have need to be taught . . ."
Ministers, ye have need to be ministered to.
Visitors and invitors, ye have need to be visited and invited.
Evangelists, ye have need to be evangelized.
Helpers of others, ye have need to be helped yourself.

I. FIRST PRINCIPLES.

"Ye have need that one teach you again which be the first principles of the oracles of God" (5:12).

A. The first principles must first be established — Supposed already to be.
  1. Building cannot be built until foundation is laid.
  2. American haste is impatient with foundations, builds tall on little, spiritually and educationally. (High school students know neither spelling nor grammar — so spiritually also.)
  3. C. C. Morrison says if he were a pastor again he would preach doctrine.

B. There is often need of laying again the foundation of first principles.
  1. "Wherefore I shall be ready always to put you in remembrance of these things, though ye know them, and are established in the truth which is in you" (II Pet. 1:12, ASV).
    "To write the same things to you, to me indeed is not irksome, but for you it is safe" (Phil. 3:3, ASV).

464

2. Perhaps the foundation was not well laid.
   (The workman jacks up the house and bolsters the floors.)
3. There come storms and stresses which shake the foundation of faith.
   — Flood damages a building, weakens it, and re-building is necessary.
4. The natural ravages of time and forgetfulness.
   — The brick needs pointing up occasionally.

C. What are the first principles?
   1. Repentance from "dead works" (self trust) or "works of death."
      — There are still some in the church who think that the form suffices.
   2. Faith toward God.
      — So we must sound again and again the clear notes of the Gospel.
   3. Baptisms — to the believer, baptism into Christ.
      (For them, Christian baptism compared with cere-monial washings.) Methodist preacher refused to preach on it: "Settled in our church."
   4. Laying on of hands — teaching of apostolic authority. Making of Christian workers.
   5. Resurrection — Christ's and our own.
      Christian life in the atmosphere of eternity.
   6. Judgment — "He shall come to judge the quick and the dead."
      Rewards and punishments. . . . Many would seek eternity without it.

II. DEVELOPMENT.

Press on to perfection.
   — We cannot, we must not stop at the starting point.
A. "Go on or get off."
B. One comes to his preacher asking removal — is put to work instead.
C. "For he that lacketh these things is blind, seeing only

465

what is near, having forgotten the cleansing from his old sins" (II Pet. 1:9, ASV).

III. FATE OF THE UNDEVELOPED.
   A. Warning against the apostasy which comes with stagnation; this is not a pleasant prospect.
   B. Some try to dodge this picture by "once in grace always." — Describe the "tasters" as those who have not shared fully . . . but . . .
      "He tasted death for every man" (Heb. 2:9).
      "Ye have tasted that the Lord is gracious" (I Pet. 2:3).
   C. Note development of those who are described as being lost in backsliding.

IV. REASONS FOR HOPE.
   "We are pursuaded better things of you" (v. 9).
   A. There must be a reason for that pursuasion. This writer is not like the fortune teller who prophesies only good. — Nor like the Jewish storekeeper, who says "I'll give a special price just because it is you."
   B. "For your work and love" — These are demonstrations. "You have ministered to the saints."
   C. Most of those present are among those who bear marks of faithfulness. Hence conclusion.

CONCLUSION —

First accept Him according to the first principles.

THE OLD AND THE NEW
(Hebrews 8)

INTRODUCTION — Remember Marcion, who very early insisted that Paul was the real authority in Christianity and that all Jewish influence was to be rejected.

Like the modern liberal, he went too far in making distinction between old and new.

I. BOTH THE OLD AND THE NEW ARE REVELATIONS FROM GOD. (See Heb. 1:1.)
   A. Each is given as it is ready to be received.
   B. Same God—Characterized by love and justice. Judgment is found also in New Testament. Power and Fatherhood.
   C. Scholars are gaining increased respect for Old Testament. (Moonlight from same source in the sun.)

II. THE OLD IS THE FORESHADOWING OF THE NEW.
   A. "The law was our schoolmaster to bring us unto Christ," (Gal. 3:24).
   B. The tabernacle foreshadowed the church.
      1. Outer court and the world.
      2. Altar of burnt offering → fruits meet for repentance.
      3. Laver—sacrifices washed, and priests purified → baptism.
      4. The holy place → the church.
      5. Table of "presence bread" renewed each week → Lord's Supper.
      6. Seven branched candlestick → "Thy word is a lamp . . ."
      7. Altar of incense before the veil → prayer.
      8. The veil before the holy of holies → rent at death of Christ.
      9. Mercy-seat in holy of holies → presence of God in Heaven.
   C. The priests and Christ.

467

D. Sacrifices without blemish → the Passover, fulfilled in Christ.

III. THE OLD IS FULFILLED IN THE NEW, WHICH IS BETTER.
   A. In each of the provisions of the Law, there is perfect fulfillment in Christ.
      1. Sacrifice.
      2. Priesthood.
      3. Law and prophets.
      4. Sabbath—"I will give you rest."
   B. The new is better.
      1. Better promises—Forgiveness and eternal life.
      2. Put into the mind—"Written not in tables of stone, but in flesh by tables of the heart" (II Cor. 3:3).
      3. A universal covenant—to the Jew first and also to the Greek.

IV. THE OLD IS FULFILLED AND READY TO PASS AWAY.
   "One jot or one tittle shall in no wise pass from the law, till all be fulfilled" (Matt. 5:18).
   A. In Christ the whole law is kept, and its purposes wholly fulfilled.
   B. It is a fatal error to try to carry into Christianity the forms of the old: sabbaths, holy seasons, laws of meats, priesthood, sacrifices, and circumcision as a religious rite.

CONCLUSION — An invitation hymn typical of the new covenant—"Just as I Am."

Charlotte Elliott, invalid, unable to help in church bazar, recalls words of evangelist, "Come to Him just as your are." Writes the hymn. It is published in pamphlet by a friend, and later presented to Miss Elliott by her physician.

John B. Gough's story: A repulsive man next to him in the pew sings "awfully"; asks for line of stanza: "Just as I am, poor, wretched, blind"; says "That I am, blind and a paralytic. The hymn is for me."

LET US . . .

(Hebrews 10:19-25)

INTRODUCTION — Christians have frequently been like the disciples of the Lord one stormy night on Lake Galilee, tossed and thoroughly frightened. Jesus came to them, walking on the sea. Peter asked to come to Jesus, and did, but "when he saw the wind boisterous he was afraid, and beginning to sink, he cried, saying, 'Lord, save me'" (Matt. 14:22, 33).

A. So, some thirty years later, the Hebrew Christians.

B. The Hebrew letter written to encourage and strengthen; it speaks of the *better* relation to God in Christ.

C. We are priests under the High Priesthood of Christ.
   1. This provides new relationship
      to God — let us draw near.
      to self — let us hold fast the profession of faith.
      to brothers — let us consider one another.
   2. Not entirely separate, but all relate in some way to the "assembling."
      a. Congregation — the gathered flock — permanent.
      b. Convention — the coming together — temporary.

I. LET US DRAW NEAR IN FULL ASSURANCE.

A. Priestly sanctification.
   1. Hearts sprinkled from evil conscience, compared with sprinkling of Aaron and his sons with blood from the altar and with anointing (Exod. 29:21).
   2. Bodies washed with pure water, compared with washing Aaron and his sons at the laver at the door of the tent of meeting (Exod. 21:4).

B. Priestly service — Not an honorary position. Now accepted, we assist others to gain acceptance.
   1. Draw near to God, as Christians, in preparatory fellowship.
   2. Where do you like to be, and with whom?
      James L. Kraft (Kraft Cheese): "I go to church on every possible occasion, because as a follower of God I desire to go to God's house."

II. LET US HOLD FAST THE PROFESSION OF OUR FAITH WITHOUT WAVERING.

A. The profession—declaration—and not just the faith itself, is to be maintained. (Don't just stand there—say something!)

The silent, undeclared faith is not the faith described in the New Testament. *Motivation*—God is faithful; "He cannot deny himself."

B. The wavering can be in either of two directions.

1. Weakening, because of faltering faith, going along with unbelievers.

2. Drifting into mere condemnation of the unbelievers, reacting negatively.

C. This problem is faced in the church.

1. She must refuse to follow a course of faltering, false doctrine.

2. She must also refuse to make herself merely a protest assembly, but be firmly declarative.

3. Thus it has something to offer to the faith of each one attending.

III. LET US CONSIDER ONE ANOTHER.

A. "Look not every man on his own things, but every man also on the things of others" (Phil. 2:4).

B. Call forth (provoke) to love and to good works.

(*Provoke* is a word whose meaning has skidded badly under weight of human nature.)

1. To love—the understanding and concern that come with acquaintance.

2. To good works, through example, concern, teaching, instruction.

B. Neglect not the assembling.

This is part of the mutual consideration! The motivation is not selfish.

C. Exhorting—What happens on platform sets tone for what people do. Sing! Speak! Pray! Encourage!

CONCLUSION — You see the Day approaching.

— *Then* we'll know how good our meeting was!

470

THE JOY OF THY LORD
(Hebrews 12:1-6)

INTRODUCTION —

   A. Do you really want to "enter into the joy of thy Lord"? It may involve more than you think.

   B. Consider the experience of Him who was the "Author and perfecter of our faith" (ASV).

I. FOR THE JOY THAT WAS SET BEFORE HIM.

   A. That phrase has two different meanings, either or both possible.

      1. The Goodspeed translation goes in one direction, saying, "In place of the happiness that belonged to him . . ."

      —Thus the "joy" is the heavenly glory Jesus left to endure suffering on earth.

      2. *Today's English Version* goes in the other direction, saying, "Because of the joy that was waiting for him . . ." —Thus the "joy" is the result of the suffering He endured.

      3. Most translations leave the choice with the reader, saying, "For the joy . . ."

   B. In context, the passage indicates the "joy" which motivates an athlete to "run with patience the race that is set before" him.

      1. We are to run the kind of race that Jesus ran.

      2. Psalm 19:5 speaks of the sun's daily course in which it "rejoiceth as a strong man to run a race."

   C. Jesus knew several kinds of joy, all of which might have been included.

      1. His glory in heaven before and after His sojourn on earth.

      2. The "strong man's" joy in going all-out to meet an ultimate challenge.

      3. The obedient Son's joy in pleasing the heavenly Father, and thus accomplishing His purpose on earth.

4. The joy of bringing other children to God. It is like the joy of a mother in bringing new life into the world (John 16:21). — None of these is the pleasure of self-indulgent luxury, and all have their cost.

II. HE ENDURED THE CROSS, DESPISING THE SHAME.

A. We have known our childhood heroes who ignored pain and injury on their way to winning some conflict or competition.
  1. The wounded soldier saving his comrades.
  2. The football player who couldn't remember the last half of a brilliant game.
  3. The basketball player who didn't feel the floor burns and bruises until a soapy shower afterward revealed them.

B. These are as nothing in contrast with Jesus' willing endurance for our sakes.
  1. Consider Him that endured such contradiction of "sinners against himself" (v. 3).
  2. See Him at Nazareth calmly walking away through the crowd that would have cast Him off the precipice (Luke 4:28-30).
  3. See Him in Gethsemane, delivering Himself into the hands of soldiers (John 18:3-8).
  4. See Him silent in trial, then making His way, bleeding and with spittle on His face, to Calvary.
  5. Hear His prayer for the forgiveness of His tormentors (Luke 23:34).

C. His followers share in the motivating joy and the suffering.
  1. "These things have I spoken unto you, that my joy might remain in you, and that your joy might be full" (John 15:11). (Compare Nehemiah 8:10: "The joy of the Lord is your strength.")
  2. Peter and John "departed from the presence of the council, rejoicing that they were counted worthy to suffer shame for his name" (Acts 5:41).

3. "But rejoice inasmuch as ye are partakers of Christ's sufferings; that when his glory shall be revealed ye may be glad with exceeding joy" (I Pet. 4:13).
   —After we have entered into this "joy of the Lord," we shall be prepared to enter that which is to come.

III. HE IS SET DOWN AT THE RIGHT HAND OF THE THRONE OF GOD.
   A. Thus was answered His prayer for the renewal of His eternal glory: "O Father, glorify thou me with thine own self with the glory which I had with thee before the world was" (John 17:5).
   B. It was God's way of recognizing the self-sacrifice of Jesus: "Being found in fashion as a man, [Jesus] humbled himself, and became obedient unto death, even the death of the cross. Wherefore God also hath highly exalted him, and given him a name which is above every name: that at the time of Jesus every knee should bow, of things in heaven, and things in earth, and things under the earth; and that every tongue should confess that Jesus Christ is Lord, to the glory of God the Father'" (Phil. 2:8-11).
   C. His glory in Heaven becomes triumph over His enemies: "Sit on my right hand, until I make thine enemies thy footstool" (Heb. 1:13; Psalm 110:1).
   D. His glory in Heaven leads to His return in judgment: "When the Son of man shall come in his glory, and all the holy angels with him, then shall he sit upon the throne of his glory: and before him shall be gathered all nations; and he shall separate them one from another, as a shepherd divideth his sheep from the goats" (Matt. 25:31, 32).

CONCLUSION — The return of a master taking account of his servants is the basis for the symbolic plaudit, "Enter thou into the joy of the Lord" (Matt. 25:21, 23).

Are we ready for it? We shall be, if we have entered into His joy—(1) in going all-out to accomplish His purposes, (2) in serving so as to please the Heavenly Father, and (3) in bringing other children to God.

473

SWIFT TO HEAR
(James 1:19-27, cf. Acts 19:33)

INTRODUCTION —

    A. Story of boys waiting for employment in a large office. Routine matters coming over the intercom; then, "Come into office four for employment interview." One goes immediately, and is hired. The rest didn't hear.

    B. So James: "Let every man be swift to hear."

    C. What you get out of a sermon or Sunday School lesson depends as much on your listening as it does on the speaker's message. As with a radio, broadcasting is worthless without reception. You demand a trained minister and teacher—what about trained hearers?

I. TO RECEIVE THE MESSAGE ONE MUST *COME*. (Cf. "We are all here.")

    A. Obvious? But how often do you come?

    B. If there is something to be gained this week, then why not every week?

    C. If a preacher refused to preach at night, or to hold mid-week services, his refusal would be resented, but as far as most of the members of the church are concerned, there are no such services.

    D. Those who come are on the way to efficient listening.

II. TO RECEIVE WELL ONE MUST COME IN THE RIGHT *ATTITUDE*. (Cf. "Before God.")

    A. "Son of man, thou dwellest in the midst of a rebellious house, which have eyes to see, and see not; they have ears to hear, and hear not; for they are a rebellious house" (Ezek. 12:1).

    B. If you come wondering what you are going to have to put up with today, you will receive very little.

    C. Why was teaching of G.I.'s in wartime effective?
    —They knew it was a life-and-death proposition.

    D. "Blessed are they which do unger and thirst after righteousness: for they shall be filled" (Matt. 5:6).

III. TO RECEIVE THE MESSAGE ONE MUST BE ABLE TO HEAR.

A. The advantage of the center section of seats.
B. The disadvantage of the choir, should be sympathized with by others.
C. We hope the hearing aids will help; tell folks about them.

IV. TO RECEIVE THE MESSAGE, PAY ATTENTION. (Cf. "To hear.")

A. You are responsible in this matter as much as the speaker is.
B. You can train yourself to pay attention.
    1. Take notes. — "What are the main thoughts?"
    2. Discuss with someone else later.
    3. Report to someone who didn't hear. A shut-in laments not hearing sermons.
C. Christ's challenge: "If any man have ears to hear, let him hear" (Mark 4:23).

V. TO BENEFIT BY THE MESSAGE, DIGEST IT.

(Cf. All things that are commanded thee of God.")

A. "Search the Scriptures daily to see if these things be so.
B. Is the message shallow? Then go on from there.
C. Is the message deep? Then get what you can and learn to swim.

VI. TO COMPLETE THE HEARING, "BE YE DOERS OF THE WORD, AND NOT HEARERS ONLY."

A. "He that heareth these sayings of mine and doeth them . . ." (Matt. 7:24-27).
B. You have heard of Christ. You have heard His command. Then do!

CONCLUSION — "Hear, O Lord, when I cry with my voice; have mercy also upon me, and answer me" (Psalm 27:7).
God is a good listener! Let's be His children!

475

SHOW ME YOUR FAITH
(James 2:14-24)

INTRODUCTION — Radio's child entertainer, "Uncle Don," sings "What are little boys made of? Snakes and snails and puppy dog's tails" and concludes, "I don't really believe that."

You know that before he says it; he doesn't act as though he believed it.

Some "Christians" quote their creeds and sing their songs in the same fashion.

I. SHOW ME THY FAITH APART FROM THY WORKS
   — it can't be done!
   A. James was writing concerning some who had twisted the meaning of Romans 3:28, "We conclude that a man is justified without the deeds of the law."
      1. *Faith* here is inclusive: "We are not of them that draw back unto perdition; but of them that believe to the saving of the soul" (Heb. 10:39).
      2. Works of the law are the rituals of the old order.
      3. But some, then as now, were teaching, "Only believe, and be saved."
   B. Even those who teach that doctrine do not believe it! Illustration — A preacher argues that faith-alone saves; then refuses to accept into membership of the church the young man he considers not morally straight!
   C. Faith and life will find a common level; life rising to faith, or faith declining to the level of life.

II. "I BY MY WORKS WILL SHOW THEE MY FAITH."
    You can't help it!
    A. "As he thinketh in his heart, so is he" (Prov. 23:7).
    B. "What kind of a man is he? What kind of God does he worship?"
    C. We show our faith by our confession.
       1. The words carry the message.
       2. The act gives it meaning. We believe in Him who confessed the good confession before Pilate.

476

3. Yet even this is not enough: See Mark 1:23, 24: The devils believe, and tremble.

D. We show our faith by our baptism. Our faith is in Christ.
   1. The act declares our faith in Him who died, was buried, arose "for me." "We are buried with Him by baptism into death" (Rom. 6:4).
   2. It is an act of faith in His cleansing power. "Arise and be baptized and wash away thy sins, calling on his name" (Acts 22:16).
   3. It is the symbol of the loss of self in Him. "As many as have been baptized into Christ have put on Christ" (Gal. 3:27).
   4. It declares our faith in His power to give new life. "Like as Christ was raised . . . so we should walk in newness of life" (Rom. 6:4).

E. We show our faith by our faithfulness in the Supper.
   1. "Ye do show forth the Lord's death until He comes" (I Cor. 11:26).
   2. Each one partakes—His death is for each one.
   3. He gave His body and blood.
   4. He is coming again.

F. We show our faith by Christian growth.
   1. How big is your Lord? Remember the fable of the toad that swelled till he burst trying to be as big as an ox? "I am trying to show what my Lord is like."

G. We show our faith by forgiving others. —"Even as God for Christ's sake forgave you" (Eph. 4:32).

H. By generosity—in the name of Him who gave to all life and breath, and all things.

I. By kindness—in the name of Him who touched blind eyes and made see.

J. By justice—tempered with His mercy.

K. By purity—"Know ye not that ye are the temple of God and the spirit of God dwelleth in you" (I Cor. 3:16).

CONCLUSION —

Your faith is known this morning—"Lord I believe; help thou mine unbelief!" (Mark 9:24).

OCCUPATIONAL HAZARDS IN THE MINISTRY
(James 3)

INTRODUCTION — James 3 sounds like an un-recruiting sermon for Christian service.

A. It came from a man who had been preaching Christ for thirty years; he was not quitting; he was guiding!

B. Don't accept the responsibilities lightly; if you do, you'll never meet them!

C. Three paragraphs in the chapter deal with three hazards in the preaching-teaching ministry.

I. THE WEIGHT OF RESPONSIBILITY (vv. 1, 2).

A. This ministry leaves one without excuse in judgment.
1. Having given God's teaching to others, he is bound to it without compromise. "You are without excuse, every man of you who passes judgment, for in that you judge another, you condemn yourself; for you who judge practice the same things" (Rom. 2:1, NASB; see also Rom. 2:21-23).
2. (The teacher cannot indulge in the excuse of the youngster who tattled, saying "They're older, and know better, and I don't.)

B. This ministry deals with irreplaceable values.
1. (The highway marker at the edge of town admonished motorists to "Watch carefully for our children; they are not replaceable.")
2. Jesus was even more severe: "Whoever causes one of these little ones who believe in Me to stumble, it is better for him that a heavy millstone be hung around his neck, and that he be drowned in the depth of the sea (Matt. 18:6, NASB).

C. This ministry deals with unchangeable values.
1. Jesus said, "Heaven and earth shall pass away: but my words shall not pass away" (Luke 21:33).
2. We have not the book-publisher's privilege of bringing out new editions to correct the mistakes in the old.

II. THE WAY OF WORDS (vv. 2-12).
   A. The preacher's basic tool is the tricky tongue.
      1. It is that with which he is most likely to offend.
      2. It is the implement last conquered in development of Christian maturity.
   B. The tongue has awesome power (vv. 3-5).
      1. Its power for evil is described.
         a. Impure words spread defilement like a contagion.
         b. Vicious words start fires of destruction.
      2. Its power for good is basic to prophets and apostles.
         a. Jesus relied on the spoken word (demonstrated) for His own ministry.
         b. The very book of James is most like a transcript of a spoken message.
      3. Part of our danger is that we so fear saying wrong things that we say nothing, and so partake of the wicked servant's condemnation (Matthew 25:24-30).
   C. The tongue is most difficult to control (vv. 7, 8).
      1. "Slips of the tongue" are familiar embarrassments.
      2. More serious are the undisciplined words that are remembered long after we no longer mean what they said in haste.
         (Here is the answer to the one who pridefully is "honest enough to say what he thinks." How long will he think that way?)
      3. The skilled speaker, like the skilled carpenter or dressmaker, will "measure twice, and cut once."
   D. The tongue is capable of vast contradictions (vv. 9-12).
      1. Blessing God means little if we curse God's people.
      2. Prayers in church are too often negated by nagging and scolding at home.
      3. Lying—that shift of gears between thought and word—is the worst of contradictions.

III. THE WISDOM OF THE WORLD (vv. 13-18).
   —This gains significance with development of the all-dominant-pastor system.

   A. It is praised by men as a way to succeed.

479

1. A noted "pastor" boasts that he is not hampered by any such things as elders, to thwart his program.
2. The world knows that "you have to have an authority figure." (Authority figure Jim Jones succeeded marvelously all the way to Jonestown.)
3. The world knows that trusted colleagues will leave you alone in trouble as Paul (II Tim. 4:9-16).
4. The world knows that trusted colleagues will betray and deny you, as Jesus was betrayed and denied.

B. It is condemned by Scripture as "jealousy and selfish ambition" (NASB).
1. It is the plague that followed the very apostles until Christ died.
2. James calls it earthly—it's success is temporal and material. James calls it sensual—there is selfish pleasure in its sense of power. James calls it devilish —as Satan promised the world, for worship of him (Matt. 4:8-10).

C. It is contrasted with the "wisdom that is from above."
1. Pure—singleminded to the glory of God, as John the Baptist was.
2. Peaceable and persuadable.
3. A living quality expressed in *meekness* and *mercy*.
4. Without pretense (to infallibility) or paritality (giving favors for advantage.)

CONCLUSION — "Let the elders that rule well be counted worthy of double honor, especially they who labor in word and doctrine" (I Tim. 5:17).

(A tour group went a considerable distance to see a recently finished crucifix, and to honor the sculptor who had carved it in stone. But consider: The sculptor worked in cold stone; the preacher-teacher works in living souls. The sculptor used tools of true steel; the teacher must use the tricky tongue. The sculptor's thrust was with balanced mallet; the teacher's his Christlike life. The sculptor carved the physical likeness of a dead Jesus; the teacher molds the spiritual image of our living Lord.)

Double honor to him who braves the hazards and accomplishes the task!

PREACHING THROUGH I AND II PETER, I, II AND III JOHN, AND JUDE

THE EPISTLES OF PETER

These letters, written to Christians in five provinces of Asia Minor, give evidence that the Apostle Peter had been among these people for some time. His First Epistle was written to encourage believers to stand fast in the face of persecution which the Emperor Nero had started against them. The Second was written as a warning against their being led astray by false teachers among themselves. It is thought that both were written a short time before Peter's death, or about 67 A.D.

ANALYSIS

I Peter 1   The Christian's incorruptible inheritance.
         2,3 Practical exhortations for the earthly pilgrimmage.
         4,5 Exhortation to stand the "fiery trial."

II Peter 1   The Great and precious promises.
         2   Warnings against false teaachers.
         3   The second coming of Christ.

THE EPISTLES OF JOHN

The Apostle John spent the later years of his life ministering in the province of Asia, about Ephesus. The First Epistle is a circular letter to the churches, and seems to have been written especially to warn against the false teachings of the Gnostics. These were some who had mixed Greek philosophy with Christian teaching and claimed to possess certain mystical knowledge of God and of truth which others did not. Their boasts of superior wisdom were not borne out in their lives, and John shows their pretenses to be false.

ANALYSIS

1   God is light, revealed in Christ.
2   Walking in the light demands holy living.
3,4 Righteousness, love, and sound faith are necessary for the Christian.
5   The Christian's assurance is in God's promises.

The Second Epistle of John is a personal letter to the "Elect Lady" (perhaps a symbolic name of a church) to warn against

481

false teachers. The Third Epistle is personal letter to the "beloved Gaius" to encourage him in helping faithful preachers.

JUDE

The brother of Jesus and of James (Mark 6:3) writes to Christians probably in Asia Minor, to warn them against false teachers and to urge them by sound teaching and holy living to "contend earnestly for the faith once for all delivered unto the saints."

Sermon Outlines Provided:

"Ye Were Redeemed" (I Pet. 1:12-25)
"Liberty, Limited" (I Pet. 2:16; Rom. 6:12-23)
"You're God's Man!" (I Pet. 5:1-5; Acts 20:28-31)
"An Old Grad Remembers" (II Pet. 1:12-18)
"For Our Sins" (I John 1:5—2:3)
"Fellowship in Love" (I John 3:1, 2, 11-18; 4:7-12, 16-21)
"Not Every Spirit" (I John 4:1-3)
"Helping God's Servant" (III John)
"Jude Speaks for Restoration" (Jude)

QUESTIONS OVER I & II PETER,
I, II & III JOHN, JUDE

1. What does Peter say is the end of your faith? (I Pet. 1:9)
2. Peter links the validity of baptism to what fact in Jesus' life? (3:21)
3. Peter exhorts elders to tend the flock of God in what way? (5:2, 3)
4. How does Peter say that prophecy came? (II Pet. 1:21)
5. Who is called a "preacher of righteousness" by Peter? (2:5)
6. What does Peter say will happen at the coming of the day of God? (3:10)
7. What does John promise if we confess our sins? (I John 1:9)
8. How does John define sin? (3:4)
9. Perfect love casts out what? (4:18)
10. If any come that bring not the doctrine of Christ, what are we to do? (II John 10)
11. Who was Diotrephes? (III John 9)
12. Jude says we are to earnestly contend for what? (Jude 3)

YE WERE REDEEMED
(I Peter 1:12-25)

INTRODUCTION — We re-examine a contract to find what there is in it for us; as in case of insurance policy.

Thus Peter writes to Christians under persecution to remind them of the power and benefits of their faith.

I. REDEEMED.
   A. Definition: "loosed, by a price."
   B. Imprisoned, the prisoner is freed by payment made by another.
   C. In faith and life you are not your own; you are bought with a price (I Cor. 6:19, 20).

II. REDEEMED *FROM:*
   A. Ignorance.
      1. Had the church so early established schools? (v. 14).
      2. "Not fashioning yourselves according to the former lusts in your ignorance."
         —Ignorance of the will and goodness of God (in which many wish to remain).
      3. In Christ you know God—the supreme knowledge.
   B. (Not mentioned here) the guilt and the power of sin.
      —This slavery cannot be relieved except in Christ.
   C. The vain manner of life (empty, unrewarding) (v. 18).
      1. It is the life without purpose.
      2. "Received by tradition from your fathers," it is bound on you by social habit.
         (Redemption demands the turning from ancestor worship to God's will.)

How great is our redemption? He that is saved from falling in, is more favored than he who is pulled out, half drowned.

III. REDEEMD *BY:*
   A. Not silver and gold.
      1. These might buy the body of a slave, but never the love of a son.
      2. The world's greatest treasure is not sufficient to the purpose.

B. The blood of Christ (v. 19).
  1. The cost to heaven is beyond comprehension.
  2. The cost to Him is reviewed (Phil. 2:5-11).
C. Measure the cost by its purpose:
  "That He might be just, and the justifier of him which believeth in Christ" (Rom. 3:26).
D. Measure the value of the redemption by its cost:
  If it is worth so much to my Lord, it can't be insignificant to me.

IV. REDEEMED *THROUGH:*

A. Redeemed through obedience to Him (v. 22).
  — The division between God's children and the children of this world turns on obedience to God.
B. Redeemed through the living word (v. 23).
  "Faith cometh by hearing, and hearing by the word of God" (Rom. 10:17).

V. REDEEMED *TO:*

A. Love of the brethren (v. 22).
  — Here is the uniform by which the soldiers of Christ are to be recognized (John 13:35).
B. A living hope—through the resurrection of Christ (v. 21).
  — Because of this you do not sorrow as unbelievers do (I Thess. 4:13).
C. Faith unfeigned—trust based on the knowledge of God's love.
  — Faith becomes a natural part of one's personality.
D. Continued obedience (v. 14).
  — Saved through obedience, one does not become a rebel afterward.
E. Holiness (vv. 15, 16). (Compare Lev. 11:44; 19:2).
  — This is the child's increasing resemblance to his Father.

CONCLUSION —

"I've been redeemed and I know it.
I've been redeemed; I must show it;
Show it in my walk, show it in my talk,
Show it in my song, halleluia!
I've been redeemed and I know it."

484

LIBERTY, LIMITED
(I Peter 2:16; Romans 6:12-23)

INTRODUCTION — From the occasion, the Fourth of July.

A. We are proud and jealous of our freedom.

B. It means little to say that millions have fought to preserve it; it means more to say that it is the heritage that our own family and friends are offering themselves to defend.

C. Peter wrote the text, with its verse on freedom shining like the north star, to Christians whose freedom we would doubt.

I. BE FREE. Are we as free as we think we are?

A. Just now we are held in by legal fences that touch every phase of life, but that is not the slavery that concerns us.

B. Can we worship freely, or are we prevented by cares, concerns, and ambitions that crowd into the very Lord's hour of the Lord's Day?

—And what of the burden of guilt that keeps out the light of God's love?

C. How many will yield to the tyranny of tobacco before they reach home, or immediately thereafter?

1. Hunters in the dry autumn woods, deprived of their smokes at the gate, are back within two hours, pleading for relief.

2. No human tyrant could boss as many Americans as completely as the cigaret does.

D. Drink—only a mention as the next step.

1. I want to be free to drink or not to drink—I want my neighbor to be the same.

2. The way to remain free is to say "no."

E. Society yields to the tyranny of the dance and the card game.

—College parties, where constructive imagination should be present, follow a slavish pattern.

F. Boy-girl relationships tyrannized by customs of disrespect and familiarity.

1. The individual is left hardly free to choose his own conduct.
2. Genuine choice is a struggle against the pressure of what "everybody's doing."

Be free, and stay free.

II. NOT USING YOUR FREEDOM FOR A CLOAK OF MALICIOUSNESS. That destroys freedom.
   A. Freedom of speech can become malicious slander.
   B. Freedom of religion can become indifference and freedom of irreligion.
   C. Freedom from want can become slavery to property.
   D. Freedom from fear can become complacent slavery.
   E. The real danger lies in liberty's becoming license.
       In every case mentioned, the slavery has grown out of misuse of freedom.
   F. Illustration — The dairyman's freedom-loving heifer finds herself in quicksand, where she can't move at all.
   G. One thoughtless act in an hour of freedom can fashion a yoke for time and eternity.

The way to stay free.

III. AS *SERVANTS OF GOD.*
   A. The only real freedom lies in choosing voluntarily the will of God — any other course destroys freedom and destroys self.
   B. Read Romans 6:15-23.
       "Ye cannot serve God and Mammon" (Matt. 6:24) — it is impossible likewise to serve neither. You will serve some god!
   C. "Ye are not your own. Ye are bought with a price" (I Cor. 6:19, 20).
       The "servant" is *Doulos* — a slave bought and paid for.

CONCLUSION — If the Son [who purchased you] shall make you free, ye shall be free indeed" (John 8:36).

486

YOU'RE GOD'S MAN
(I Peter 5:1-5; Acts 20:28-31)

INTRODUCTION — An elder's request for help in understanding his work brings letters that become a book.

"Pete, You're God's Man." — Not only God's man, but God's partner in the ministry of Psalm 23.

You have not been given an honorary degree; you've been given a job, and what a great one!

Pastors and assistants!

I. *WHAT IS THE JOB?*

— Pastors-shepherds as seen in Psalm 23. The concept is hard to understand, because we don't see the prototype.

A. Feeds.

Psalm 23	*I Peter 5*	*Acts 20*
"Maketh me to lie down in green pastures"	"Feed the flock of God"	"Feed the church of God"

B. Leads.

"Leadeth me beside still waters"	"Being examples to the flock"	"Take heed to yourselves"

C. Protects.

"Restoreth my soul" — "in the presence of enemies"		Take heed to the flock "Grievous wolves"

D. Directs.

"Guides in paths of righteousness"	Taking the oversight	"The Spirit has made you overseers."

"Apt to teach" — "Holding the mystery of the faith in a pure conscience." — "Holding fast the faithful word . . . to exhort and convince" (Tit. 1:9).

Why do we not have more detailed job descriptions? They wouldn't always fit. The job description needs to be developed by the elders for the congregation.

II. HOW IS IT TO BE DONE?
A. Not of constraint, but willingly. (They were already elders.) —"If a man desire the office of a bishop he desireth a good work" (I Tim. 3:1). The Lord's army is made up of volunteers.
B. Not for (money), but of a ready mind.
John 10:11-14, contrasts the hireling and shepherd.
C. Neither as being lords over God's heritage, but being examples. Beware the Diotrephes-Boanerges syndrome. (Young people asked an elder, 84, to talk to them about dating! —An elder exercising his authority!)

III. WHO IS TO DO IT?
Qualifications are just that—the person for the job.
A. Character—positive: blameless, one-woman man, sober, good behavior, hospitable.
—negative: wine, striker, greedy, brawler, covetous, self-willed.
B. Ability.
Aptitude—apt to teach, vigilant, orderly.
Experience—rules well his own house, not a novice, well reported, given to hospitality.
C. Equipment—good name and good wife.

IV. WHY? —Compare I Peter 5:6-9. It is for your life!
A. January 1975 *Reader's Digest* has "A Psychiatrist Looks at Pro Football." He was employed by the San Diego Chargers to improve their performance. He came up with a personality profile for every position, and applies it generally: "Appropriateness of success and happiness." —But the Chargers still lost their games!
—And arguing about the qualifications for office hasn't done much to improve their performance among our churches. What then?
B. By contrast—
Young mother lifts the riding mower off a little boy's foot—she had to!

CONCLUSION — So I Peter 1:6-11 —With men it is impossible; with God all things are possible!

AN OLD GRAD REMEMBERS HIS TEACHER
(Commencement)
(II Peter 1:12-18; 3:17, 18)

INTRODUCTION — Consider your college yearbook:
- A. You will look it over many times, with enriched meaningfulness.
- B. Suppose that you had a complete record of lifelong ministry, related to student days.
- C. The Apostle Peter had such an album of memories, and shares some of it.

I. RECRUITMENT (John 1:40-42).
- A. It wasn't exactly a college recruiting tour that Jesus made to Judea, but it turned out that way for Simon.
- B. The active recruiter was brother Andrew.
- C. Jesus set forth the possibilities.
  - 1. He saw what Simon was, a person, the natural product of a family. —There was danger that Simon might be satisfied with that, not seeing need.
  - 2. He declared what Simon could be, by the influence of Christ: "Cephas." —There was danger that he might be discouraged, not seeing possibilities.

II. REGISTERING (Luke 5:1-11).
- A. The seaside encounter and call led Peter to leave his family business and sign with Jesus as a full-time student.
- B. In the event we see what brought Teacher and student together. It spells LORD.
  Leadership (in Jesus) and following (in Peter).
    —The request for a pulpit-boat, supplied.
  Oversight and obedience.
    —The ridiculous demand to resume fishing in the daytime, submitted to.
  Reward and recognition.
    —Boatloads of fish, and acknowledged "Lord."
  Direction and discipleship.
    —"Thou shalt catch men," an invitation immediately accepted.

489

III. RECITATION (Matt. 16:13-23) AND TESTING.
  A. The merit-award recitation, confessing Christ (vv. 13-18).
    1. "Who do men say I am?" The student must know what's going on.
    2. "Who do you say I am?" The student comprehends and is committed.
    3. The student at the head of the class.
      a. Information came from the right source.
      b. The honor name (Cephas, Peter) is conferred.
  B. The failed test, professing his own mastery of the subject (vv. 21-24).
    1. The subject matter (suffering, death, resurrection) was difficult.
    2. The student failed to comprehend, and resisted.
    3. The resistance became a tacit denial of Jesus' Lordship.
    4. The student at the foot of the class.
      a. Information came from the wrong source.
      b. The rebuke fitted the seriousness of the error.

IV. REVIEW (Matt. 17:1-8).
  A. The transfiguration re-emphasized the glory of Christ.
  B. Peter's proposal of three "tabernacles" revealed again his faulty comprehension.
  C. The divine "Hear Him" reemphasized the authority of Christ.

V. THE NIGHT OF THE SENIOR BANQUET
  A. Competition over "who is most likely to succeed."
    1. Then the Teacher started shining shoes!
    2. This must not be! "Then you have no part with me." "Then give me the full treatment."
  B. Warning that all would be ashamed of the Teacher.
    1. "Others perhaps, but not I," Peter professed (of himself).
    1. "You especially," Jesus warned.
  C. Puzzling and depressing predictions; then a prayer session in a park.

1. "Watch while I pray," Jesus requested; but Peter and the others slept.
2. A band of terrorists came to take Jesus. Peter used his switchblade on one of them, but Jesus patched the fellow up!
3. Jesus let the blackguards take Him away, and Peter stumbled along at a distance.

D. There was a trumped-up trial in the priestly palace, Peter trying to be not too uncomfortable.
   1. "Hey, you're one of His men!" "Not me!" came the automatic, scared, defensive.
   2. "Sure you are!" Is a scared liar going to *confess* immediately to the repeated charge? Rather, he who will tell a lie will swear to it!
   3. The cock's shrill morning cry pierced Peter's ears and his heart. He crumbled and fled!

VI. REINSTATEMENT (John 21:1-17).
   A. Resurrection day provided Peter a brief encounter with the Lord (Luke 24:34).
   B. Fuller conversation came later in Galilee.
      1. A night's fruitless fishing was followed by another miraculous catch, at Jesus' direction.
      2. Seven disciples breakfasted on grilled fish sandwiches with Jesus; then questions to Peter, and answers without boast or profession:
      "Do you have more God-like love for Me than these others do (as you have boasted before)?"
      "I'm really fond of You." "Then feed My sheep."
      "But do you have that God-like love for Me?"
      "I like You a lot!" "then tend My lambs."
      "Do you really like Me as you say?"
      "You know everything; You know I like You!"
      "Then feed My lambs."
   C. Jesus addressed Peter again as Simon; but He still had work for him to do. (Neither Peter nor we have to be perfect for the Lord to use us. We must be willing.)

491

VII. COMMENCEMENT (Acts 2).
 A. The Holy Spirit made the introductions, and Peter was salutatorian.
 B. His address a bold affirmation (confession) of Christ:
  1. Jesus of Nazareth was approved of God but rejected and slain by you (v. 22).
  2. God raised Him from the dead. Prophecy had shown that it would happen (vv. 24-35).
  3. God has made Him Lord and Christ (v. 36).
  4. You are to repent, and be baptized in the name of the One you killed, so your sins may be forgiven (v. 38).
 C. The church began with that commencement.

VIII. POST-GRADUATE WORK.
 (He did not cease to be a student after he graduated.)
 A. Peter's ministry was always confession of Christ; never more profession of his own faith.
 B. At the healing of the lame man at the Temple: "You killed the Prince of life, whom God raised from the dead" (Acts 3:15).
 C. Before the Council when it tried to silence him: "In the name of Jesus Christ of Nazareth doth this man stand before you whole . . . neither is there any other name . . . wherein we must be saved" (Acts 4:10,12).
 D. Again before the Council: "The God of our fathers raised up Jesus, whom ye slew. Him did God exalt with his right hand to be a prince and a Savior"(Acts 5:30, 31).
 E. "They ceased not to . . . preach Jesus as the Christ."
 F. In the house of Cornelius: "[Christ] is Lord of all!" (Acts 10:36).

CONCLUSION —
 Peter turns from remembering to admonishing:
 A. Beware lest ye also . . . be led from your own steadfastness (as I was, in denying).
 B. How can we be safe? "But grow in grace, and in the knowledge of our Lord and Savior Jesus Christ."
 C. "To Him be the glory both now and forever. Amen."

FOR OUR SINS
(I John 1:5 – 2:3)

INTRODUCTION –

Sin is not a popular subject, and it is going by many names, but the thing that used to be called sin is wrecking the world, life by life.

I. SIN IS A REALITY.
   A. "If we say we have no sin . . ."
      1. A tendency to sin is in the nature of man.
      2. Perhaps the grosser sins crying for expression, and finding it too oft.
      3. Perhaps the subtler sins of selfishness and pride.
   B. "If we say we have not sinned . . ."
      1. Shall we look into the dark recesses of every concience?
      2. Can we say we have taken every advantage of our opportunites before God?
      3. In the Sermon on the Mount we see the spiritual Xray probing innermost ills.
   C. Shall we add "If we say we cannot sin . . ."?
      1. Captain Hazael replies to Elisha's prediction of his treachery against his king, "Is thy servant a dog, that I should do this thing?" (II Kings 8:13).
      2. As Simon Peter, "All men may be offended in Thee, but I never" (Matt. 26:33).
      3. General Braddock dies in Washington's arms, sighing, "Who would have thought it?"

III. IF WE CONFESS OUR SINS . . .
   A. No one is left out.
      1. John includes himself, thus rebuking those who sit in judgment.
      2. Paul says "pray for us" (I Thess. 5:24) – each must pray for other, and Christ for all.
      3. The book is written to Christians, and not to sinners of the world.

B. There is the modern idea that a sense of guilt is not wholesome.
   1. Explains wrong actions as left-overs of animal ancestry, or unavoidable result of unfortunate heredity or environment.
   2. The result is rampant, unbridled sin.
   3. Amoral or immoral, the result is the same.
   4. In Christians it becomes the careless, "continue in sin, that grace may abound" (Rom. 6:1).
C. There is the other extreme, seen in "St." Augustine, spiritually lashing himself for trivial offenses of long ago. — This becomes the attitude of hopelessness.

III. HE IS FAITHFUL AND JUST TO FORGIVE US.
A. Pardon is the only hope.
   1. We can't plead "not guilty."
   2. We can't bear the just punishment.
B. The blood of Jesus Christ His son cleanses us from *every* sin.
   1. In this is the limitless cost of our offenses.
   2. In it also is the personal application of His sacrifice to each sin.
C. We have an Advocate (one standing alongside) with the Father.
   1. "He ever liveth to make intercession for them" (Heb. 7:25).
   2. He that is without sin is not casting stones.
D. He is the propitiation for our sins.
   1. Atonement — the only possible payment.
   2. Sin-offering — the one perfect, complete, and eternal sacrifice.
   3. Means of appeasement.
   4. Reconciliation — "God was in Christ, reconciling the world unto himself" (II Cor. 5:19).
   5. Propitiatory — the Mercy seat, presence of God among His people.

CONCLUSION — And not for ours only, but for the whole world. How shall He become their Advocate? Through us! "Freely ye have received, freely give" (Matt. 10:8).

FELLOWSHIP IN LOVE
(I John 3:1, 2, 11-18; 4:7-12, 16-21)

INTRODUCTION —

    A. John presents Christian fellowship as a strong cord of three braided strands:

        (1) Fellowship in light — the truth of Christ — doctrinal.

        (2) Fellowship in life — the way of Christ — moral.

        (3) Fellowship in love — the care of Christ — interpersonal.

    We deal today with the third strand.

    B. By definition and language we recognize three "loves" — romantic, affectionate, and godly. An enrichment of the Greek language was necessary to express God-like love. The word chosen was *agapé*.

    C. There are two distinct postures in fellowship:

        1. Face to face, as noted especially in David and Jonathan.

        2. Shoulder to shoulder, as noted especially in Paul and Timothy. We deal with both.

I. WE RECEIVE GOD'S LOVE TOGETHER (shoulder to shoulder).

    A. It is godly love, in the divine nature that could not be known until God sent His Son (John 3:16).

    B. It is first love.

        1. "Herein is love, not that we loved God, but that he loved us, and sent his Son to be the propitiation for our sins" (4:10).

        2. He who interprets love as some other person's responsibility toward him has missed the whole point of God's initiative.

    C. It is inclusive love, shed abroad to the whole world. — Who, then, are we to be particular with the distribution of our love?

    D. It is love that acknowledges: "Behold, what manner of love the Father hath bestowed upon us, that we should be called the sons of God" (3:1).

E. It is self-forgetful, sacrificial love: "He laid down his life for us" (3:16). —Matthew 9 tells of a series of incidents in which Jesus' acts of mercy were met with skepticism and scorn; yet He continued to give Himself unfalteringly, because He saw the needs of the people and had compassion on them.

II. WE RESPOND TO GOD'S LOVE TOGETHER (shoulder to shoulder).
   A. We love (Him), because He first loved us.
   B. We enjoy the removal of fear.
      1. We are not terrorized by God's presence nor fearful in the presence of men.
      2. Thus we are safe for others to be around. It is typically the frightened animal, or man, that is dangerous.
   C. We are equipped with boldness in the day of trial.
      1. We may speak freely of Christ, as did Peter and John (Acts 3, 4).
      2. We may sing while persecuted, as did the martyrs of Roman oppression.
   D. We are under obligation to continue in love.
      —Revelation 2:4 rebukes those who "left their first love," betraying Christ as the object of their love, and shaming Christ by slacking their devotion.
   E. We are exhorted not to love the (anti-Christ) world.

III. WE REFLECT GOD'S LOVE IN RELATION TO ONE ANOTHER (face to face, especially).
   A. Since God so loved us, we are to love one another.
   B. We thwart love when we act as Cain, whose works were evil (3:12).
      1. The fellowship in moral behavior having been broken, the fellowship in love couldn't stand the strain.
      2. When tempted to be viciously critical, look within. What are you trying to cover or excuse?
   C. We express love in material ways (3:16-18).
      1. Verbal expressions are not enough; deeds establish the truth of words.

496

2. Love is generous with what it has, though that may be little (II Cor. 8:1-5).
3. Love lays down its life for the beloved (3:16; John 15:13).
    a. The "laying down" may be acceptance of death, as Christ on the cross.
    b. It may be the daily bestowal of time, rights, etc., as Christ in ministry. "I would be giving and forget the gift."

D. We accept love from those who love the Lord, and love us for His sake.
1. God sought, even required, the love of His people (Deut. 6:5).
2. Jesus, as Lord, required the love of His disciples (Matt. 10:37).
3. So we also need to be loved, and others need to give the love we accept.
4. The love given and accepted is sometimes imperfect.
    a. (See the Greek or a careful translation of John 21:15-17: "Do you have God's kind of love for Me?" "I am fond of You.")
    b. The Lord still uses our imperfect love to His purposes if we allow it.

E. We do not limit our love to the circle of those who love us.
1. God requires our love to His people, and He has some who do not love us.
2. Jesus commanded, "Love your enemies" (Matt. 5:43-48).
3. God loves us beyond our deserving; we are to be like Him.
4. Some of His people love us beyond our deserving; we can be like them.

CONCLUSION — An important element in any fellowship is the opportunity for a deepening and broadening acquaintance. God is love; let's enlarge our acquaintance with Him!

497

NOT EVERY SPIRIT
(I John 4:1-11)

INTRODUCTION —
  A. Burma missionary's story of communist spies in Burma.
     —The city did not want to be told that there was danger,
     or that its respected citizens were spies. It was prelude
     to disaster.
  B. Thus the church in this day shudders from those who
     would warn them of anti-Christian elements.
     1. We are not saying that all those who are not com-
        pletely Christian are deliberately designing its de-
        struction—that is the danger.
     2. Yet it is as dangerous to be unwarned of spiritual
        misleaders.

I. BELIEVE NOT (TRUST NOT) EVERY SPIRIT.
   (*Pisteuo*—"to place confidence in, believe, trust.")
   A. False prophets do, and will, exist; folk should be warned
      against them.
   B. The warning is not toward suspicion, but toward intel-
      ligent evaluation.
   C. The nature of the false prophets.
      1. Those who would destroy the Messiahship of Christ.
         Here is a touchy issue with our Jewish neighbors.
      2. Humanists—the term is more exact and descriptive
         than "modernist."
         a. Humanisn not as anti-Christian, but humanism
            disguised as "Christianity."
         b. Human Bible; human Christ; human salvation;
            human hope; human development.

II. THE DIVINE TEST—"Every spirit that confesseth not
    that Jesus Christ is come in flesh . . ."
    A. Humanists in religion are to be known more for what
       they do not say than for what they do. A consistent omis-
       sion of reference to cardinal facts of the Gospel is at
       least a good hint that they don't believe them.
    B. Course for a Young People's Conference on Life of
       Jesus says, "Those young people who find intellectual

498

difficulty in accepting the divine generation of Jesus should be allowed to study him as the son of a normal Jewish family." — This course never mentions Christ. It makes only vague reference to the "survival of Jesus" — no clear declaration of His resurrection.

C. Such is suicide for Church of Christ.
  1. Having denied every head except Him, we must not destroy Him!
  2. Having rejected every book but the Bible, we cannot afford to destroy that.

III. BELIEVERS ARE OF GOD. DISBELIEVERS ARE NOT. Two distinct conditions.

A. This is a basis of understanding, and is not inconsiderate.
B. The Jew resents this idea, and tries to destroy it.
  1. He has edited the Bible to remove historic references to Jewish opposition to Christ.
  2. Here is real danger to neighborly relationships; let him reject Christ if he must, be he shall not be allowed to destroy Him again!
  3. If the Christian world wakes up in future generations to find that the Jew has robbed him of all that is best in his religion in exchange for a false "brotherhood," it will not be good for the Jew.
C. The Jew has nothing to fear from the New Testament Church. — His bitterest enemies are political and non-Christian.
D. Nothing is to be gained by confusing the issue.
  — A Christian preacher leads a VBS class in visiting a Jewish synagogue, where the rabbi shows the elements of Jewish worship. Preacher closes the session with prayer, in Christ's name. Rabbi expresses appreciation that Christians engage in Christian prayer.

IV. AND CONCLUSION — Love toward all is the fruit of real faith. Dr. Shelton gives his life in Tibet to the people of that country — not because they are his brothers in Christ, but because they are not!

HELPING GOD'S SERVANT
(III John)

INTRODUCTION — "What did I do?" It's a question often asked by one who is credited with some good deed or charged with some crime, when the deed was performed by another.

    A. Accessories to the fact are dealt with by law as responsible for what is done.

        1. So we try the "lookout man" or getaway driver or hideout helper in a bank robbery.

        2. In similar fashion the sports statistician records "assists" as well as goals.

    B. Second John and Third John deal with "assists" to religious teachers.

        1. Second John warns against encouraging false teachers.

        2. Third John commends Gaius for helping and encouraging traveling teachers of truth.

I. WHOM SHOULD WE HELP?

    A. Teachers of truth.

        1. Truth is tested by acknowledgment of Christ in the flesh (I John 4:1-3).

        2. Truth is tested also by the nature of one's "walk."

    B. Shepherds rather than hirelings (v. 7).

        1. They do not deal with godliness as a way of gain (II Tim. 6:5, 6).

        2. Undemanding, yet dependent on the provision of God through His people.

    C. Demetrius cited as an example (v. 12).

        1. Recommended by those who know him.

        2. Recommended by comparison of his words and works with the Word of God.

        3. Recommended by the apostle.

II. WHY SHOULD WE HELP?

    A. Because the servant needs help.

        1. (Fund raising organization says it won't raise a dollar; it will show your people how to raise all they need.)

        2. So the servant of God cannot do the work that needs

to be done; he can lead, teach, and encourage to all that is required.
3. The newcomer and stranger especially needs help, as one vulnerable, perhaps lonely.
B. Because the Christian needs to give the help (v. 8): "Fellowhelpers to the truth."
1. "Where our missionaries go, we go with them."
2. A church is blessed in calling a young preacher, not for what the young man could do for them, but for what they could do for him. Together they grew!

III. HOW SHOULD WE HELP?
A. In a manner worthy of God.
1. Because he is God's servant and you love God, you help him with your best.
2. Because you are God's servant, you act as a representative of God.
3. (Comparison: when the Avon lady calls, her respect for her employer will make her act like a lady; and the customer's respect for Avon will make her treat the representative kindly.)
4. How much more royally a Christian should deal with God's servant!
B. In encouragement for his service to another.
1. "Receive" and "bring them forward on their journey." We are not the only ones they need to serve.
2. Christians cannot afford to be selfish.
C. In thoughtful reflection of the Golden Rule.
1. Cooperate in what we ask him to do.
2. Express appreciation for conscientious effort.
3. Accept and benefit from the teaching and service he renders (Compare I Thess. 3:8).
4. Be thoughtful and considerate to his family. He can't accomplish his work if they are unhappy.

CONCLUSION — You'll meet him later, at a convention or at the judgment. Let him greet you warmly, saying, "You helped me to whatever accomplishment I have made in the ministry!"

Philemon 7: "The hearts of the saints have been refreshed through you, brother."

JUDE SPEAKS FOR RESTORATION
(Jude)

INTRODUCTION —

    A. Here is restoration: (1) Something so inherently right that departure from it becomes wrong; (2) A departure so substantive that it demands correction; (3) The acceptance of responsibility for making the correction; and (4) Implementation of the renewal.

    B. All this we find in Jude's one-chapter book dealing with the theme, "Contend earnestly for the faith which was once for all delivered unto the saints" (v. 3, ASV).

  I. LOOK AT WHAT IS GIVEN (vv. 1-3).

    A. The Giver is God.

      1. He is the Father, revealed in Old and New Testaments.

      2. He is wholly good, and mindful of His children.

      3. He has spoken, variously at various times, but finally through His Son (Heb. 1:1).

    B. The recipients are "the saints," those who are committed to His cause (v. 1).

      1. They are called by the Gospel.

      2. They are beloved of God, having received the gift of His Son (John 3:16).

      3. They are kept, or preserved, by the power and for the sake of Christ.

    C. The gift is "the faith"—that which is believed by those who are Christ's.

      1. It is *salvation;* that which saves becomes the identifying mark of those saved.

      2. It is the common salvation, available alike to all mankind in every time and every clime. Those who are one *with* Christ become *one IN* Christ.

      3. It is impossible that there be another faith delivered, as it is impossible that there be another Christ, or only begotten Son, given.

II. LOOK OUT FOR DEPARTURES (vv. 4-16).
— Much of the New Testament is restorationist here.
 A. Moral defections, "turning the grace of our God into lasciviousness."
  1. Romans 6 warns against continuing in sin.
  2. I Corinthians 5 and 6 decry immorality among the saints.
 B. Doctrinal wanderings, "denying the only Lord God, and our Lord Jesus Christ."
  1. I John 4 warns of those who deny that Jesus Christ is come in the flesh.
  2. Galatians warns against mixing the authority of Moses with that of Christ.
  3. I Corinthians 1—4 warns of challenging the Lordship of Christ through loyalties to men.
 C. Personal vagaries, especially in the rebellious, quarrelsome spirit—
  1. Despise dominion, and speak evil of dignities (v. 8).
  2. Murmurers, complainers, walking after their own lusts (v. 16).
  3. Verse 11 introduces a terrible trio:
   a. Cain, whose jealousy led to murder.
   b. Balaam, whose greed led to betraying Israel.
   c. Kore (Korah), whose prideful ambition stirred rebellion against Moses.
   — There was not an atheist in the bunch; all were active in the fellowship of folk worshiping the true God; but they had a vicious spirit.

III. LOOK INWARD TO YOUR OWN RESPONSIBILITIES (vv. 17-23).
 A. The spotlight turns from "them" (the defectors) to "you" (the readers).
  1. "You" may have wandered and need to be restored— thus said Old Testament prophets.
  2. "You" may see a brother wandering, and need to restore him (Gal. 6:1).
  3. "You" (all of us) need to be warned and protected against wandering (II Pet. 3:17).

503

B. Jude's admonitions:
  1. Remember the warnings given earlier by Christ and the apostles (vv. 17-19).
     a. Don't be misled into following the defectors.
     b. Don't lose your confidence in Christ.
  2. Reenforce your faith (vv. 20, 21).
     a. Build yourself up; grow in grace and the knowledge of Christ (II Pet. 3:18).
     b. Pray, both for yourself and for others.
     c. Live in God's love.
     d. Grow in eternal hope. (Restoration is a goal, not an accomplishment. It is a chart to follow, not a log of finished journey.)
  3. Relate to fellowmen in the experience (vv. 22, 23).
     a. Have compassion and reach to save.
     b. Snatch the sinners from burning, but cautiously.
     c. The "restoration plea" must be a *plea, pleading,* saying *please.*

IV. LOOK UP, TO THE SOURCE OF POWER AND JUDGMENT (vv. 24, 25).
  A. Jude has set forth problems and responsibilities too great for us. —Good! Now we are where God wants us, depending on Him.
  B. God can keep from stumbling.
     1. Into excesses, of sin, or of abhorrence of the sinner.
     2. Into self-satisfaction that we have not so wandered.
  C. We honor Him by allowing Him to do for us and in us what He wishes.

CONCLUSION —

In a Christ-centered God-consciousness is the fine balance of humility and confidence that belongs to restorers at their best. The faith once for all delivered is not our invention, so we have nothing of which to be proud. It is God's provision, so we have nothing of which to be ashamed. His be the glorious reign, forever!

PREACHING THROUGH REVELATION

THE KING'S ART GALLERY!

In word pictures, full of symbolisms which at times escape the understanding, but always challenge the interest, there is presented in this book the message of the glory of God and His Christ, and the ultimate triumph of His church. As serious art, the book attempts to convey ideas rather than material presentation of fact.

THE APOSTLE JOHN

The writer was the Apostle John, who spent his later days in and about the city of Ephesus in Asia Minor. The book was God's message to the Christians in that area as they faced the rigors of persecution inflicted by command of the Roman emperor Domitian, about A.D. 96. John received his visions while in exile on the rocky island of Patmos, his exile being a part of the current attempt to stamp out Christianity.

TODAY'S READERS

Present readers of the book fall into two distinct classes. There are those who love the spectacular, and love to speculate. They dwell greatly on this book, as they do also on the Old Testament Apocalypses, Ezekiel and Daniel. There are those of more practical mind who admit that they cannot understand it, and neglect it almost entirely. Both are wrong. Revelation is a part of the Bible, neither more important nor less important than other parts. It has an inspiring message for all, not depending upon the detailed interpretation of its images.

UNDERSTANDING REVELATION

Interpretations of Revelation fall into four general lines:

(1) The Preterist (past), which holds that the book deals only with things which "must shortly come to pass" following the writer's own time.

(2) The Historical, which finds in Revelation a pre-figuring, in more or less detail, of world and church history from the time it was written to the end of the world.

(3) The Futurist, which holds that most of the events described in Revelation will take place in literal and material form in the last seven years before the consummation of all things.

505

(4) The Spiritualist, which denies any special reference to historical events in the figures of Revelation, but holds that they present spiritual principles which apply with equal force to the events of any age.

All agree that the book deals with the sufferings and trials of the faithful, and inspires them to continued faithfulness in order that they may share in the final glory of God.

OUTLINE OF THE BOOK

Chapter 1 Introduction: John's vision of Christ.

2,3 Special letters to the seven congregations in Asia.

4,5 Christ the Lord and Ruler of all.

6-11 Judgment: opening of seven seals, and sound of seven trumpets.

12-14 Enemies of the faithful.

15-16 Judgment and wrath poured out.

17-20 Overthrow of the enemies and of Satan.

21-22 Eternal glory of heaven.

Sermon Outlines Provided:

"The King's Art Gallery" (Rev. 1)
"The Spirit and the Day" (Rev. 1:4-11)
"I Know Thy Works" (Rev. 2)
"A Crown for the Faithful" (Rev. 2:8-11)
"Worthy Is the Lamb" (Rev. 5)
"A New Song" (Rev. 5:1-14)
"Measuring the Temple" (Rev. 11:1, 2)
"He Shall Go Into Captivity" (Rev. 13:1-10)

Other Sermon Topics Suggested:

"Out of Great Tribulation" (Rev. 7:9-17)
"The Accuser and the Friend" (Rev. 12:7-12)
"Her Name Is Mystery" (Rev. 17:1-7)
"The Bride" (Rev. 19:6-10)
"The Completed Word" (Rev. 22:16-21)

QUESTIONS OVER REVELATION

1. Revelation 1:1 says it is a revelation of whom?
2. What did the seven candlesticks represent? (1:20)
3. What church had left its first love? (2:1, 4)
4. Which church had a name that it was alive, but it was dead? (3:1)
5. Which was the lukewarm church? (3:14, 16)
6. Who was worthy to open the sealed book? (5:5, 6)
7. Those who had come out of the great tribulation had had their robes washed white in what? (7:14)
8. Who ate the little book the angel held? (10:9, 10)
9. How long did the two witnesses prophesy? (11:3)
10. Those saved overcame the accuser of the brethren by what three things? (12:11)
11. What is said about those who die in the Lord? (14:13)
12. What is inscribed on the forehead of the woman in Revelation 17? (17:5)
13. The Lamb is Lord of lords and King of kings and those with Him are the what? (17:14)
14. Of the one on a white horse called Faithful and True Revelation 19:13 says his name is called what?
15. What happened to the beast and the false prophet? (19:20)
16. What happened to Satan before he is loosed to deceive the nations? (20:1-3)
17. What will become of those whose names are not found in the book of life? (20:15)
18. What is the last invitation in the Bible? (22:17)

THE KING'S ART GALLERY
(Revelation 1)

INTRODUCTION — A VISIT TO AN ART GALLERY.

1. The serious artist has a message in each piece of his work, not necessarily photographic.
2. The pictures may be related, but they are not connected.
3. There is symbolism (See in Hoffman's picture "Gethsemane," rough rock, sharp lines, dark, thorn.)
   Much of this is not known to the casual observer, and not noticed. Nevertheless it makes an impression which grows with the study of the picture.

Revelation is the King's art gallery — all these things apply.

I. TO UNDERSTAND IT YOU MUST UNDERSTAND THE BACKGROUND.
   A. Time of Domitian's persecution of the church A.D. 95.
   B. Province of Asia, rich and favored, sought still more favor by enforcement of emperor worship.
   C. Business boycotts successfully used.

II. WRITTEN TO THE CHURCHES THEN UNDER PERSECUTION.
   A. Must be delivered, censored, by soldiers of the Empire.
   B. Message to tell of the final overthrow of the Empire, success of the church.
   C. Spoken in figures that the intended readers would know, and that the soldiers (and we) would not.
   D. Record that it did have a powerful effect in stiffening faith.

III. IMMEDIATE MESSAGE IS ALSO A MESSAGE FOR THE WHOLE CHURCH.
   A. Three different views of interpretation.
      1. Preterist — things past and passing at time of writing.
      2. Futurist — things wholly in the future.
      3. Historic — outline of all history of the church.
   B. Our own thought that it dealt especially with things rather close to the time at hand.

C. Secondary application to later circumstances.
  1. History repeats—and as often as it repeats, this message is applicable.
  2. The Alpha and Omega—principles are eternal.

IV. CHARACTERISTICS OF THE PICTURES PAINTED.
  A. That God is the King and ruler of the universe.
  B. His majesty, power, and judgment are uppermost. —We need this emphasis in a day which would make him a kind of Santa Claus.
  C. Christ the Lamb, glorified, Son of God and Son of man. —Atonement plainly taught.

V. THE FIRST PICTURE.
  Couldn't put it on canvas, any more than you could photograph any other word picture.
  A. Christ among the churches—"Lo, I am with you."
  B. The stars—the messengers of the word in the churches —are in His hand.
  C. Long robe—Priest—"after the order of Melchizedek."
  D. Golden girdle—accoutred as king.—"Hosanna, thy king cometh."
  E. Brightness of glory of His countenance—Compare Moses at Sinai.
  F. Feet as of bronze—glorious and strong.
  G. Voice as of many waters—to be heard everywhere.
  H. Sword proceeding from mouth—Sword of spirit, which is word of God.

CONCLUSION — I fell at his feet!

"The head that once was crowned with thorns
Is crowned with glory now;
A royal diadem adorns
The mighty Victor's brow.
The highest place that heaven affords
Is His, is his by right;
The King of kings, and Lord of lords,
And heaven's eternal light."

509

THE SPIRIT AND THE DAY
(Revelation 1:1-11)

How inclusive is Christian worship!

I. THE WORSHIPER.
  A. John—exiled to Patmos. Tradition says that he labored in the quarries.
  B. The Lord's Day—he is the first to go on record with that term.
    1. Others—Barnabas, Ignatius, Dionysius, Justin Martyr followed.
    2. Day of the resurrection, first day of the week (Acts 20:7; I Cor. 16:2).
  C. In the spirit—at worship, but more.
    1. His apostleship demanded more in this occasion.
    2. Visions took him out of time and place (Cf. Peter, Acts 10:10; Paul, II Cor. 12:2).
    3. Messages were given to the churches.
    4. Christ's promise fulfilled by the Spirit:
       "For he shall not speak of himself; but whatsoever he shall hear, that shall he speak: and he will show you things to come. He shall glorify me; for he shall receive of mine, and shall show it unto you" (John 16:13, 14).

II. HIS LINK TO THE PAST.
  A. This event harks back to another first day of the week about sixty-five years before.
  B. Then it was not John alone, but other Ten apostles, and more.
  C. The Day—Pentecost. (See Lev. 23:15-17.)
       Implored blessing in the harvest.
       Recognized the giving of the Law.
       (Here was a new law and a new harvest.)
  D. The coming of the Spirit—prepared for by a period of prayer.
    1. Evidenced by sight and sound.

510

2. Tongues of fire and tongues of speech.
3. Power given to the Word—but no conversion without the Word.

D. On that day there came into being the church, to help which John wrote.

(Perhaps John wrote to some of the same people who were among the original three thousand.)

III. HIS LINK TO OUR PRESENT.

—The important things of that Lord's Day continued through John to us.

A. The day—the resurrection day.
   1. Time of worship; time of stewardship; time of service.
   2. All is in the name and for the sake of the risen Lord.
B. Same Spirit working through the same Word.
   Promised to all—abiding in all; giving life to all.
C. The same Gospel, completed, sealed, unchanged.
D. The same Church, identified by plan of pardon, ordinances, life.
E. The same blessing to those who will be in the Spirit on the Lord's Day.
   1. It takes preparation.
   2. It takes participation—public and private worship, two arms of one body.
   3. Blue Monday denotes wrong colors mixed on Sunday!

CONCLUSION — the message of the Day and the Spirit is Christ.

Baptisms took place at Pentecost—Today?

I KNOW THY WORKS
(Revelation 2)

INTRODUCTION — A preacher in Michigan made headlines —and trouble—with his claims to know the doings of his neighbors, and the members of his church.

—In Christ the claim is real, perfected, and for the good of all. In all the letters of Revelation 2 and 3 there is the same outline.

I. I KNOW THY WORKS.

(Compare Psalm 139:1-12.)

A. Concern of the average man for what the preacher knows. It is a concern misplaced.

B. See special troubles of these churches—Persecution and pagan and heathen infiltration.

II. TAKE NOTICE OF AND APPROVE THE GOOD.
Christ's sense of value.

A. Ephesus' toil and patience—(2:2).
1. Would not bear with bad men; tried false apostles and found out.
2. Hated the works of the Nicolaitans—evidently licentious Gnostics.

B. Smyrna's tribulation and poverty (2:9).

C. Pergamos did not deny the name of Christ—Antipas the martyr (2:13).
—Pagan authorities sought to make them curse the name of Christ.

D. Thyatira held to love, faith, and patience.
—Her last works were greater than her first (2:19).

E. Sardis had a few faithful in spite of the general decline of the church (3:4).

F. Philadelphia had a little strength (3:8).
Kept the word of patience.

G. Even Laodicea had the potential for repentance (3:19, 20).

III. TAKE NOTICE OF EVIL AND CONDEMN IT.

A. Ephesus left her first love (2:4, 5).
1. She no longer loved *what* she did at the beginning.
2. She no longer loved *as* she did at the beginning.

512

B. Pergamos suffered false teachers in the midst. Baalam, Nicolaitans (2:14).

C. Thyatira "suffered the woman Jezebel"; claimed to be prophetess, mistaught (2:20).
(Some say a sybil, half heathen, half Christian — false church.)

D. Sardis had a name for being alive, but was dead. No works completed before God (3:2, 3).

E. Laodicea neither hot nor cold (3:15-17).
Boasted of wealth and felt no need.

IV. I KNOW YOUR NEED FOR REPENTANCE.

1. Ephesus: repent and do first works (or I take candlestick away) (2:5).

2. Smyrna: be faithful unto death (2:10).

3. Sardis: be watchful, and establish what remains (3:2).

4. Philadelphia: hold fast that which thou hast (3:11).

5. Laodicea: "Buy of me gold, . . . and raiment."

V. MY VERY CHASTENING IS AN EXPRESSION OF TENDER LOVE.

CONCLUSION — Not only, "I know thy works," but "I know the end of things."

A. Two were not chided: Smyrna and Philadelphia (little strength). The cities remained as centers of Christian population. Gibbon says Philadelphia "a column in the sea of ruins, a pleasing example that the paths of honor and safety may be the same." Smyrna is to Mohammedans a "city of infidels."

B. Two were warned. Pergamos and Thyatira, still stand and have Christians.

C. Ephesus (capital); Laodicea (wealthy) and Sardis long ceased to exist. "I will take thy candlestick out of its place."

D. "He that confesses me, him will I confess."

A CROWN FOR THE FAITHFUL
(Revelation 2:8-11)

INTRODUCTION —
  A. Tribulation and poverty.
  B. The church in Smyrna—
    1. A proud and wealthy seaport, 100 miles north of Ephesus.
      —Wore its crown of beautiful buildings about a rounded hill.
    2. In contrast, materially and spiritually, the church. Last stronghold of Christianity in Asia Minor when Moslems overran "the infidel city."

I. I KNOW.
  —There is acknowledgment as well as knowledge. Comfort in the words.
  A. "The Lord knoweth the way of the righteous"—comfort to believers.
  B. Contrast "Depart from me, ye that work iniquity; I never knew you."

II. FEAR NOT.
  A. There is little that is bright in the picture of persecution, but there is the assurance of God's presence.
  B. There is not the dread of the unknown.
  C. See Luke 12:4, 5.
  D. "Fear not: for they that be with us are more than they that be with them" (II Kings 6:16).

III. BE THOU FAITHFUL.
  —Full of faith in Christ according to His word (not credulity, nor confidence only in power over God).
  A. Belief. "Ye believe in God, believe also in Me" (John 14:1).
  B. Trust. "Be like the bird, That pausing her flight, awhile on boughs too slight, Feels them give way beneath her and yet sings, Knowing that she hath wings."

C. Obedience—"The acid test of faith"

"One dared to die; in a swift moment's space
Fell in war's forefront, laughter on his face;
Bronze tells his fame in many a market place.

Another dared to live the long years through,
Felt his slow heart's blood ooze like crimson dew
For duty's sake, and smiled, and no one knew."

IV. UNTO DEATH.

A. It is more than "until death do us part."

B. "If we be dead with him we shall also live with him; if suffer, we shall also reign with him" (II Tim. 2:11, 12).

C. "Ye have not yet resisted unto blood, striving against sin" (Heb. 12:4).

V. I WILL GIVE UNTO THEE.

A. The reward is not earned, but it is prepared for.
   (A son prepares to take over his father's business.)

B. "Henceforth there is laid up for me a crown of righteousness, which the Lord, the righteous judge, shall give me at that day: and not to me only, but unto all them also that love his appearing" (II Tim. 4:8).

C. David Livingstone underlined Matthew 28:20: "These are the words of a gentleman, and I know that they are fulfilled."

VI. CROWN OF LIFE.

A. Contrast second death (Rev. 20:6, 14; 21:8)—Powerless over faithful.

B. (I Cor. 9:24, 25.)

CONCLUSION — Polycarp of Smyrna: "Eighty and six years have I served my Master and He has done me no wrong; how can I now deny Him?"

515

WORTHY IS THE LAMB
(Revelation 5)

INTRODUCTION —

Another of the portraits of Christ from the divine art gallery. — Bold and symbolic. They show, not Jesus of Nazareth the great Teacher, but the King of kings, the Prince of Heaven in His glory.

I. THE BOOK THAT WAS TO BE OPENED.
   A. The revelation of the things that were soon to be — the mysteries which God has in store for men. It was in the hand of Him on the throne.
   B. Written within and on the back — *a scroll* — regularly written on one side.
      1. This is written full — the message is complete.
      2. Part seen by the eye of man, part is not.
         — Things which are seen are temporal, things not not seen are eternal.
   C. Close sealed with seven seals.
      1. Completely sealed from the unworthy.
      2. Part opened at a time.

II. NONE FOUND WORTHY TO OPEN IT.
   A. Who is worthy to open the book of the mysteries of *your* life?
      1. Not yourself; you have made it less than it should be.
      2. No man can perfectly advise; many will betray confidence.
      3. "We have this treasure in earthen vessels."
   B. "Wept much."
      1. Because the mystery was not to be known?
      2. Because of the unworthiness of all.

III. PORTRAIT OF THE WORTHY ONE.
   A. Lion of the tribe of Judah, the Root of David — Jesus' kingly line.
      "The sceptre shall not depart from Judah, till Shiloh come."

B. Hath overcome, to open the book.

"Fear not, I have overcome the world" (John 16:33).

C. In the midst (between) the throne and the four living creatures.

"One mediator between God and man" (Tit. 2:5).

D. In the midst of the elders—"God with us"—never aloof.

E. The Lamb, slain (John looked for a Lion).

(Be not materially literal.)

"Behold the Lamb of God, that taketh away the sin of the world" (John 1:28).

F. Seven horns—"All authority hath been given unto me" (Matt. 28:18).

G. Seven eyes, which are the seven spirits of God, sent forth—

"Lo, I am with you always."

IV. RESPONSE TO THE WORTHY ONE.

A. We consider the worthiness of Christ.

1. His spotless life—"Which of you convicteth me of sin?" (John 8:26).

2. His deeds of power—disease, demons, life and death, the natural forces subject to Him.

3. His matchless teaching, plumbing the depths of the eternal soul.

4. His works of mercy. He went about doing good.

B. But what does the Word say?

1. "God hath highly exalted him" (See Phil. 2:5-11).

2. God provides that we may partake of His worthiness. (See I Cor. 1:22-25.)

"But God, who is rich in mercy, for his great love wherewith he loved us, even when we were dead in sins, hath quickened us together with Christ, and hath raised us up together, and made us sit together in heavenly places in Christ Jesus" (Eph. 2:4-6).

CONCLUSION — Read verses 11, 13.

517

A NEW SONG
(Revelation 5:1-14)

INTRODUCTION — They say the darkest hour is just before the dawn—and the greatest songs are sung at the dispelling of that darkness.

"O say can you see by the dawn's early light what so proudly
    we hailed at the twilight's last gleaming
Whose broad stripes and bright stars, through the perilous
    fight,
    O'er the ramparts we watched were so gallantly streaming?
And the rockets red glare, the bombs bursting in air
    Gave proof through the night that our flag was still there.
O say, does that star spangled banner yet wave
    O'er the land of the free and the home of the brave?"
                                        — *Francis Scott Key*

I. SONGS IN SCRIPTURE.
    A. Song of Moses and of Miriam, at the crossing of the Red Sea (Exod. 15:1-21).
    B. Song of Deborah, at the victory over the armies of Sisera the Canaanite (Judges 5).
    C. Song at the bringing of the Ark of the Covenant to Jerusalem (I Chron. 16:7-36).

II. OCCASION FOR SONG IN REVELATION.
    A. The scroll, written full of the mysteries of life and the world, close sealed with seven seals.
    B. John's despondency that there was not one worthy to open and to reveal.
    C. There arises, according to promise, One who is worthy —there is a new song.

III. SINGING OF THE LAMB WORTHY TO REVEAL THE MYSTERIES.
    A. The first question: Why is evil in the world? Whence has it power? How shall the power be broken?

"There was one who was willing to die in my stead
That a soul so unworthy might live,
And the path to the cross He was willing to tread,
All the sins of my life to forgive.
They are nailed to the cross;
they are nailed to the cross.
O how much He was willing to bear!
With what anguish and loss Jesus went to the
cross,
But He carried my sins with Him there."

B. Second question: Does God care?

"Marvelous grace of our loving Lord;
Grace that exceeds our sin and our guilt,
Yonder on Calvary's mount outpoured,
There where the blood of the Lamb was spilt.

Grace, grace, God's grace;
grace that will parden and cleanse within.
Grace, grace, God's grace;
grace that is greater than all our sin."

C. Third question: If a man die, shall he live again?

"I know that my Redeemer liveth,
And on the earth again shall stand.
I know eternal life He giveth,
That grace and power are in His hand."

D. Fourth question: Why do the righteous suffer?

"There are days so dark that I seek in vain
For the face of my Friend divine;
But tho' darkness hide He is there to guide,
By the touch of His hand on mine.

When the way is dim and I cannot see
Through the mist of His wise design,
How my glad heart yearns and my faith returns,
By the touch of His hand on mine."

E. Fifth question: What is the meaning of life?

"All the way my Savior leads me;
What have I to ask beside?

> Can I doubt His tender mercy,
> Who through life has been my guide?
> Heavenly peace, divinest comfort,
> Here by faith in Him to dwell,
> For I know whate'er befall me,
> Jesus doeth all things well."

F. How shall we sing when evil is rampant?
  When England was at its worst, Isaac Watts wrote:

> "Joy to the world, the Lord is come;
> Let earth receive her King;
> Let every heart prepare Him room,
> And heaven and nature sing!"

IV. CHRISTIANS SING.
  A. Paul and Silas in prison, were heard singing hymns at midnight (Acts 16:25).
  B. "I will sing with the spirit and I will sing with the understanding also" (I Cor. 14:15). (Concerning conduct of worship.)
  C. (In a passage that speaks of the Christian's home life): "Be not drunk with wine, wherein is excess, but be filled with the Spirit; speaking to yourselves in psalms and hymns and spiritual songs, singing and making melody in your heart to the Lord; giving thanks always for all things unto God and the Father in the name of our Lord Jesus Christ (Eph. 5:18).
  D. "Let the word of Christ dwell in you richly in all wisdom; teaching and admonishing one another in psalms and hymns and spiritual songs, singing with grace in your hearts to the Lord" (Col. 3:16).

CONCLUSION — The new event of Christ's coming again will be accomplished with the New Song. Till then:

> "All hail the power of Jesus' name;
> Let angels prostate fall.
> Bring forth the royal diadem,
> And crown Him Lord of all!"

MEASURING THE TEMPLE
(Revelation 11:1, 2)

INTRODUCTION — In his vision the apostle John was asked to take a poll.

    A. He was asked, not to learn what the people thought about an issue before them, but to learn and to tell what the Word of God said about the people before Him.

    B. His measuring of the temple could not be a material measure of the literal temple in Jerusalem; that had been destroyed some twenty years before John wrote.

    C. The measurement, then, must have a symbolic meaning, clear to Christians in first-century Asia Minor, to whom Revelation was addressed.

        1. The stick to be used in measuring was God's Word.

        2. The temple to be measured was the Church.

        3. The altar to be measured was the worship, its object and procedures.

        4. The worshipers to be measured were the people who made up the church.

I. THERE WAS NEED FOR MEASUREMENT (v. 1).

    A. Maintain constant reference to a divine standard.

        1. It can warn of departures as they develop.

        2. It can provide a basis of correction.

        3. The Lord's seven letters to the seven churches in Asia (Rev. 2, 3) served as such a measurement.

    B. The need for measurement becomes greater with the passage of time.

        1. Divisions and contradictions develop within the church.

        2. As the church is Christ's, it either pleases or disappoints Him; it needs a frequent report on what it is doing.

    C. Refusal to measure and be measured rests on human whim, not divine will.

        1. The immature ones say, "I am right and you are wrong."

2. The humanists say, "I am right for me; you are right for you."
3. Christians must say, "Let's both get right with God."

II. THERE WAS AND IS A BASIS OF MEASUREMENT, GOD GIVEN (v. 1).

A. The measuring rod has its counterpart in the "Little book" of Rev. 10:8-11.
   1. Scripture (the book or rod) has about it an attractive beauty, sweet and pleasant.
   2. Digested to discover its meaning, it disturbs with its rebukes and demands (See II Kings 22:10-13).
B. For the New Testament church the given yardstick is the New Testament Scripture.
   1. It presents the Gospel and the commands of Christ.
   2. It leads the way to salvation in Christ.
   3. It instructs and corrects, directing the life in Christ.

III. THE TEMPLE—THE CHURCH—IS TO BE MEASURED BY THE GIVEN STANDARD (v. 1).

A. Its message is to be compared with the words of Christ.
B. Its creed is supplied in the apostles' confession of Christ (Matt. 16:13-18).
C. Its name is that which identifies it with its Lord.
   —Forbidding Scriptural names is as wrong as adopting unScriptural names.
D. Its organization is seen in the directions given in Acts and the epistles.
   1. Christ is the Head: under Him all are brothers.
   2. Elders and deacons (overseers and servants) minister to the church in a free and flexible society.
   —Flexible adaptation to the local scene is a part of the given pattern.
E. Its necessary oneness is demanded by the oneness of God and His revelation (Eph. 4:1-7).

IV. THE CHURCH'S WORSHIP—THE ALTAR—IS TO BE MEASURED BY THE GIVEN STANDARD.

A. Its ordinances—baptism and the Lord's Supper—are supplied by the example and direction of Christ.

522

B. The center of its worship—both attitude and action—is Christ, and especially the Christ of the cross.

C. The manner of its worship—in spirit and in truth—is directed by Him (John 4:23, 24).

D. The extension of its worship, in personal dedication, is the acceptable "living sacrifice" (Rom. 12).

V. THE CHURCH'S WORSHIPERS ARE TO BE MEASURED BY THE GIVEN STANDARD.

A. In purity of life the measure is the example of Christ.

B. In love of the brethren it looks to His insistent command (John 13:34, 35; see also I John 3 and 4).

C. In Christian service it hears the Sermon on the Mount and the judgment prophecy of the Lord (Matt. 25:31-46).

D. For spiritual growth it looks to Christ (Eph. 4:13).

VI. GOD'S SERVANT IS NOT AUTHORIZED TO MEASURE THE WORLD (v. 2).

A. In John's vision the measuring stopped at the entrance to the holy place. — Outside was the court of the Gentiles, for which he was not responsible.

B. Paul agrees: "What have I to do with judging them that are without? Do not ye judge them that are within? But them that are without, God judgeth" (I Cor. 5:13).

C. Christians waste much time trying to bring communities and their uncommitted citizens into conformity with Christian standards of faith and life. It can't be done. It is hard enough to get Christians to act like Christians, without expecting non-Christians to act like something they are not.

D. Bring the citizen and Christ together; then measure according to the Word.

CONCLUSION — Ye are the temple of God, and thus subject to measurement! "Search me, O God, and know my heart; try me and know my thoughts, and see if there be any wicked way in me, and lead me in the way everlasting" (Psalm 139:23, 24).

WHAT KEEPS GOD'S PEOPLE GOING?
(Revelation 13:1-10)

INTRODUCTION — Do you ever feel that you have come to the end of your string, that you can't keep on as a Christian?

A. Consider the folk to whom the book of Revelation was first sent.
   1. Bitterly persecuted for their refusal to worship the Roman Emperor.
   2. Position, property, and friends taken from them, their lives were in jeopardy.

B. Consider the message that came from John on the Isle of Patmos.
   1. It had to be delivered by officers of the Empire.
   2. Thus it was written in symbols and figures the Romans could not understand, but were known to the Jewish Christians from such books as Ezekiel and Daniel.
   3. The message in brief: You are on the ultimately winning side; keep on keeping on!

I. THE ENEMY IS DESCRIBED (vv. 1-9).

A. The ravening beast is the persecuting Roman Empire.
   1. Coming up out of the sea: Roman forces approached Asia Minor through the Aegean Sea.
   2. The ten horns conform to ten emperors who had reigned up to that time.
   3. Seven heads, with blasphemous titles, conform to seven of the emperors who had been and were worshiped as gods.
   4. The power to overrun and persecute was evident in the Roman military power.

B. The Roman persecution is limited.
   1. Terribly severe, it was still but for a time and would end. "Time and times and half a time" comes to three and one-half years.
   2. It is still not ultimate destruction: "Fear not them which kill the body, but are not able to kill the soul:

but rather fear him which is able to destroy both soul and body in hell" (Matt. 10:28).

C. The Roman persecution was subtle.

   1. It did not forbid the worship of God in Christ; it simply demanded the worship of the Emperor as one among many gods.

   2. Christians' refusal to worship anyone or anything but God seemed intolerant and unpatriotic; but for this "intolerance" they gave all.

   3. Application: What competing loyalties tempt *you* to less than complete service to God? Employment? Business? Peer pressure? Property? Social obligations?

II. THE ASSURANCE IS GIVEN (v. 10).

The basic text of Revelation 13:10 admits to two interpretations:

A. "Whoever makes captives, he will be led into captivity; whoever kills with the sword, he must be killed by the sword" (*The Berkeley Version*).

   1. This reiterates Galatians 6:7: "Be not deceived, God is not mocked, for whatsoever a man soweth, that shall he also reap."

   2. The Empire that enslaved its captives would diminish its own freedom in the process, and would ultimately see its own citizens enslaved.

   3. Recall Jesus' words to Peter in Gethsemane: "Put up again thy sword into his place: for all they that take the sword shall perish with the sword" (Matt. 26:52).

   4. "Woe to thee that destroyest, and thou was not destroyed: and dealest treacherously, and they dealt not treacherously with thee! When thou hast ceased to destroy, thou shalt be destroyed; and when thou hast made an end of dealing treacherously, they shall deal treacherously with thee" (Isa. 33:1).

   5. Christians were sustained by assurance of ultimate justice.

B. (Alternate interpretation) "If anyone is to go into captivity, into captivity he will go. If anyone is to be killed with the sword, with the sword he will be killed" (*New International Version*).

1. This accords with Matthew 6:25-34 in renouncing worry over matters beyond one's control; leave matters in the hands of God.
2. "Dearly beloved, avenge not yourselves, but rather give place unto wrath [God's judgment]: for it is written, Vengeance is mine; I will repay, saith the Lord" (Rom. 12:19).(Compare Deuteronomy 32:35-37.)
3. "Christ also suffered for us, leaving us an example, that ye should follow his steps . . . who, when he was reviled, reviled not again; when he suffered, he threatened not: but committed himself to him that judgeth righteously" (I Pet. 2:21, 23).
4. Christians were strengthened by assurance that God's control of the situation was adequate, and better than their concern (II Tim. 1:12).

III. GOD'S PEOPLE RESPOND (v. 10).

—The basic text of the final statement admits of two interpretations:

A. "On this fact rests the endurance and fidelity of God's people" (Goodspeed, *An American Translation*).
   1. The assurance of ultimate justice makes patient continuance possible.
   2. "If we be dead with him, we shall also live with him: if we suffer, we shall also reign with him: if we deny him, he also will deny us" (II Tim. 2:11, 12).
   3. So the courage, faithfulness, and mild behavior of persecuted saints has always amazed the persecutors.
   4. (The scoffing farmer bragged about receiving more for his crop than did his Christian neighbor. The Christian replied with a smile, "What ever gave you the idea that God settled all His accounts on October 1 each year?")

B. (Alternate interpretation) "This calls for patient endurance and faithfulness on the part of the saints" (*New International Version*).

526

1. Unable to prevent or control their affliction, they would need strong faith to survive. Thus the passage becomes part of the exhortation, "Be thou faithful unto death, and I will give thee a crown of life" (Rev. 2:10).
2. Compare the stubborn faithfulness of the three Hebrews facing the fiery furnace (Dan. 3:17, 18).
3. It is the ultimate faith in God without specific promise of immediate help: "I know whom I have believed, and am persuaded that he is able to keep that which I have committed unto him against that day" (II Tim. 1:12).

CONCLUSION — We see a confrontation between two "eternal cities." Rome, which had lasted a long time, but its ancient ruins speak of final destruction; The New Jerusalem, to be the home of God's people forever.

Between the two is this distinction: "All that dwell upon the earth shall worship (the beast/Rome), whose *names are not written in the book of life* of the Lamb slain from the foundation of the world" (Rev. 13:8).

INDEX TO SERMON OUTLINES

Precise indexing of sermons is, of course, impossible. No sermon is wholly doctrinal, and none is wholly practical. None deals with one doctrine to the omission of all others. We have, nonetheless, tried to provide a helpful and usable index, based on the principal thrust of each sermon, and keyed to the basic sermon text as it appears in the book's arrangement, from Genesis to Revelation.

DOCTRINE

Of the Bible

General
- Exod. 20:1-20 21
- I Kings 22:12-24 107
- Psalm 119:9-15, 105 ..175
- Jer. 36:20-32 217
- Amos 8:11-14 245
- I Tim. 1:1-7 441
- II Tim. 3:14-17 454
- Heb. 1:1-4 461
- Rev. 1..............508

Covenants
- Jer. 31:27-34 215
- Mark 12:28-34.......297
- Heb. 8 467

Of God

General
- Job 42:1-10 157
- Psalm 19 163
- Psalm 42 167
- Psalm 90 171
- Psalm 98 173
- Prov. 15:3 185
- John 1:1-14 329
- II Tim. 2:13........449

The Name
- Num. 6:22-27 37

Judgment
- Joel 2:27-32 243

False Gods
- I Sam. 4:1-11....... 81

Of Christ

General
- Job 9..............151
- Job 19:25-27 155
- II Cor. 9:8-15 413
- Phil. 2:1-11 431
- Heb. 1:1-4 461
- Heb. 12:1-6 471
- I John 4:1-11 498
- Rev. 2..............512

In Prophecy
- Exod. 12........... 19
- Num. 35:9-15 43
- Isa. 53 209
- Hos. 11:1, 2........237
- Zech. 9:9, 10 257

His Character
- Eccl. 2:1-11 193

His Power and Authority
- Matt. 8 267

His Life and Ministry
- Mark 1:1-15........283
- Mark 1:35-39.......286
- Mark 7:31-37.......295

529